# ARCHITECTURE, ANIMAL, HUMAN:
## *THE ASYMMETRICAL CONDITION*

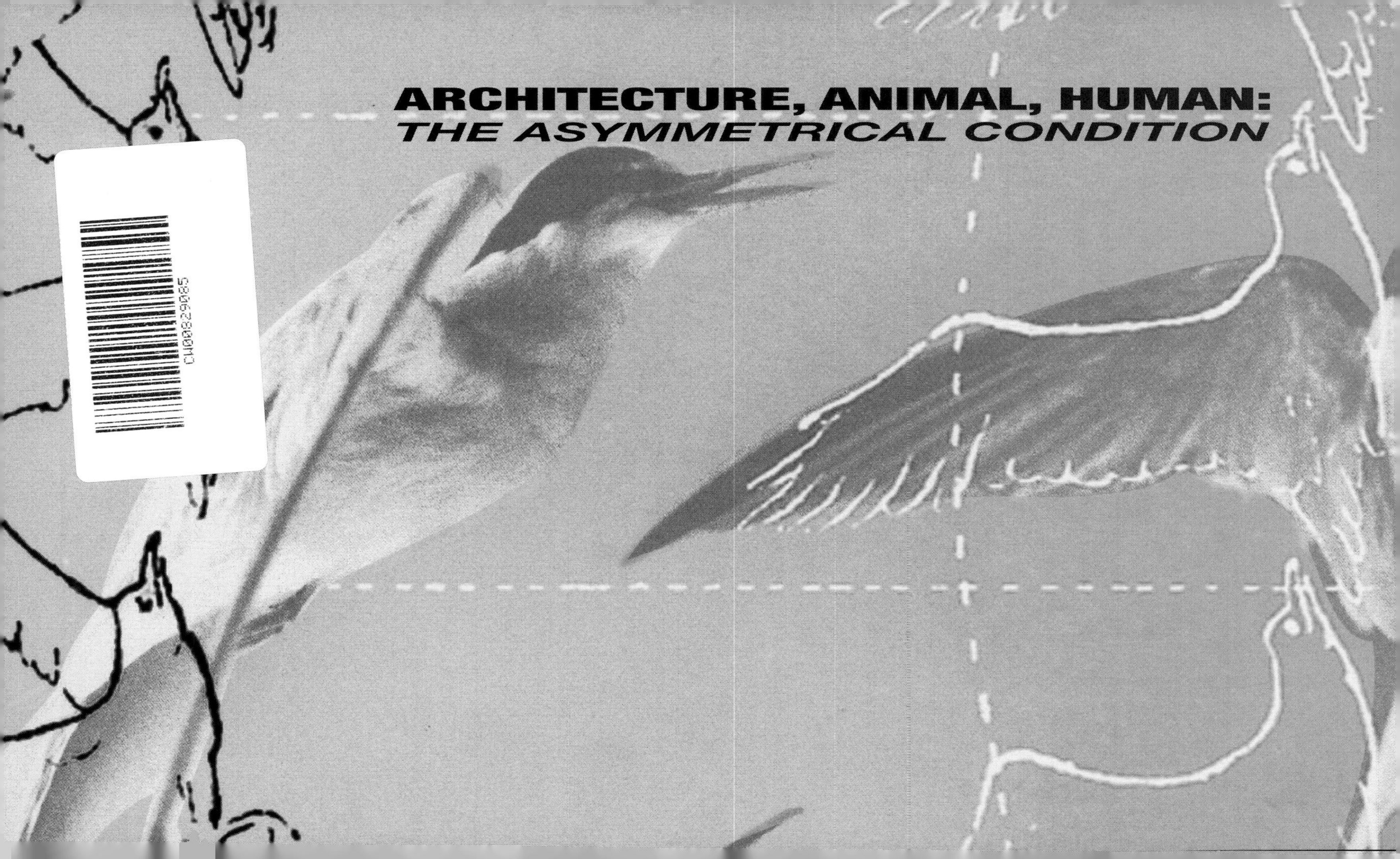

The relations between the organic and inorganic, animate and inanimate, natural and technological, are of paramount importance to the field of architecture, both in current digital architectures and in classical debates and practices.

This book looks at specific instances in the Renaissance, Enlightenment, and our own time, when architectural ideas and ideas of biological life come into contact with each other. These convergences are fascinating and complex. Life privileges itself above all else, and seeks to continually expand its field of expression. Architecture, for its part, depends on life, but is also necessarily indifferent to it. This is the "asymmetrical condition" of the title, and to understand it is to gain important new theoretical perspectives into the nature of architecture.

**Catherine Ingraham** is Professor of Architecture at Pratt Institute. She is the author of *Architecture and the Burdens of Linearity* (Yale University Press, 1998), co-editor of *Restructuring Architectural Theory* (Northwestern University Press, 1989), and was an editor of the critical journal *Assemblage* from 1991–1998.

ROUTLEDGE
Routledge
Taylor & Francis Group
LONDON AND NEW YORK

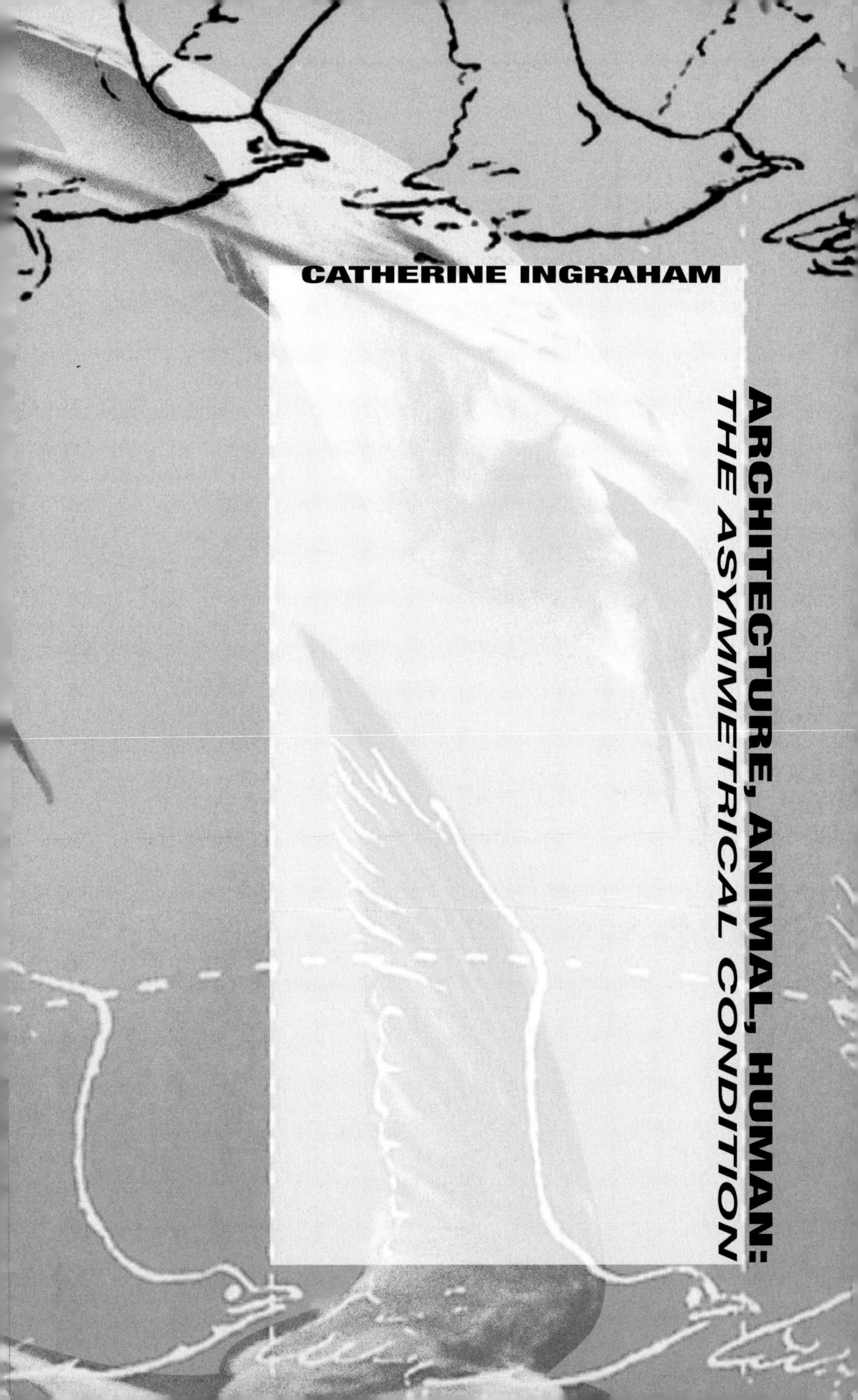

CATHERINE INGRAHAM

# ARCHITECTURE, ANIMAL, HUMAN: *THE ASYMMETRICAL CONDITION*

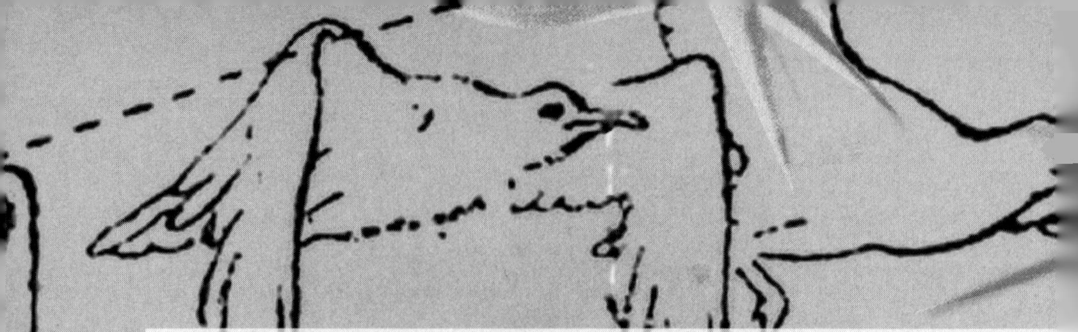

First published 2006 by Routledge
2 Park Square, Milton Park, Abingdon, Oxon, OX14 4RN
Simultaneously published in the USA and Canada by Routledge
270 Madison Ave, New York, NY 10016

*Routledge is an imprint of the Taylor & Francis Group*



Typeset in Baskerville by Mark Rakatansky Studio
Printed and bound in Great Britain by TJ International Ltd, Padstow, Cornwall



*British Library Cataloguing in Publication Data*
A catalog record for this book is available from the British Library

*Library of Congress Cataloguing in Publication Data*
A catalog record for this book has been requested

ISBN 0-415-70106-6 (Hb)
ISBN 0-415-70107-4 (Pb)

Book and cover design by Mark Rakatansky Studio

Cover images:
Background birds: Copyright 1983 Jeremiah Dine from Natural Selection (London/Stuttgart: Editions Hansjörg Mayer, 1983). Foreground birds: Etienne-Jules Marey, *"Tableau synoptique des attitudes successives d'un Goéland au vol projetées sur trios plans différents,"* included in Siegfried Giedion, *Mechanization Takes Command* (New York: Norton, 1969): see Fig. 8.3.

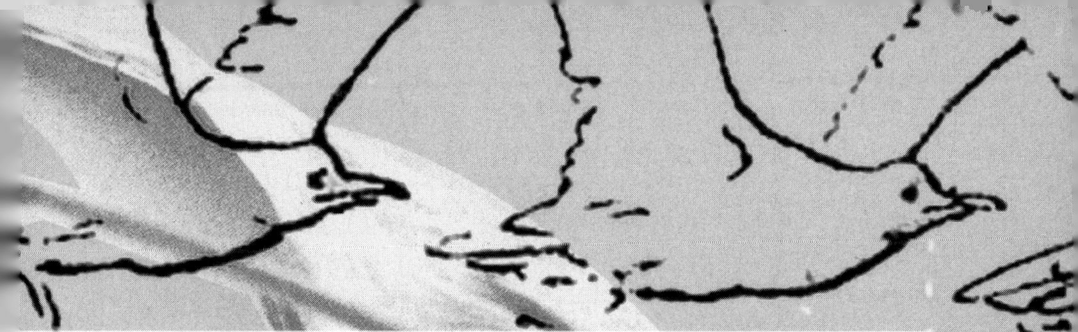

# TABLE OF CONTENTS

# ACKNOWLEDGEMENTS

There are many people to thank, almost all of them for their support of my work through a time that was very full of other responsibilities.

Thank you to those who allowed me to take time off, Robert Segrest and Tom Hanrahan; to those who afforded me time off, Iowa State University and Pratt Institute, the amazing MacDowell Colony, and the generous Graham Foundation for Advanced Studies in the Fine Arts; and to those who suffered my time off, Mark and Max. Thank you to those who watched my back while I was gone, Gary Hill and Regina Scully.

Thank you to those who invited me to teach and lecture on this material, which was crucial for the development of the book: Bernard Tschumi, Mack Scogin, Rafael Moneo, Mario Gandelsonas, Ralph Lerner, Sylvia Lavin, Wolf Prix, Moshen Mostafavi, Mark Cousins, Mark Wigley, Nasrine Seraji, and Stephen Cairns. Thank you to the many wonderful students in my seminars and studios at Iowa State University, Pratt Institute, Harvard University, Princeton University, and Columbia University, whose live intelligences always took the material into new places.

Thank you to those who wrote recommendations, read early drafts, published chapters: the editors of *Grey Room* Reinhold Martin, Felicity Scott, Branden Joseph; Michael Sorkin, Alessandra Ponte, Mark Jarzombek, Michael Bell, Keller Easterling, Diana Agrest, K. Michael Hays, Laurie Hawkinson, Cynthia Davidson, and Paulette Singley.

Thank you to Mark (MR Studio), William Arbizu, Shannon Beauchaine, Lauren Panepinto, Ben Porto, and Jason Vigneri-Beane for this beautifully designed book. Thank you to Caroline Mallinder, of Routledge, for her support of architecture and architectural history/theory.

Thanks, lastly, to my mother, sisters, and brother–Elizabeth Ingraham, Christine Ingraham, Anna Grady, Michael Ingraham–for their humor, courage, and talents. Mark, thank you again for many things (Bernini, for example) and Max, you too.

# INTRODUCTION



You may want to know, in particular, about the animal. And you may want to know which "asymmetrical condition" the title is making reference to. *Architecture and Life*, or, more specifically, *Architecture and Post-animal Life*, were provisional book titles at different stages of the project. The question of life in architecture is very much the framework of this book. And it is the relation between architecture and what I call post-animal life, architectural/biological life after the Renaissance, that particularly interests me. The subject of life always raises the stakes. We anticipate in it something so powerful and so pleasurable we are willing to risk any number of forays into the subject. Whenever we bring life to mind, the terms of discussion instantly shift into a different register. It is as if an explosion of energy and interest suddenly animate placid dispositions of the "argument." The very force of this curiosity and desire is part of the reason why, between architecture and life, there is a relation of asymmetry. Architecture, which is the exact artistic and technical discipline for which human biological and psychological life are a necessary precondition, must always be, at some level, indifferent to the life within it. And life, for its part, privileges itself above all else, and seeks continuously to expand its field of expression. This is true of both animal and human life, although animal life has rarely been of architectural interest.

Erwin Schrödinger described his project in *What is Life?* as a study of how the "events in *space and time* which take place within the spatial boundary of a living organism [can] be accounted for by physics and chemistry." Because architecture has belonged, since the Renaissance, to both mathematics, "the physicist's most dreaded weapon," and life, which is "too involved to be fully accessible to mathematics,"[1] Schrödinger's project is also, in part, the project of anyone who is interested in the problem of life in architecture. This is true in spite of significant changes in the field of both genetics and physics since the writing of *What is Life?* The problems of quantum physics in the 1950s—which were concerned with the statistical analysis of large numbers of atoms that make both organized patterns of events, and random disorganization in the physical world—are also the problems of contemporary architecture in some form. But architecture is additionally concerned with the problems of living organisms, which ". . . in relation to the statistical point of view differ . . . entirely from that of any piece of matter that . . . physicists and chemists have ever handled physically in . . . laboratories or mentally at . . . writing desks."[2] A physicist's usual objects of study, non-living matter, are "periodic crystals." Living organisms are "aperiodic crystals."

For life, reproduction and genetic repetition produce a new product, another life. For technical production—the material aspects of architectural work—reproduction and repetition produce inevitable disintegration and decay, the entropic decline of the second law of thermodynamics. When "like produces like" in animals or humans, everything is renewed and the species is given another chance. Schrödinger's specific question about how quantum physics and biology are related focuses on the ways in which reproduction, through heredity, produces something like "permanence" through time. Biological permanence, or the relative permanence acquired through the passage of genetic information from generation to generation, is a form of order. In terms of quantum physics, it must therefore depend on the operation of a large number of atoms. In physics, the "co-operation of an enormously large number of atoms" is required for statistical laws to "begin to operate and control the behavior of these assemblies. . . . It is in that way that events acquire truly orderly features."[3] But, as Schrödinger argues, in living organisms the number of atoms is not large enough to justify the order of hereditary permanence; nor are there enough atoms to, statistically, produce what we apprehend as the orderly coordination of our intellectual life with our bodies. In addition, normative human perception is very crude compared to the microscopic dimensions of atomic theories of matter. In fact, "incredibly small groups of atoms, much too small to display exact statistical laws . . . play a dominating role in the very orderly and lawful events within a living organism."[4] He formulates the question as follows: "Why must our bodies be so large compared with the atom?"

I discuss some of these issues later in the book, but I mention them here because, in some peculiar way, the difference in "size" between architecture and the body is very great and this difference affects everything: the meaning of various occupations of space, the nature of time, duration, organization, orientation, adherence to physical laws, the nature of permanence, and so forth. We usually speak of the difference between the technical and biological as self-evident. But Schrödinger suggests that since both physical structures in space, such as buildings, and the physical body of living beings must accord with physical laws of space, we can, and should, bring these "objects" into the same place and compare their operations. One invariably brings the other to mind. There are, of course, innumerable ways of doing this that do not involve reducing everything to a molecular level and most of my discussion is not about Schrödinger's, or other physicists', view of the problem. But it is worth noting that Schrödinger's analysis does not, as one might expect, lead him to an argument that reinforces a material reductionism or empiricism, which, for architects, has been both the temptation and the failing of most of its engagement with modern physics. Instead, his analysis leads to problems of mind and matter—the most profound and complex difference that makes a difference in life and architecture. The very fact that the human mind cannot, even now, be located in a physical place—not yet on the inside of the body, contrary to the mind's powerful sense of itself as existing in an interior, nor, in any direct sense, outside the body[5]—continues to complicate the status and meaning of the formulation "architecture and life" in all its manifestations. The mind is known, in some respects, by its actions and its labor, although what is known, how it is known, and the effects of such knowledge on the world, constitute the most intricate and diverse philosophical debates of the last three hundred years.

We already know much of this to be true, even before the terms of my discussion are clear. Architecture is a discipline that, like many disciplines, has attended to its own standing up, its own internal history, logic, and style of technical development. François Jacob, a geneticist, when writing the history of heredity describes the gradual bifurcation of the biological from the technical as a split that is based precisely on the difference between animate beings that reproduce and inanimate matter that is reproduced—the split, in some sense, between an active and passive voice.[6] Architecture belongs chiefly to what Jacob calls "mental memory," cultural memory. Life, on the other hand, is neither art nor discipline, although capable of being disciplined. Life too is concerned with its own logic and its own standing up, and it belongs to what Jacob calls "genetic memory." Very little from mental, or cultural, memory becomes inscribed in the genetic memory by which the body is reproduced over time, although almost everything about the body and its biological life has been a subject of inquiry in contemporary cultural life. Schrödinger remarks extensively on the irrelevance of our cultural lives to genetics. We know that this can't possibly be completely true but the terms of its untruth are difficult to pin down. These two types of history, mental and genetic, are radically different and any attempt to historicize the body in culture, or culture in the body, runs into the conflict between these two histories. Taking account of these two worlds is, nevertheless, the philosophical and practical work of both architect and inhabitant, and it has typically seemed to be accomplished almost effortlessly, as part of our acceptance of, and simultaneous ambivalence and resistance toward, our artistic/technical/biological nature and history. The philosophical paradoxes of the "active" living in the "passive," or the animate in the inanimate, or the genetic in the mental, have been left, in contemporary architectural analysis, largely to the philosophers and writers—Plato, Aristotle, Hegel, Heidegger, Kant, Bataille, Lyotard, Foucault, Wittgenstein, Lacan, Levinas, Derrida, Deleuze and Guattari, Rilke, Coetzee, and others—many of whom use architectural metaphors and examples routinely but have not found it particularly interesting to address the question of life from the side of architecture. From the side of architecture, certain classical philosophical oppositions that have almost always, since antiquity, accompanied the analysis of life—necessity and contingency, stability and mutation, divisions between the mind and the body—are made to coexist side by side in a provisional, and complicated (because illusory and ultimately unharmonious), cooperation. Architecture is thus alert to the ways in which stability, for example, must depend on, rather than contest, change. But my point is not to confirm, once again, architectural work as a good place to demonstrate philosophy. Instead it is to suggest that architecture has, in some way, leveled the playing field for these canonical oppositions—made them work out their differences in provisional ways in spite of their respective structural privileges and prejudices. A certain backing up from architecture, rather than philosophy, into questions of life suggests that while historically our dwelling places have appeared to serve as the static ground for the variability of our biocultural lives—our "permanent address," so to speak—it may be that this stasis or constancy actually has been supplied by a biological homeostasis, not an architectural one. Architecture, the externalized and material body, thus provides the variability and variation, the vicissitudes of a milieu, the machinic phylum, while the interior body of the occupant projects an internal orderliness into the space of its occupation in order to stabilize itself around a "way of life." More accurately, however, it is most certainly a ceaseless exchange and oscillation between milieu and body, each of which has a different stasis and variability, that constitutes the relationship. The body lives on the noise shed by its milieu and the milieu lives on the order produced by the body; the body lives on the order produced by the milieu and the milieu lives on the noise shed by the body. In light of this oscillation, certain contemporary questions of "sustainability" in architecture, for example, would not tend to be based on a limited, material-based, analysis, but, instead, on a set of "live" exchanges between an asymmetrical pairing of life/milieu. Architecture has been practicing this kind of sustainability since the Renaissance because it first began, in that period, to understand itself in terms of life processes.

At the very least, it is extremely odd that, over our long period of development as biological beings, we have more or less predetermined our own niches and almost taken ourselves out of the evolutionary stream. Nothing is new about this oddness in the biological sciences but, in architecture, the question of life's adaptive powers and counter-formation of niches has been sublimated into the many ideals of architectural work. The "commodity, firmness, and delight" of Henry Wotton (after Vitruvius) in the seventeenth century is only one of numerous rhetorical attempts in architecture to contend with architecture in the face of life. Almost all architectural theory since Vitruvius has attempted to unite the issues of biological life ("needs," Wotton's *commodity*) with the technical, tool-based, work of human beings (*firmness*), in order to produce the various fields of meaning that architecture claims for its intellectual and artistic work: aesthetics, ethics, social forces, politics (*delight*, often pejorative and broadly understood).

Human life has not always had the biological privilege it seems to enjoy today. And neither has architecture always been the secular techno-aesthetic practice we know it to be today. The asymmetry between life and architecture has, itself, evolved, if it makes any sense to speak this way, with the different evolutions of architecture and life. To some degree, it is only in the face of an expectation that architecture can be linked with human biological life—an expectation that, surprisingly, cannot be take for granted—that any asymmetry asserts itself. In *The Human Condition*, Hannah Arendt suggested that contemporary human life had lost its "preserve" of artifice: ". . . as though we had forced open the distinguishing boundaries which protected the world, the human artifice, from nature, the biological process which goes on in its very midst as well as the natural cyclical processes which surround it, delivering and abandoning to them the always threatened stability of a human world."[7] Architecture, among other arts, has maintained preserves of human artifice by means of Arendt's "distinguishing boundaries," but architecture, unlike other arts, takes the idea of preserve quite literally. It allows biological life to circulate "in its midst" and cyclical processes (weather, for example) to surround it. And it maintains an insistently human enclave inside its borders. This has allowed architecture both a conservative and constructive role in human history. But architecture has also maintained a crucial and confusing permeability because biological life, in order to survive, has always required something like a free passage between inside and outside; some vital movement from protected to open air. I am not speaking metaphorically or poetically. Buildings require literal doors and windows, and architecture requires both literal and symbolic openings; these openings are an integral part of any architectural treatment of its interior space and its boundaries. There is no architecture, in the modern sense, without them. A biological history of the window might see windows and doors as trace references to some nascent relationship between interiority and exteriority in human developmental history, not as amenities that had to be added to, or punched out of, a solid architectural wall. Or, perhaps the window could be seen as a kind of reference to a hypothetical "open field" which humans lived before architecture—keeping in mind that the word "field" itself prevents us from imagining that the moment we "became human" was anything other than a moment of also "becoming architectural." When Rachel Whiteread makes a cast of a house in plaster—making of the house a solid mass with the windows and doors cast into relief on the surface—she, in effect, entombs and calcifies the material and biological life that is a defining condition of architecture. And, in fact, the catalog from her 1996 exhibition of these casts is called *Shedding Life*.[8] Calcification is certainly one of the most powerful points of her work but its chilling beauty belongs not to the sublimity of, say, the architectural ruin, but to the sublimity of sculpture. Whiteread's work, as with Bernini's work, continuously causes us to weigh the vacuity of space and hard outlines of volumetric enclosure against a solid infill of mass.

The "asymmetry" that I have introduced as a difference between one thing, life, which privileges itself, and another thing, architecture, which is indifferent to this privilege, mimics, to some degree, the asymmetry between a biological organism and any ecological milieu, with the obvious but very problematic addition of a motivated connection between artifice and artificer. This connection has changed over time depending on the relative status and value of human life and the relative status and value of architecture.

The discipline of architecture itself, officially formed as a discipline only in the eighteenth century, has always claimed a central role in human life, but seems to have remained, with respect to biological life, pointedly oblivious to the multiple paradoxes of its own position. Architectural historians and commentators such as Vitruvius, Laugier, even Rowe, Wittkower and Murray, frequently argue that these paradoxes emanate from the classic three (or sometimes two) part problem briefly mentioned above in Wotton's work: that is, the relations between art/aesthetics, science/technology, and need/function. But the sense in which all three of these complex categories are biological, as well as cultural and technical, would make of architecture a particularly tricky, almost unmanageable, form of life science.

It is certainly somewhat true to say that this book is about the relation of architecture to the history of the idea of biological life, since now it is impossible to evoke the category of life without bringing to mind its biological complexity, although this also was not always true. At the same time, it is also impossible to render biological life as something that can be disentangled from political and social life.[9] Architecture designs the space, environment, and context within which most of biological/social human life passes. And, as suggested above, insofar as architecture is a spatial and technical practice that responds to forces in the world, it, like a biological milieu, is "governed by laws indifferent to the intrinsic needs of living beings."[10] But many architects would disagree categorically with this statement. What else has architecture ever been but a response to the needs/culture of living beings? Speaking quite generally for the moment, it is only insofar as architecture can suspend its preoccupation with spatial and technical interests that it apprehends the life of the beings who live inside it; overcomes its indifference to "needs." By means of this suspension architecture organizes a mode of life, a program, for the occupant, although, paradoxically, such modes of life are conditioned and infiltrated by the very spatial and technical terms put into suspension. The familiar relation in the discipline and practice of architecture between space and life—which is inscribed, for example, in the modernist relation between plan and program, or the contemporary relation between surface and program—is a relation that prescribes precise ways of operating in architecture. But this relationship also always sustains a level of false consciousness, from which multiple historical and theoretical debates have been precipitated for hundreds of years. One aspect of this false consciousness has come to rest inside the words "occupant" and "user," which are the impoverished modern terms by which we now describe life in architecture. "The user's space is *lived*," Henri Lefebvre laments,[11] which means that it "bears the stamp" of life's childhood, maturation, private/public existence, animal/human formations, the history of the species, ideologies of the body, psychological phantasms. Nothing in the word "user" suggests the depth and complexity of the human, or animal, use of space.

Thus, the asymmetry produced by architecture's indifference to life, on the one hand, and life's self-privilege, on the other, is not just one issue among many in architecture. It is, in a sense, the always-there, always-prevailing, issue. But, of course, because of this the subject is too vast. My interest in the way life, particularly human and animal life, has been defined biologically since the Renaissance is an attempt to limit the subject to (a mere) five hundred years, rather than the millions of years that life has existed on earth and that architectures, or at least elaborated structures, have been built to house that life. As a further expedient, I take only three, although canonical and therefore thick, historical points of intersection between ideas of life and architecture in Western culture: the Renaissance, the Enlightenment, and our contemporary time. I gather from these three periods essentially what I need, which is another way of saying that my point has not been, could not have been, to exhaustively reiterate work that has already been done on visibility, the eighteenth century body, medical representation, the history of ethical philosophy, the history of science and humanism, or the huge number of studies on architecture in the Renaissance and the Enlightenment. Many very insightful scholars have already examined significant aspects of architecture and life during these periods. And yet the question of how biological life bears on architectural work during these periods seems to have eluded significant mention. The vastness of the subject clearly cannot be completely controlled, for reasons I only partially articulate in the book, by historical analysis. Perhaps there is a degree of impossibility to this question, or perhaps it is only recently in the face of contemporary genetics, evolutionary work and developmental biology, and computational work, which have raised new ethical questions for philosophers—that this question has developed any meaning or interest. This book only, finally, begins to frame the subject of architecture and life in what I see as a preliminary way. The energy of the book has been expended—in, of course, what I hope is a meaningful direction—on the formulation of fruitful questions around this very complex subject matter, almost all of which beg for further elucidation.



### Post-animal life

In light of these introductory remarks, then, instead of looking at something called "life" as a unified idea in architecture, or "architecture" as a unified idea in life, the three periods in history I pick are times when certain terms/clusters of, in particular Western, ideas around architecture and life are brought into particularly intimate relation to each other. First, in the Renaissance, there is a general emergence of what we know, in its different guises, as a much-debated "humanism" that linked a number of diverse developments: an increasingly secularized and civic human life, specific ideas about the acquisition of knowledge, and specific theories of the role of the divine and the ideal in human practices such as architecture and mathematics. Second, the Enlightenment is a period when human life is definitively separated from other forms of biological life, biology itself is invented as a discipline and architectural history, more or less simultaneously, is invented using the life sciences as a model for organizing a history of building types and specific ways of life. The third period is the current time, our time, when theoretical work in architecture and biology, particularly genetics, coupled with computational technologies, is suggestively critiquing ancient divisions between the animate and the inanimate. Our current time is also a time when it has become possible to pose certain kinds of theoretical questions in architecture that it would have been difficult to pose during many other periods of history, although the presumption of this claim will prove problematic. Barbara Herrenstein Smith, for example, argues that post-classical theory renders the difference between specific classical oppositions, such as the animate and inanimate, as undecidable.[12] But we use these oppositions on a daily basis not simply out of ignorance or recalcitrance but because we still find support for these oppositions—often rendered as fantastical or utopian—in everyday life, not least architectural life.

Biological life itself has developed very slowly—the human body has changed very little since prehistoric eras. But, of course, it is impossible to speak of some base condition of the human body, which is always, as our current most enlightened philosophical work has shown us, a social/political construction that has changed drastically over time. At the same time, the relation, frequently oppositional, between biological humanness and social/political humanness has never been entirely without meaning. Even before there was a specific discipline of biology, there were venerable philosophical splits and dualisms between body and mind, carnal and spiritual intelligence. Biological being is classically both an unruly being and an unruly category of being. Since the nineteenth century—particularly since Claude Bernard and Charles Darwin—the meaning of biological bodies in the world has almost always been involved the operation of both constancy and variation, although Darwin's theory of natural selection based on "small, continuous, accidental" variation has undergone important revisions. It is discontinuous, episodic mutations, without intermediate forms, that have replaced Darwin's variations because mutations, unlike variations, are passed through the hereditary structure.[13] Biological bodies pursue both the constancy of homeostasis and continual although rare variation based on mutation, species opportunism, inside, as it were, the vicissitudes of social/political lives, which have no apparent direct effect on biological development. It is this relation of constancy/variation that architecture, in particular, has responded to almost more profoundly than to the social/political being—the symbolic being—that architectural history is largely concerned with. But it is very hard to see how this constant/varying being has been rendered in architecture without narrowing the discussion to the usual reductive functional analysis. Enter the animal; or, rather, what I call "post-animal life."

My interest in the subject of life and architecture had a peculiar beginning. While writing an earlier book, I reread Le Corbusier's *The City of Tomorrow*[14] to remind myself of Le Corbusier's claims that the existence of right angles and straight lines are primary evidence for the "rightness" of the human mind, particularly the "uprightness," i.e. propriety, of the architectural mind. However, it was not enough, for some reason, for Le Corbusier simply to make this claim and go on. In his text, human life was opposed to another kind of life, a non-architectural, not right or upright life, mainly animal life—a donkey. The wandering, mindless donkey, for Le Corbusier, was the instructive foil to the straightness of the lines that humans draw in the world. Thus, ancient cities organized around animal paths are, according to Le Corbusier, sites of congestion and disease, while modern cities exhibit their health by means of straight avenues based on right angles. As is evident, the donkey has massive ethical and aesthetic implications in these texts. It is not incidental that most of contemporary philosophical work on animals understands the animal as a challenge to human ethics and the hegemony of reason—not only the killing of animals, but also, in the case of Derrida for example, the violence of generalization that places, with apparent indifference, vastly different kinds of animals into one category, "animal." Peter Singer—professor at Princeton University and author of much controversial work on animal rights—claims, among other things, that animals have equal moral status to humans. These ethical arguments, in particular about the relation of humans to an unreasoning, unself-conscious, "other," in which the animal always plays the part of the other, are tied to the massive theoretical debates in Europe and America about history, human freedom, knowledge, and politics in the late nineteenth and twentieth centuries. Ethical questions in architecture have been notoriously difficult to pin down because of the ambivalence of a practice and profession that historically has always been suspended between intellectual/artistic work and commercial work. My point here is simply to have it all ways, while pursuing only a few ways. "Post-animal life," in other words, connects, as a subject, with the deepest strands of philosophical debate in Western culture, but insofar as this life is part of a series of architectural questions, these debates are subordinated in almost every case to the questions that press, in both profound and profoundly limited ways, on architecture. Not all of the limitations are embraced but neither are they ignored.

The donkey, in Le Corbusier's writings, remained, for me, a repository of unresolved ideas in architecture, some but not all of which are concerned with ethics and philosophy. Le Corbusier's odd, and diverse, invocations of the donkey over and over in his writing opens up a subject matter—animals—that is difficult, if not impossible, to absorb into architecture and architectural history/theory for reasons that are quite interesting. Why, or how, a trivial, typically comical animal such as the donkey came to oppose the right angle, held as one of the most significant abstract productions of the human mind, the deep mathematical heart of Western architecture itself, is one aspect of a complex set of issues. My general inquiry into life and architecture, in this book, thus came to include the problem of animals.

Animals represent, generally, a form of life that is even more radically antithetical to architecture than human life. Architecture is a human endeavour, but this does not guarantee its "sympathy" with human life: even less does it guarantee a sympathy with animal life. But animals cannot be detached from human life; indeed, human life is also animal life, although this means different things at different times. So the animal invariably complicates, and confuses, any picture of human life. The animal itself, whatever that might mean, is not the main focus of my discussion for reasons I explain in different parts of the book. And for this I apologize. Nothing, in my view, would be more intriguing than if we could see animals for themselves—bees, horses, lions, a bird, a snake. The extraordinary intensified presence of these living beings in the world is deeply satisfying and more interesting, in some sense, than anything else we see or think about. Sanford Kwinter, who has been studying evolutionary developmental biology—in the interest of suggestively critiquing our animal relation to architectural form ("we may be hard-wired as a species to see form," he commented recently)[15]—is fascinated, in particular, by the morphology and behavior of super-predators such as lions and hyenas. As he remarked, in a public lecture, the "shape of the animal is everything that the animal does" and its behavior and morphology are connected to both contemporaneous and ancestral animals. A bird is the bird's actions, the nest, the forest, other birds, other animals that co-inhabit its territory as well as broader ranges, predators and prey, and so forth.

Animals, who exhibit life in highly concentrated and diverse forms, have the power to completely alter our way of thinking about ourselves, both the form of ourselves and the forms we make, live in, and respond to. But imagining a paradigm shift in architecture in which animal life would play a part is an extremely difficult task. The sight of animals in the wild is always riveting and fills us with an inarticulate desire that almost immediately results in rampant speculation: what do these animals mean?; how can anything like a lion still exist? To which there are no satisfactory answers. These animals literally bring us, our complex systems of inhabitation and living, our understanding of form, matter, energy, and resources, to life. But they also elude us. Part of my discussion—almost against my will because some of my scholarly sympathies lie with Elizabeth Costello's (that is J. M. Coetzee's) blunt and incisive observations about human and animal life rather than the convoluted discussions of the ethical philosophers or the simplistic discussions of the humanist historians[16]—has been to try to understand the resistance that architecture offers to the subject of life in addition to speaking directly about what a "life-architecture" paradigm shift might mean for architecture and urbanism. In some way that evolutionary developmental biology also recognizes, particularly in its fascination with animal behavior, we cannot really see these animals, so buried are we, and they, in a human life-privileging from which there seems to be no escape; indeed, is the very definition of autonomous humanity since Kant.[17] "Man," as Darwin said, "is so incomparably better known than any animal."[18] The animal, too, is buried in its own species-privilege, but we have no idea what this means to them apart from the impoverished idea of "mere survival." The various kinds of studies that have observed animals behaving as "architects," for example, depend on so many unexplained and ultimately embarrassing, if not horrific, projections and presuppositions about animal and human life, as well as architecture, that in the end they qualify as sinister, although fascinating, fairy tales about ourselves. Alexander Kojève enigmatically wrote, at one point, that if post-historical man were to become an animal again he would build the way spiders do. But we don't know what spiders have in mind when they spin webs; that is, we don't know what their architectural theory might be. And it would be impossible, of course, to spin a web from the human body, Spiderman notwithstanding. But Kojève is sly. He perhaps meant that when we become, again, "purely biological," abandoning the "unidirectional history" that gained its significance through accumulation, we would keep, in what he calls our "animal happiness," a desire to construct networks, cages, cul de sacs, scaffolding, bridges.[19] There are, as well, ways of spinning webs that do not involve literally imitating a spider.

At the same time, specific animals and their characteristics are crucial to the architectural questions asked in the book. As one of my students astutely noted, if you are riding a donkey or carrying things by donkey then the much-maligned "donkey paths" that Le Corbusier proposes replacing with more "rational" avenues are, in fact, the more rational of the two pathways.[20] But this would also suggest that we were, at some point in history, able to allow the donkey an autonomous movement and identity, i.e. that we were able to yield to what I called in an earlier book "donkey urbanism."[21] The phrase "post-animal life," which I use to label both human and animal life since the Renaissance, simultaneously stands guard over and disallows the animal *qua* animal, the autonomous animal. "Post-animal life" denotes animal life that has been divested of any autonomy it ever had, and human life after its animal aspect has, for the most part, been put under the supervision of science and psychology. But "post-animal" also refers to the historical slippage between architectural modernity, which I argue (with Manfredo Tafuri) began in the Renaissance, and biological modernity, which began in the late eighteenth century. Generally, post-animal human life has lost much of its animalness but gradually acquired a biological identity that is now given equal, or even advanced, status compared to human intellectual and spiritual life. Post-animal animal life, on the other hand, has lost biological status and a complex identity, as well as, in many cases, life itself. Animals, even wild animals, are universally seen by humans as valuable primarily for their potential contribution to human life. This is a cumbersome way of speaking—too many twists and turns—but the benefit is that it might give us a way to speak, in architecture, of animals and, through the animal, to speak of something like a "biological human" or a "human-animal" without our usual architectural tendency to project generalized, and often extremely nostalgic, forms onto life. Typically we can't even speak of the subject of biological humanness in architecture, much less the animal, without being rendered almost speechless. Sentiment, which, under certain circumstances, has been marshaled as a form of critique of the certitudes advanced by philosophy and rationalism, also has no legs to stand on in architecture. In other words, the sentimental other—rendered as animal, either benevolent or malevolent—might have the ability to challenge our belief in something like the primacy of language (since animals apparently have no language)[22] were it not for the fact that architecture is a "semantic nightmare" as Rem Koolhaas has noted.

The question of "autonomy," which has accompanied us during our three-quarters of a century study of architectural modernism, has referred, typically, to the autonomy of the human subject in architecture. The phrase "post-humanist," used by Michael Hays and others to describe the loss of autonomy in the humanist subject—in favor of the dispersed or fragmented subject of Jacques Lacan existing in a post-modern world—does not speak, typically, of humans both acquiring, and shedding, their animal part or of animals losing their identities as whole beings. In a post-animal world, which begins with Renaissance humanism and humanist presuppositions—the endlessly interesting inventions of perspective in painting and architectural representation, secularization, and the mathematical adjudication of architecture and the human body—humans begin to sublimate the identity that mixed them up with animals. This sublimated animal aspect is gradually recovered, formalized, and made "scientific" by the nineteenth century sciences of biology and psychology. But by then the human is, in a sense, a different animal than before. During the Renaissance, the literal animal also begins to be discovered and brought out of its wild state into the human enclave. There was a (short) moment of speculation about whether, for example, Palladio's villas were, in effect, co-inhabited by farm animals. This incidental, somewhat ludicrous, fact, if true, does not tell us about the wild animal per se, but it might contradict part of the impression we have formed of Palladio's humanist project; that is, the impression that the project was exclusively for human beings. At the same time, our architectural interest in Palladio's work would be almost completely unaffected by the possibility that the human occupants of these structures were flanked by animal occupants. The "occupant"—even the word speaks of the bureaucratized formation of living beings tuned to a particular architectural task, i.e. "occupancy"—clearly belongs to a different order of being than the building. And its species-identity has not been in question since at least the Enlightenment.

The animal brings with it, among other things, a danger and fascination that comes from outside architecture and is never fully assimilated or appropriated by it. It raises, as a live subject, serious aesthetic, performative and ethical expectations that are almost never met. Our knowledge of animals is the scene of our seduction by them, a seduction that makes us so nervous that we invariably trivialize the question of the animal both as it presents itself in our lives in general and as it comes into play in architecture. One of the problems of the animal in architecture is that it is alive in a way that is identical to the aliveness of human beings, i.e. organic or biological life, but its life is clearly held to be of lower value, which one might initially think would make its architectural value also lower. In fact, the reverse is true. The animal is not only alive, and therefore eligible as an occupant—subject to some of the same laws as the human occupant, such as the need for/fulfillment of shelter and warmth—but it has traditionally been used in both symbolic and structural ways in buildings. The animal can cross into, and be endangered as well as ennobled by, the formal realm of the building in a way that human life generally cannot. The animal can be *literally* represented in the architectural building and, in fact, is frequently asked to carry heavy symbolic burdens in the interest of architecture's claim for its aesthetic excess over building. Since the Renaissance, and even before, human life has been held away from this realm.

Architecture *as* animal—Alberti's words—was an ideal of Renaissance architecture and describes a different aspect of the same issue. Alberti argued for an architecture that had absorbed organic principles of organization into its inorganic structure, making of it a "body" that was comprised of the assembly of parts and wholes, as part was to part, member was to member.[23] This is an identification that architecture sustains in various ways throughout its history, and it is not meant primarily as a metaphor. It is meant to grant architecture the same depth or organization, mobility, aliveness, that characterizes the life that lives within it.

Both Michel Foucault and François Jacob characterize the Renaissance as a time when all life is interconnected by means of analogies and loose linguistic and imagistic (surface) affiliations. The idea of "life" is swamped by the undifferentiated pervasiveness of what Aristotle called "animate principles." Palladio's villas might be said—specifically, even, since Palladio himself was a careful scholar of Renaissance theories of appropriate forms for the divine (universal) and the human (subjective)—to be built for human and animal life that is undifferentiated from vegetable and mineral life. But it is telling that we rarely raise the question of life in this way. Most historical studies take for granted the value of human life over animal, for example, and studies of historical architectural production such as Palladio's concentrate on the various developments of metaphysical theories, not on the possible weirdness of animals sharing Renaissance living spaces.

As Colin Rowe so ingeniously reminds us in *The Mathematics of the Ideal Villa*,[24] when we speak of architecture and life, we immediately add to biological life (or "bare life," as Giorgio Agamben calls it) a cultural/technical aspect; we typically speak not of life, but, as mentioned earlier, of *ways* of life. Architecture's primary response to biological life has been to organize its animate potential, to set it in motion down a path or through a program of occupation—to send it on its way through the world of the city, the site, the building. The motion of the occupant and architect alike—his/her/its pursuit of a "way" under architectural command—produces, in architectural space, further asymmetries based on the relation between the static and the moving. Paradoxically, one of architecture's historical responses to these asymmetries, which it, itself, cultivates and about which much more needs to be elucidated, has been to invent anchoring technologies that are, for the most part, symmetrically arranged, at least on the surface. In light of this, Rowe's comparison of Palladio's architecture of carved "niches," which produces a free section, to Le Corbusier's architecture of the free plan, is particularly interesting. In both cases, he argues, the problem is how to geometrically reconcile the vicissitudes of everyday life with the problem of a mathematically reasoned structure. The (apparently) non-reasoning animal being and the reasoning human being are, of course, united in the human occupant. But architecture historically has joined first theology, and later philosophy, in the careful and crafty partitioning of large parts of "animal being" away from the reasoning being that is the human "occupant." Rowe's opposition between "everyday life" and "mathematical structure" thus becomes, in effect, almost a complete tautology. Reasoning/mathematical beings produce rational/mathematical architectures for reasoning/mathematical beings. Indeed, modern architecture could be said to be have been founded on the attempt to realize this tautology; to erase the idea of "vicissitudes of everyday life." As is evident, it is difficult to hold the ethical philosophers at bay once the animal comes into the picture since "reason," which is also self-consciousness, is the fundamental measure by which we determine our value as a species. But there are many paradoxes in these positions because, as mentioned above, architecture has a peculiar identification with animalness in its own form and in the form of its occupants.

Because of the eventual containment of all biological life in the cages of the Renaissance (perspective) and the cages of the Enlightenment (taxonomy/classification)—cages which are jointly defined by architecture, art, and science—human and animal lose much of the spatial difference that was based on, in particular, the idea of a wild nature versus the cultivated space of culture. In some sense, they come closer together. However, during this same time period, humans gain their own evolutionary branch and definitely separate from animals, at least for a time. Biology discovers and invents, in the nineteenth century, *Homo sapiens*, a creature that makes possible the idea of a "human-animal" who is formally alive but scientifically detached from ideas of inner life or psychological history, sexual or otherwise. By finding a place for the human in the animal—a place that gives *Homo sapiens* biological persuasiveness but also makes the human more human than animal—biology both includes and distinguishes the human in/from the animal. Biological predominance is thus added to the intellectual and spiritual dominance of humans during pre-biological history. This human-animal, which is some kind of amalgam of the post-animal human and the post-animal animal, will prove to be peculiarly useful and interesting to architecture. In spite of the formidable development of the psychological sciences in the nineteenth and twentieth centuries, architecture continues to invoke the nineteenth century biological human—again, this human-animal—until genetics begins to again alter the understanding of human life in the late twentieth century. The human-animal is one kind of "post-animal life." Part of what I want to say is that, since the Renaissance, the human-animal, in one form or another, is the being whom architecture has brought to mind whenever it has brought "life" to mind. This is a large, and largely speculative, claim. Its point is not to offer a didactic argument about how architecture sees life in less-than-human terms. Instead, its point is to begin to define architecture precisely as the surreptitious form of life science that its theoretical history has attempted to mediate and even refuse.

## History

Another part of my answer to the question "What is this book about?" concerns the use of the word "history" already mentioned earlier in this introduction—the "history of the idea of biological life" and the "history of architecture." Both the subject and fact of life enforce an examination of history and historical practices. Inevitably, the book takes on some of the issues associated with contemporary historical and theoretical practices in architecture, and the relation of these two academic practices to architectural practice itself. There are many polemical relationships between different styles of thinking about, and practising, architecture but one of the book's aim is to show how architecture, architectural history, and theories of biological life converge at certain moments in their respectively diverse histories. This aim requires a somewhat more theoretical approach to architecture and biology: I do not use theoretical arguments in order to demonstrate the virtues of theory over history or vice versa, but, instead, to get somewhere that it might otherwise be hard, if not impossible, to get to. The complex subject of life, which is simultaneously always historical (we are the products of our biological history) and ahistorical in its lived state (the biological arrow goes only one way in time, toward the future) requires a double approach that from one point of view is historical and, from another, is not. This approach is not meant to make the subject matter more complicated, but to change the style of question one might ask. Certainly the style of questions I ask in this book are often different from what an historian or practitioner would ask. But theory is neither ignorant of, nor irresponsible toward, history and practice. It has been, in architecture, precisely the ability of theory to occupy a middle, although not neutral, ground between history and practice that has made it useful and interesting.

The point of view of the book and its critical framework are oriented, therefore, in several directions. On the one hand, the book responds to a set of themes and concerns in architecture, and in architectural history and theory, some of which have been under discussion for thirty years or more: architectural representation, modernism and its various phases, post-classical theory, digital architectures, and computational theories. These themes unavoidably include questions of "architectural meaning"—philosophical, symbolic, social/political, and material—as well as more specific issues such as the pivotal importance of the eighteenth century in the formation of architectural history that Anthony Vidler made us vividly aware of in his book *The Writing of the Walls*.[25] On the other hand, the book is as much as possible a precise investigation into specific ideas about biological life in order to pose—in a different vein than most studies—a series of questions about human life and architecture that view the gradual emergence of the category of the "human" in biology and paleontology as significant for architecture, and ask how that emergence necessitated a radical change in the way the world was viewed. How does a change in the status of human life in culture affect architectural ideas? When biology and architecture officially come together—since architectural history and biology are both formed as disciplines during the Enlightenment—they exchange metaphorical terms such as *structure, typology, organization, evolution,* and *development*. This explicit exchange ceases, after a time, to be noteworthy, but these metaphors subsist beneath both disciplines over the next two centuries. Viewing architecture from the point of view of life—in its full array of manifestations—also suggests that we might now understand life-figures and "aliveness" in architectural work, both theoretical and built, in a different way.

Architecture's articulated "humanist" view of life was a specific cluster of ideas in Renaissance architecture around issues of scale, mathematics, proportion with respect to the human body, the revival of classicism, the secularization of civic life, and the idea of human life as a worldly, serene, principled, and beneficent force. "Architectural humanism"—a humanism referred to, in different ways, by Rudolf Wittkower, Siegfried Giedion, Andrea Palladio, Peter Murray, Michael Hays, Manfredo Tafuri, Geoffrey Scott, Jacob Burckhardt, and many others—was a movement that postulated, simultaneously, a "scientific" basis for architecture, the *sprezzatura* (studied recklessness) of multiple kinds of knowledge, and an understanding of human life that rested on ideas of "unchanged values," and "unchanged constancy."[26] What is recognized in the nineteenth century as the force of biological homeostasis is, in the fifteenth century, articulated as a desire for human life to hold itself still in the face of the ideal. This early concept of constancy supports the possibility of an idealization of architectural work. In the Renaissance, without too much exaggeration, one could say that humans, animals, plants, minerals, and crystals are still scientifically, metaphysically, and materially undifferentiated from each other. The animate and the inanimate are still significantly mixed up with each other—monstrosity is not hypothetical—in the fifteenth century. And yet, architecture is already in the process of becoming modern. It founds, and serves as foundation for, "representation" and gives itself, as a result, "symbolic form." This form locates and fixes things and beings in space; as Panofsky argues, the construction of Brunelleschi's perspective was the construction of metaphysical space itself with its potentials and limit conditions. The internal biological constancy that Bernard later hypothesizes for both animal and human is defined, in the Renaissance, as an external constancy of representational and symbolic space that emanates from the two centers of the human body, the displaced navel of the Vitruvian man, and the human eye that forms the vanishing point. So one revised formulation of Renaissance architecture might include an inquiry into how such preliminary ideals of modernity can house life that still possesses a very real relation to the monstrous.

Before concluding, I should say that part of the difficulty of writing this book had to do with finding a way to refer to the "Renaissance" and "Enlightenment" while maintaining the ahistoricity of the subject of life—ahistorical because it makes no sense to speak of Renaissance biological life versus Enlightenment biological life. In Jacob's remark that biological life is, at any given moment, a precise record of its history means that it biologically depends on everything that has come before it. Humans live in something we call history but life as it is lived in the body cares nothing for historical process. I am also a theorist; so my sympathies usually lie with historical inquiry that has been heavily bracketed—the "Renaissance" caged in the ubiquitous quotation marks of the theorist. But it has been exceptionally interesting to look at some of the classic architectural histories of the Renaissance and Enlightenment. These periods have been understood, by most historians and theorists, to be pivotal in the formation of modernity in both architecture and the biological sciences, even if it requires, in most cases, the nineteenth century to confirm this modernity. Nevertheless, while I have tried to resist the grand summaries so endemic to Renaissance and Enlightenment scholarship—partly because of ongoing arguments about what actually constitutes their boundaries and influences—I too refer to these periods in the time-honored way, using phrases like "roughly in 1550" or "around the late eighteenth century." This is a little like the *tremolo* in singing, or the wavy line used in sketching. Both cover the fact that one's voice, or hand, is a little tenuous when it comes to holding one note or one line in its pure enunciation. But, of course, there is no one note or path in the case of historical interpretation or drawing, and probably not in singing either. We are incurable in our desire for such a note, and have devised ingenious ways of both having, and not having it, at the same time.

**Computation**

Finally, the book also takes some account, particularly in the last chapter, of current discussions around animation and movement in architecture—specifically in computational architectures—since any investigation of architecture and life by necessity runs into the physics and metaphysics of time and motion. This part of the book responds to the "contemporary moment," but its deeper thematic connection has to do with how architecture, *vis-à-vis* the computer, has absorbed some of the changes in the status of life associated with contemporary genetics. Genetics has been re-opening certain doors between species that were closed, in a decisive way, in the late eighteenth and early nineteenth centuries when Darwin, in particular, adopted the tree, with its branching structure, as the operative figure of species development, i.e. each species gets its own branch, never to return to the fork of divergence that initially differentiated each from the other. The field of genetics is, without question, changing our view of life, returning to those "forks in the tree," suspending the orthodoxies of species origins and so forth. Under its influence, post-animal life certainly will give way to something else.

A final anecdote that might give us some inkling of how to situate such questions. I was recently participating in an academic final architectural jury where students were designing buildings for a site in Queens that New York City has designated for the 2012 Summer Olympics, should New York win the bid.[27] Using biological terms such as "evolution" and "adaptation," the projects attempted to create what students called an "evolutionary surface" that would allow different aspects of the program (spectatorship, eating, media coverage, athletic competitions) to seamlessly merge into each other; an architecture of continuous surfaces, differentiated by various isoparms, or crests, that spilled activity from one place to the next, from leisure to work, from work to spectatorship. The projects suggested, as a number of architects have been suggesting for the past five or six years, that architecture no longer belongs to the rigid geometries that have been its structural (geometric, philosophical) heritage, nor to the rigid programs of typological construction. But the power to change form in biology does not happen at the individual level, nor is its spatial character clear. It is not a poignant moment, a crest or watershed, because the meaning of the process of change on the whole direction of the form of a particular species is only understood at the provisional end of a long process of change. And it is a statistical event, based on a huge array of random possibilities. Change, in biology, is never heroic (a point of arrival) or even anti-heroic (a shared, interstitial, boundary line). Change happens through time in biology. And biological change is reliant on life processes—dependent, as least as we have theorized it to date, on random mutations and unpredictable internal and external pressures. We rarely think of architecture in this way. Architecture, as an act of design and construction, is, by definition, always at a remove from life processes. One of its primary technical roles is to regulate the exertion of external force on organisms in the form of light, materiality, enclosure, heating/cooling, and so forth. If architecture becomes evolutionary in imitation of the biological body—even if this is only at the figurative or metaphoric level—there ensues what can only be called a "mimetic crisis" between organism and milieu. Architecture begins to mistake itself for an organism and life for a technology, both of which "mistakes" describe some of the aspirations of recent work in the field. These are sometimes fruitful mistakes and may even be an accurate way of describing, philosophically, what would need to be done to achieve a seemingly much desired cyborgian or hybrid architecture, a radically "inter-disciplinary" architecture. The aspiration is also, now, toward a generative architecture. A cloned architecture would possess the regenerative principles of biological reproduction rather than the entropic principles of classical physics. The computational universe that both architecture and biology can now share (along with every other discipline) allows each to appear to slip into the other in some way; but this universe is also advancing its own cybernetic visions and arguments, not necessarily specific or friendly to its various users.

One of the results of architecture's use of biological metaphors in the age of genetics (which short-circuits adaptation and variation in a different manner than, say, nineteenth century breeders) is this illusion of quick change, movement that is coterminous in time and space with the movement of ourselves through space as we might go, or desire to go, from one function to the next. The fixed axes, the counter-bracing, of the horizontal and the vertical, leaden as they are, irrelevant as they are to the mobile human body that must poise itself on the narrow base of its feet or the flexible forces that impinge on any built structure—wind, water, networks of organizational energy—are, nevertheless, extremely hard to replace in architecture. It is still somewhat easier to theorize life as a technology, as Foucault attempted, than theorize technology as alive, as Deleuze attempted. The diagonal, or the ramp, which suggest movement and movement averaged, is, structurally, still a bracing up of the horizontal and vertical. At the same time, as questions in contemporary architecture shift, what we can do is no longer accord the diagonal its classical geometric and philosophical status in relation to volume and structural stability. I discuss these issues, primarily, in the final chapters of the book, but my point in this introduction is to say that the students' work in this study—which was virtuoso contemporary work in architecture—raises, at this moment in time, more questions than it answers.

But, finally, I don't want to be too disingenuous. The students' work in this studio was attempting to make, ultimately, not a biological or genetic argument about time and change, but a series of computational arguments in architecture that privilege flows and fluid processes. The use of developmental surfaces, made possible by computers, as well as the intellectual provocation of biological and genetic terms, may represent an apotheosis of what I am calling the "post-animal," the point at which both human and animal pass back into each other in a different way, and re-enter a new period of co-dependency and co-genesis. The pig, under certain genetic modifications, may be able, in quicker-than-evolutionary time, to become not a human but a part of a human, an organ. This new co-dependency will certainly bring with it new ideas about structure and space/time. We are already able to "back-engineer" life from fossil remains with much greater accuracy and detail. The ubiquitous T. Rex, who used to stand upright and possess reptilian skin, now is bent and possibly feathered. Certainly the ever-present and pressing questions of "sustainability" in architecture, some of which were mentioned at the beginning of this introduction and which ask not simply for a green building practice but also for remediation and renovating technologies that can address huge landscapes and urban systems, will be deeply served by digital architectural techniques in ways we are only beginning to understand. The surface meshes of computational architectures carry the potential not only for acting as some kind of living surface but also for making profound fields of reparation beyond their immediate boundaries. The word "interactive" does not even come close to describing the potential of this work. But whether architecture can or should exploit or build itself as an epigenetic, or remediation, surface is not the question of this book, although these are the questions that might arise out of this book. For the purposes of this book, my interest is in how our recent interests in a mobile architecture—an architecture that attempts to refute the metaphysics of the vertical and horizontal (which is also the metaphysics of volume) in favor of a metaphysics of surface, and an architecture that finds its metaphors in the domain of an increasingly intricate idea of biological and political/cultural life—fits into architecture's long history of adjudication with its living occupants.

**"Life is that which resists partition."**

—Georges Bataille

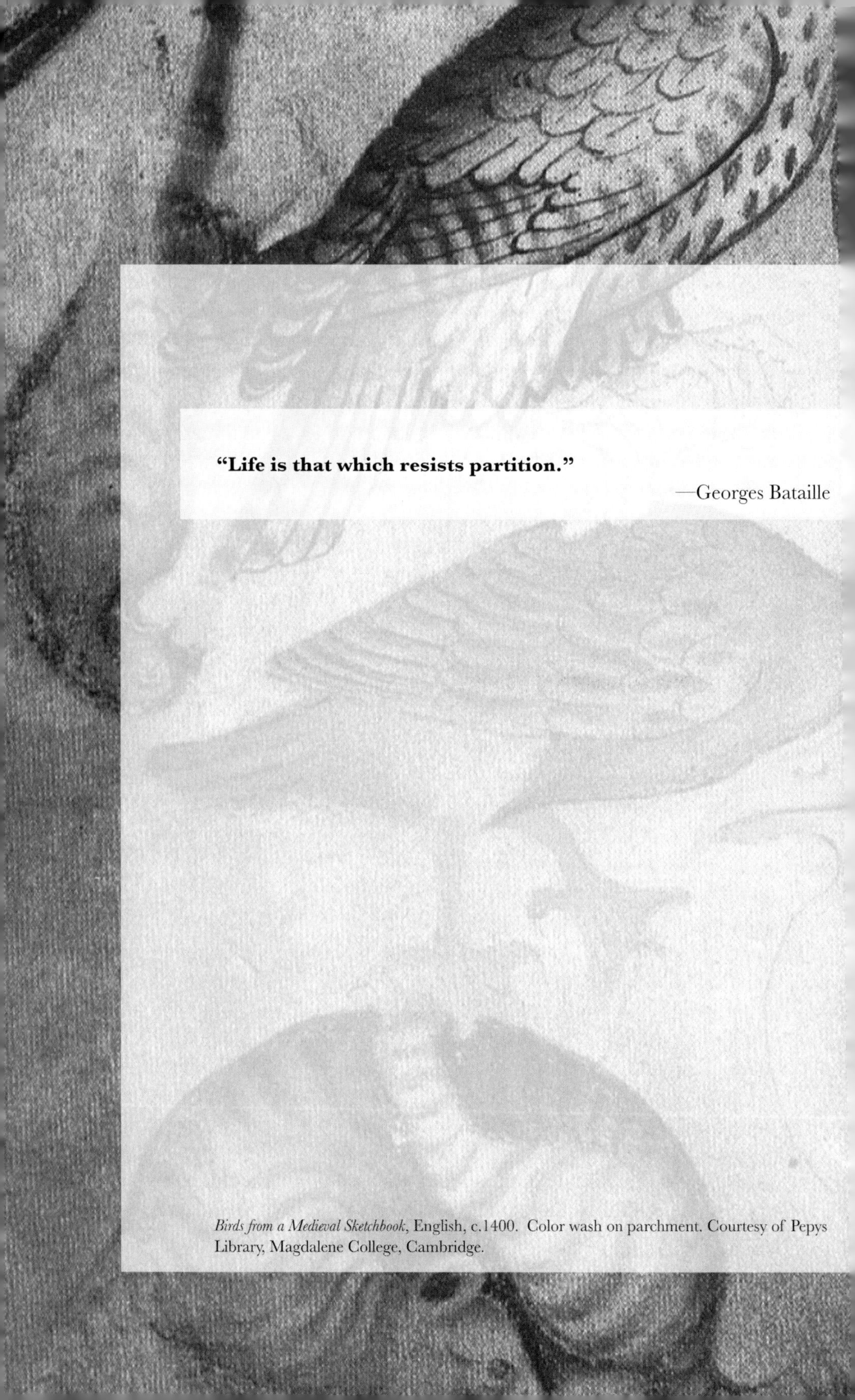

*Birds from a Medieval Sketchbook*, English, c.1400. Color wash on parchment. Courtesy of Pepys Library, Magdalene College, Cambridge.

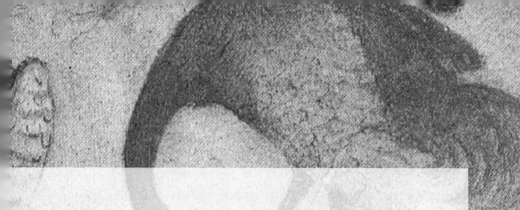

# 1: PARTITIONING THE ORTHOPEDIC WHOLE

Almost all definitions of living beings, since Aristotle, wrestled in some form with the problem of separating the living from the non-living, the vital subject from the dead object.[1] Georges Canguilhem reviews this history as one of similarity and difference between and among "life forms" that are themselves differentiated, *vis-à-vis* Aristotle, from non-living forms by being "identified with animation . . . the life-soul is the form, or act, of which the living natural body is the content." Canguilhem further writes:

> All the medical philosophies that held, down to the beginning of the nineteenth century, that life was either a unique principle or somehow associated with the soul, essentially different from matter and an exception to its laws, were directly or indirectly indebted to that part of Aristotle's system which can equally well be called biology or psychology.[2]

Or, tautology: living beings exhibit life; life is different from non-life because it is infused with a life principle. Because Aristotle, particularly in his *Parts of Animals*,[3] regarded the classification of "parts"—organs, actions, functions—as a way of directly recording the effects of this soul or life force, subsequent attempts at making the world systematic, until Bichat, were more or less able to sidestep the direct question of life in favor of increasingly refined combinations of parts. Agamben remarks that this "thing," life, "that remains indeterminate gets articulated and divided time and again through a series of caesura and oppositions that invest it with a decisive strategic function . . . everything happens as if, in our culture, life were *what cannot be defined*, yet, precisely for this reason, must be ceaselessly articulated and divided."[4]

When the Renaissance architects Andrea Palladio and Leon Battista Alberti[5] looked to classical antiquity for architectural principles, they also found Aristotle, as well as Plato and Pythagoras, standing watch over the formation of architectural cosmology. This was not the "Aristotelian scholasticism of the Middle Ages"[6] but the Aristotle of epic tragedy, the *Poetics*, and the metaphysics of universal principles.[7] Aristotle defined rationality in terms of a synthetic logic of parts and wholes,[8] and he made of architecture, as well as animals, a composite of parts.[9] In Aristotle's animals, these parts are bound together and animated, infused with a soul, by the (imperially translated) "unmoved mover" who is empowered without limit. In Renaissance architecture, the imputed universal binding principle, which also implied a cosmic mathematics, was harmonic mathematical proportions. As Wittkower argued:

> The conviction that architecture is a science, and that each part of a building, inside as well as outside, has to be integrated into one and the same system of mathematical ratios, may be called the basic axiom of Renaissance architects. We have already seen that the architect is by no means free to apply to a building a system of ratios of his own choosing, that the ratios have to comply with conceptions of a higher order and that a building should mirror the proportions of the human body; a demand which became universally accepted on Vitruvius' authority. As

man is the image of God and the proportions of his body are produced by divine will, so the proportions in architecture have to embrace and express the cosmic order.[10]

Architecture, like Aristotle's animal body, is constructed in the Renaissance out of marked parts bound together by divinely controlled principles. Already in the Renaissance architecture as a "science" objectifies the relation of parts to each other.

Human life, as we understand it now, typically wields its privilege by means of a felt wholeness of a body, however illusory that wholeness. This was, in part, Jacques Lacan's point. Our illusion of our "orthopedic" wholeness is put together from two sides, between which there is an uncrossable gap. Our physical bodies and the image of our bodies reflected back to us by the mirroring eyes of the mother make up the psychological and musculoskeletal coordinates by which we navigate the self and the world. These sides are both symmetrical—reversed, mirror images of each other—and asymmetrical: one reflection comes from a place outside the body, the other is a three-dimensional "house" in space, a body with an interior. The asymmetry between outside and inside has also accounted, in some way, for the gap between the body and the technical work of the body, such as architecture. In either case, this asymmetry manifests itself as a kind of oscillation in focus between the outside and the inside. Many contemporary theories of change and adaptation in biology are also concerned with this asymmetry. Morphological differences seem to be co-produced by tensions that extend beyond, and outside of, the organism understood as a genetic cluster proper to itself. The asymmetry between inside and outside conditions in advance the relation of part to whole—partitioning and resistance to partitioning—that has characterized our understanding of life.

Even before any idea of "life's privilege" is understood in medical, physiological, or psychological terms, human biological life resists, out of necessity, its own partitioning or objectification on behalf of architecture. Leonardo da Vinci's Vitruvian man, architectural aspirations

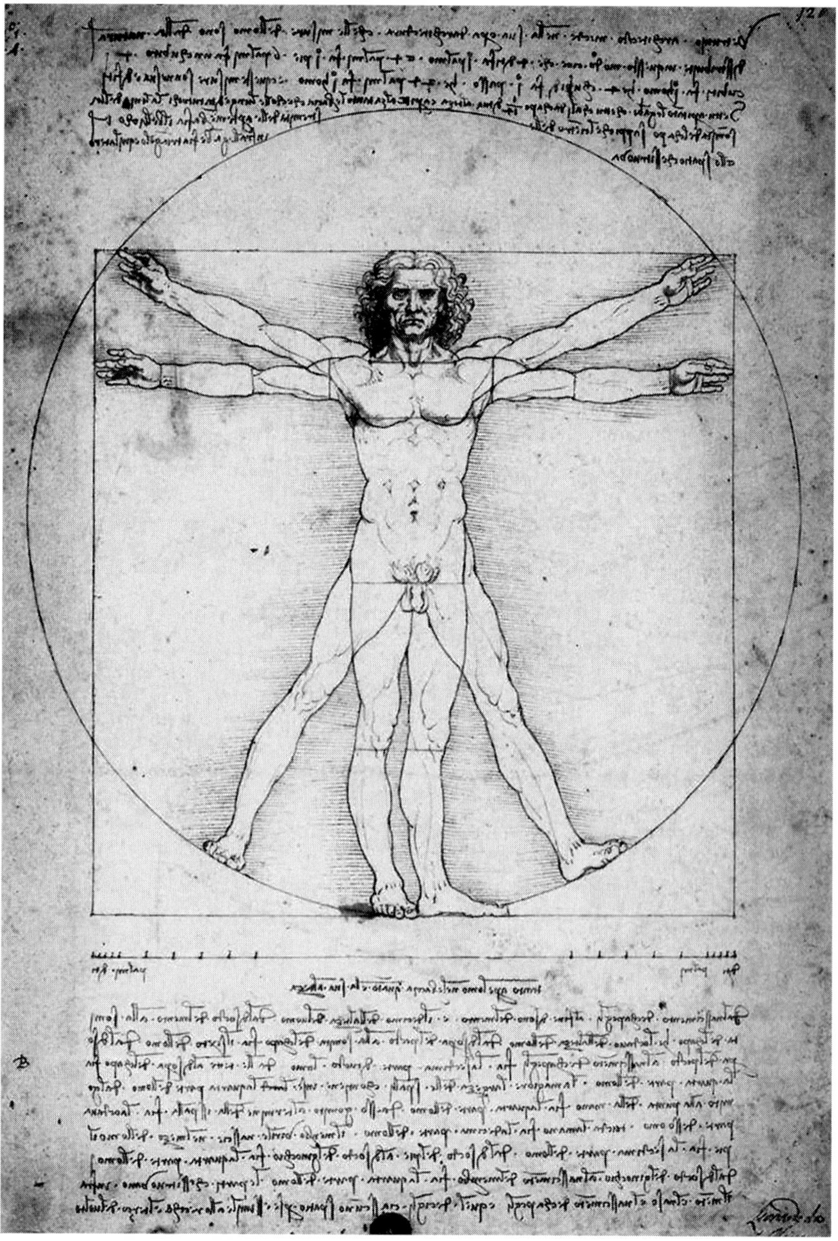

Figure 1.1: Leonardo da Vinci, *Vitruvian Man*, 1492.

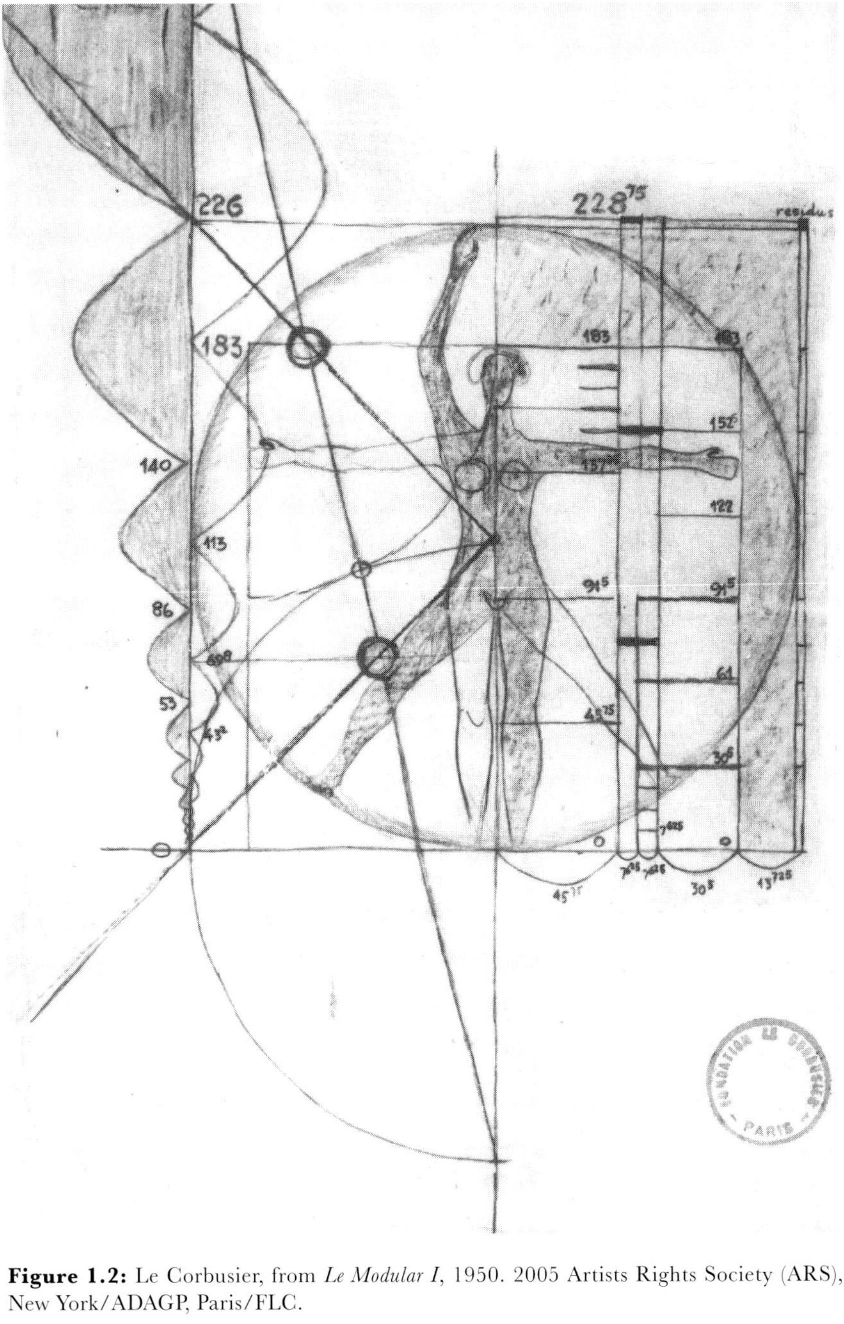


**Figure 1.2:** Le Corbusier, from *Le Modular I*, 1950. 2005 Artists Rights Society (ARS), New York/ADAGP, Paris/FLC.

notwithstanding, could not be used as a proportioning system in any rigorous sense because it refers, in spite of its idealization and channeling of the divine, to both ideal and non-ideal human life, a morass of theological and animistic theories in which life forces are undifferentiated. The "parts" that might make up a system of proportional ratios cannot be clearly broken out. Le Corbusier's Modular—another attempt at the idealization of the human body with respect to architecture—fails as a measuring instrument for different reasons, but sustains the resistance of life to partitioning. Bataille remarks that life itself is, in fact, that which "resists partition."[11] The idea of proportion in the Renaissance, which describes a harmonized relation between parts and attempts to inscribe the symmetrical human body in mathematical space, inaugurates two opposing ideas about human life in architecture—one, that life is a relation of parts (ratios), and the other, that life is whole (circumscribed). Both strands of this description, and its discontents, continue to weave in and out of architecture for centuries.

The Renaissance sculpture-architect Bernini, differentiating architecture from sculpture, remarked: "First [in architecture] it was necessary to reflect on the material, then on the invention, thereafter on the ordering of the parts, and finally on giving them the perfection of grace and delicacy." "Delicacy" (*tenerezza*), Franco Borsi suggests, refers to the "softness and gentleness" that Bernini brought to the "cold art" of architecture.[12] In the sculpture "Pluto and Proserpina," as well as other Bernini sculptures, Borsi notes that the sculptural space "divides . . . into parts," and uses this as proof of the "predisposition" of Bernini's sculpture toward architecture. But this sculpture, in particular, which was done just prior to Bernini's first architectural work, suggests a more troubled relation between parts, the human figure, and architectural space. The imprint of Pluto's fingers on Proserpina's soft thigh and back, the alarm of three-headed Cerebus, the molding of the curls of the hair, the "classical citation" of the torsion of the two torsos, all suggest that the writhing figure of Proserpina is, in fact, trying to escape the "sheath of space" of the sculpture as a proto-architectural space. Her eyes are wide open, looking out of the sculptural space, two marble tears on her cheeks. It is hard to read that look, in which the whole narrative mythos of the statue is held. It is certainly an appeal, and a look of fear—this is a rape—but her eyes have no relation, for example, to the eyes of the animal in the scene, which are rabid and spaceless, or Pluto's eyes, which are forbearing but still deeply within the sculptural space and argument. The animal, which symbolizes here an even more deeply wild aspect of the god, is from Hades. Proserpina, as a young girl, is from the union of sky and earth (Zeus and Demeter). The capture of her body, *her* torsion away from Pluto (both torsions, according to Borsi, placing huge stresses on the marble), is not in the same space that Pluto holds down with the weight of his powerful body. Let go, her resistance against him would rebound with enough force to throw her out of the frame. She is the object of his desire, a goddess, but her live body against his anchored body is fighting the framing, figuralization, and division into "parts" that predisposes this sculpture to an architecture. Proserpina is "becoming human" in the sculpture, in a sense that foreshadows her paradoxical role as a goddess of the fertile earth as well as of the underworld. And it is her humanness that asserts itself against the partitioning of the proto-architectural space.

As this sculpture in some way portends, the human body, since at least the Renaissance, can be objectified but, in spite of the gap that composes its (modern) wholeness, it cannot be easily partitioned. There have been, and continue to be, extreme circumstances in history when the human body was literally partitioned, but most occur during periods of war or terror, when "humanness," as an idea, explodes into an animal existence that belongs, always, to some prehistoric being: to mythical animals such as Hades' dog Cerebus in Bernini's sculpture, in which the animal stands for sheer brutality and violence. The body is also partitioned in modern medical practices. But the issues associated with surgery, for example, are very different. Theoretically, medical practice attempts to penetrate the epidermis of the human body without, in some sense, breaking into the orthopedic whole. In modernity,

 **Figure 1.3:** Gianlorenzo Bernini, *Pluto and Proserpina*, 1621-1622. Courtesy of Museo Borghese, Rome. Photograph by Michael Herrman.

**Figure 1.4:** Gianlorenzo Bernini, *Pluto and Proserpina* (detail), 1621-1622. Courtesy of Museo Borghese, Rome. Photograph by Michael Herrman.

as Giorgio Agamben has written in *Homo Sacer*, human life is sacred, but sacred in a way that allows it to be "killed but not sacrificed." Among other things, sacrifice would entail breaking up human bodies in a sanctioned, ritualized context that grants deep significance to each part. It would also make the human body available, as ornament, to architectural work, as is attempted in several other Bernini projects (as well as other architectures in the Renaissance and after); the domes, for example, in the Fonseca Chapel, the Alaleona Chapel, the Sant'Andrea al Quirinale are filled with sculptural figures of cherubs and angels. These bodies are heavenly, which is why they are allowed to occupy the dome, but they are also, of course, modeled on human bodies. The human aspect of Bernini's cherubs, their babyish quality, perhaps makes it appear as if these figures are trying to crawl to the opening at the center of the dome where the light comes in—trying to find a way out of their architectural containment which makes them an ornamental part, on the one hand, and a whole figure caught in the circumscription of the dome, on the other.[13]

When mathematical and musical ratios are no longer used as analogs for the problem of assembling parts into an architectural whole, the practice of architecture—in what amounts to a kind of historical abandonment of the problem of life—continues to put faith in the subordination of parts to a whole that is meant to exceed the parts. The relation of parts to whole in architecture is also a lingering metaphysical mechanism that still underwrites our belief that architecture is essentially the continuation of one kind of building, a building without symbolic import, into another, a building that is architecture. Because one aspect of architecture requires an intense concentration on the assembly of parts, their transportability, composition, adhesion to each other, manners of assembly, it is always profoundly indebted to a material and, until recently, a mineral history. Even more exotic synthetic materials—the new building materials we are interested in today, such as polymers, DuPont's bulletproof Kevlar, aerospace metal composites, goat milk spider wire[14]—continue the argument that architecture, in order to make a conceptual whole, must master the material part, even if that part is now, itself, almost alive. The part, for a long time, carries the weight of an empirical (materialist and positivist) determinism that the architectural whole (symbolic, conceptual) must both accommodate and exceed. It is only in relatively recent attempts, first in modernism with the standardization of parts—which was both fetishistic and meant to reduce the hegemony of part over whole—and then in digital architectures that attempt to model monolithic surfaces, that the empiricist role of the part in architecture begins to be challenged. "From Klee to Le Corbusier, the protagonists of modern art have silently transformed the fragment and absence into motives for a profound reflection on totality and semiotic plenitude," Tafuri wrote,[15] knowing well the problems that will arise from these aspirations toward plenitude and totality, but marking the crucial departure of modernism from an empire of parts. Digital architects, among other things, want to produce a whole that is not indebted for its philosophical persuasiveness to the underpinning of material parts. The much decried "floating" character of digital architecture in the computer, its de-materialization, its insistence on the problem of flows, and its search for modeling and fabrication systems that are seamless are different versions of a resistance to an historical dominance of the part in architectural thinking. Both modernism and digital architecture share the pitfalls and benefits of an idealism that rests on a whole without parts. But one interesting outcome of this idealism in digital work has been the character of its interior spaces, which are increasingly grotto-like,[16] niches or folds of space that have been placed under great pressure by an unsympathetic and lumbering external form. And the question remains: What kind of occupant is implied by these grottos? It is not obvious that the implied occupant—a media-laden, hyperconnected, neurotic, Prozac-sedated, pierced navel (Leonardo's center adorned) individual, an individual that no longer demonstrates any anxiety about, or interest in, part and whole—is the most plausible. As usual, architecture is almost always going at a different historical speed—and with different historical concerns—than the life that inhabits it.

Although the relation of parts to whole is relentlessly general as a philosophical principle (how else could one proceed?), its force in architecture can be mapped quite specifically because it follows the familiar lines of opposition between the material and the conceptual—the material part, the conceptual whole. The analytic intelligence that takes the world apart to examine its parts (Aristotle and early Socrates) and the synthetic intelligence that elaborates a vast synthetic system to explain everything (Aristotle, late Socrates) are both present in architectural history and architectural work. And it is hard to separate the two, at least in Western architecture. But these are also logics that, while inscribing ideas about life for many centuries, have not touched the "logic of life" itself. The logic of life ultimately resists both ancient and classical, as well as later, analytic/synthetic attempts to account for its relation of part to whole. When Deleuze and Guattari, following Leibniz, critique Western metaphysics by substituting movement, assemblies and emergences for discrete parts and wholes, their project was to unlock some of the hard oppositions by which Western technologies have advanced themselves—to follow, specifically, a live hydraulics, a hylomorphic world of "variable intensive effects"[17] a "fluid" or "flow," a continuum. Flow, however, is not quite what Jacob means when he titles his book *The Logic of Life*. He means, instead, that biological life, through heredity, is governed by neither whole nor part, divine nor secular powers, materials nor concepts, but by its own specific set of genetic events, its own precise reproductive adventure through history. A living organism, in his view, is, above all, an agent of transition between past and future.[18]

•

But we are still before all that. In the Renaissance, the human body is represented as both idealized and hollow. Leonardo's drawing of the Vitruvian man dreams of an impossible symmetry between music, architecture and the human body. This diagram, and others like it, are intriguing—certainly as art and descriptions of a particular cosmology, but also for their proposition, already somewhat framed above, about the wholeness of bodies, organic and architectural. Wittkower calls the inscription of various human figures in geometric diagrams "anthropomorphic devices."[19] Leonardo's man is, of course, without internal organs; not because they are unimagined—one has only to look at the detailed renderings of anatomical interiors by the Renaissance artist-anatomist Vesalius—but because they are irrelevant to the idea, and role, of human life in the Renaissance. The interior and exterior of the body are not yet connected. And an idea of an architectural interior connected to an exterior, such as we now hold, was also missing in the Renaissance. There were, to be sure, the Renaissance cabinets and alcoves within which private life unlocked itself, within which curiosity could be gratified. But they are like storage boxes inside buildings, not integrated "interiors." Is Palladio's niche-carving into thick structural walls in the sixteenth century a possible instance of an interior architecture? Perhaps these niches begin an idea of architectural interiority, but it is rudimentary. Rather than "thinking" the interior or allowing the architectural interior a form of expansion that benefits from the flexibility and optics of its containment, such as later, particularly Baroque, architects will do, the anatomies and architectures of the early and mid-Renaissance are almost entirely dependent on exterior views. The organic life Leonardo's figure suggests, inside the astronomical and cosmological frame that both inscribes him and is inscribed by him, is that of a complete "outline," a finality and totality that is formed from the human body's status as both instrument of measurement and "immediate datum."[20] In the eighteenth century, when Auguste Comte makes of the organism a "consensus of organs and functions," Leonardo's figure of life/cosmos would begin to gain, were it to be redrawn as a medical rendering, a more complex interior, but it remains a "total outline" until the nineteenth century. "Between Immanuel Kant and Claude Bernard . . . finality, in the guise of totality, [is still] an essential element of the definition of an organism."[21] It is only with Bernard and Darwin that the idea of life, human life in particular, gradually loses its ability to be inscribed, from the outside, as a finality. Finality and inscription, as desirable states of being, do not completely disappear with the development of the idea of an organic interior, but they migrate to other, non-biological, accounts of human life.

According to Wittkower, it is by means of the classical relation between parts and wholes implicit in harmonic proportions that architecture is first "elevated" from a manual to a liberal art. Harmonic proportions, Wittkower writes, established a theoretical foundation for architecture, which was, as mentioned earlier, the "great achievement" of the Renaissance artists.[22] Architecture is simultaneously delivered from both its lowly status as manual building and its exalted status as an abstract work of God. It begins to take its place as a humanist discipline among the other Renaissance humanist disciplines, poetry, other language arts, music. Manual architecture—in the slightly cartoonish version that the word "manual" brings to mind—assembled the parts of a building through the skill of craftsmen whose "architectural designs" were based on whatever building technology offered and on meanings and formulas handed down from monarchical, theological, even mystical sources.

The humanist architectures of the Renaissance are, then, an early hypothesis, still ensnared in idealisms, about what it might mean for architecture to control the assembly of parts through mathematical principles of generation in conceptual work—the ratios are esoteric and hard to fathom, but they help overcome a deeply felt incongruence between building and body. The regulating, perhaps even mediating, force of the human figure in this process raises, modestly at first, only as an outline or even an accident, the bare presence of a mundane and problematic human biological occupation. Once raised, such a presence might well have disappeared again into the blur of living beings, had there not been at the same time a slight withdrawal, more a coming down to earth, of the power of the divine, one agent for which was the rigid diagrammatic contribution of perspectival construction. Perspective, in Panofsky's terms, appears to assist both sides of the equation. The theologians could see finally what "infinity" looked like, and the secularists could see finally the meaning of earthly bodies in space. This was one of the effects of architecture's alliance with the humanist arts. It prevented Proserpina from leaving the space of Hades—everything about that scene could be easily represented and contained in abstract mathematical space. The earth, and above and below the earth, had become a spatial and temporal continuum, almost, but not quite, a milieu.

Alongside the practice of a theoretical architecture designed in light of an idealized body, then, is also the appearance of a human body, but not in any contemporary sense. The human biological body—both its obviousness and complexity held at bay in Leonardo's man—appears first not as a body per se but as a "way of life," an in-scribed life-motion of the human figure itself that is present in certain architectural narratives. The Renaissance way of life is not a building plan or program per se, but a narrative path that circumscribes the architectural project. The "Virgilian way of life," for example, that Colin Rowe imagines for the owner/occupant of Palladio's Villa Capra-Rotonda does not simply describe the building, it also theorizes the occupant's position in, and perspective of, the building. Generally, the so-called "humanist architectures" begin to accommodate both the autonomy of future scientific life (that is, more than one point of view and the scientific ideal of "objectivity") and the insistence of life on "having its way." Architecture cannot remain wholly indifferent to the life within it because ways of life—about which I will say more later—increasingly suggest that the milieu must bend not only in the direction of the movement and ideology of its inhabitant, and vice versa, but also toward the complex biological and evolutionary development of a species.

Overall, then, the idea of human biological life in the Renaissance is still radically undeveloped, and architecture, while increasingly sophisticated in technical ways, still has its back turned on the life it houses. It is not until the nineteenth century that architecture can be seen with any clarity from the standpoint of the life within it, that ideas of ways of life begin to be figuralized and systematized as programs in civic and institutional spaces in particular, and that both biological and psychological interiority gains ground. And it is not until the twentieth century that life, as an idea, acquires a sufficiently complex definition to offer serious resistance to architectural claims to autonomy and universality that arise from ancient logics of parts and wholes.

•

I am not attempting a comprehensive gathering of the many strands of human history in, and since, the Renaissance—a history for which there are large and fruitful archives, extraordinary existing art and buildings, and on which extensive and powerful scholarly work has been expended by Jacob Burckhardt, Wittkower, the Viennese scholar Panofsky, Manfredo Tafuri and many others. But my summary of some of the issues associated with this history feels the tremendous temptation, as do many more comprehensive studies, to relate everything to everything else in that history; to strive, as those theories strive, for a unified theory of the Renaissance that has specific bearing on architecture. This is partly, I think, the deep temptation of the logic of parts and wholes in architecture and partly the sticky effect, in architectural terms, of Renaissance ideas.

Tafuri names part of the problem, after Foucault, as that of "the production of meaning . . . during the era that we have become accustomed to call the Renaissance."[23] "We are immediately confronted," Tafuri argues, "by notions of transgression and license that imply the problem of the limits," a "thematic ensemble" to which the term "*sprezzatura*, or studied carelessness" has been applied.[24] Knowledge, in the form of "splendid, elegant words," was gathered in the Renaissance from everywhere, forming a pluralist base for artistic production. Linguistic transgression as a basis for linguistic law, Tafuri suggests, is the "notion of a language in perpetual metamorphosis [under which] a dynamic relationship is established between a 'collective that speaks' and the individual subject."[25] Assemblies of knowledge in Renaissance architecture were based on diverse and imaginative renovations of antiquity—a quasi-nostalgic set of recoveries that served as a diverse and rich hermeneutical resource for architectural re-imagining.

"Antiquity"—before our more limiting contemporary conception of historical epochs was installed—was a far broader, and more diverse, era than we now characterize it. For example, as Tafuri also writes, Bramante had eclectic interests in, on the one hand, the Basilica Aemilia (a temple with mixed orders) and, on the other, early Christian and Byzantine architecture, as well as, perhaps, the Hagia Sophia (which he might have deduced, it is suggested, from a plan drawn in Giuliano da Sangallo's *Libro*).[26] Others were interested in the Imperial era, the "infinite variety of the antique models" and the thrilling "fragments." The implied classical principles of architecture that Vitruvius forwards—the rules—are part of the innovation game, a "language game" appropriate to an age of representation. To transgress the rules, to act in the face of the rules, "established the norm." To Wittkower's establishment of a theoretical foundation for architecture in the Renaissance, Tafuri adds the "experimental impulse," a "concealed transgression" in the midst of a collective inquiry into the past. This might be called Renaissance humanist architecture "aslant."[27]

The experimental renovation of a rule-bound antiquity in Renaissance architecture is a particularly compelling idea, if we agree with Tafuri, because, for the first time, architecture acknowledges itself as actively hermeneutical—subject to a nearly reckless play of meaning brought to it, gratis, by the language arts and, simultaneously, playing by precise rules of organization and composition based on the "correct" ratio of parts. We feel compelled, it seems, to return to this set of paradoxes over and over, finding them in early to late Renaissance, in Il Redentore (the carnival church), Venice proper, in Milan, Florence, and then in the strewn fragments of the Roman ruins. Certainly it seems as if Renaissance artistic and humanist ideals, many of which were supposedly corrupted or dead by the time the Baroque begins to twist around on itself, nevertheless installed themselves, not as ideals so much as ideal paradoxes that retain a place in human consciousness and culture as it modernizes itself. An epistemological style in architecture that brings the rule and its interpretations into a dialectic mode, if that is the right phrase, influences diverse organizations of human knowledge henceforth, although there are also profound regressions, and renovations, of this kind of knowing. Modernity begins here, in other words. The "disappearance of representation" by the end of the seventeenth century that Foucault remarks on is not a conclusive disappearance. It is always henceforth evident, even when that evidence is lamented, that "architecture is founded on [at least] two principles." Claude Perrault, in 1673, recovers these two principles in his commentary on Vitruvius: "the first is positive [useful, necessary, 'commodity, firmness, and healthfulness']" and "the second arbitrary." Perrault names the arbitrary principle as "authority and custom," i.e. culture, but the category of the arbitrary recoups, as well, the arbitrariness of language and its work in ideology and culture that is the work of Renaissance representation. [28] Perrault also was a physician and hygienist. Tafuri, arguing with Antoine Picon, suggests that it was "in the field of anatomy that Claude proposed a distinction analogous to the one he introduced when searching for a definition of beauty: *vérités de fait* and *vérités de droit* form a conceptual pair comparable to the one that pitted nature against institutions."[29] This is the subject of a longer discussion that I will not investigate here in any rigorous way, but it is to be noted that the Renaissance inspired, literally breathed life into, the subject of humanness in the midst of the human's simultaneous rigidity and blurriness so curiously represented by Leonardo's man. And all the conceptual pairs by which we have argued architecture since the Renaissance—classical notions of "opposition" put to many different kinds of work over time—are at one point or another presented in the architectures of the Renaissance.

The subject is so rich, once we admit its instability. Humanism—the means by which the past is recovered before the "past" exists in any precise historical sense—perhaps initially proceeded something like the *nostoi*, the return narratives of Homer, by importing into fifteenth century Florence fragmented memories, and memories of fragments, from a classical and heroic age, the armature for which had to be almost completely reconstructed in contemporary terms. In some cases, such as Alberti's architecture, the armature is left deliberately incomplete in order to celebrate the fragment. Like the *nostoi*, much of the authority of these humanist narratives came from their apparent link with an already distant and finished past; in architecture, the usual source, the only dedicatedly architectural source of authority, was Vitruvius. But Vitruvius is opaque and limited on many details; he is a powerful, but rather clumsy, figure in the Renaissance pantheon of far more sophisticated practitioners and theorists. All the so-called "antique authorities" permitted both specific and generalized associations. The "Renaissance Man," *uomo universale*, becomes, thus, a kind of expert shopper, picking up here and there fragmentary classical evidence to form—through mixed associations supplied by social custom, classical tradition, as well as desire, memory, imagination—both a contemporary scene and, as Anthony Vidler discusses, a story of origins.

The twentieth century philosophical, scientific, and medical histories of life by Michel Foucault, Georges Canguilhem, and François Jacob, among others (which are treated more expansively in Chapter 3), summarize the fourteenth to sixteenth centuries in terms that correspond, to some degree, to Tafuri's Renaissance, but they make short work of it. As mentioned earlier, these are periods during which living and non-living beings are known and identified, falsely in many cases, by means of surface associations and analogies. The habit of analogy stretches "back to antiquity."[30] While the "analogical topos has no place in [Alberti's] *De re aedificatoria*," Tafuri writes, ". . . the comparison between man and animal appears consistently . . . according to an inverted scale of values."[31] "Inverted" in the sense that the animal finds a tighter concordance, metaphorically, with architecture than man. And this is, in part, because the animal can be partitioned. The analogy between architecture and music in the Renaissance, Tafuri claims, is used instrumentally by Alberti and others to forward the idea of "the architectural organism as *animal*."[32] Through the animal, then, architecture initially acquires an idea of interiority and wholeness that depends on the relation of parts—organ to organ, member to member—that will later become a deep interiority that enables, in different ways at different times, the fantasy of orthopedic wholeness.

## 2: INSIDE AND OUTSIDE

Bernini's actual architectural "debut," the bronze Baldacchino in St. Peter's—which Franco Borsi explicates according to Wittkower's theme of "centrality,"[1] is a rudimentary interior enclosure—a highly ornate geometric outline of a chunk of space that started out with the delicacy characteristic of Bernini mentioned earlier, but soon gains thickness. This outline is not unlike Leonardo's man—a finality without an interior; not an orthopedic whole. But it is also a definitive stab in the direction of interiority as an architectural idea, although still in the idiom of the Renaissance cabinet. Since the Baldacchino is Bernini's first move away from sculpture into architecture—a sculptural event inside a central-plan temple—it takes its form, as outline, from his early hypotheses about architectural space. In other words, he draws lines around a rectangle of space and holds it together with ornate twisted columns.

The commission was a risky one. Bronze had to be pillaged from the Pantheon portico and Michelangelo's dome exerted its dominance over the spatial "crossroads" that was the site for the Baldacchino. The Pope issued, in so many words, a mandate that Bernini was to make this "like the temple of Solomon"—a neat trick, to erect a temple inside another temple. Bernini of course had the ability, by means of drawing, to carry out an "advance study of the effect the Baldacchino would make in perspective when viewed from the nave;" he also formed multiple models in wax, personally cast the bronze columns, and included the pontifical arms of the three bees.[2] These models dissimulated an interior that, in some sense, had no interiority.

The columns are twined around with vines—a classical vegetative referent—and the structure uses both "real architecture," the calculation and support of material loads in space, as well as architecture symbolized by elements such as pieces of temple fronts.[3] The interesting thing about the interior suggested by the Baldacchino is how, in spite of its exalted position in the center of St. Peter's, it is still only an outline of an interior, a cabinet of space. Renaissance private life took place in alcoves, inner chambers, cabinets, sometimes indistinguishable from closets, which were located inside otherwise undifferentiated spaces of the house. In these locked rooms were a family's valuables, including the virtue and vice of marital relations. Renaissance cabinet spaces, though meant for the gratification of curiosity, were not the hybridized curiosity cabinets of the eighteenth century, which gathered ornamental grotesques from the intervening years of decorative experimentation, perhaps in a late homage to a pre-classical age of rampant association between things and beings in the world.[4] Brunelleschi had also "made use of a few elements of interior furnishings such as choir stalls and altars" in Santa Maria del Fiore that were like these cabinet-interiors that typified domestic architectures.[5] Palladio used section drawings to reveal structural support, but the section is not an inside view of the circulation of air and bodies through a building, nor is it an intellectual idea about interiors; it is merely the inside of an outside conception of the building, artfully represented.

•

I was trying to leave my small hotel in Capri, in order to see the Blue Grotto. But I kept losing things in that room because all the interior

**Figure 2.1:** Gianlorenzo Bernini, *Baldacchino*, 1631, St. Peter's, Rome. Photograph by Michael Herrman.

surfaces—furniture, floor, walls—were covered with patterned wall paper or fabric. My keys were camouflaged by the pattern of the tablecloth; clothes that had fallen on the floor became part of the carpet pattern; the bed blurred into the wall. Specific figure-ground relationships between objects and background were erased—with the exception of myself, as always, who preserved a point of view. Such an interior, for some, might represent the perfect final purpose of architecture that has gained knowledge, so to speak, about the body's interior—to house our private bodies in an interiority that is like the deep physical interior of a liquid body, still understood to be entirely distinct from, although protected by, the exterior. Decoration, even if unplanned and chaotic, would be one way to achieve this.[6] But decoration leans toward an inhabitant's life "taste," whereas architecture leans away.

The struggle between the inside and the outside of both building and inhabitant has produced a long and interesting series of events in architecture, much of which is a struggle not with interior decoration, whose allegiance is clear, but with ornament, applied to exterior and interior surfaces, whose allegiance is mixed. The famous, and histrionic, criminality of ornament of John Ruskin and Adolf Loos—"criminal" because aesthetics in architecture is seen during certain periods as morally excessive, beyond the basic needs of the inhabitant—was an argument for which biological life served as a moral anchor. Ornament, exterior or interior, applied or integral, is always playing both sides of the life/architecture equation. The idea of interiority—of both life and building—is connected, then, to the relative coherence and possibility of biological interiority not simply as a visual, but also as a structural, idea. The interior cannot be induced to reveal itself as an "opened" space until it is shown to be connected in more than superficial ways with the structures and skins of the exterior. Beginning with perspectival representation, which seems to pass with equanimity through inside and outside—although, according to Wolfgang Lotz's seminal essay,[7] it could not be immediately used to draw out the interior space of architecture—it remained to supply this "merely representational" system with a system of structural persuasiveness. Interiority in architecture and life is connected also to the construction of ways of life referred to briefly earlier, because ways of life, directed initially toward the external realms of building and property, also served as an early formulation of the modern idea of the individual and of the private life, which both includes and occludes biological life, that interiority supports and advances. In architectural terms, this means that the wall, as it is understood in an interior rendering, must be represented, as Lotz notes, as a solid enclosure of an interior, not just a divider.[8] Filarete was the first to do an interior perspective, according to Lotz, that seemed to take seriously the idea of enclosure.

My Capri hotel was a derivative (and cheap) version of a hyper-interiority that started in highly "decorative" eras of architecture that followed the Renaissance, particularly the Baroque and Rococo. Modernism gradually repudiated this version of an interior architecture by placing the outside and inside on the same existential axis, displaying the inhabitant's life as a form of cinematic or psychoanalytic interior contained within a transparent envelope. But modernism also invited another form of collapse between being and space, by bringing the figure of structure closer to the ground of space, often using those same transparent materials. Both the inhabitant's and the building's transparency are part of modernity's "optical unconscious." The neo-psychological drama of the architectural interior and exterior, from which both explosive decorative impulses and the spareness of modernism arise, depends on conceptions of interiority that are not present in the Renaissance in any elaborated way.

Nor is the interior of the human body, and its connection to its exterior, well understood until the middle of the eighteenth century, when (as will be discussed in more detail in subsequent chapters) beings and things begin to be pulled apart from each other in space, named and classified. In the late eighteenth century, this classification deepens into an account not simply of the surface of organisms but also of their interior structures. This deepening is partly due to, and accompanied by, medical changes in the understanding of human anatomy, which, in turn, are connected to changes in the depth and importance of time. Everything, using Foucault's formulation, becomes suffused with history. The "discovery" of an anatomical interior—which happens against the backdrop of, by then, an almost fully modernized idea of the architectural interior—brings with it the discovery of "inner life," i.e. the rudiments of a psychology that uses architecture metaphorically to structure theories of consciousness.

When Wittkower looks into the interior of Palladio's churches, he seems to find, already, evidence of an interior that displays a psychological-optical drama. In the Redentore, for example, which "tackled anew the old problem of the 'composite' type of church in which a centralized domed structure is joined to a longitudinal nave," Palladio detaches the longitudinal nave from the centralized area and then renders this detachment, according to Wittkower, in optical terms: "The unification of separate spaces is achieved by the creation of corresponding vistas across large spaces rather than by the uniform handling of wall articulation, as was customary in central Italy."[9] The screen of free-standing columns near the altar is an "optical and psychological" barrier and link that "invites us to let the eye wander into the space beyond—a space to which the congregation is not admitted."[10] But I think to call the barrier "psychological" is stretching it. The optical as an incisive instrument that opens space and is linked to a "mind's eye," upon which a full conception of interiority will depend, is not yet fully in place here, although it is prefigured in perspectival representation. The Redentore, like other Renaissance architectures, is still a locked cabinet of space. Renaissance architects, looking to Leonardo's Vitruvian man, tried to weld the circle and the rectangle together by employing the circle of the head and the length of the legs (another of those anthropomorphic devices) as a template. However, the center of Leonardo's man, the navel and the middle (the milieu) of the composition—which, in fact, had to be moved up in order to hold the center of Leonardo's geometric argument—is not connected to any interior biological genesis of the body or to a psychological construction of wholeness that would imply an interior. The still astounding narrative images of Vesalius' anatomical figures (*De humani corporis fabrica* 1543), as François Jacob wrote in *The Possible and the Actual*, display the architecture of the body in postures of everyday life at the same moment in history that Copernicus' work was published, shifting the sun to the center of the solar system.[11] These are images of the interior of the human body, as much a subject of art as science. They are not, however, images of an interior that has a discernible effect on the exterior of the body—that is, on the life of the body in the world. Diseases of the body during the Renaissance can come from any place—God, ill humor, forms of excess, etc. The idea of interiority in anatomy, as I mentioned above, is not yet functionally connected with the exterior of the body, nor with the effect of bodies on each other and on a still nascent milieu. As a result, these images of flayed bodies, and the musculo-skeletal structures they reveal, do not yet describe a profound interior milieu. The consequences, in biology, of a missing interiority—the "doctrine of internal finality" with which the interior of the bodies of animals and humans were viewed until Darwin's theory of natural selection—meant that "each individual . . . is made for itself, that all its parts conspire for the greater good of the whole, and are intelligently organized in view of that end without regard for other organisms."[12] The inside and immediate outside of the body, as well as the more remote outside of the external milieu, are not connected to each other in time and space.

The closed anatomy at the end of the Renaissance yields eventually, as mentioned earlier, to anatomical research that begins, through various comparative methods, to bring differing structures and organisms into relation. The increasing depth of the interior body brings with it a more elaborated and significant set of external relations, and this eventually, over a period of several centuries, results in both a deepening of space, such that interiors can be connected to exteriors, and a deepening of time. It is, in part, by observing the work of eighteenth century comparative anatomists, who were able to construct the time line of an organism by means of morphological developments, that architectural historians begin to draft a time line for different kinds of buildings in different cultures. Architecture acquires some conception of a spatial interior long before biology, but architectural history—which is a discipline of exterior forms as well as of the relation of architecture to modes of life—can only be formed when the static spatial interior, and its connection to exterior structure, can be connected to the history of life. As Jacob writes of biology, it was "[o]nly through such comparison of forms and structures, through the idea that their distribution in space actually reflects a distribution in time, [that] . . . a theory of evolution becomes possible."[13] It is, for both biology and architecture, the comparison of exterior bodies distributed in space and time, from which a more profound sense of architectural, anatomical and biological interiority is achieved.

Foucault remarks that there is a twenty year period, 1775 to 1795, when the extraordinary taxonomies of Linnaeus and others, which formed the "character" of a plant or animal and which were based on careful observational techniques, yield to the examination not of surfaces but of underlying "organic structure." As he writes:

> [C]haracter resumes its former role as a visible sign directing us towards a buried depth; but what it indicates is not a secret text, a muffled word, or a resemblance too precious to be revealed; it is the coherent totality of an organic structure that weaves back into the unique fabric of its sovereignty both the visible and the invisible.[14]

The function of the organic structure is, then, not merely a static, inside, structure but a set of relationships between inside/outside structure that are dynamic, i.e. life-filled and life-defining. A mobile sovereignty of function eventually comes to both define and differentiate the living being from other living beings and to enlist the milieu in its operations.

Interiority, in nineteenth century biology, does not oppose exteriority. The exterior is sublimated in the interior in the sense that organs and processes of reproduction, respiration, digestion "weave into" (Foucault's words) and form the surface of the living body. The surface of a body is a structure that is literally, simultaneously, visible and invisible.

I suggested, in my introduction and earlier in this section, that the opening of space in the eighteenth century between different forms of life (living and non-living) occasioned by concepts of time and space is related to the "invention of space" that Panofsky claims attends the invention of Renaissance perspective. Further, in this and the previous chapter, that these two openings conspire to make up a conception of both an anatomical and architectural interior/exterior "whole." Of course, these two openings happen approximately four hundred years apart, and one might ask, with respect to architecture in particular: What is happening during all that time? Several of the following chapters attempt to map some of this period. But the two "openings," which are two different kinds of history, are difficult to connect. It is as if the consequences, at first only theoretical, of the symbolic and mathematical construction of space that perspective finds on behalf of representation in Renaissance art and architecture begin, after a while, to seep into the world itself. Relatively soon after perspective was invented, in fact, its world-changing ambitions and powers became evident. The first architectural interior perspectives appear, as mentioned earlier, in Filarete's work.[15] The fact that perspective was "merely a construction"—not an accurate reflection of how we see in psycho-physiological space, where, among other things, space is curved—was repressed surprisingly quickly. The human eye seemed to compensate, fairly quickly, for the inaccuracy of perspectival space, and it effectively adopts perspective as not just a good representation, but the best representation.

So perhaps it is not surprising that insofar as the taxonomic sciences had the power to organize all living beings by separating and identifying them in space, they also complied, to some degree, with the capture of this life inside the geometric space-box already in place. When the space around life becomes an opening by which differences are marked and classified, this space-box reaches beyond its artifice in the world of art/representation and into the world of science/objects. Architecture, first captured by the grid in the Renaissance, receives, by the late eighteenth century, a living occupant that is comprehensively identified in terms of visible attributes. By the middle of the nineteenth century, architecture receives a living occupant that is further identified by means of invisible interior structures, and a precise placement in time and space—an occupant who has become highly sympathetic, in other words, to architectural space. Architecture sees the human "as an (architectural) organism" and humans see architecture "as a (human) milieu." In this highly synthetic proposal—which leaps over years of adjudication between life and architecture in social, political, and biological ways—it is thus not merely in the spirit of its time that architecture looks to natural history to organize itself historically and typologically: it also looks to natural history to get a life.

Architecture, which had already achieved, in the Renaissance, a systematic way of locating and representing itself in space, continues in its technological development. Human beings thus try to find in architectural space (the space-box), over these four hundred years, what Heidegger grants to them, up front, ontologically—their right to the possession of the "open" and the "disconcealed:" that is, self-consciousness. In seeking accommodation for a self-conscious biological being in space—the very definition of modern humanness—the open comes to include, rather than oppose, captivation. In this way, the modern human is definitely human, self-conscious, disconcealed, but, simultaneously, animal, that is, captured, and on occasion concealed, formally by architectural space.

I don't mean to charge the discussion, at this point, with the many contemporary political/philosophical resonances surrounding the words "open" and "captivation" that will later come into play.

Captivation, in Heidegger's terms, defines the ontological state of the animal, not the human; presumably, in his terms, this is a state that has held the animal in its thrall for all time. What it is (we know something already about what it is), or if he's right, are questions that will need to be addressed. Certainly, the captivation of nature, particularly the animal, through the art and science of classification is part of an impulse toward "knowing" that knows no bounds—the very definition of the Enlightenment is to know everything without reserve. At the beginning of our own century, over two hundred years after the Enlightenment project began, nothing happens in the jungle free from our desire to know about it; most species of animal and plant life have been identified and subjected to the processes of classification—mode of life recorded and entered into the historical record, habitats mapped and located, populations counted, organic structures compared and so forth. Interconnected webs of knowledge, now historical in the most profound sense, that were made possible by the opening of space between beings, surpassed, but did not do away with, the early eighteenth century desire to "nominate the visible." Taxonomies of the surface and the visible lead to taxonomies of the invisible, the inner structures of life. The opening of the inside makes of classification a body of knowledge that captures not just the surfaces of life, but over time *all* modes of life, exterior, interior, individual, collective, public, private, revealed, concealed. It is an almost, but not quite, as I suggest in different places, complete capture.

In a literal sense, the web of inner and outer knowledge of life has, particularly in contemporary culture, been taken for a literal space of capture, a net, or a system of cross-hairs: nations require identity cards, Global Positioning Systems (GPS) are used to locate and identify animals in hunting safaris, radar detects enemy planes. But we still believe the pursuit of knowledge to be, if not always objective, at least benevolent, which was one of the promises of both secularization and science: to remove knowledge from the biases of special interests, including theological ones, and pursue it objectively as a set of internal and external relationships between bodies in the world, for the betterment of the world. If it makes any sense to speak of capturing life by opening a space between beings and, subsequently, defining an interior, it was, until relatively recently, understood as a benevolent capture, made in the interest of this knowledge and architectural humanity. Indeed, it would be hard to know what the alternative would be, enmeshed as we are in our project of humanity. At the same time, the pursuit and accumulation of knowledge about interior structure also revealed itself to be a mechanism of power that began to be seriously theorized in the twentieth century. Modernity brought with it, for example, what Agamben and others define as a bio-politics in which bare life—the biological life of the body—serves new political purposes.[16] How this changes or qualifies the capture of the open and "opened" post-animal human in architecture is still to be seen. As Agamben wrote in his book, *The Open*:

> Heidegger was perhaps the last philosopher to believe in good faith that the place of the polis (the *polos* [pole] where the conflict between concealedness and unconcealedness, between the *animalitas* and the *humanitas* of man, reigns) was still practicable, and that it was still possible for men, for a people—holding themselves in that risky place—to find their own proper historical destiny. He was, that is, the last to believe . . . that the anthropological machine, which each time decides upon and recomposes the conflict between man and animal, between the open and the not open, could still produce history and destiny for a people.[17]

# 3: LIFE (BEFORE)

Before what, exactly? A short list would be history, taxonomy, Darwin, ecology, biology, architectural modernism, metal, certain kinds of space, deep time, theories of organic organization, mechanization, computation, gravity, and *Homo sapiens*.

François Jacob, in the highly condensed *The Logic of Life: A History of Heredity*, characterizes the natural world up to the seventeenth century as primarily combinatory: ". . . each mundane object, each plant and each animal can be described as a particular combination of matter and form."[1] Matter consists of four elements—earth, air, water, fire—and is indestructible; otherwise everything would have already been used up. "[A]n object," Jacob remarks, "is . . . characterized by form alone. . . . The hand that confers form on matter to create stars, stones or living beings is that of Nature . . . [which is] an executive agent, an operative principle working under God's guidance." Reading nature is a matter of deciphering clues about relationships and similitude that might reveal this divine intention. Resemblances between things argue for the overarching existence of a "designer." "The resemblance of a plant to the eye," Jacob writes, "is . . .

the sign that it should be used for treating diseases of the eyes. The very nature of things is hidden behind the similitudes."[2]

"Similitudes," in Jacob's book, are the "resemblances" of Foucault's *The Order of Things*. Both refer to surface identifications of objects as they appear in the world, but also to how those objects are animated by their resemblance and physical proximity to other things in the world. The world, as Foucault remarks on this same pre-classical period, is like a chain. Things are linked together in a "graduated scale of proximity." Marks on the surfaces of things, "signatures," tie objects to both divine and natural origins. Such a world, Foucault suggests, produces vast systems of related attributes, comprehended by means of resemblance and analogy. Jacob writes that form "distinguishes one animal, or being, or thing, from the next, [but] form does not fix this being in one place:"

> When Aldrovandus deals with the horse, he describes its shape and appearance in four pages, but he needs nearly three hundred pages to relate in detail the horse's names, its breeding, habitat, temperament, docility, memory, affection, gratitude, fidelity, generosity, ardor for victory, speed, agility, prolific power, sympathies, diseases and their treatment; after that the monstrous horses appear, the prodigious horses, fabulous horses, celebrated horses, with the descriptions of the places where they won glory, the role of horses in equitation, harness, war, hunting games, farming, processions, the importance of the horse in history, mythology, literature, proverbs, paintings, sculpture, medals, escutcheons.[3]

Because of the vast, diverse and interrelated set of references that make up each being, the living world cannot be organized in terms of form alone; form does not contribute anything specific to the identity of a living being, as happens later with comparative anatomy and the classification of species. Further, the non-living world does not exist separately from the living world; everything possesses some degree of animation/spirit, if only by association with animate beings. The significance of things is unusually mobile. Ordering systems such as cartography and linear historical narratives that, in the eighteenth and nineteenth centuries, will organize landscapes and life increasingly in terms of measurable, static locations and formal descriptions tied to larger contexts are absent, although ancient forms of mapping, as well as narratives of passage, allow some coherent movement and commerce between different cultures. Various Aristotelian distinctions between plants, animals and man that persist during this period refer not to notable distinctions between forms but to distinctions between the kinds of souls invested in them. And while the separation, on largely metaphysical or theological grounds, between humans, beasts, and minerals is almost always discernible, where resemblances between forms are noted, "it is difficult to decide where one domain begins and ends."[4] Monsters and hybrid beings have access to the human enclave by means of this system of diverse association. Monsters are, in effect, evidence of the degree to which analogies formalize life during this period. As Jacob writes, "none differs entirely from what can be seen at every turn . . . a monster with a bear's head and a monkey's arm," "the man with the hands and feet of an ox," "the child with the frog's face."[5] These monsters are entirely unlike the monster-experiments now underway in both contemporary genetic research and tissue engineering projects, such as the fascinating and disturbing experiment in growing frog "meat," an amorphous growth of living tissue that never acquires the identifiable form of a frog.[6] Some of these contemporary monsters are fabricated from recombinant DNA (although not the frog meat project) and their subsequent generative capacity, to a degree still uncertain, can be somewhat controlled—indeed, the control of reproduction is the whole point of the recombination. Sixteenth-century monsters are composed of jumbled, but not arbitrary, external forms with no generative capacity. The largest missing piece in understanding life in the pre-classical era is the

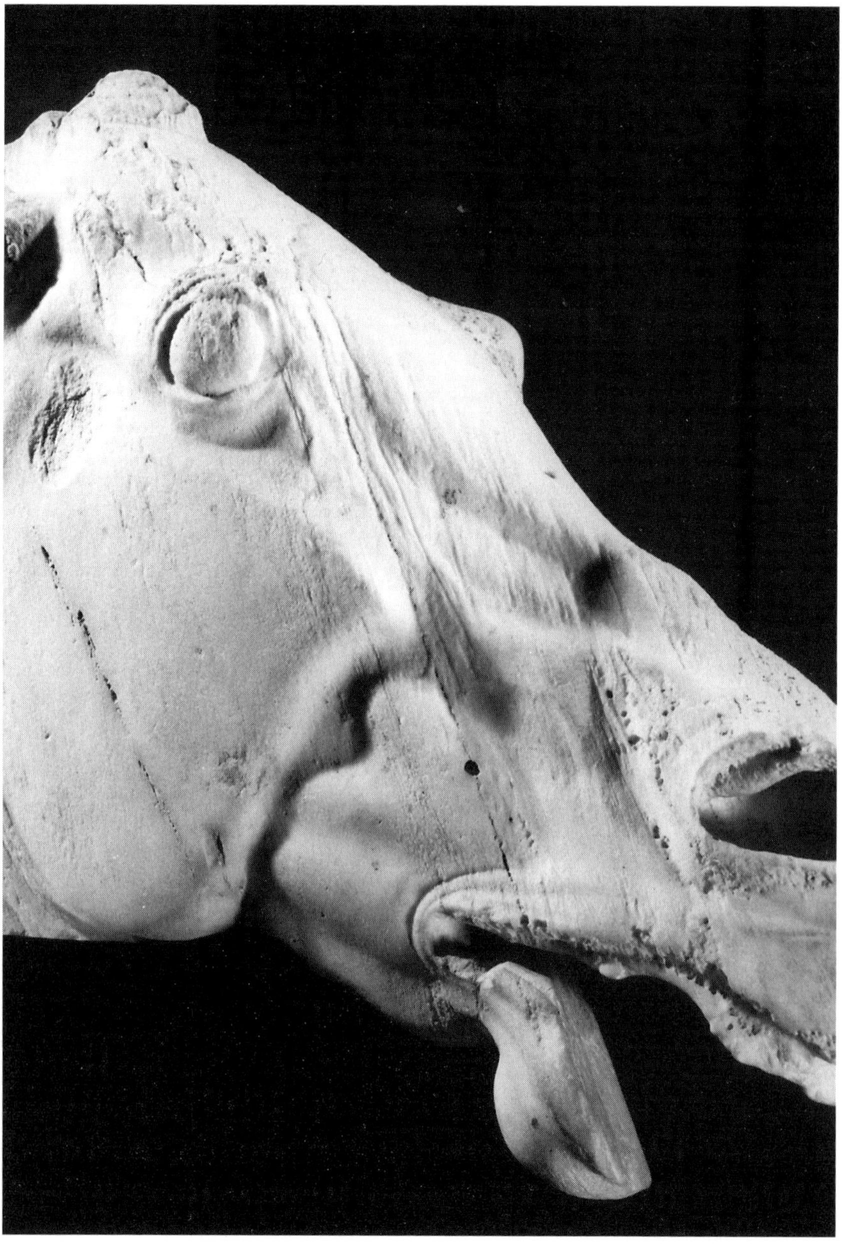





**Figure 3.1:** *Horse of Selene, Parthenon*, 447-432 BC. Courtesy of The British Museum, London. Now detached from the east pediment of the Parthenon, the Horse of Selene originally emerged from the lower corner of the pediment. It is pulling the chariot of the sun. Its eyes and the posture of its head clearly indicates that it is working, and in motion. But the head was also caught in the corner of the pediment as if in a headlock.

understanding of the process of reproduction. There is no theory of inheritance or reproduction that structurally controls the generation of life. Each being is separately created, and the observable fact that "like produces like" is held as evidence of nature's divine harmony, not of its reproductive or evolutionary operation.[7]

In the subsequent seventeenth and eighteenth centuries, living bodies—the thickly layered and thinly stretched horse of Aldrovandus—are "scraped clean" of their encrusted sets of relations in order to "appear in all the nakedness of their true outer shape." Evidence of generation—the genetic likeness passed from parent to child—begins to support the classification of life as something that acts according to laws of nature. The seventeenth century accords "new privileges" to observation.[8] It is also a century of both confusions and pivotal advances in theories of animation, mechanism, and scientific method. It is the century of Descartes: "Two things alone have to be considered . . . ourselves who know and the objects themselves which are to be known;"[9] and Galileo: "Philosophy is written in a great book which is always open before our eyes, but we cannot understand it without first applying ourselves to understanding the language and learning the characters used in writing it;"[10] and Harvey, who carried out experiments on blood circulation similar to those Galileo carried out with stones; and Leibniz: "The art of discovering the causes of phenomena . . . is like the art of deciphering." And, of course, Newton. Newtonian science organizes the world in terms of a mathematical language that expresses universal laws that can be applied to all aspects of nature. Newton also adds the element of space—for him, "a void in which particles are in motion"—to Descartes' world of matter and movement.[11] The calculation of the force of gravity (attraction), the origin of which was still unknown, linked the "mechanics of heaven and earth." Jacob writes of this period, still following Foucault:

> The analysis of objects now . . . requires that . . . objects . . . be represented by a system of signs. The sign is no longer the

> stigma [signature] placed on things by the Creator to enable man to divine his intentions. It becomes an integral part of human understanding, both a product elaborated by thought for the purpose of analysis and a tool necessary for exercising memory, imagination or reflection. Among the sign systems, mathematics is evidently supreme. By means of mathematical symbols it is possible to divide up the continuum of things, to analyze them and rearrange them in various combinations.[12]

When the analysis of all animate life is narrowed, for part of the seventeenth century, to the analysis of moving, mechanical, physical objects (on the earth and in the sky) that are subject to laws, attempts are made, yet again, to bring birds down to earth. Stephen Jay Gould, the evolutionary paleontologist, maintains (with important differences) some of these seventeenth century mechanistic assumptions by beginning with the proposition that animals are "physical objects" whose size and shape is determined, in large part, by the geometry of space.[13] Gould also suggests, somewhat reductively, that architecture, particularly the church architecture of the medieval period, should be analyzed similarly for its status as a physical object in space. The length and width of these churches, Gould proposes, were determined by an inverse ratio between interior space and surface. As surface area grows, interior space diminishes. Before animals, mammals specifically, evolved lungs, which are a series of interior folded and filtered surfaces through which air can pass, they needed large exterior surfaces, and relatively smaller bodies, in order to breathe. The medieval church behaves in the same way, according to Gould. Because it had no artificial lighting source, it could only increase its surface area through "out-pouching," which brought in more light. The interior remains relatively small until various technologies of the interior—structural, electrical, mechanical—can free it from dependence on the exterior.[14] The idea that both biological and other objects share "physical objecthood," which means they share an atomic structure and are subject to physical laws, was the basis, as mentioned in my introduction, of Schrödinger's attempt to analyze biology from a quantum physics point of view and to find in it the operation of similar principles.

In the seventeenth century, birds manifested the perfect management of the "mechanics of heaven and earth" in a new world ruled by gravity. Galileo, more than Descartes, noted that the bone structure and body size of animals cannot be increased indefinitely "without destroying the unity and hampering the normal functioning of organs,"[15] In birds, there is a necessary relationship between body weight, wingspan and muscular power. "Even if he had wings," Borelli (1685) wrote, "man could never fly, for want of sufficiently strong chest muscles." Birds demonstrate the necessity of nature and are, as is usually the case, situated as object lessons for human life. Flight and the sky were the one movement and the one space, for millennia, completely denied to humans.[16] But nature, in Galileo's and Borelli's view, is as it must be. Birds in the sky affirm the existence of a perfect "fitness" between organism and milieu—although part of the language is wrong for the seventeenth century. There is no idea yet of space as specifically meaningful for organisms, in which even the sky can be stratified and understood as an ecological niche. The bird's fitness, by which the morphology of a body is limited by gravity, surface tension, and organ function, is mechanical, based on the idea (shared by Gould) that living bodies, as well as inanimate bodies, act as physical objects in space. This idea of fitness lays the groundwork for the later assumption that space acquires meaning, as do bodies, from the relationship between them. The sky thus eventually acquires a certain definition in relation to the birds that "use" it. When Henri Lefebvre, in the mid-twentieth century, claims that space makes physical bodies symmetrical, he is using, in some form, this seventeenth century teleological idea of "fit" without the theological overtones.

There have been innumerable experiments, since antiquity, in which humans attempt bird-like flight, some of which are meant as parodies of the human condition. Castel Fallboys, in Peter

Greenaway's film *The Falls* (1980), for example, has a gait like a starling and has vainly attempted "to perfect human flight" by "ruthlessly streamlining his body by excessive exercise and diet, growing very lean in the leg, muscular in the shoulders, long in the arm and short in the neck."[17] Fallboys' struggle to acquire the fitness of the bird to its milieu is, of course, both comic and tragic, but the bodily "fit" into the birds' milieu is withheld not so much by some corporeal reality (i.e. his humanness) as by what Greenaway calls "the theory of the responsibility of birds," which beckons humans (catastrophically in *The Falls*) to bird-like flight and bird-like views but denies them the visual-physical equipment for either.

As is well known, Darwin's nineteenth century theory of random variation and the "survival of the fittest"—which elaborated on the spirit of the eighteenth century inquiries into nature—did not mean, as it was often thought to mean at the time, that organisms and milieu find the fittest "fit," but only that they find a viable fit. Xavier Bichat's definition of life at the beginning of the nineteenth century rejected, famously, any idea of a "fit" between living organisms and a milieu by arguing that the milieu is indifferent to the life within in. Auguste Comte later modulates this antagonism to a consensual relationship between organism and milieu that "does not go beyond what actual life requires" but is, nevertheless, arranged to permit existence.[18] Both Bichat and Comte advance, in complexity, the terms of the relation between living and the non-living. Darwin, looking at his flocks of finches on the Galapagos Islands, was thus able to pick out the birds from the geological background and, simultaneously, understand the birds in terms of their background. Darwin is able, in effect, to hypothesize a far deeper field of vision in the nineteenth century than could have been imagined in the classical era because the concept of background—space, as well as time and historical process—and its relationship to life is thicker and more extensive.

As Georges Canguilhem remarks in *A Vital Rationalist*: "[Georges] Buffon and Carolus Linnaeus could describe and classify life forms without ever defining what they meant by 'alive.'"[19] It was therefore a moment of revelation, in the field of medical research, when Bichat began his *Recherches physiologiques sur la vie et la mort* (1800) with the statement, "Life is the collection of functions that resist death."[20] Bichat defines life, as Canguilhem writes, "in terms of a conflict between, on the one hand, a body composed of tissues of specific structure and properties (elasticity, contractility, sensitivity) and, on the other, an environment, or *milieu* . . . governed by laws indifferent to the intrinsic needs of living things."[21] The definition of life includes here, and henceforth, an exterior milieu, which, *governed by laws indifferent to the intrinsic needs of living things*, forces the question of the milieu, in spite of its exteriority and indifference, to comport itself inside the question of life, and vice versa. That death is the result of a long conflict in life—in its internal functions, and against the external forces that wear it down—is an idea that enlarges and opens the idea of life to include what lies outside, but is necessary to, its own self-perpetuation. The "essence" of life, in Bichat's definition, is to resist the entropic forces of the environment that it needs to live in the first place. This opening of the idea of life to a milieu also begs the question of life's difference from its milieu. After centuries of various misinterpretations of the specific boundaries between animate and inanimate, Bichat's definition requires ever more precise differentiations, which, in turn, contribute to the formation of the "discipline of life"—biology. His statement is published, in fact, one year before the term "biology" is first used in Germany by Gottfried Reinhold Treviranus and in France by Jean-Baptiste Lamarck.[22] Biology instantiates itself as the science of studying life—not merely its parts and manifestations but also, implicitly, its "essence"—at a moment when life itself is being defined as that which resists, but nevertheless is dependent on, an apparently indifferent milieu within which it resides.[23]

Comte's biological philosophy confirmed that biology was a "great scientific revolution which, under Bichat's leadership, transferred overall priority in natural philosophy from astronomy to biology."[24]

The correlation that Comte made between "milieu" and "organism" is different from Bichat's. Comte took the word "milieu," used specifically in seventeenth and eighteenth century mechanics and the physics of fluids, and transformed it "into a comprehensive, synthetic concept" that helped establish the modern, still positivist, dualism between life and matter, the living and the non-living.[25] He was also instrumental in removing the teleology from biology. "Conditions of existence" meant that "within certain limits . . . everything is . . . arranged in such a way that existence is possible."[26] The relationship between an organism and its environment, as mentioned above, thus gradually became one of viability, not necessity.

Buffon's and Linnaeus' classification of species in the eighteenth century, essentially the beginning of natural history, continue a process of opening secular space between different types of living beings, and between life and its milieu, that both Bichat and Comte further advanced. Nascent ideas about the role organization itself plays in biological life were still confined to summaries based on visible evidence. So while the living and non-living are becoming separate categories of bodies in the world, as Jacob argues, their separation by means of organization still produces confused taxonomic distinctions, as, for example, between "brute or unorganized Beings, organized and inanimate Beings, organized animate Beings, and finally organized, animate and reasonable Beings."[27]

Foucault famously argues that the classical age, mid-seventeenth century, is inaugurated by the first of two radical "discontinuities" in the *épistème* of the world since the Renaissance and, in some less clear way, since antiquity. The classical age, Foucault remarks, relied on a "coherence . . . between the theory of representation and the theories of language, of the natural orders, and of wealth and value." This configuration changes in the nineteenth century. "The theory of representation disappears as the universal foundation of all possible orders; language as . . . the primary grid of things, as an indispensable link between representation and things, is eclipsed in its turn."[28]

"Despite. . . our possible belief that the classifications of Linnaeus, modified to a greater or lesser degree, can still lay claim to some sort of validity," Foucault warns us, the "quasi-continuity" of events through these two epistemological breaks is only a "surface appearance."[29] During the second break, happening roughly between 1775 and 1810, a "profound historicity penetrates into the heart of things, isolates and defines them in their own coherence, imposes upon them the forms of order implied by the continuity of time."[30] Through the aperture of this "discontinuity" the idea of "modern man" emerges—"a recent invention, not yet two centuries old, a new wrinkle in our knowledge . . . that will disappear again as soon as that knowledge has discovered a new form."

Foucault exposed what continues to be a central controversy in contemporary historical work. Historical accounts, he argues, attempt to write the history of life before life or history as ideas existed. All that existed, prior to the nineteenth century, were "living beings" and "histories." The tendency of modern traditional history was to arrange matters so that one era appeared to arise out of another. Seeing history as a sequence of connected events was almost universally adopted as an organizing principle by a multitude of disciplines formed at the same time as the discipline of biology, architecture among them. Since life, after Darwin, was newly understood to include the problem of time, these disciplines formed themselves around sequences as both a temporal and spatial idea. Architectural history, for example, formed itself around the sequence of architectural types, although typology and temporal sequence are not necessarily congruent forms of order. In all cases where time has an impact, the weight of life is also felt, because time, as mentioned earlier, requires a living body. Foucault complained that the fixation of history on sequence blinded it to the discontinuities and irregularities in the continuum from which history draws its evidence and cuts its cloth. Studies of history in which "man" must play a part—in truth, all histories—tend to obscure the fact, Foucault argued, that:

> the study of [man], supposed by the naïve to be the oldest investigation since Socrates . . . is probably no more than a kind of rift in the order of things, or, in any case, a configuration whose outlines are determined by the new position he has so recently taken up in the field of knowledge. Whence all the chimeras of the new humanisms, all the facile solutions of an "anthropology" understood as a universal reflection on man, half-empirical, half-philosophical.[31]

Numerous historical accounts of the mid-seventeenth century, for example, suggested that the discipline of Natural History arose out of the failure of Cartesian mechanism to account for the "richness" and diversity of nature. Foucault remarks that "[O]ne science can arise out of another; but no science can be generated by the absence of another, or another's failure. . . . In fact, the possibility of natural history . . . is contemporaneous with Cartesianism itself, and not with its failure."[32] And he continues:

> For natural history to appear, it was not necessary for nature to become denser and more obscure, to multiply its mechanisms to the point of acquiring the opaque weight of a history that can only be retraced and described . . . ; it was necessary—and this is entirely the opposite—for History to become Natural. In the sixteenth century, and right up to the middle of the seventeenth, all that existed were histories: Belon had written a *History of the nature of birds*; Duret, an *Admirable history of plants*; Aldrovandi, *A History of serpents and dragons*. In 1657, Jonston published a *Natural history of quadrupeds*. This date of birth is not, of course, absolutely definitive; it is only to symbolize a landmark . . . the apparent enigma of an event. This event is the sudden separation, in the realm of *Historia* of two orders of knowledge henceforward to be considered different.[33]

What happened is that the semantic network within which life was held, prior to the eighteenth century, has disappeared. In the nineteenth century—the second break—representation, and the taxonomies it enabled, are displaced by "organic structures," "internal relations between elements whose totality performs a function." These organic structures are governed by principles of analogy and succession (time and the identity of relation that no longer includes visibility) and the functions they perform.[34]

What Foucault performs on these histories and ideas of order, as many have said, is an operation. The history of life, in which the idea of life itself does not coalesce until the eighteenth century, nevertheless is imagined in our contemporary world as if life had proceeded from coalescence to coalescence. And, since I want to trace architecture's path alongside the development of ideas of life, as we have imagined life over time, so we have imagined architecture. Foucault showed us that all the instances of coalescence we attribute to life in its long history are, in fact, evidence of the need for coalescence in a relatively modern discourse, the discourse of history as it looks back. "Nature" does not wait to be seen for what it is at any given moment; it is, simultaneously, utterly dependent on time and without a historical view. Through the various techniques of Foucault's "event" we move, then, always doubling back, between modernity—and its various historical claims—and the thick, multiple, oscillatory modalities of life, under and in which we have lived as a species, and by which we have formed ideas of our biological being and our spaces. There will have to be much more about the eighteenth century, of course. Between the confusion about biological life that prevailed for centuries and the often mis-leading lucidity that modernity seemed to bring to the subject, there are numerous interesting developments.

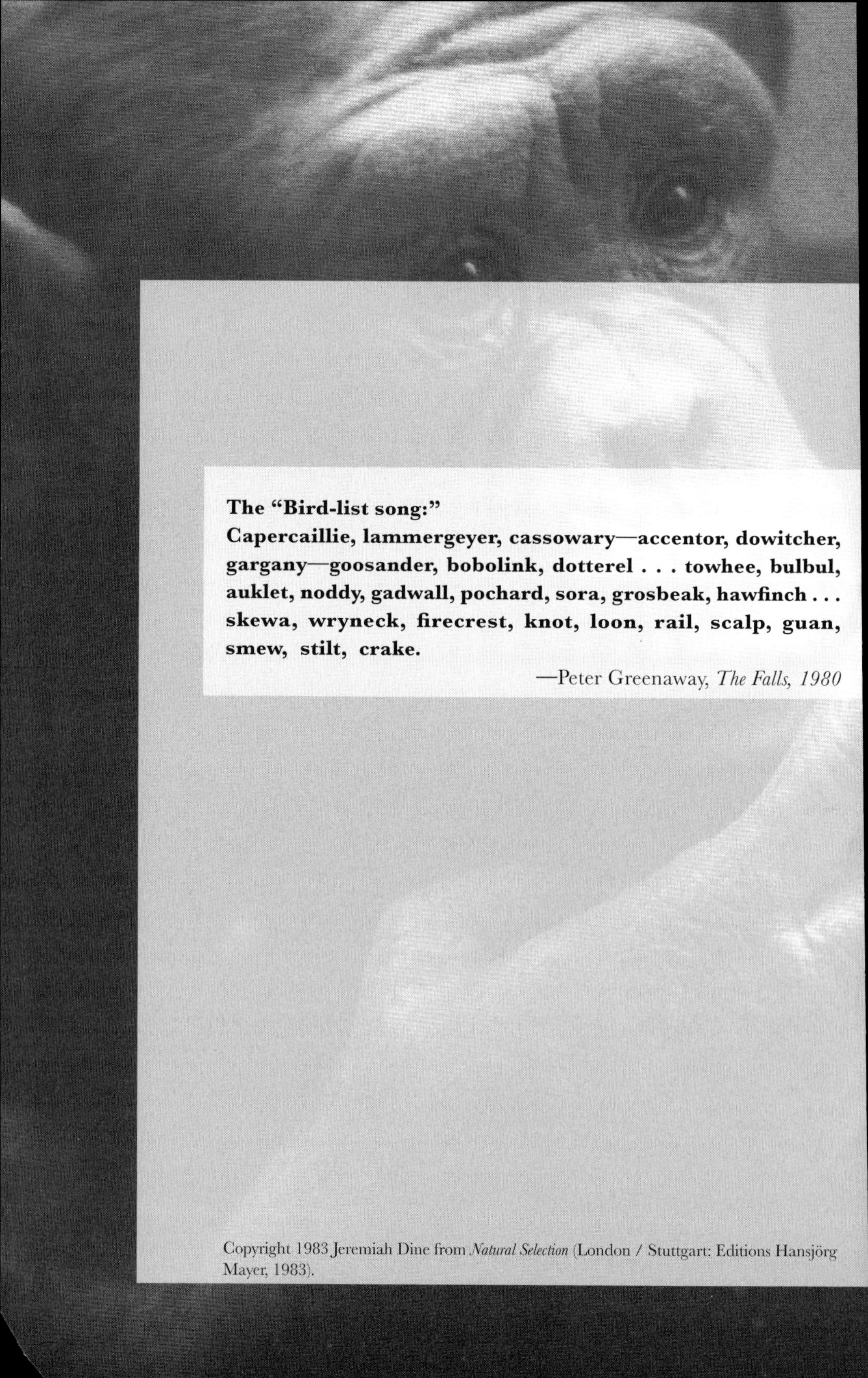

**The "Bird-list song:"**
**Capercaillie, lammergeyer, cassowary—accentor, dowitcher, gargany—goosander, bobolink, dotterel . . . towhee, bulbul, auklet, noddy, gadwall, pochard, sora, grosbeak, hawfinch . . . skewa, wryneck, firecrest, knot, loon, rail, scalp, guan, smew, stilt, crake.**

—Peter Greenaway, *The Falls, 1980*

# 4: POST-ANIMAL LIFE



*Post-animal life* is a description of life that both links and slips between architectural and human/animal "life" history. It takes note, as a description, of the fact that the status and value of human and animal life changed drastically from the Renaissance to the present and also makes the supposition that ontological shifts in the meaning of life affect, and are affected by, shifts in the meaning of architecture. As is evident, I have adopted the much disputed, but arguable, view that modernity, for architecture, begins in the Renaissance, whereas modern human and animal life do not begin until the late eighteenth century. The period of slippage and consolidation between these two modernities is post-animal because animal life itself—as an idea, form, and reality—is taken hostage by the various disjunctions between architecture and human/animal life. The problem of post-animal life and architecture is thus simultaneously historical and theoretical.

In the nineteenth century, to be "human" means to have been finally, and definitively, separated from animals (which make a genetic comeback in the late twentieth century—but that is a later part of the story). To be "animal" means to have been divested of psychological autonomy and power in such a way that continued existence in the world becomes increasingly precarious. Many of the things that happen during the eighteenth and nineteenth centuries—the usual things we are familiar with from reputable histories—result from the sudden convergence of an already modern architecture faced with an emerging modern human being, now an autonomous, individualized and secularized being placed at the center of everything. During the same period, architecture also houses what could be called ongoing atavistic bestial life, in the form of the disappearing animal inside the human. Only the last part of the previous sentence would seem strange to those reputable historians. The "dispersal of the subject," or "post-humanism," of the late twentieth century, which subsequently dismantles ideas of human autonomy—an idea of autonomy that dates back only several hundred years, to the moment "humanness" found its place in the world—might have calculated some of the cost of the loss of human autonomy in terms of what we knew already in the eighteenth century about the loss of animal autonomy.[1] And the "inverted values" of a Renaissance architecture that is "animal" continues in a different form. But this, too, is a later story.

Recapping where we are: architecture captures "objects in the world" in the Renaissance by means of spatial coordinate systems, which eventually, in Panofsky's skillful words, enable the "claim of the object to meet the ambition of the subject." Part of the "ambition of the subject" to which the collateral ambitions of Renaissance history routinely testify is to universalize architectural principles in a way that accounts for almost everything about architectural objects: their meaning, construction, placement on a site, design, authority as artistic objects and status as theoretical objects. Part of the claim of the object in the Renaissance is to be mathematically "known" in space. The definitive separation between animate and inanimate objects based on bio-ontological differences—life and death, movement and stasis, biological and astronomical time, generative and reproductive capacities—are not yet in place in the Renaissance, but one beauty of the invention of perspective is that it treats all objects in its domain, living or non-living, as equal, and all space in its domain as full.

Beginning in the late eighteenth century, architecture captures, specifically, human life, which is in the process of gaining biological autonomy from animal life. Architecture captures this life in what is now not only a net of analogic relations, and a sophisticated interior, but also a field of space—space that has been enlarged beyond representational space by sixteenth and seventeenth century science and new theories of time. In subsequent eras, human life biologically consolidates what had been, since antiquity, its philosophical and theological centrality. Human life, as it grows in biological complexity, analytically matches, and in some cases surpasses, its historic intellectual and spiritual privilege with biological privilege. These developments are registered in architecture through the secularization and formalization of "public space," the formation of architectural history and typology (which models itself initially, as mentioned earlier, after the natural sciences), and the design of new institutions based on new disciplines such as medicine, sociology, anthropology, and politics. Architecture also registers these developments by becoming envious and desirous—the euphemism is perhaps too dramatic—of the intricate motion, depth, and organization of the body it houses and increasingly understands. And, from the other direction, the constancy and variability of human life, now formalized into "ways of life" that are analogous to what we recognize, in contemporary terms, as a kind of biosocial homeostasis, impose new types of order and disorder on architecture. With the opening of space between beings and things, and between human and animal in the eighteenth century, the distance between architecture and biological life, paradoxically, begins to narrow. One of Agamben's points in *The Open*, which takes little account of space or architecture, is, nevertheless, the same. The human body has always been thought to be a combination of natural and divine, or natural and social—part animal, part something else. Instead, Agamben argues, humanness "results from the practical and political *separation* of humanity and animality."[2] This separation is particularly potent in the post-animal age, which is post-Renaissance for architecture and post-Enlightenment for human and animal life. The animal is withdrawn from the human scene in the Enlightenment, "liberating" humanness into its various modern good and bad humanities.

When Siegfried Giedion traces this same history in architectural history, a large segment of his scholarly focus is brought to bear on how architecture contends both with the movement and space that is augmented by mechanization (*Mechanization Takes Command*), and with the movement and space that is increasingly implied by modern theories of time (*Space, Time and Architecture*). Alongside the deep technical interests that architecture has in moving structures and in structures that must sustain movement, and the philosophical and scientific fascination with time and space are the issues of biological movement in space and time. Post-animal human life moves more freely in the world and claims, for itself, territory formerly accorded to animals. Architecture confronts, in this life, an effect that cannot be easily assimilated into physical space: the human psyche, the inside of the inside, inner life.

The Renaissance and Enlightenment increase the range and intensity of architecture's relation to ways of life—through the mechanisms of perspective and the opening of interior spaces and structures that result over time in the architectural program—but also encounter, in the nineteenth century, the Freudian unconscious, the dark protector of contemporary human consciousness. Rosalind Krauss' grasp of modern painting (which I discuss in a later chapter) as a surface through which the eye moves with lightning speed, supplying dimensions (but not the "optical third dimension" of Clement Greenberg), constructs the eye itself as the "optical unconscious." The eye brokers what is seen in the external world with the restless constructive motion of the unconscious and of Lacanian desire, the internal world. Architecture, in assuming that human life was, for architectural purposes, primarily a body-in-space, felt itself able to sidestep the complex skein of developments that understood human movement to be evidence of a particular kind of mind, not a particular kind of body. For architecture, the perfect occupant has been, and to some degree still is, a living being chiefly identified by means of its form and the (limited, encaged) movement of its body, the humanized animal, or "human-animal" of the post-animal world. It is not, of course, as if humans were given any choice as to what kind of consciousness they have, nor do they have much say over their form. It is simply that the restraint that architecture places on human bodies in architectural space is almost purely formal. This formalism is routinely overcome by movement—the movement of the body through space. So movement and form are essential to our conception of architecture and the modern architectural program. Human consciousness, however, is not, although it would be impossible to design, build, or live in architecture without such a consciousness.

Psychological life, in architectural terms, remains naïve. The nineteenth century architectural subject is, thus, definitively human in form, its "needs" are known, and it has human privileges (it can enter and leave enclosures as it pleases), but it remains closer to what the animal has become than what the human, in other parts of its life, has become. Prior to the eighteenth century, for example, animals were understood to have magical powers (analogous to psychological powers), and these begin to evaporate once taxonomic sciences begin to be more precise about the divisions between different kinds of life. In architectural terms, both animal and human, in the post-animal age, are increasingly understood as physical forms uniquely amenable to capture; that is, the newly discovered human and the reformed animal of the nineteenth century do not offer any psychological resistance to the act of being housed or caged—in fact, the reverse. The interior of the house comes to stand as a metaphor for the interior life of the human—it takes over, in some sense, the space of interiority that the human psyche claims for itself when it leaves the surrogate interior of the house. To be permanently "outside the house" is, at the same time, a pathological life, a homeless life.

There are, of course, reservations on all sides. As I suggested earlier, human and animal retain reserves of "wildness." For animals, we have only this word and its slippery meaning; for humans, there are numerous words—schizophrenia, legendary psychasthenia, claustro-phobia, the uncanny, all the spatial phobias and aphasias such as autism, agoraphobia, attention deficit disorder—many of which had their origins in the nineteenth century clash of human life with mechanization and industrialization but all of which raise the specter of the animal and the animal caught by space. I do not want to romanticize these terms or the conditions of resistance they imply. I simply want to mark the possibility of a reserve that cannot be fully assimilated by an account of post-animal architectural life. We are familiar with the argument that this reserve or wildness is human consciousness itself, the interior of the human mind that is unable to be housed by architecture and thus acts as a wild card. But I also think this reserve belongs not to the human mind, as Freud imagined it, but to the part of the animal that lives outside humanness. This is not the rat of the Ratman or the wolf of the Wolfman, nor the rat and the wolf as they might play the role of the "other," but the rat and the wolf as they are unknown, rather than known, by humans. The particular balance between form and restrained movement that defines the animal in the post-animal world makes the human-animal an ideal architectural occupant. Using, again, Heidegger's problematic but provocative terms, the "open" and "disconcealedness" of human consciousness, and much that it contains—the various humanisms and "world-making" of its history—humans thus find, specifically in architecture, a foregone animal identity that they make contemporary with themselves. Post-animal life in architectural space is thus the paradox of an "open captivation." Architecture sustains and defines some aspect of the animal in the human long after it has been, apparently, eradicated by science, and long after the human political and social being has been brought into the fully separate place of humanness.

I also do not mean to say that architecture should, somehow, be more human, or more humane, than it is. Perhaps it should, and could, be. But the extreme difficulty, even the impossibility, of any direct reference, on the part of architecture, to the self-conscious aspect of human life—in spite of the obvious fact and paradox that architecture is designed by self-conscious human beings—is not necessarily meant to indicate a dire condition that needs correction. Instead, it is a kind of explanation for many facets of architecture that we have tried—from Renaissance harmonic proportions that were meant to make buildings and human bodies commensurate to Daniel Libeskind's obtuse architectural lines of concordance with human history—to account for in terms of life and, above all, in terms of a felt disjunction or asymmetry between life and architecture. Perhaps having such a view changes, at the very least, the way certain images are read. One might notice more acutely, for example, how images of human and animal life are almost always missing from architectural images, or, when they do appear, how heavily stylized they have become. In early Renaissance drawings of building interiors, there is no human figure to give scale to the buildings—"giving scale" to buildings is what human figures, as one humanist ideal, were meant to do.[3] We place the building in its own transparent artistic cage in order to see it better. Notable exceptions are, as always, Le Corbusier and his inheritor, Rem Koolhaas, who craft their figures of life as if they were characters in a movie, stylized, backs turned, beautifully dressed, highly formal, profoundly inenigmatic. Beatriz Colomina reads Le Corbusier's images of human figures as if they are actors inside architectures that act like camera lenses—an "architecture as mass media" that breaks the distinction between the public and the private.[4] Koolhaas inexplicably includes an animal, a giraffe, in his photograph of the Villa dall'Ava in Paris, a house with two "apartments." Why a giraffe? The giraffe is poignant in the photograph. It is a scaling diagram, like the modular, but also contributes a trace of its characteristic posture to the structure of the house, which rides on splayed *pilotis*.

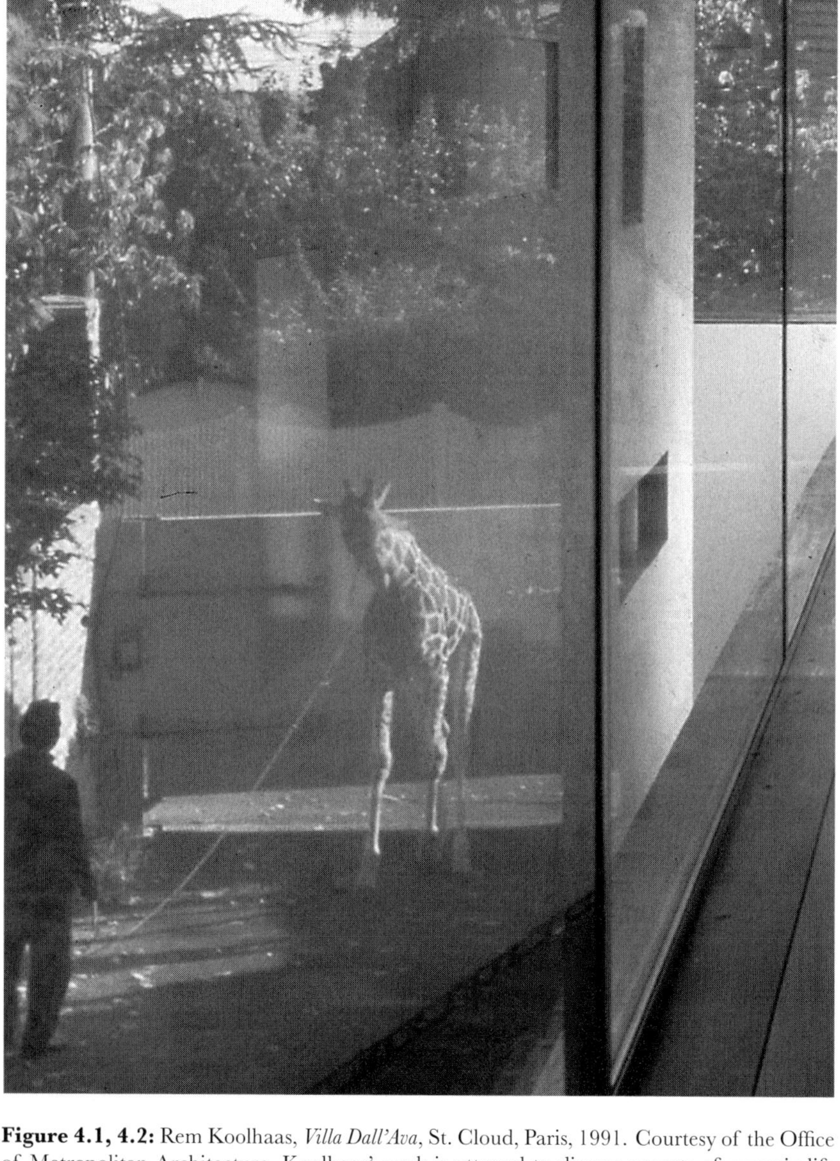



 **Figure 4.1, 4.2:** Rem Koolhaas, *Villa Dall'Ava*, St. Cloud, Paris, 1991. Courtesy of the Office of Metropolitan Architecture. Koolhaas' work is attuned to diverse aspects of somatic life sublimated in metropolitan and domestic architectures.

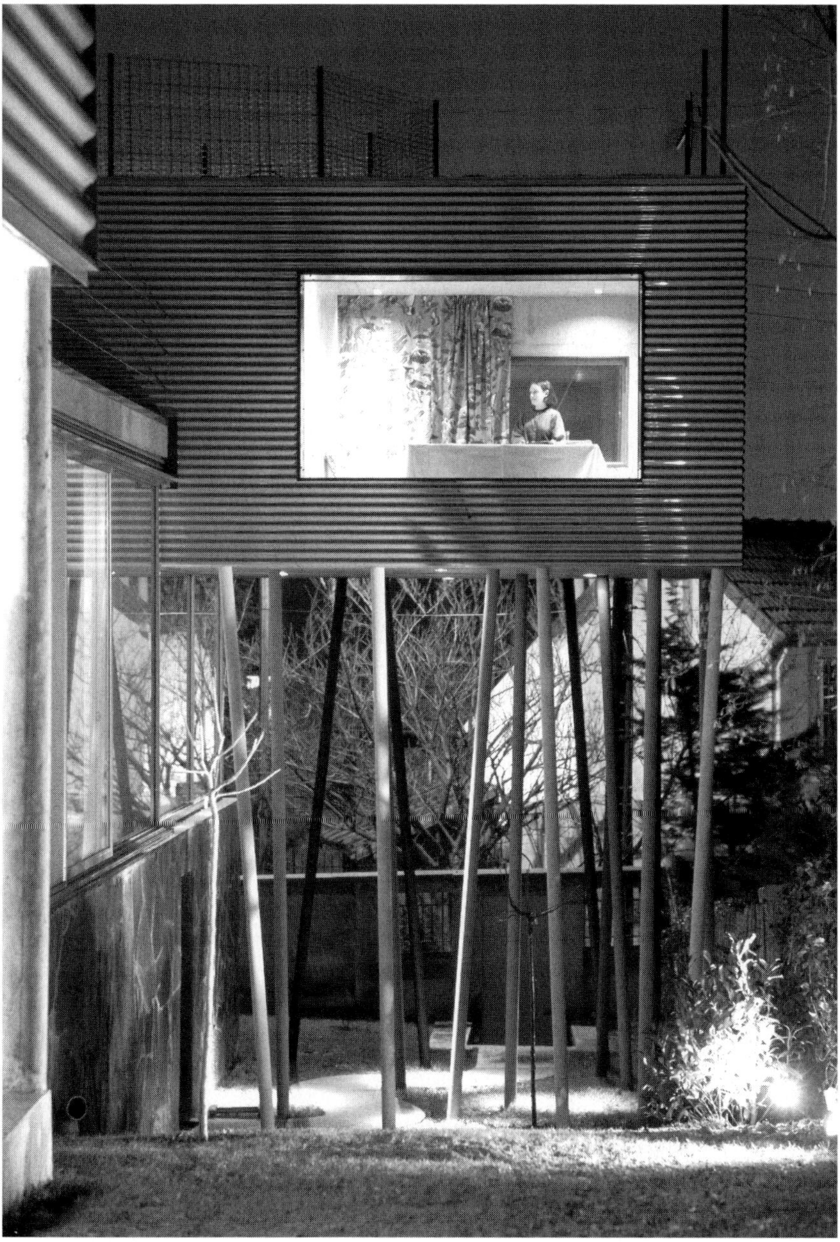

The expansiveness of *SMLXL*, which records these somatic architectures—their "splendors and miseries"—is laden with narratives and images from a human planet that lies open to an animal interior; thus a building can be carried on long spindly legs.

Or perhaps the giraffe is a figure of lost human grace or a symbol of a wild captivity that marks post-animal life. It is, as always, hard to read the "image effect" of such gestures—was the giraffe digitally pasted into the scene or hauled to the site, or does it, any longer, matter? Perhaps, given what has been laid on the table, we will eventually have to look at some other kind of story.

# 5: AFTER



It is familiar because it is quite close—life after Darwin, molecular biology, quantum physics, museums with fossils (which have become a quaint novelty), genetics, cybernetics, medical technology, deep time, Foucault (always there is Foucault).

It has been, certainly, a long time since I first read Foucault's *The Order of Things*, where, as Martin Jay wrote, "hostility to traditional notions of visual primacy and the critique of humanism were intricately linked."[1] I remember what it was like to walk into that book for the first time as a graduate student. I did not then know what was at stake, so the arguments were opaque to me, but the character of the book itself was to have an enormous impact on how I subsequently thought about scholarly work. The many controversies surrounding Foucault's early work—historians' skepticism about his historical method; an involved writing style that deferred its summary remarks for page after page, folding in layer after layer of insight; the problems of grasping and practicing historical criticism in light of theories of discontinuity, and so forth—were much discussed during my graduate education. I have since taught Foucault routinely in architecture, particularly *Power and Knowledge,* for its discussions of the politics of space and the panoptic machine.[2] But rarely have I taught *The Order of Things*, or, if so, almost always only the first chapter, on *Las Meninas*. This book's virtuoso ability to pass through four hundred years of natural and cosmological history, reversing the orthodoxies with incredible, devastating insight, is so methodologically powerful that a class on this book would quickly become a methods-in-theory class. Architecture students are often avid students of theory, but they are poor students of intellectual method. Analytic methods, in architecture, if they are taught at all, are taught in the design studio.

Foucault's opening remarks are about the order of things and words: "The fundamental codes of a culture establish for every man, from the very first, the empirical orders with which he will be dealing and within which he will be at home." At the other end of the spectrum, he argued, were the philosophical or scientific interpretations that explain why order exists in general. "But between these two regions . . . [of] the already "encoded" eye and reflexive knowledge there is a middle region . . . [which] insofar as it makes manifest the modes of being of order . . . is the most fundamental of all." "What I am attempting to bring to light is the epistemological field," Foucault wrote, ". . . [that] manifests a history which is . . . that of its conditions of possibility. . . . Such an enterprise is not so much a history . . . as an archaeology." The "quasi-continuities" of history are doubtless, everyone will remember Foucault saying, "surface appearances."[3]

We are, by now, a long way down the road of Foucault's archaeologies, a class of inquiries that fundamentally revised the practice of history into what is now called historiography—history as a study, although not an exclusive study, of its own processes and discourses. The transformation that historical scholarship, cultural theory, the history of science, and other fields have gone through in the past thirty years, partly as a result of arguing with and assimilating Foucault (as well as other philosophers), is staggering. And yet there is almost nothing of Foucault's intellectual adventurism, innovation, and courage in this new historicism. One of the defining characteristics of his work, his ability to wield writing as a method of inquiry that had direct bearing on the inquiry itself, has been burned up in the reconstruction. Certainly the euphoric inauguration of various theoretical investigations in architecture has now almost abated. Perhaps, in retrospect, very few writers or practitioners (although there are notable exceptions) working during the complex twenty year period between the mid-1970s and the mid-1990s could maintain their balance in a field where it was necessary to be an expert in at least three or four types of practices: theory, history, both scholarly and literary writing, architectural design. It was almost too rich and diffuse a mixture.

Part of the driving force of doing architectural theory in light of post-structural philosophy was the problem of how to comport theoretical arguments inside the resistant, materialist discipline of architecture. It is an oversimplification of recent events to say that it was inevitable that the field of architecture would retake its practice from the various practitioners of something other than architectural practice in order to revive empiricist and formalist approaches to material and (now-digital) technology in architectural practice, and to "get back to specifics" in scholarly writing. It might be more accurate to say that once history was theorized, theory had to be historicized. History did not disappear, in other words, as many had thought it would. The Berlin wall actually fell and things changed, yet again, in the world, accounts of which had to be given in historical terms. These terms were not, however, the same terms as before.

I am generalizing a set of conditions, in this brief introduction to eighteenth century theories of life, because I want to offer an apology, in the classical sense, for bringing in Foucault, rather than just doing Foucault or some version of Foucault, or doing post-Foucault, whatever that might mean. In my view, none of the importance of those twentieth century, mostly French, philosophers has been diminished or exhausted with respect to early twenty-first century architectural work in either its renovated modernisms or the computational studies of non-linear and dynamic systems theory. In particular, the attachment of post-classical theory to contemporary science, especially biology, does not yet seem to fully stand apart, in theoretical terms, from discussions of the past thirty to forty years. The widespread preoccupation with computational work among architecture students, on the one hand, and questions of ecology and sustainability in architecture, on the other, give evidence of an ongoing interest in some of the precise issues raised thirty-five years ago by Foucault in *The Order of Things*, where language, information and the economy of the world, cultural and natural, are structurally entwined with each other.

Having said all this, it is also true that we, architects, historians, theorists, and it, architecture, are now alert to other influences, many of which derive from the disciplines of cybernetics and genetics, fields that were forming themselves around the same time that Foucault was writing. These other lines of development reflect in very different ways on the nature of history and the status of the event. Like eighteenth and nineteenth century biological sciences, these sciences are altering the ontological status of human and animal life. How this will affect architecture—and it has already—is a question that is, at this moment, influencing the work of many people.

•

First, to complete the initial foray: Between 1750 and 1850 underlying orders of the world are subjected first to "powers of nomination," classification, and natural history; and, second, to what Foucault calls the discovery of internal structure. These orders are brought into focus and elaborated by human systems of knowledge. The movement from exterior to interior constituted a seismic shift, and its consequences are still at work in the life sciences today. Oddly, the world itself seemed to yield up some of its secrets in response to these developments, although the idea of "yielding" is, of course, wrong—as if nature were deliberately obfuscating its own processes. But it is often the dark secrets of natural processes, such as the work of reproduction in biological evolution, that seem to enlighten Enlightenment knowledge; nature is not an inert substance illuminated by the mythical blinding light of human understanding. The interior structures of the world are eventually, in every sense, constructed by leaping over the exterior evidence and then reconnecting interior to exterior. As Barbara Stafford has perhaps most profoundly elucidated, it is difficult to pry open, in any orderly or meaningful way, the "invisible interior" of organic bodies, or, for that matter, any object or system in the earthly and planetary world. To do so, as suggested earlier, the intricate logics of a relation between interior to exterior already have to have been solved at some level. Stafford writes that the hunt for the "unseizable other" is inevitably a "hunt for definitive origins or documentable beginnings of aesthetic, ethical, biological, cognitive, and social experience."[4] As François Jacob writes of this same period: "It was [now] within living bodies themselves that the very cause of their existence had to be found . . . the parts . . . gave meaning to the whole. The surface properties of a living being were controlled by the inside, what is visible by what is hidden."[5]

A form of reconciliation between outside and inside, in the case of biology, was made possible through the concept of organization, which "assembled the parts of the organism into a whole, enabled it to cope with the demands of life and imposed forms throughout the living world." Jacob continues, "[T]hus, . . . a new science was to appear. Its aim was no longer to classify organisms, but to study the processes of life."[6] The idea of organization itself required that the "dualistic construction of the physical and corporeal cosmos inherited . . . from the seventeenth century" be expanded into "wider fields of inquiry."[7]

In general, in the eighteenth century, and continuing into the nineteenth century, questions of evidence become paramount.[8] As Denis Cosgrove remarks on the history of maps, observational accounts made possible by increased travel gradually revised former universalized mathematical and cosmological diagrams and maps of the world.[9] Eyewitness accounts, filled with detailed information about other cultures, landscapes, and botanical life, as well as interpretations produced by the hubris and lament of observation endemic to long, complicated, and often lonely voyages, change the content as well as the style of the world's representation. Different strands of knowledge begin to be integrated. In paleontology, fossil discoveries support various accounts of time and the part that time has played in the formation of the earth's geology and life forms. The discovery of "deep time"—the beginning of the geological time we are now familiar with—fundamentally affects the organization of all knowledge. Eighteenth century assemblies of evidence link seeing to knowing in a way that results in systems of knowledge that are seemingly capable of ordering everything in the world, both known and unknown, first into classifiable parts, and then into linked structures. This recalculation of the world is profound.[10] Seeing and knowing are not simultaneous forms of apprehension; they operate both together and against each other. "Seeing into," in particular, was the potent eighteenth century metaphor for the construction of knowledge as well as for the meaning of life itself.[11] Humans become the species that not only see the world in all its richness but also see into themselves.

The Enlightenment—it is often said—consolidated a certain potential for visuality that was already somewhat present, in a much more narrow sense, throughout the pre-classical age. Various theories extend the reach of the visible through instruments that see more, such as the microscope, and also through internal mechanisms and structures that are newly theorized as open structures. These can be correlated with other structures not simply through surface comparisons but also as systems of internal cellular or tissue organization. This is a result, in part, of gradual transitions in anatomical research from the seventeenth to nineteenth centuries: attempts, for example, to understand the circulation of the blood (William Harvey, 1600s); theories of tissue organization (Bourgery, 1797–1849, and Bichat, 1800[12]); and related developments in corpuscular theories of elementary matter (Buffon, late 1700s).[13] The interior, as an idea and a space, comes to light, literally and figuratively. The sight of the surface of the monster gives way to a fascination with the interior of mutated forms and structures (now rendered knowable), and, thus, the monster disappears, because it depended, as a category, on keeping significant parts of itself concealed or enigmatic—its genesis, final shape, hybrid parentage, the degree to which it was familiar or strange, its ability to procreate.

Some of these shifts in the natural sciences intersect with architecture. In addition to the comparative anatomical studies by Georges Cuvier already mentioned, which are imitated by architecture in the interest of formalizing a history of types, architecture also begins to think of itself as a discipline of historical sequences, with immature periods leading to mature periods leading to decline.[14] Architectural ruins, like fossils, seem to suddenly align themselves into demonstrable evidence that architecture has "evolved," like an organism, over time and space. "[E]very single organism living today represents the last link of a chain uninterrupted over some three thousand million years. Living beings are . . . literally creations of history."[15] Further, if living beings are historical and the fossil record broken (most fossils are teeth; rarely is a whole body found), architectural remains and ruins might also serve as evidence, it was reasoned, for the history of life itself. These remains and ruins are, thus, repositories of knowledge and mythologies about human life history. This idea works most effectively during the eighteenth and nineteenth centuries when the history of life and the nature of time are being deduced and pieced together from actual fossils and geologies. Later, in the early twentieth century, when molecular biologists begin to look at organisms at a much deeper level, architectural ruins as a repository of living history will feel precisely like many fossils now feel: out of date and out of scale to the detail of life; useful and picturesque, but somehow dusty and inarticulate about the soft tissue. But in the mid- to late eighteenth century there is a moment of concordance between the historical construction of living beings and the evolving history of architectural type and structure.

This moment can be found nowhere more, and less, so than in Piranesi's work, which is at once contemporary, historical, geological, archaeological, theoretical, idiosyncratic, anatomical,[16] artistic and architectural, with an extreme interiority, a fascination with the ruin and fragment, anthropological in a primitive sense, and concerned with tracing the architectural marks of those living and those dead. Leafing through the tomes of architectural history, looking intently at neoclassical eighteenth century English country estates with names like Strawberry Hill (1750, Walpole's "cottage enlarged and Gothicized" at Twickenham in west London), Stourhead House (mid-eighteenth century, "an artificial lake . . . a pantheon and a rustic cottage)," Kew Gardens (1763, "Chinese Pagoda") and so forth,[17] it is easy to see that architecture is still attempting to bridge the old and the new, but it is not easy to see any theory of human, or other, life. The Neoclassical pavilions constructed as deer, monkey, and bird houses (dovecotes) that can be found on these estates do not seem promising. In the midst of all this Englishness the Venetian Piranesi theorizes a history of the world, through etching, in terms of Roman structures. His is not exactly the Neoclassicism practiced by eighteenth century English architects; among other things, he advances Rome as central evidence for the entire spectrum of modern human civilization. "Piranesi's radical experimentation with etching . . . permitted him to perform perceptual rescue work. He artistically unearthed the mutilated corpus of Italian antiquity."[18] The Carceri, of course, are part of Piranesi's argument—"free-floating interiors" in which the interior is seen as a dense involution of life and architectural form. Tafuri claims for these etchings the promise of human collectivity that will mark the modern age, but the depiction of the human figures in these scenes are disassembled, rather than assembled, as a collective body—an interior that is not sublime, in Burke's terms, so much as unearthed from its sublimation in an earlier era of heavy grandiose surfaces. One thousand drawings devoted to the city of Rome.

"An English gentleman's education," Spiro Kostof wrote, "was not deemed complete without the Grand Tour which culminated in Rome.[19] To the French Academy on the Corso came, for a three year stay, the winners of the Prix de Rome, the highest award of the American Academy in Paris." Johann Joachim Winckelmann, "the chief defender of Greek supremacy," who was particularly interested in the outer form of a building "presenting its inner construction," lived in Rome.[20] Stafford suggests that Piranesi's etching technique was drawn from eighteenth century surgical procedures and anatomical representation—Cowper's in particular—to "turn the still-living fabric of architecture inside out."[21] Weirdly, these anatomical artist-physicians are after not only anatomical information but also the way anatomical information might intersect with the body in its daily activities—the body embedded in a way of life, not just the body proper. Skeletons are posed as if reading a book or paying bills. Sectional cuts through bodies in these anatomical portraits maintain the unsectioned face in poses of everyday life and thought. Piranesi, who was to die from the fumes released by the acids he used to etch his drawings[22] (and of which Stafford makes so much of interest—the cutting into the paper itself is an unearthing and textural process that can "flay" the buildings in the interest of knowing more),[23] declared himself up to the task of designing a new universe. Indeed, many aspects of universe making are implied in his body of work—classification documents, plans, sections, elevations, conduits, connective tissue, support infrastructures, waterworks, cages for the animals, civic and government structures. This is an architecture of the earth, and below the earth (no renderings of the heavens and gods), and an architecture of gargantuan enclosures for the stylish or incarcerated "loiterers" ("acquisitive tourists"[24]) that show up in other parts of Piranesi's vision; in it human life is dwarfed by the scale of its enclosures and yet perfectly at ease. The scale of Piranesi's drawings sets the scale and style of subsequent

**Figure 5.1:** Giovanni Battista Piranesi, *View of the animal cages built by Domitian*, 1784. Courtesy of Biblioteca Nazionale Centrale di Roma.

**Figure 5.2:** Giovanni Battista Piranesi, *Ruins of an ancient building in the Villa Barberina*, 1764. Courtesy of Biblioteca Nazionale Centrale di Roma.

nineteenth century natural history museums, in which, if possible, the entire evolution of life had to be staged through the figural presentation of the evidentiary bodies and bones that were to make the case for both the eighteenth century turn toward the interior of bodies and, simultaneously, the explosion of insight into origins and identifications of life occasioned by that turn.

But why would Piranesi imagine that a new universe was needed? The short answer, certainly not Piranesi's in any explicit historical sense, but just as clearly intimated in his work, is that a type of life known as *Homo sapiens*—a specific biological being with a complex interior and a specific biological history—is about to make its debut in the world. This debut will cause an erasure of certain confusions about human life, a gathering of definitiveness around the animal part of humanness, and the beginning of the deaths of animals themselves. It is also a move from skin to structure, exterior to interior. Piranesi's "etching" of the interiors of building, to follow Stafford's probative metaphors, is dermatological (the skin is pocked by acid) and also surgical (the skin is cut open to reveal the interior).

To bring to mind some of what else is happening during this period: in the mid-1700s, the same period in which Diderot is writing the *Encyclopedia* (1751), a "universal dictionary of sciences and arts;"[25] Claude Ledoux theorizes and builds an "architectural encyclopedia" that is both a "tree of knowledge"[26] and a symbolic architecture that suggests ways of life that are not fully realized until the 1900s—a life of rural and urban labor and production over which Jeremy Bentham's panopticon, which resets humanist values;[27] later becomes the controlling metaphor; Boullée designs a monument to Isaac Newton, a planet-shaped building for the philosopher of the planet. "There set in a violent reaction to Baroque and Rococo forms, as well as a resistance to the authority of Vitruvius and classical canons—both ancient and recent. An earnest search was underway for . . . a universality more encompassing than that of Greece and Rome."[28]

In 1735, the Swede Carl Linnaeus classifies living beings in such a way as to definitively establish the zoological position of humans, who thenceforth became a species, *Homo sapiens*. "Fifty more years had to pass before the logical order of living species found its counterpart in the chronological series of fossils."[29] From 1749 to 1788, Georges Buffon writes the thirty-six volumes of his *Natural History* and "brings up within a mass of still shaky documentation the two problems that were to inflame nineteenth century thought: Our zoological nature and the immense antiquity of geological eras."[30] In 1764, J. J. Winckelmann writes the *History of Ancient Art*, which Anthony Vidler places in the "methodologically heterogeneous climate of mid-eighteenth century historical connoisseurship."[31] Like those of the early natural historians, Winckelmann's history is an account of the past that arranges things in "sometimes chronological [order], sometimes heterotopic, sometimes arranged by juxtaposition, similarity, or resemblance."[32] The entire restructuring of the idea of the human—the image of the human self, and the relation of this self to knowledge—happens in this, and the next, century alongside the restructuring of the fossil record. Theories of human physical and mental development reach into a deeper and deeper past, and the world literally becomes more ancient. N. de Maillet, in 1755, assembles documents that intimate that the earth is several hundred thousand years old,[33] the oldest the earth had ever been. The modern idea of directional time, the breaking of time into eras, the depth of time, the dating of space that is geological in character but also abstract, these enable history in general to develop as a discipline that, to begin with wants, as Vidler writes, to "begin at the beginning"[34] and then is sufficiently in control of concepts of space and time to conceptualize complex, non-theological, non-creationist beginnings.

As Vidler also elucidates, architecture in the eighteenth century is increasingly concerned with the civic and secular realm in which reformations are under way in institutional organizations, systems of knowledge, medical technologies, industrial techniques, and urbanism. Architecture attempts to organize, in some form, a clear set of directions for the construction of appropriate modern spaces while maintaining various connections with classicism and ancient symbolic realms newly theorized.[35] The increased desire of architecture to make itself clear—as a discipline and practice—increasingly enlightens the category of space itself so that, eventually, it becomes a revealed, exteriorized, orderly, and "principled"[36] space against which the by now increasingly named and categorized activity of life can take place. An architectural "interior"—not simply a literal interior that is spatially theorized but an organization of parts that has a direct effect on the exterior—is thus opened.

Georges Cuvier wrote in the late eighteenth century:

> It is a mistake to look upon [life] as a mere bond holding together the various elements of a living body, when it is actually a spring that keeps those elements in constant motion and shifts them about . . . the state or composition of the living body changes from moment to moment . . . the instant of absolute rest, which is called total death, is but the precursor of further moments of putrefaction.[37]

This "spring" keeps life going, and it also keeps the environment going or, rather, makes of an indifferent environment and a self-promoting organism a "device" of energy/order exchange—life-plus-milieu defines life itself, although the precise role of the milieu in the development of the organism remains contested, even now. Thus might the organism be said, as Schrödinger later says in *What Is Life*, to "suck its orderliness" from its surroundings, a statement that will be both tempting and tricky when we speak of architecture since, of course, architectural "surroundings" are designed by the human organism itself. A key question for Schrödinger is how living organisms avoid decay, "thermodynamic equilibrium death." His answer is that they eat and drink but also stay "alive . . . by continually drawing from [their] environment negative entropy."[38] The human being, in an architectural milieu, sucks some of its orderliness from ideas of orderliness—the inside from the outside from the inside—and this has been, in some sense, the subject of architectural history for three hundred years. But it must also absorb, as a biological being, negative entropy from the materiality of this environment. It is able to return to the material environment a "constancy" that assists in maintaining that environment. The everyday habits of maintaining a house or living space—actions that make up, in large part, a way of life, which, in turn, is inscribed in architectural typology—offer a kind of evidence for the extension of biological homeostasis into the milieu. Because architecture is a container put in place by the contained, just as the head and brain are defined and understood by the mind, none can speak to the other, by definition. There is, nevertheless, an intimate relationship and co-structuring between all parts. Schrödinger had a slightly different way of saying this: "Mind has erected the objective outside world . . . out of its own stuff. Mind could not cope with this gigantic task otherwise than by the simplifying device of excluding itself—withdrawing from its conceptual creation. Hence the [objective world] does not contain its creator."[39]

There will be much more to say about this strange absence of the live architect in the objectified architecture, which is of course part of the "asymmetrical condition" of the title of this book.

Architecture eventually gets assembled into the familiar time line by which we still navigate the past—ancient, medieval, Renaissance, baroque, Enlightenment, Industrial Revolution, modernity—and histories of architecture, henceforth, follow what is essentially a developmental model of structure. The idea of "type" which, in the analysis of living beings and matter, is abandoned in the mid-nineteenth century for statistical mechanics and the study of statistical variations in populations (evolution), persists much longer in architecture because the statistical analytic model that replaces it in the sciences initially makes no sense in architecture.

Anthony Vidler writes "The idea of type in architectural theory, with its omnibus meaning of concept, essential form, and building type, was formalized as a part of academic doctrine for the first time in the eighteenth century."[40] Further:

> Natural scientists such as Buffon and Adanson had already made [the] connection between typicality and characterization, on the one hand identifying what Adanson called "general and particular characters," the visible signs of the type and its variations. For the botanist Carolus Linnaeus, the question of character had become central to taxonomical procedure, for the purpose of identifying fixed, formal properties of the species in question that characterize its type.[41]

"The principles of observation outlined by Buffon," Vidler argues, ". . . formal discrimination, selection of types, and ordering of species—are also applied to architecture."[42] The idea of type is joined, on the one hand, to historical continuity, and, on the other, to social continuity. Each type reflects a way of life and, in turn, consolidates, partly through the operation of history, how each way of life is connected to architectural acts and vice versa. This eventually results in a sublimation of "social relations" and ideas of historical continuity into architectural typologies, which also opens the portal to theories of psychological space, the interior of the interior.

Architecture, until very recently, organized its history of the ensuing two hundred years as a progression from the primitive to the civilized, from the less perfect to the more perfect. This history, also until recently, was meant to refer to the connection of building types to both the ideals of geometry (as always) and life typologies. This is why the study of type, in spite of its multiple confusions, is so interesting. It is only, for example, in the last thirty years that ideas of primitive versus civilized have undergone a profound restructuring. The Enlightenment belief that man was at the center of the universe served regressive ideas about culture and race, including the idea that less technologically developed architectures automatically signified less developed cultures, i.e. primitive cultures. Cultures that were still using nature directly as an intellectual and material resource—such as North American Indian cultures and African cultures—were seen, until the late twentieth century, to be architecturally, politically, and socially less developed than industrialized cultures. At the same time, in ways difficult to align precisely with the history of industrial and scientific developments, architecture continued to evolve as a secular milieu, an environment that sustained, increasingly, all aspects of life and a form of production that has its own evolutionary path, apart from life.

Vidler also argues that the development of comparative analysis is linked with antiquity and the Vitruvian theorization of architectural origins: "These texts [Seneca, Lucretius, Vitruvius] were valued not so much for their narrative forms, which described the origins of building according to a formula often repeated since the Renaissance, nor simply for their content, which seemed mythical enough to a materialist *philosophe*, but for the authority with which an antique notion of commencement might invest a modern idea of improvement."[43]

The idea of "improvement" over time—progression toward some kind of betterment—so compelling to architecture in its humanist and futurist manifestations, is precisely what statistical analysis in the sciences attempted to eliminate. By doing so, science opposes what becomes a defining principle in the historical disciplines: transformist, progressivist, and value-laden ideas. Although the sciences and history, as disciplines, arise at the same moment, the newly formed humanities, including architecture (in spite of its long alliance with engineering) diverge almost immediately from science, the life sciences in particular. The architectural collectivity becomes not a population but a public with tastes and styles.

Jacob describes the transformation from type to statistics as a fundamental shift in the way we look at collections of objects—either living beings of the same species or molecules of a gas:

On the one hand, they can be considered as a group of identical bodies, all members of the group being true copies of the same pattern. In the living world, the forms are thus classified according to the structure perpetuated through successive generations, i.e. the permanence of the type. It is not the objects themselves that have to be known, but the type they represent. Only the type has any reality. Objects merely reflect the type. . . . Deviations from the type are negligible quantities or insignificant defects. On the other hand, the same collection of objects can be seen as a group of individuals which are never identical. Each member of the group is unique. There is no longer a pattern to which all individuals conform, but a composite picture, which merely summarizes the average of each individual's properties. What has to be known, then, is the population and its distribution as a whole. The average type is just an abstraction. Only individuals, with their particularities, differences and variations, have reality.[44]

"The passage from the first to the second," Jacob continues, ". . . marked the beginning of modern scientific thought."[45]

The shift from type to statistical analysis in the natural sciences was prompted by the work of Wallace, Boltzmann and Gibbs, and, later, Mendel. Darwin's theory of natural selection is based on large populations of any given species whose reproductive success—whose fecundity—allows a larger number of opportunities for mutation to arise, some of which may further benefit the species. Linnaeus' earlier division of animals into species, which was a way of typing animal groups according to shared attributes, does not disappear in statistical analysis. Speciation becomes a general form of organization inside of which populations undergo continual change across a spectrum of possibilities, some of which may be across species barriers.

Contemporary biology is gradually altering the categorical idea of species in favor of more fluid definitions of animal differences according to genetic makeup, rather than attributes and characteristics. Statistics also eliminated the Lamarckian belief that variation had to represent an improvement in advance. The idea that an organism was whatever it should be at any given time—the "fit" discussed in an earlier section that also fuelled transformationist ideas about progress and human development with respect to animals—was replaced by the view, as Jacob further writes in the same section of *The Logic of Life*, that "nature favors what already exists. . . . Production comes before any value judgment on what has been produced . . . there is no Manichaeism in the way nature produces novelties, nothing of progress and regression, of good and evil, of better and worse. Variation occurs at random . . . without any relation between cause and result. Only after a new being has emerged is it confronted by the conditions of existence."

"The equilibrium of the living world," after the middle of the nineteenth century, again according to Jacob, "was established through a kind of dialectic of permanence and variation, of identity and difference." "What is called 'progress' or 'adaptation' is only the necessary result of the inevitable interplay between the system and its surroundings." Reproduction was the "meeting point of determinism, responsible for the formation of the like forms, and contingency, responsible for the appearance of new forms." Reproduction is the way in which what is "selected" can shape both identical and different forms. As Jacob says:

> Its regularity moulds a child in the image of his parents. Its fluctuations create novelties. Living beings are born. . . . Then they are judged by the country they live in and the organisms around them; by those they hunt and those that hunt them. . . . The verdict is final and without appeal; it is measured by the number of descendents.[46]

In a section of his book that refers to the relation of architectural history to the comparative models of the natural sciences more specifically, Vidler discusses Defoe's *Robinson Crusoe*, the myth of the civilized man in nature. The "discovery of genuine savagery" in America, and Joseph-François Lafitau's astute, but also picturesque, observations and interpretations of North American Indian tribes (early ethnological documents) were an example of a comparative analysis of cultures in which architecture featured prominently.[47] Lafitau's comparison of contemporary dwellings in "savage" populations to historical and biblical structures of ancient nomadic tribes established the architectural time line and a sense of progression and continuity from antiquity to the present referred to earlier. The interest in primitive cultures in the eighteenth century was simultaneously exploratory and colonialist. It was an attempt to marry the modern work ethic, the "economic man," to different myths, some ancient, of the "natural man." Robinson Crusoe's dwelling, which Vidler says is built according to Henry Wotton's recommendations for the healthful and proper positioning of buildings on a site, demonstrates the "principled behavior of man in a wild state" and models the utopian myth of development of humans from a wild to a civilized state.[48] The treatment of a building site as a coordinated set of events that included the quality of water, air, waste systems, storage—all of which eventually coalesce into a healthful composite site—is fundamentally an understanding of the site as a life-support system for the occupant. Life, in this case, means evolved life, life that has reached a level where it can exercise technical support on its own behalf and prolongation. This is, quintessentially, understood to be human life.

"No sociability is yet evident" in Crusoe's story. Sociability, the origin of culture, according to Rousseau, would have transformed Crusoe's defensive castle into domestic and public space.[49] So Crusoe's dwelling—built to support a "principled" human existence in the wild on a healthful and appropriate site—is still built against an animal enemy within and without,[50] against the regressive, unprincipled animal in the wild, and against the regressive, unprincipled animal in culture, the "savage."

Darwin's "tree of life," the tree that Robinson Crusoe would find in the wilderness were he building in the century following his own, points directly toward a common heritage for human and animal. Each species get its own branch, which continues to diverge from the other branches. Darwin, as a traveller, studied networks of interactions between living beings in geographically distinct places.[51] On the Galapagos Islands, diverse species of finches serve as evidence for a community of descent: "All the species of this family are thus linked together," writes Darwin, by "indirect lines of affinity of various lengths going back into the past through a large number of predecessors." As François Jacob remarks:

> Birds seem to be profoundly separated from other vertebrates, because a large number of forms connecting their ancestors to those of other forms have vanished. . . .
>
> [Darwin claimed that] "All true classification is genealogical, that community of descent is the hidden bond which naturalists have been unconsciously seeking, and not some unknown plan of creation, or the enunciation of general propositions, and the mere putting together and separating objects more or less alike. . . . Each island has its own birds, . . . [b]ut all these birds have a family likeness with each other. . . . It is as if the differences stood out on a background of resemblances, as if these various species of birds were all derived from a common ancestor, and their individual characteristics were only the result of their isolation in their geographical territories."[52]

The distinctness of species is due not to multiple origins for living beings but to the tree of divergences whereby a small number of ancestors eventually branch into a large number of adaptive offspring. Difference is a matter of degree in the sense that clear-cut distinctions "are due to the extinction of intermediate forms."[53] Within this sense of continuum, there is also, however, "contingency." No overarching plan governs the picture: According to Darwin, "There is no sudden appearance of new organs which seem to have been specially created for some purpose. The emergence of organisms represents the consequence of a long struggle between opposing actions, the result of contending forces, the outcome of a conflict between the organism and its environment."[54]

This linking of all animate life with other animate life competing for survival in diverse environments was the pretext for the significant attacks on Darwinism, in the nineteenth century and after, by those in whose advantage it was to keep the origins of life—and of the earth in general—shrouded in a quasi-theological haze. These advocates of the false theories of the Great Chain of Being, and various kinds of theism, which even Darwin partially believed in, keep humans connected to the biological stream but place them at the head of the pack. Even the Museum of Paleontology in the Jardin des Plantes, which houses Cuvier's amazing collection of bones, has, at the head of a literal herd of fossils, a human skeleton that has been fleshed out, given facial and bodily expression that no other animal seems to get. Darwin's birds, and other birds, will return shortly.

# 6: WAYS OF LIFE



> Unaccommodated man
> is but a poor, forked animal.
> —William Shakespeare, *King Lear*

*King Lear* will come up more than once.[1] Perhaps at this moment we can suspend Lear's literary status and use his life as an example of a life that is without a "way." The problem for Lear, living in a prehistorical world where humans identify themselves, in effect, as divine creations that maintain a bare life existence, is that once he leaves the unintelligible interior of his kingdom, he is exposed, literally, to storms of space—a madness and landscapes that have no limits. Lear goes into an open that is neither enlightened (human) nor illuminated (divine), but is, instead, the monstrous and paradoxical space of limitless being. "Limitless being" has no definable character, no value, no power of relation, and no place to stand, and is therefore at the mercy of the multiple forces around it—other animals, weather, fools. Nothing about the (medieval) castle enclosure that Lear leaves—indeed, we barely know its outlines—or what seem to be infinitely flexible formulations of his own or others' lives institutes a way of life that extends beyond the castle's primal protection. And, once left, it is impossible to get back; there is no path of return. This idea of space is, in effect, also a theory of motion. Lear moves chaotically through space. The "humanness" of his motion descends, gradually, into a blind and jerky prehistoric occupation of wild space. He has lost his way and lost his motivation. Lear's life might oppose itself to that of Robinson Crusoe, for whom a way of life—"civilized," "English," "human"—is the resourceful ground upon which his primitive hut is built. As important as Crusoe's literal building in the wilderness is, it has more meaning as the establishment of a way of life, which, in turn, implies a path, a way of going out and returning that connects the inside and outside of his enclave in a modern way.

Yet "way of life" still seems too general a term. Going from Lear's castle to Crusoe's dwelling certainly describes a certain fantastical passage from darkness to light, from placelessness to place, waywardness to path, that describes, in some received sense, architectural history from the Middle Ages to the eighteenth century. Lear's world is without a program. The modern architectural program, which documents ways of being and moving in space—repetitive movements that emanate from both internal and external sources—and also, implicitly, values and ideologies associated with specific kinds of organization and modes of being, is a consolidation of ideas about life that include, necessarily, a "way." Way of life is an architectural idea here but it depends on the motion and privilege implicit in the idea of life itself, life as a body and mind. Cuvier's "modes" and "flows" name life as "turbulence."[2] When Claude Bernard discovers *homeostasis*—the constancy of the internal environment of the organism that is self-regulated by various internal mechanisms—he names the organic internal counterpart to what a way of life suggests in an external environment.[3] Comte's "consensus of functions"—organization—draws the internal and external milieux into closer proximity. Cities are formed and organized in some kind of imitation of this internal consensus of biological functions, although most attempts at organic/functionalist theories of urbanism have failed to maintain the tension between the internal and external milieux. To have a way of life, as human or animal, unites, for a period of time (a "life"), the constancy of the internal environment of the body with the variability of the external milieu. It extends biological constancy into environmental variability, habits and routines of everyday biological life into an indifferent milieu. The architectural program codifies modes of life, taking consensus for granted, and it attempts to erase the question of value from architectural space.

In that still most amazing of essays *The Mathematics of the Ideal Villa* Colin Rowe links Palladio's remarks on the site of the Villa Capra-Rotonda and Le Corbusier's remarks on the Villa Savoye:

> [Palladio] The site is as pleasant and delightful as can be found, because it is on a small hill of very easy access, and is watered on one side by the Bacchiglione, a navigable river; and on the other it is encompassed about with most pleasant risings which look like a very great theater and are all cultivated about with most excellent fruits and most exquisite vines; and therefore as it enjoys from every part most beautiful views, some of which are limited, some more extended, and others which terminate with the horizon, there are loggias made in all four fronts.

> [Le Corbusier] *Le site: une vaste pelouse bombée en dôme aplati. . . . La maison est une boîte en l'air . . . au milieu des prairies dominant le verger. . . . Le plan est pur. . . . Il a sa juste place dans l'agreste paysage de Poissy. . . . Les habitants, venus ici parce que cette campagne agrest était belle avec sa vie de campagne, ils la contempleront, maintenue intacte, du haut de leur jardin suspendu ou des quatre faces de leurs fenêtres en longueur. Leur vie domestique sera inserée dans un rêve virgilien.*[4]

Both architects join accounts of the ideal life of the villa with accounts of the site and aspects of the building's design. Rowe writes that the "Virgilian dream" named specifically here by Le Corbusier, but also pertinent to the recovery of "Roman virtue" in the Renaissance, places the villa's owner "within a fragment of created order" from which he can:

> watch the maturing of his possessions and savor the piquancy of contrast between his fields and his gardens . . . reflecting on mutability, he will contemplate throughout the years the antique virtues of a simpler race, and the harmonious ordering of his life and his estate will be an analogy of paradise.

Both Palladio and Le Corbuiser, according to Rowe, understand the "poignancy of contrast" between the disengaged cube and its setting in *l'agrest paysage* (geometrical volume and appearance of unimpaired nature). "If architecture at the Rotonda forms the setting for the good life," Rowe comments, "at Poissy it is certainly the background for the lyrically efficient one;"[5] each architect claiming for architecture a style of virtuous life appropriate to his time.

The owner, from the architect's view, looks from inside the building to the outside; from inside their fragment of order out to a scene of nature that reaches into the distance. The owner's view, again from the architect's point of view, also includes the view from the outside in, seeing the whole building, in plan, elevation and from three hundred and sixty degrees around it—the "loggias made in all four fronts," the "quatre faces de leurs fenêtres." The architect's view thus forms in advance, for the occupant, a way of coming and going, entering and exiting, standing and moving, owning and operating, seeing and being seen, framing and being framed. This opportunity for the passage of biological life in a particular place is what an owner acquires, and adapts to, when the house itself is acquired. It does not matter who the owner is precisely, although a sociopolitical identity will be fundamental to what kind of life is established. Like all environments, artificial or natural, architecture places constraints on the life that first inhabits it and establishes, for that life, modes of living and modes of organization. For ways of life to become the modern architectural program, human beings needed to emerge as a distinct species. Palladio's villa occupant has cultivated a sharp sense of the nature that surrounds the building, but has only a vague sense of where he or she might be biologically, and existentially, located. In effect, Palladio's inhabitant, in the passage cited by Rowe, is not even on the ground but is looking down from the sky like a bird, just barely a bird with a bird's-eye view. None of this existential discomfort can be read in the buildings themselves because part of what modernity accomplished was an erasure of the idea of life per se. Architecture is understood, in the ideal terms of modernity, as both destined for occupation and removed from the sphere of occupation. Science, and the neo-scientific view that modernism eventually adopts, "denies values life imputes to different objects" and attempts, instead, to evaluate the relations between objects.[6] When we look back to Palladio from the era of Le Corbusier, it is through the neo-scientific, although not value-free, eyes of Le Corbusier that we look.

"In the life sciences," Canguilhem remarks, "what we hope to discover is the obsessive presence of certain unscientific values at the very inception of scientific inquiry." He continues:

> Even if objective knowledge, being a human enterprise, is in the end the work of living human beings, the postulate that such knowledge exists—which is the first condition of its possibility—lies in the systematic negation, in any object to which it may be applied, of the reality of the qualities which humans, knowing what living means to them, identify with life. To live is to attach value to life's purposes and experiences; it is to prefer certain methods, circumstances and directions to others. Life is the opposite of indifference to one's surroundings.[7]

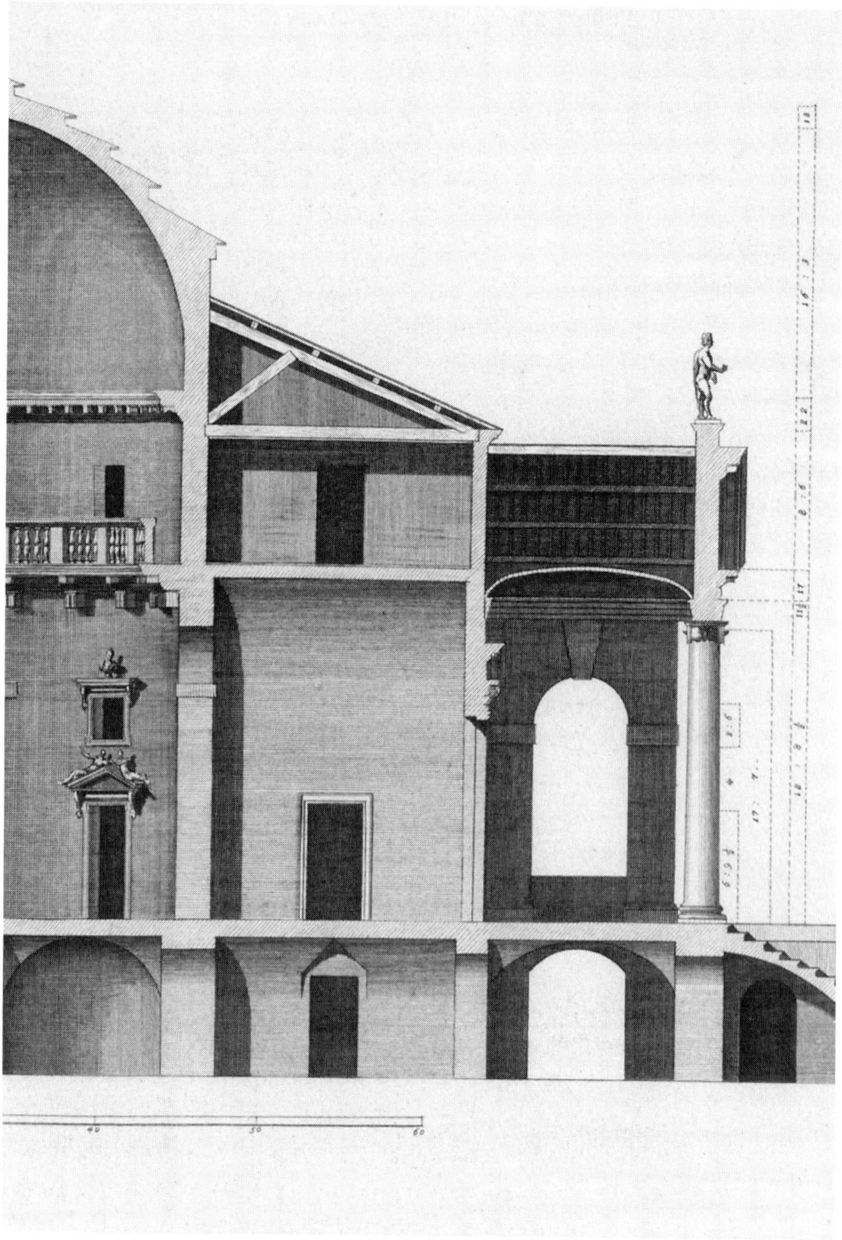



**Figure 6.1:** Andrea Palladio, *Villa Capra-Rotonda*, Vicenza, 1556, section. Courtesy of the Centro Internazionale di Studi di Architettura Andrea Palladio, Vicenza.

**Figure 6.2:** Le Corbusier, *Villa Savoye*, Poissy, 1929-31, interior. Photograph by Jeffery Howe, 1996.

The knowledge of the Renaissance architect, which treated architecture as a quasi-mathematical science, according to Wittkower, also lies in this negation, in the object to which it is applied, of the "reality of the qualities" that humans identity with life. Unlike other forms of human scientific knowledge, however, architecture is continually challenged to respond to life at the level of its "way"—its programmatic enactment in space, its needs, its pressures.

The "Virgilian dream," as Rowe ingeniously applies it, is of a cube in a pastoral landscape that attempts to bridge the terrible distance between human and non-human, geometry and variability. Rowe's paragraphs on this subject, intricate and virtuoso, articulate how both Palladio and Le Corbusier realize the "Platonic archetype of the ideal villa to which the fantasy of the Virgilian dream might be supposed to relate." He continues:

> The realization of an idea, which is represented by the house as a cube, could also be presumed to lend itself very readily to the purposes of Virgilian dreaming. For here is set up the conflict between the absolute and the contingent, the abstract and the natural; and the gap between the ideal world and the too human exigencies of realization here receives its most pathetic presentation.[8]

My point in turning to Rowe has been to suggest that human life, as a way of life, begins in the Renaissance with the invention of two versions of, essentially, the same thing—perspectival representation, which allows for the privileging of the architectural/artistic eye, and Renaissance humanism, which allows for human life, still biologically poorly understood, to achieve enough congruency with the mathematical cube of the villa to "house" and ground it—literally, to bring it down to a secular plane of existence. Secularity is a means of grounding the body and bringing its "irreducible polymorphousness" and "condition of carnality" under more local control.[9] The owner's lived life thus acquires both a formal position and plural ways of being from architecture. Both perspective and humanism favor the mathematical and artistic, which emanate from the reassuring context of a recovered classicism. The same combination of elements—mathematics, artistry, classicism, humanism—make for the hybridized new culture of pagan temple fronts attached to domestic structures that are radically unlike the classical structures from which they are drawn.[10] The architectural organization of life at this point organizes, for the inhabitant, many of the almost tragic, as Rowe intimates, and confused polarities of nature and culture, polarities that still exist, in a different way, when Le Corbusier eulogizes Poissy. In doing this, architecture brings its quite specific material and intellectual powers to bear, in a thousand ways, on the value of human life—which is still an idealized life, to be sure, but also a life whose biological self-privilege begins to spread through the world and gain value by means, literally, of its own eyes. One milieu of this eye, architecture, is sympathetic to this development and, in a sense, patiently awaits its moment.

Agamben locates the opposition of "simple natural life" (*zoē*) to "qualified life, a particular way of life" (*bios*) in the early Greeks. *Bios* includes political life, which is life that has acquired specific values. Simple life—bare life—is reproductive life (subject to Jacob's "logic of life") and remains, for the most part, within the domesticity of the home. We are familiar with these distinctions and, in some sense, still sustain them in our ideas about our own animal and cultural life. Agamben is interested, as was Foucault, in marking a difference between Aristotle's understanding of man as a "living animal with the additional capacity for political existence" and "modern man [who] is an animal whose politics calls his existence as a living being into question."[11] "Biological modernity," Agamben writes in the same section (referring to Foucault) is "situated at the point at which the species and the individual as a simple living body become what is at stake in a society's political strategies." According to Foucault, man is "bestialized" through sophisticated bio-political techniques that both protect biological life and "authorize a holocaust." Agamben points to Hannah Arendt's work—which Foucault does not refer to in his *History of Sexuality*—on *homo laborans* (laboring life) and *homo faber* (conditional life), a composite biological being that is at the "very center of the political scene of modernity." For Agamben, "the entry of *zoē* into the sphere of the *polis*—the politicization of bare life—constitutes the decisive event of modernity and signals a radical transformation of the political-philosophical categories of classical thought."[12] The place of architecture in these analyzes seems at best complicitous and at worst trivial with respect to the larger political and cultural forces at work. Still, I do not believe that biological modernity begins specifically as an abstract confrontation between the biological and the political. I think it begins in the place that is rendered as backdrop, rather than player, i.e. in the house. And this happens most definitively in the first claims that biological life makes over space in the eighteenth century. Modern space thus is in place in advance of biological self-definition. It was Foucault who insisted that modernity be connected with problems of space, and the distribution of sovereign power through space, in order to capture the body in a particular, disciplinary, way. Aristotle makes this connection as well:

> Among living things, only man has language. . . . Language is for manifesting the fitting and the unfitting and the just and the unjust . . . [which is] proper to man as opposed to other living beings, and the community of these things makes dwelling and the city.[13]

For Agamben, and for us, it has been the city as *polis*, as the political qualification of bare life, that is interesting. Bare life in Agamben's account is sacred man, *Homo sacer*, again, the being that "can be killed and yet not sacrificed."[14] This being is the "key," according to Agamben, by which sovereignty and political power "will unveil their mysteries." What I want to pick up from Aristotle's statement is the dwelling and the city as *polis*, of course, but also as material installations of spatial theories that play specific roles in the drama of biological and political modernity. On the cover of Agamben's book, *Homo Sacer*, is an image of Auschwitz—the "dwelling and the city" in which biological and political modernity found their most sinister manifestation. Auschwitz was a prison camp and yet the plan, if we did not know what it was, could be mistaken for almost any early twentieth century housing settlement. Nothing of the life that was held and taken in that place has been entered into the plan. The plan, per se, does not care about the precise individual life with a precise political identification. In this indifference, it acts typologically (a concentration camp *is* a housing settlement) and, in some peculiar way, statistically; it is based on a large sampling of human life conditions in which extreme aberrant life conditions, such as incarceration, have almost no meaning. The plan's banality, in the face of the horror associated with both the name and fact of Auschwitz, seems to argue, also, for a chilling neutrality. In fact, it is not neutral in all respects. The modernist plan includes, in a way that pre-Renaissance plans do not, the assumption that the very site and possibility of its generation is evidence of a self-conscious humanity that uses the plan in order to describe a particular way of life. From a political standpoint this is radically inadequate because this knowledge, which is architectural knowledge that has been embedded in the knowledge of humanness, does not differentiate the political options so apparently available to it. Were it to do so, how could such a plan be drawn in the face of the way of life it portends?

The effects of sovereign power, in and around architecture, have been studied in different ways by a number of scholars: Tafuri, certainly, and, in different ways, Bataille. In very precise ways, architecture adds value to whatever life scene it houses, even in cases where the architecture is punitive and the property relations corrupt. Punitive and corrupt structures themselves result from investments of life in structure. "Value" means the existence of opposing relations. To attribute value to life calls for a structure within which values oppose each other to form economies.[15] Once value is concentrated in human life, in particular—making a "way" that opposes other "ways"—architecture accommodates life in a different way. The poetics of a way of life of an inhabitant living inside architectural space—space that must contend with its own excess over building—has often, particularly in phenomenology, been summarized under the category of experience. The sophisticated philosophical and material management of light, space, and surface in high modernist buildings, for example, has been often ridiculed as cold or bare based on an analysis of life value, and the collapse of the intellectual work of architecture, into the terms spelled out by a sociology of experience. Some might say this collapse is portended by the architecture itself—its proclivity for reduction. One of the abiding mantras of socio-empirical work in the twentieth century has been the separation of life and life experience from space, such that a cause–effect structure can be erected between life and space; in a sense, space is not allowed to "tempt" us into its geometries and voids.[16] Bachelard's poetics of perception, by which objects in the world are rendered complex by human psychological complexity (simple objects, complex subjects), made this idea of experience almost palpable to architecture.

I think also, in the Renaissance, that architecture becomes fundamental to the establishment of ways of life for human beings not merely because people live inside buildings, which they had been doing for centuries, but also because instruments of architectural design and construction, in and after the Renaissance, simultaneously are understood to be instruments of location and identity. Architectural accounts of the design and construction of buildings henceforth attempt to resolve the ensuing asymmetry between inanimate objects, buildings and landscapes, and animate objects, life and life forces. The oppositional relation of animate to inanimate produces the value of each inside the architectural structure. Thus, Palladio as well as Le Corbusier equally attempt to chain "together a potentially endless lattice each unit of which . . . would imply the infinity of the extension . . . the microcosm in which 'everything' in the whole would be expressed."[17] "Life" in architecture therefore is gradually made a "way of life," and architects express this in the technological and descriptive accounts of their work. Ways of life for human beings are at least partially, in almost every case since the Renaissance, architectural and urbanist accounts. Most would say, for example, if asked how they lived, something like the following: "I live in *x* city, in such and such a neighborhood, in *y* house built during *x* historical period;" or, simply, "we have a house or apartment in *x* or *y* place." Architecture, in spite of its historical allegiance to divine forces, can be seen as an early agent of secularity for human biological life. A way of life does not imply a good, or bad, way of life; the question of value is not about some absolute value that architecture brings to life, or vice versa. We draw order or disorder from the milieu and extend, to the milieu, a biological variability and constancy, but whether we thrive in this situation—or whether architecture thrives in this situation—is totally fortuitous, although not fortuitous in exactly the same way as an organism in a biological milieu. As the Frankfurt School's critique of the dialectic of enlightenment argued, an architectural dedication to betterment and knowledge—the modern project in most respects—does not necessarily lead to a benevolent life; often, in fact, the reverse is true.[18]

With the Renaissance, then, ideas about ways of life specific to human beings begin to be opened, and held open, in architecture (as discussed in the earlier chapter "Life (before)") although the human as a biological being is not fully defined as distinct from other kinds of biological beings until the nineteenth century. This does not mean that everything and everyone is henceforth free from the dangers of "unaccommodated man" and limitless space/being; there is no final transcendence of any aspect of human history, natural or otherwise. The continued existence of war, bio-politics, prisons, migrancy, oppression, and totalitarianism remind us continuously of how ways of life are as radically provisional as life itself was before we lived as fully in the property of the house as we do now. We are also reminded, by the same drastic examples, of how relentlessly human life, as a species, has maintained itself—certainly by means of both its biological constancy and its ability to adapt—in the face of its tendency toward socio-political extremism. A way of life is, of course, an illusion of security and constancy in variability. But it is a very powerful illusion that frequently works on behalf of episodic social and political stability. Architecture adopts, initially, nothing more or less than what other Renaissance practices adopt—a generalized humanism, attempts to bring parts of the cosmological puzzle together into unified ideas, idealized references to the human body, a belief in certain values from antiquity, and a studied carelessness with respect to knowledge. Architecture's own evolution as a milieu, though, which predates the understanding of evolution in terms of the life that it inhabits, begins in the Renaissance. The villa is a domestic structure with institutional intentions, in its adoption of the grand façades of antiquity. Institutional life—which is not fully formulated until the nineteenth century and which, more intensively, arises from the birth of architectural typologies of the eighteenth century—is a Darwinian extension of some kind of individual life into the life of populations, the private into the public.

In some sense, architecture invents human life—as the owner of the villa is invented in Palladio's description—as the omnipotent master of all light and space, in order to offset the various forms of darkness lingering from the past, varieties of darkness that are symbolized by animals and demons and later take the variety of names of the psychological. Even when definitions of life come to include, in architecture and medicine, ideas of health and normativeness in the eighteenth century,[19] human beings, in their everyday lives, continue to be driven by forces of the pre-conscious and the unconscious. The notorious houses of the mad and nineteenth century sanatoriums testified to this. Thoughout these periods, these darker forces are named "animal forces;" there is a tacit recognition that the human, although always held in a more elevated position, is still part of a larger amorphous world that includes animals. Of course, the relation of darkness to enlightenment is related to the whole human history of the metaphor of "light"[20]—from its divine to secular meanings. We drag all the humanness there is with us as we enter the so-called animal part of humanness. No comparable move exists with respect to animals; it makes no sense to speak of enlightenment and darkness in animals. Animals just "are," or, as is more often the case, "are not." To enter the animal part of humanness is, then, as we know, an existential journey as well as a metaphoric journey. We go from light to dark by passing from one kind of knowledge (enlightened) to another kind, instinct (unenlightened). The terms of the enlightenment are, by definition, beyond the reach of the animal, and after this period it is increasingly difficult to "get back" to the animal. As we know from Freud, this darkness of the unconscious human mind belongs not to an exteriorized historical set of events—although the formation of history in light of this darkness is exceptionally interesting—but to the structure and function of the mind itself.

So how have ideas, however specious, of humanity's progressiveness been carried forward? Classical idealisms—including the illusion of constancy and habit that allows us to appear to exercise our knowledge on our own behalf—often enable historical movements by transcending the disruptive exigencies of being human, whatever they might be. We know that these ideas of progress existed and worked in some sense, because of their effects: the literal surgical cuts through cities that reduced their congestion, the curing of diseases, the construction of scientific knowledge and related technologies, and so forth. The effects of these movements on architecture were profound: architecture becomes a formal and autonomous discipline, it drafts a history, a theory of origins, it shapes itself as a practice that is publicly accountable, it relinquishes most of its mystical and theological connections. History happens. But these effects are measured, traditionally, from the same vantage point as the idealism that was their goad. Humanism is measured by the instruments of measure put in place by humanism, rationalism by rationalism. I want to step outside that tautology for a moment in order to consider the following proposal.

In architecture, I am arguing, these ideas of progress were carried forward, as already discussed in another context, by carefully partitioning the human away from its animal parts. This is a tricky business because, on the one hand, until humans are definitely separated from animals taxonomically, animals still have tremendous power over humans. A "way of life" is one way of bringing this position about. The human way of life that begins to emerge in the Renaissance—with its various connections to architecture and civic life—begins to produce a human with less and less animal in it. In the Enlightenment, when animals have lost most of their power—caged by both spatial constructs and taxonomies—this partitioned human being grows even more insistent in its humanness. Yet the very fact of partitioning makes of this human an animal. Again, from Freud, to partition human life to make human life fully enlightened, as both Palladio and Le Cobusier want to make it by removing the blindness of the human eye (which cannot see everything at once and which is a metaphor for the refusal of the inner darkness we routinely name as animal)—is a kind of sacrifice of human life. It is ethically wrong in modern life, as Agamben synthesizes, to sacrifice human life the way we sacrifice animal life, to ritualize the killing and partitioning of it. Architecture and urban discourse (the civic discourse that arises in the Renaissance with secularism and the city-state) inadvertently produce, at the moment they produce humanness by organizing a way of life for the "owner," a humanized animal. So the animal slips back into the human and is sustained not in its own form but in human form, by means of architecture. The humanized animal—a human that can now be partitioned (and possibly sacrificed)—who lacks the interior depth of the unconscious, which is the defining aspect of human life, but possesses both form and mobility, is a being peculiarly amenable to enclosure.

Architectural humanism, about which so much has been written and whose aura we are still embedded within, was also the dawning of ideas, in architecture, about what it meant, in a preliminary way, for humans to live in architectural space (i.e. symbolic space), although I want to avoid Geoffrey's Scott valorization of this idea as a unique form of architectural appreciation. It is not accidental that Renaissance humanism expended much of its time on the problem of adjudicating the scale of buildings to the idealized body of its putative occupant. The movement of this occupant—still, so to speak, in its earliest stages—is what the inauguration of ways of life portends, which is why, ultimately, the largely static, elaborate, and misguided proportional calculations of the Renaissance humanist architects—of whom Palladio is the outstanding example—fall by the wayside. Palladian architecture, however, does not. It remains occupied and comes to stand, in some sense, for the first site of a moving consciousness: humans gradually becoming aware of occupying space as humans, secular beings, an evolution organized for them, in advance, by architecture. Humans will benefit massively from these Renaissance inventions; animals will not.

# 7: HYENA:
## TOTEM ANIMAL OF THE LATE TWENTIETH CENTURY

> The jaguar's vision, unlike the panther's, is not blunted. On the contrary his eyes drill through the darkness of space. The cage has no reality to him, he is elsewhere. He is elsewhere because his consciousness is kinetic rather than abstract: the thrust of his muscles moves him through a space quite different in nature from the three-dimensional box of Newton—a circular space that returns upon itself. . . . So—leaving behind the ethics of caging large animals—[Ted] Hughes is feeling his way toward a different kind of being-in-the-world . . . [t]he body is as the body moves . . . [this is] poetry that is not about the animal, but is instead the record of an engagement with him.
>
> —J.M. Coetzee, *The Lives of Animals*



Joanna Greenfield, now a wildlife management scientist, published an article in 1996 about being severely bitten by a hyena.[1] The hyena was in a cage and she was putting water into the cage when the hyena bit her arm, dragging her into the cage. After that it attacked her leg, taking out the calf in three bites. Greenfield, by her own account, had crossed the line—so infrequently crossed by human beings in the modern world—into the domain of predator and prey. Her experience, like many accounts of being attacked by wild animals, had to do not so much with the pain—which the body is initially insulated against through the mechanism of shock—as with the atavistic horror of being attacked by a live being with whom there is not only no hope of reasoning, but also no grounds for reasoning, missing radically what Jacques Derrida calls the "principle of calculability."[2]

The hyena has been the darling of many philosophers of calculation, Georges Bataille among them, and Gilles Deleuze, who desired of the hyena that it show us the meaning of deterritorialization and pack organization in our flight from the Oedipal. The animal, as mentioned earlier, has been regarded by twentieth century philosophers primarily as presenting an ethical challenge to humans, less frequently as aesthetic object, evidence of life's excess and demonstration of possible meanings of the always too-naturalistic term "wildness."

It is the ethical dimension of this story that is most chilling—because it cuts off the possibility of any philosophical discussion. It occurs at the moment when Greenfield describes the look in the hyena's eyes as it ate away at her arm: ". . . all the time those black, blank eyes evaluated me . . . calm, and almost friendly."[3] There was nothing malicious in the eyes, she recalls. They were just eyes looking into the middle distance while eating; a calm, speculative looking. The eyes of the hyena were of particular interest to Greenfield because she herself had been born without the neuro-optical ability to construct depth perception. "My eyes," she writes, "do not work like two halves of a whole, and I have no perception of depth, so human faces blend into their background and are unreadable. . . . I had to learn about emotions, which are subtle and often masked, from animals, who signal theirs so much more clearly, with mane and tail and the position of the body."[4]

Animals were also easier, apparently less complicated, for Greenfield to read because their identities—from the moment we began to pose questions about modern human and animal identity in the eighteenth century—came to rest more in their form than in their faces.[5] The post-animal animal is allowed less range of motion, less territory/range in the world, than the post-animal human. Formal identification of the animal, according to various identification techniques, renders even the living animal's existence almost equivalent to that of a taxidermic specimen. The post-animal animal is always in the process of arriving at, if it has not already arrived at, an arrested state. It is important, in other words, that the hyena in the story is caged. It is no longer able to lay down its scent on the plains, the means by which its difference from the place fixed lion and the Oedipal human is announced.

The article also states, incidentally but interestingly, that after the wounds were finally healed (infection from hyena wounds is especially profound because hyenas are scavengers and eat rotten meat, so healing takes a long time and the wound should not be closed initially) an animal trainer told Greenfield that even the slightest limp in a human who has been bitten by animals is easily detected by other animals and that that human henceforth belongs to the world of prey. It was not clear whether this trainer meant that animals could differentiate a limp resulting from an animal attack from some other kind of wound, but the import of the remark is that humans routinely assume themselves to be masters of the animal world; to be disabused of that assumption because of a limp would come as a cosmic surprise. The scale and improbability of such a surprise is an indication of the depth of isomorphism and existential comfort with which humans move in the post-animal world.[6]

The hyena, in this amazing story, is also radically non-inscribed in the ethical universe of human consciousness, at least as we have practiced that consciousness since the seventeenth century.[7] It cannot be part of what Kant called the "insurmountable wickedness" of humans because of this radical non-inscription;[8] it cannot even be called "bad." It is, in fact, almost (but not quite) neutral in this most primal of acts, eating. And it is precisely the almost-neutral, non-inscribed, aspect of the hyena—the example also, gratuitously, includes a cage and problems of "seeing"—that aligns it with the neutrality and neo-scientific attitude that architecture began to desire for its occupant in the Renaissance. The architectural forms this Renaissance desire takes predate, by several hundred years, the appearance of a human form that is amenable to this kind of capture. As I remark earlier, the Renaissance begins architectural modernity, but it is not until the eighteenth century that human and animal life becomes "modern." The modern dining room, as we have programmed it routinely—once human, animal, and architectural modernity coincide—imagines just such a "diner:" a generalized being, ethically and politically barely inscribed, possessing a naïve psychological profile, breakable into functionalist parts, formally located but with no proper name, almost friendly, with eyes toward the middle distance, eating with a powerful jaw in a room that accommodates that function or behavior. The absence of fundamental human attributes, such as self-consciousness or explicit biological being (the "wild")—two attributes often thought to be the same—in architecture is also why, ultimately, theories such as Geoffrey Scott's about the formation of architecture in the image of the human (a human "aesthetic" based on emotional life) or, in a different vein, theorizations of the gendered body of the 1970s and 1980s have, to our constant intellectual chagrin, little traction or durability in architecture. We have been looking in all the wrong places.

The comparison between hyena and human in the architecture of the dining room is, of course, hyperbolic and paints a ridiculous scene. In some respects, the hyena eating and the human dining, both inside cages of a sort yet to be determined, are almost exact reversals of each other. The animal *might* eat the human in one, the human *might* eat the animal in the other.[9] In other ways, of course, these two beings, and the architectures that support and surround them, do not even inhabit the same cultural or mental universe. The hyena, in Greenfield's account, eats in a cage designed by human beings and is locked in, which may account, in part, for its unpredictable attack on Greenfield, i.e. it is a wild animal for whom a cage is, literally, the loss of the space; an induction into a pathological aphasia. The human eats inside a "cage," where the quotation marks are crucial indicators of its difference from the hyena cage;[10] that is, it is designed by human beings, which means that, provided the typology of the cage is not a prison, its occupant can walk out at will. The architectural cage, for humans, is a gain in the meaning and reality of space.

At yet another level, from an architectural position still deeply informed by Renaissance techniques of representation (the possibility of architecture *as* a cage or box, the space-box of perspectival representation) in which the animal, as well as the human, can be contained, the geometric and spatial laws of Descartes and Newton, late eighteenth century taxonomies and the invention of history, the caged hyena and the "architectural human" are intimately related. They are both inside space-boxes, the focus of their eyes is calm, untheorized and unfathomable—detached from questions of ethical calculability associated with theories of seeing, being, and occupying space. They are positioned and coordinated (Descartes); they are engaged in a "function" (eating); they are subject to accurate representation (Brunelleschi), scientific classification (Linnaeus, Cuvier), and species differentiation (Darwin). They are also subject to gravity (Newton) and they are understood, as living beings, to exist in a clear, homogeneous spatial continuum of similarity and difference (Panofsky, Darwin) that has begun to include everything within reach, animate or inanimate, alive or dead. And, finally, both hyena and human are partially set in motion, animated, sustained, or inhibited by the space that surrounds them—their way of life and morphology is enhanced or inhibited by enclosure. Living beings that can be formally inscribed and identified in enclosed space, that can be more or less contained in an interior, and that can maintain a way of life inside that container make up one of the necessary but not sufficient conditions for a post-animal architecture.

To import the question of the animal, in both its scientific and mythical mode, into a discussion of architecture and the architectural subject, whether in the dining room or elsewhere, might seem at first to be a way of freighting our contemporary view of architecture with questions that might lead us into the philosophers' realm of ethical dilemmas, as well as the realm of sentiment, inner life, and the relation of these things to the construction of form that we know architecture to be simultaneously about and not about. This line of inquiry, the "sentimental" in particular, leads us into a cul-de-sac. The animal, in different ways at different moments of its history, is a sentimental object. At the same time, we can find little ground for thinking the animal inside histories or theories of sentiment and affect, since any idea of a psychological or sentient animal necessarily impinges on crucial modern distinctions between animal and human.[11] "Sentiment," when it comes up in the modern history of the animal, is almost always intimately tied to different theories of functionalism.[12] The paintings of animals on the cave walls of Lascaux are, disputably, art and/or documentary evidence of some kind, but the animals in these paintings are also, indisputably, prey. This combination of affect and function is part of what makes the animal attractive as artistic object, sign of nature and secular or sacred ornament. Architecture, in particular, finds this combination of affect and function compelling. Like the animals in Greenfield's account, who display their instinctual life through readily discernible formal gestures, the existential position of the post-animal animal possesses enough of an interior to satisfy the need for aliveness that architecture habitually attributes to its subject (not, for the moment, including the interesting exception of the tomb and mausoleum), but not enough of an interior to shift the weight of architecture away from its primary technical activity into that aliveness. The animal is also an extremely formal form of life compared to human life. It lives inside its form in a way that humans do not see themselves as living. It is uniquely available, from a human standpoint, as both object and subject, and from an architectural standpoint, as both alive and dead, both moving surface, a live load, and inert form, no psychological radiance, no brain waves that matter.[13]

Greenfield's story is, also, a story about how animals live now. They live provisionally and increasingly in peril. The density (the intensified body) of the animal in the landscape, which signals its pivotal complexity in the order of things, has not saved animals from the territorial predation of human beings. Deleuze and Guatteri make the point, in *A Thousand Plateaus*, that animal-becoming is "not the site or point of application for myths. . . . The origin of packs is entirely different than that of families and States; they [the animals] continually work them from within and trouble them from without."[14] An animal in a cage is an animal that has suspended tasks—the tasks of the pack for example—that sustain its vitality. It has fallen idle in an entirely different way than Georges Bataille or Henri Lefebvre (both of whom do not believe animals work) might have imagined. In the epigraph to this chapter, Costello paraphrases Deleuze and Guattari without making direct reference to them, but she also adds a spatial theory of the "elsewhere" that elaborates slightly the notion of "reserve" I have been exploring as a somewhat different process/place than that of becoming-animal. Here such a reserve is not a space to which the jaguar retreats but an energy reserve that resides in its body, capable of "drilling" through darkness, springing into action, or dematerializing the very meaning of the cage. Generally, only the thinnest aspects of our powers of reasoning and laboring have dwelled on the implications of animal energy, territory, and precariousness. We marshal to their cause only our most unstable, dispensable, and ephemeral arguments—sentiment, generalized metaphors of beauty, generic global well-being, child-like protection. The maturing of representation in human history—from drawing to digitalized images—has meant that animals, including mythical animals, continue to "be present in the human scene. But these representations are deliberate de-densifications of animal being; the digital, with its pixelated surface, is, representationally, the correct analog for the animal as a contemporary object of human thought. Post-animal animal life is life that holds itself together in the human domain by means of flickering surfaces. Post-animal human life is life that definitively (at a certain moment when it felt able to be definitive) parted ways with animal life, and became predatory, in a sense, on the site of its own past. Agamben, again working inside Heidegger's idea of the open, writes that humans become more animalized as they move into the open, unconcealedness, of their own being. Heidegger adopts, and reverses, Rainer Maria Rilke's "open" from "The Eighth Elegy." In Rilke, it is the "creature-world" that beholds the open "with all its eyes" and "our eyes . . . encircle it on every side . . . like traps." In Heidegger, the animal never sees the open. The open, in architecture, is sometimes the space in which humans can remove their clothes—that is, the space of their houses. It is not accidental that Derrida tries to fathom his cat at the moment of his own nakedness. As humans move into the captivation of architecture, they become more animalized (more naked, more bored). This is not a moment of "becoming-animal" in Deleuze and Guattari's sense.[15] This is not a "discovery" or invention of other strands of, or ways of thinking about, possible existence. Architecture is a place in which, biologically, we both achieve humanness and regress. As the place of our boredom (suspension of self-consciousness) and our nakedness, it is also the place where we eat, as the hyena ate, in calm pursuit of our own survival. It is, in fact, in Heidegger's long critique of boredom that Giorgio Agamben finds man's return to his own animality—that man becomes, again, an animal.[16]

Architecture in the post-animal age—to finish the hyena story—acts conservatively in light of the big question of who will survive. It takes a little from each side—from the side of the human, the still idealized geometric form that is allowed to wander slightly outside its lines, and from the side of the animal, life without an intricate psychological profile. The hyena, if I remember correctly, was shot.

**Sovereign is he who decides on the state of exception.**

—Carl Schmitt, in Giorgio Agamben, *Homo Sacer*

**Insofar as the animal knows neither beings nor nonbeings, neither open nor closed, it is outside of being; it is outside in an exteriority more external than any open, and inside in an intimacy more internal than any closedness. To let the animal be would then mean: to let it be outside of being.**

—Giorgio Agamben, *The Open*

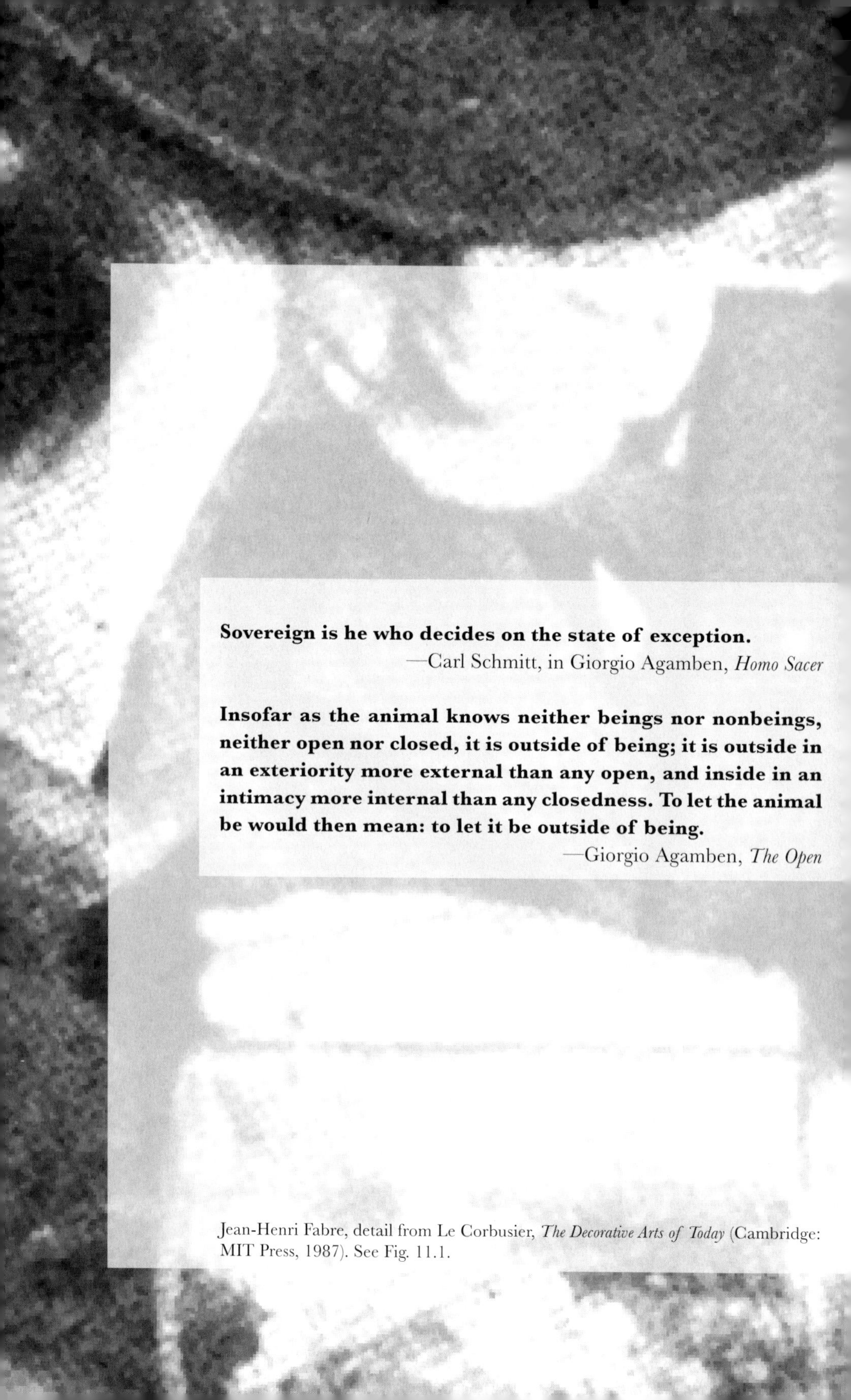

Jean-Henri Fabre, detail from Le Corbusier, *The Decorative Arts of Today* (Cambridge: MIT Press, 1987). See Fig. 11.1.

# 8: BIRDS (FROM ABOVE)



Why all these birds?
—Claude Lévi-Strauss, *Totemism*

It has been argued that while representational precision in drawings of animals does not arrive until the late fourteenth century, when it does appear, "it appears chiefly in the representation of birds."[1] Birds were apparently of particular interest to the medieval mind because "they were free, decorative and . . . unencumbered by symbolic associations. They were simply objects of delight."[2]

We can now (so sensitive is our collective radar) immediately read the signs of how this line of thought goes awry. Precision in drawing or sculpting animals that, at any given moment, "occupy man's curiosity"[3] is rarely about the animal itself, or even attributes of the animal. An attribute of the bird, such as the ability to fly, may constitute part of its attraction as a representational object, but the desire of representation to fix its object—to stop birds in flight—is the chief force that draws birds into the representational field.[4] As we also now know, this "fixing of the object" took a particularly interesting turn in the Renaissance with the invention of "accurate" perspectival representation. An accurately constructed perspective appears to capture objects pre-existing in homogeneous space, but it would be equally possible to say, as many discussions of perspective argue, that this type of representation aggressively subordinates objects and space to its own very picky requirements; it subordinates everything, first, to the symbolic visual and, second, to the ideality of a homogeneous spatial continuum whose outer conceptual reach is the concept of infinity.[5] "It is not for nothing," Rosalind Krauss writes famously in *The Optical Unconscious*, "that this geometry [of perspective] turns around the almost unimaginable limit of 'infinity,' a point that is literally reduced to nothing." She continues:

> Far from nothing coming from nothing, the truth that arises from this Euclidean meeting of parallel lines at that point beyond the limit of imagining is the solidity of the construction's basis in geometrical law. And the infinite smallness of this point in the eye from which the entire architecture is suspended is, as well, an infinite rapidity.[6]

Krauss' use of King Lear's words to Cordelia—"Nothing will come of nothing"—refers to a world (Lear's world) in which every object and subject faces the crisis of losing its form, where nothing literally threatens to come of nothing, a world without a theory of reproduction into which any monstrosity may enter. Krauss articulates here the cosmic order of the two motions of perspective, one toward the infintesimal smallness and nothingness of the vanishing point and the other toward the solid vastness of the whole world over which perspective "casts its net."[7] In a remarkably economical gesture, a bird in flight is thus simultaneously constructed and ensnared by the perspective lines drawn to represent it. The fact that birds are among the most skittish and rapid of possible art subjects, might make their capture in art particularly noteworthy.

By the end of the Renaissance—to reiterate—this represents a double capture: first, to get the animal, the bird for example, to "sit still,"[8] then to capture it in the lines of perspectival representation. By the end of the eighteenth century, this is a triple capture: to get the bird to sit still, to capture it in the cage of the drawing, and to identify it within its genus and species by means of taxonomic classification, not necessarily in that order. And, by the nineteenth century, when classification by means of visible similarities gives way to classification by means of internal structures, birds continue to be collected in the form of bones and skins, for comparative anatomies as taxidermist specimens meticulously arranged in natural history museums. The final capture (at least until some unseen future event) is, initially, through film and later through digital imaging and genetics, which have worked together since the 1950s. Birds thus might be seen as a peculiar testing ground for the artistic science of perspective, the scientific art of classification, and the digital-genetic alliance.

Not incidentally, and in ways that will eventually pertain to all these discussions, birds are also from the sky. Birds inhabit the milieu of the infinite, an oxymoron. They are dark, moving points in the sky that belong, in some figural way, to the "infinite rapidity" that maintains the theoretical vanishing point in the construction of the perspective. Like Piet Mondrian's *Plus and Minus* paintings—*Pier and Ocean* (1914–15) and *Composition in Lines* (1916–17)—which, as Krauss states, started "from the expanse of sea and sky" and throw the "net" of an "abstract grid" over "the whole of the external world in order to enter it into consciousness,"[9] birds mark an expansive context with the dark plus sign of their wings, which is not necessarily, as Mondrian showed, a mark of presence.

The sky is that problematic field of space against which buildings are stamped in perspective drawings. The amorphous field of "sky" was an interesting problem in Brunelleschi's original experiments in drawing perspectives and continues to represent a problem, representational and otherwise, throughout subsequent epochs of architecture.[10]

Quarto el ultimo disegno di perspetiua nel secondo modo p me proposto per
coregere il dello marmo
AB. linea piena del marmo
ACBD. linee orizontale
BC. linea della distancia
FP. aucheta rastremata
G. cortiuagio
le linee oculte disegnano il piano
digradato al ingiu


 **Figure 8.1:** Martino Bassi, *Second recommended improvement for the Milan Annunciation Relief.* Courtesy of Biblioteca Trivulziana, Milan.

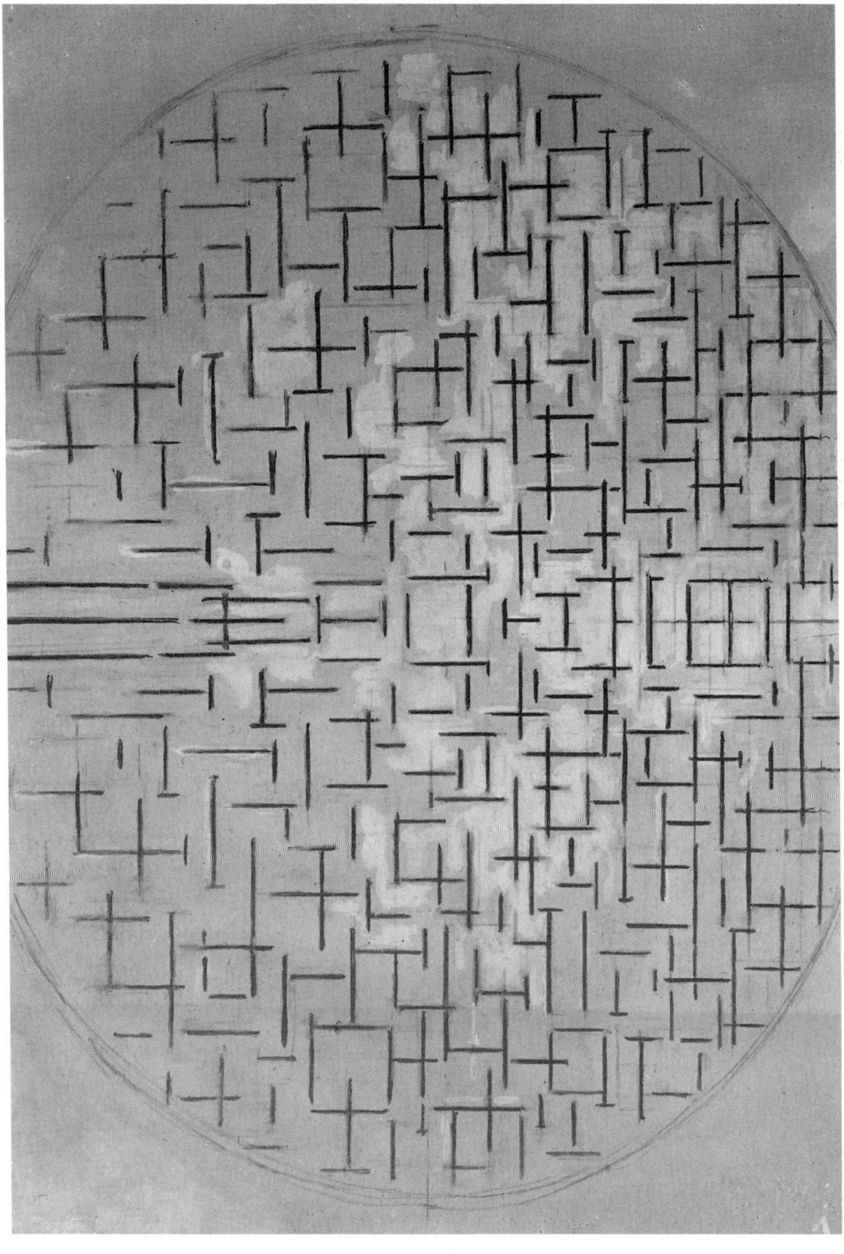

**Figure 8.2:** Piet Mondrian, *Pier and Ocean*, 1914. Charcoal and white watercolor on buff paper. Courtesy the Museum of Modern Art. Photograph 2002, the Museum of Modern Art, New York.

Sciences of the sky—astrophysics and meteorology, for example—are where crucial revisions in theories of matter and space are formulated. Recent work in dynamical systems and distributed network theories routinely uses bird flocks (and fish schools) as examples of complex systems, where sky and water are understood to be relatively open fields of operation. Krauss writes:

> The sea and sky are ways of packaging "the world" as a totalized image, as a picture of completeness, as a field constituted by the logic of its own frame. But its frame is a frame of exclusions and its field is the work of ideological construction.[11]

Birds are both occupants of, and emissaries from, this troubled and turbulent domain of the sky. It is a long way from the condition of birds in the sky and the representational (and other) puzzles generated by that condition to architecture—specifically the problem of real/virtual movement, biological and psychological human/animal life, and other forms of animation in/of architecture. At the very least, this is a two-pronged problem, with those prongs converging rather than diverging from each other: first is the problem of life already broached inside architectural structures and space and how the definition of life, its biological and existential status, the character and motive force of its movement, its composition and historical meaning, has changed over time; second is the definition of architecture and its status, character of movement, technological evolution, composition and historical meaning. The structure, as well as its occupant, moves, but these two motions refer only obliquely to each other. Living beings and inanimate objects have, at different points in history, come into more or less intimate contact with each other. During animistic periods, for example, almost everything in the world is invested with the power of movement.[12] Biology and architectural history, as formal disciplines, come into being more or less at the same moment in the Enlightenment. For the most part, though, life and architecture maintain divergent interests and divergent histories. These are surprising and problematic claims because, since antiquity, architecture has been theorized (with different degrees of attention) as the precise art and science that takes account of human life. Yet, as suggested earlier, architecture acquires a formal distinctness—a practical logic—long before human life or animal life are classified as discrete entities with specific attributes. When biological life is, in effect, "named" in the eighteenth century, architecture seems, somehow, prepared to receive it. At the same moment, however, architecture is in the process of turning its attention in other directions: absorbing, for example, the meaning of metal structure, revisiting classicism, attending to social and political changes that portend new forms and ways of life, agrarian to urban. There is almost no registration, at this crucial moment of entry into history, of the biological "human"—*Homo sapiens*—nor is there specific mention of the newly organized, by means of species, biological animal. The history of domesticity and private life—much of which has been theorized in both architectural and cultural history in the late twentieth century—contains tantalizing clues to the status of bodies in architectural space. Even as everything changes, over time, in the relationship between domestic occupant and culture, the peculiar and quick emergence of the Human Being does not immediately propose a different path for architecture. The paradox is, of course, that architecture serves, at its most basic level, this new biological being. Modern architecture typically rendered its occupant as a mediated socio-technical entity that architectural enclosure itself came to signify. This *was* a kind of architectural response to the arrival of organized life, life that is managed by science, life that is named. Architecture "dresses" this being. Acknowledgement, from the biological side, of the human being as a being that is heavily mediated by its forms of enclosure is also surprisingly rare.

It has often been noted that architecture seems to be a rear-guard practice. It absorbs culture slowly, distilling its meanings over long periods of time into architectural forms. In biological terms, in contrast, the milieu is already there in advance of the organism, although Darwin argued that the organism, at the moment of occupation, has the "first word."

What can possibly be said about the animal, the bird for example, in this context? To speak of "birds in the sky" (free animal, individual and collective) and "birds in the hand" (art, science) is a fertile, although perhaps too artful, way of initially presenting the problem of animation with respect to objects, specifically architectural objects, that submit specific attributes of aliveness—relative freedom of human movement, for example—to the requirements of form. And, one could ask, Why keep the bird in the picture at all? The bird is incidental to—merely an odd example of—the problems of free and constrained movement in space. Perhaps some of the bird's existential status as a free animal lingers inside certain architectural forms—inside the tacit will of these forms to restrict flight, or to fly. Or the bird might act as a necessary, formal signifier of the non-human; a signifier of a paradise, or purgatory, lost or foregone. Part of architecture strives to be "not-a-bird." In Diane Wells' book *100 Birds and How They Got Their Names*,[13] she reminds us that the "inferno," as in Dante's *Inferno*, referred to a place that was "without birds." It is a place "of the below." Architecture is never strictly the subterranean world of the inferno, but it clings to the earth in literal and philosophical ways, not all of which are benevolent.

In general, birds, or any animal for that matter, are typically rendered in the margins of questions about human life and architecture. It is implicitly understood that architecture is emphatically not concerned, except on rare occasions, with anything but human life.

At the same time birds, and other animals, keep cropping up in discussions of life and, in different ways, in architectural work. Darwin, on the Galapagos Islands, drafts his theory of evolution in the presence of birds. Because so many intermediary species of birds are missing, which is evidence of what biologists now call the "episodic" or dynamic equilibrium character of organic change, the diversity of bird species is paradigmatic of how diversity demonstrates the common descent of all animals, including man. When the French physiologist Etienne Jules Marey (1830–1904) attempts to graphically represent movement by rendering "the true form of movement, as it is described in space," he harnesses a dove to a "registering device . . . [that] transmits the curve of its wing beats to smoked cylinders. From these the form of the movement is plotted out point by point."[14] Or, later, when Marey begins to use photography, he points his "Photo-gun to Register Phases of a Bird's Flight," essentially the first movie camera, at seagulls. The mechanization of a bird's flight is understood to be definitive because birds, like fish, are largely defined, as a species, by their specific movements, which unfold in three dimensions. When Eadweard Muybridge, also in the late nineteenth century, sets up a series of cameras at twelve inch intervals in order to assemble frames of a moving body, he first photographs birds. The point of many of these studies is, ultimately, to understand human movement—the movement of muscles, heartbeats and blood, for example. But the bird is indispensable, not only for the plain fascination of its motion, but also for what human investigators class, illogically, as its exemplary movement—continuous, graceful, almost effortless, in concert with other birds, in the sky. Le Corbusier wrote in 1935: "By the effort of a generation the cumulative effect of the discoveries of a century . . . we have been endowed with THE BIRD'S EYE VIEW."[15] Le Corbusier is not writing about birds per se, and, in any case, the first drawings using the bird's eye view, by Leonardo da Vinci, appeared long before Le Cobusier's.[16] The bird's-eye view, or the "fly-through" in contemporary three-dimensional modeling, is generally modeled after a bird's imputed view/movement.

In a different set of developments, when the first mechanized animal processing assembly lines were designed in the United States, one of the most difficult problems was how to pluck poultry mechanically. The removal of feathers, which are individually anchored in the skin of the bird and which lie flat against each other, became an index of

Marey invited Muybridge to visit him in Paris (1881), and introduced him in his house to a gathering of Europe's most brilliant physicists, astronomers, and physiologists, who welcomed Muybridge's straightforward tackling of the problem.

Muybridge's photography of flying birds did not entirely satisfy Marey, who wished to gain full insight into the three-dimensional character of flight — as Descartes had projected geometrical forms: for the flight of insects and of

7. E. J. MAREY: Recording a Gull's Flight in Three Projections Photographically. Before 1890. *At Marey's laboratory in the Parc des Princes, Paris, three still cameras placed at perpendicular angles to the line of flight simultaneously record a seagull's passage before black walls and over a black floor.* (Le vol des oiseaux, *Paris*, 1890)

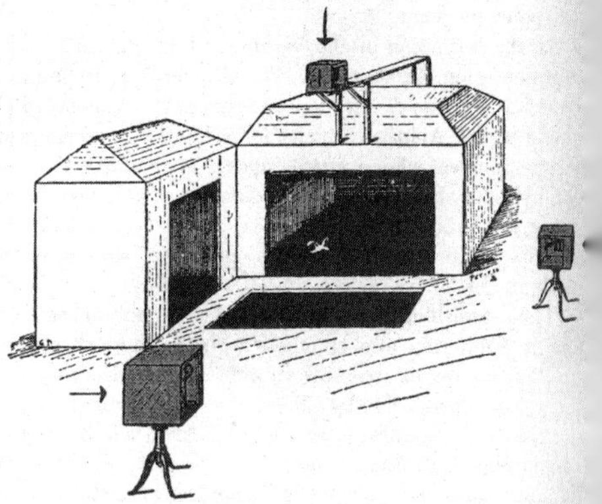

birds is spatial. It evolves freely in three dimensions. Around 1885 Marey pointed three cameras in such a way as to view the bird simultaneously from above, from the side, and from the fore (fig. 7). At his laboratory in the Parc des Princes, Paris, he set up a vast hangar, before whose black walls and ceiling the sea gull flew over a black floor. These simple realities, normally hidden to the human eye, have an impressiveness that needs no further explanation.

For better knowledge of the bird's flight, Marey later drew diagrams in which he separated the overlapping phases of the photograph (figs. 8–10). He even modeled the sea gull in its successive attitudes (fig. 9) — sculpture that would have delighted Boccioni, creator of the 'Bottle evolving in Space' (1912) and of the 'Marching Man' (1913). In his later research [13] Marey made extensive use of the movie camera, which proved not especially suited to this purpose.

[13] Marey, *La Chronophotographie*, Paris, 1899, pp.37ff., or as he calls it 'images chronophotographiques recueillies sur pellicule mobile.'

22

 **Figure 8.3:** Siegfried Giedion, *Mechanization Takes Command* (New York: Norton, 1969).

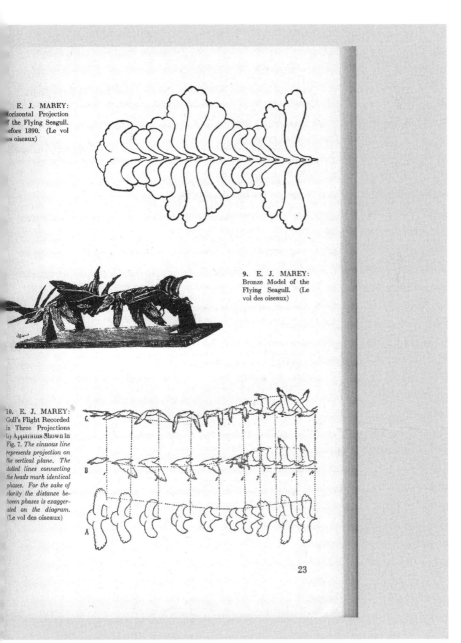

E. J. MAREY: [H]orizontal Projection [o]f the Flying Seagull. [B]efore 1890. (Le vol [d]es oiseaux)

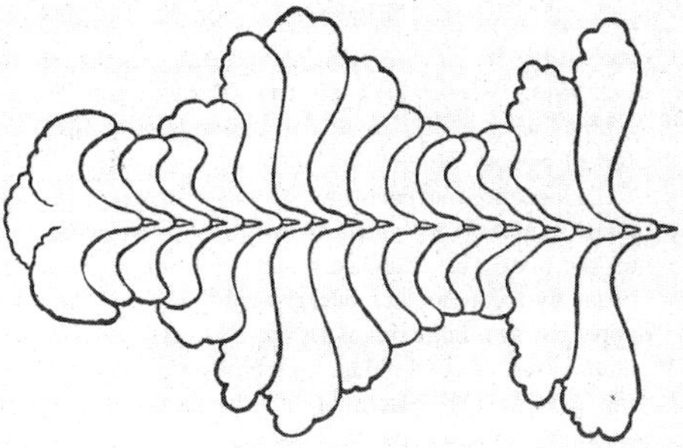

9. E. J. MAREY: Bronze Model of the Flying Seagull. (Le vol des oiseaux)

10. E. J. MAREY: Gull's Flight Recorded in Three Projections by Apparatus Shown in Fig. 7. *The sinuous line represents projection on the vertical plane. The dotted lines connecting the heads mark identical phases. For the sake of clarity the distance between phases is exaggerated on the diagram.* (Le vol des oiseaux)

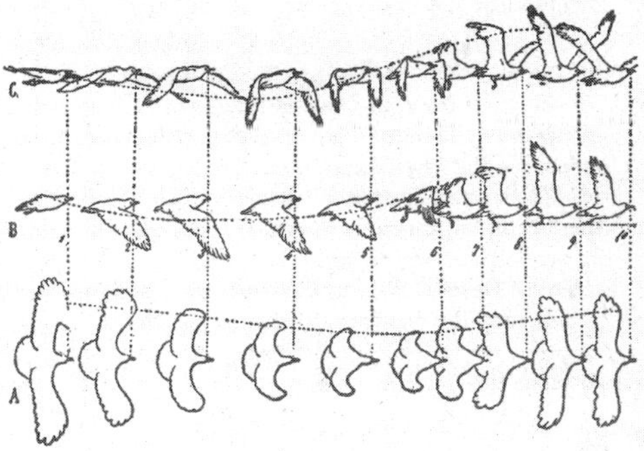

23

how refined mechanization could become, both how detailed and how ingenious its mechanical interaction could be with the irregular, soft, diverse forms of dead animals. Two out of the four eschatological animals were birds, one domestic, the other "free"—the cock and the eagle. And, of course, in 1994 through 2001, the architect-engineer Santiago Calatrava designs, to much acclaim, the Milwaukee Art Museum in a context where it still is permissible and remarkable, and not ridiculous, to form a building not only in the image of a bird but with implicit, metaphoric (a "kinetic structure") aspirations to flight. Finally, also in the twenty-first century, when digital architects look for models of distributed networks, they look endlessly, with palpable envy, at videotapes or animations of bird flocks, at the "boids" flocking studies, the emergent logics of unpredictable movement.[17]

Birds are, contrary to Clark's remarks, so heavily burdened symbolically, so completely un-free historically, that getting rid of them in a discussion of architecture, life and animation would profoundly impoverish and limit that discussion. So the "problem of birds" remains, subsists, inside this discussion. And what is it exactly? One of its first declarations might be, crudely, that humans have been animals for more centuries than they have been humans. Just beneath our use of the term "human life" and its various relations to architecture, lies animal life—bird life, for example. Birds are deeply lodged in human life, camouflaged perhaps by what amounts to a two centuries old, yet continuously modern disputation of our animal ancestry, and by other dissimulations yet to be explicated.

Here, again, we might turn to art theory. Certainly architecture is somehow automatically attuned—in the very fibers of its conception—to life and its movement in space because, of course, humans have formed it. Does it, then, make any sense to speak of a kind of artistic/technical production, such as architecture, that sublimates, yet maintains a formal reference to, some aspect of aliveness that attends the making of artistic material? Would such a class of artistic production follow the familiar lines of difference between figurative art and abstract art, for example, the difference between portraiture[18] and Frank Stella's *Hyena Stomp*, or between the exaggerated verisimilitude of Leonardo da Vinci's horses and the huddled abstract bulks of Henry Moore's sheep? And does it matter if we are speaking of paintings or sculpture or architecture? Formal allusions to "life" in art, whatever that might mean at different moments of time, use the usual paths of reference—in contemporary pre-digital art, repetition, verisimilitude, mimesis, abstraction; in ancient art, what Erwin Panofsky calls the "antique authorities"[19]—and many of these references are almost completely absent from architectural objects. Architecture as an art, by comparison with other arts, seems to be almost isomorphic with life. It uses a certain self-evidence of life to advance the myriad instances of its symbolic relation with life. And, it is worth reiterating, in almost no case is architecture's relation to life understood to be anything other than a relation to human life. This is also true of any art; the making of art, by definition, classically excludes any artfulness attributed to non-human life. There have been a few bizarre experiments that have attempted to test this definition. Steve Baker, in *The Postmodern Animal*, writes about the environmental artists Olly and Suzi, who work with the photographer Greg Williams. Olly and Suzi first do a painting of an animal, a shark, for example, using natural pigments from soil, blood, inks, and dyes. And then, "operating in . . . dangerous circumstances, as close as they can get to . . . animals," they attempt to attract a shark to the painting in order for it to "interact" with the painting. The shark's bite into the painting, as part of the performance of the art, implicitly contextualizes the art in a larger environment than the human environment.[20] However, something about this experiment, and others of its kind (elephants "painting" for example), is so forced and absurd—awash, also, in our profoundly sentimental and expectant relationship to wild animals—that it is very difficult to ascertain its lessons.

Art is that which survives, exists outside of, the inescapable logic of biology. As Hannah Arendt wrote:

> The man-made world of things, the human artifice erected by *homo faber*, becomes a home for mortal men, whose stability will endure and outlast the ever-changing movement of their lives and actions, only insomuch as it transcends both the sheer functionalism of things produced for consumption and the sheer utility of objects produced for use. If the *animal laborans* needs the help of *homo faber* to ease his labor and remove his pain, and if mortals need his help to erect a home on earth, acting and speaking men need the help of *homo faber* in his highest capacity, that is, the help of the artist, of poets and historiographers, of monument-builders or writers, because without them the only product of their activity, the story they enact and tell, would not survive at all.[21]

Architecture, like other arts, thus writes human life in order, in part, to perpetuate the human story. It extends the reign of the biological through time by carrying life histories, because, in most cases, it outlives the lives within it. It thus is a kind of genetic residue that is passed on to subsequent generations—among other things, a cultural/genetic form of binding of the body to space and time.

Both art and architecture now have saturated histories in which the formerly regressive idea of pre-historical art/architecture—caves and cave art for instance—has been largely replaced with the idea of an always already refined humanity of artistic practice. In some sense, architecture and art have always drawn on, and underwritten, whatever reservoir of "humanness," "humanity," "human value" existed at any given time, even before any equivalent of what we now call human value existed. And yet the separation of human and animal is a very complicated story. There has always been something like a human enclave in history, but its existential status has been radically different at different times. The use of animal (and plant) motifs, for example, in the form of architectural ornaments is relatively common throughout architectural history; but most of these ornaments were meant to keep the animal, particularly the evil monster, out of the human enclave. Ornamentation on buildings has a rich history.[22] Ornament acts as a supplement to architectural structure and, as such, attempts to control, from the outside, what and who is allowed—spiritually, psychologically, and actually—to enter and inhabit a building. Its supplementary character means that ornament is both a symbolic appliqué to a building, and a force that acts structurally. Ornament, particularly in periods of confusion about spiritual life, exerts sovereignty over the building; it designates who and what is included and excluded, who and what enters and exits the building. Ornaments that evoke animal or neo-animal (hybrid) life often are meant to keep both the animal and animalism—the bestial world existing both inside and outside human life—out of the world of the building, the architectural world. The biological status of humans, during many of these periods, is indistinguishable from that of the animal. Thus, the work of medieval ornament such as gargoyles was to divide the human away from its animal body—the spiritual from the bestial—before that human could enter the place of spiritual life, the church. Humanness, unnamed during these periods, is sustained in this way as (the eventually unsustainable idea of) a more immediate, more valuable, spirituality. Dividing the spirit from the body, the very basis of Christianity in medieval architecture, attempts also, in effect, to erase the fact of architecture as a human production. Medieval churches were constructions of God, transcending humanity, for which the architect was merely a translator, a medium.

Clement Greenberg, again from Krauss' *The Optical Unconscious*, wrote of modern painting:

> The heightened sensitivity of the picture plane may no longer permit sculptural illusion, or *trompe-l'oeil*, but it does and must permit optical illusion. The first mark made on a surface destroys its visual flatness, and the configurations of a Mondrian still

> suggest a kind of illusion of a kind of third dimension. Only now it is strictly pictorial, strictly optical third dimension.[23]

This optical illusion of a third dimension that belongs to modernist painting "into which one can look, can travel through, only with the eye"—a claim that Krauss will find extremely objectionable on the grounds of its recourse to ideas of transcendental pure immediacy—was also claimed, in a different way, for the flat planes of modern architecture, although architecture is complicated, corrupted, as always, by being four-dimensional space. In architecture, it is necessary to move the whole (problematic) body through space in order to grasp the paradox of the "architectural object."

So the apparent purity of seeing that erases the body but keeps the eye in front of the modern painting is never entirely possible in architecture; indeed, Krauss radically addresses the impossibility of this kind of seeing in modernist painting as well. In this she might be said, in part, to be substituting the dimensioning, moving gaze of/onto the architecture of the painting (absorbing its hidden structures) for the static gaze of/onto painting or, in her more precise words, to be substituting the psychological spatiality of an "optical unconscious" for the flatness of optical immediacy. Krauss would not agree with this attempt to draw her into an architectural reading. Architecture—particularly its "literalness"[24]—is the very thing art theory, and art itself, contests. Architecture is an art that tries to *still* the body and repress the psychological. At the same time, it must always deal with the body, even in modernity when everything conspired to pack the body into the eye. The "unconscious" of the "optical unconscious" can rarely find purchase for its desires and psychological fortresses in the literal spaces of architecture, although an unhoused unconscious is the very definition of madness. Architecture, as Benjamin taught us—through the use of that compelling word "distraction"—entails a *stop start stop start* kind of seeing that accumulates over an interval in which space and time are traversed and fit together.[25] Architecture eludes optical summation because the seeing is corrupted by the large and small movements of the body and the movement is corrupted by the willfulness of seeing. Modern architecture, as both a discipline and practice, determined the existential status of everything within its grasp by means of this seeing/movement, this eye/body construction.

In architectural history, architectural buildings have been understood to be, on occasion, extrusions of the body through the eyes (mental projections), hand (tools) and backbone (attitude/posture). One of the roles of the animal in my discussion is to prevent what has generally become, particularly in architectural history, a "poetics" of the body—both an account of its privilege and a poetic view of the body's apparent proximity to nature. The animal and the animal body is neither poetic nor subject to poetics—that is, not subject to the work of a stimulated psyche and intellect, not artistic. The shark that bites the painting is, literally, from another world than the painting. Its bite does not produce a connection between these worlds in either metaphoric or literal terms. The difficulty of maintaining a discussion of the animal without invoking these connections is also what makes such a discussion useful in thinking through the subject of architecture and life.

We have been speaking of the representation of space, not literal space—although these two things are always uniquely conflated in architecture. The architectural drawing, with the exception of the presentation drawing, is not a drawing of the building as a whole. It is a series of summary diagrams by means of which the building will be assembled. Renderings and presentation drawings "present" the building but they, too, can only summarize the building through a series of additive views. Looking at architectural drawings, the eye moves neither through Greenberg's optical dimension nor through Krauss' optical unconscious (although the question of the unconscious plagues architecture at many levels), but through a series of framed diagrams interrupted by white gaps. These gaps are, in some respects, representatives of the space of an unconscious poised behind a seeing eye

THE PROCURACIES, VENICE

*The uniformity of the innumerable windows in this vast wall on the Piazza San Marco gives the same play as would the smooth side of a room. The repetition of the same unit lends the wall a grandeur that is boundless but can be easily appreciated; the result is a type-form of a clear and simple nature. The pigeons of St. Mark's themselves add their own uniform module, providing a varied and effective note in the scheme.*

# VI

# CLASSIFICATION AND CHOICE

## (TIMELY DECISIONS)

> " It is the city's business to make itself permanent, and this depends on considerations other than those of calculation. It is only Architecture which can give all the things which go beyond calculation."

SINCE we are now in a position to know how we feel, let us choose, for our comfort, the possible methods to effect a cure for the general well-being.

*



 **Figure 8.4:** Le Corbusier, *The City of Tomorrow* (Cambridge: MIT Press, 1971).

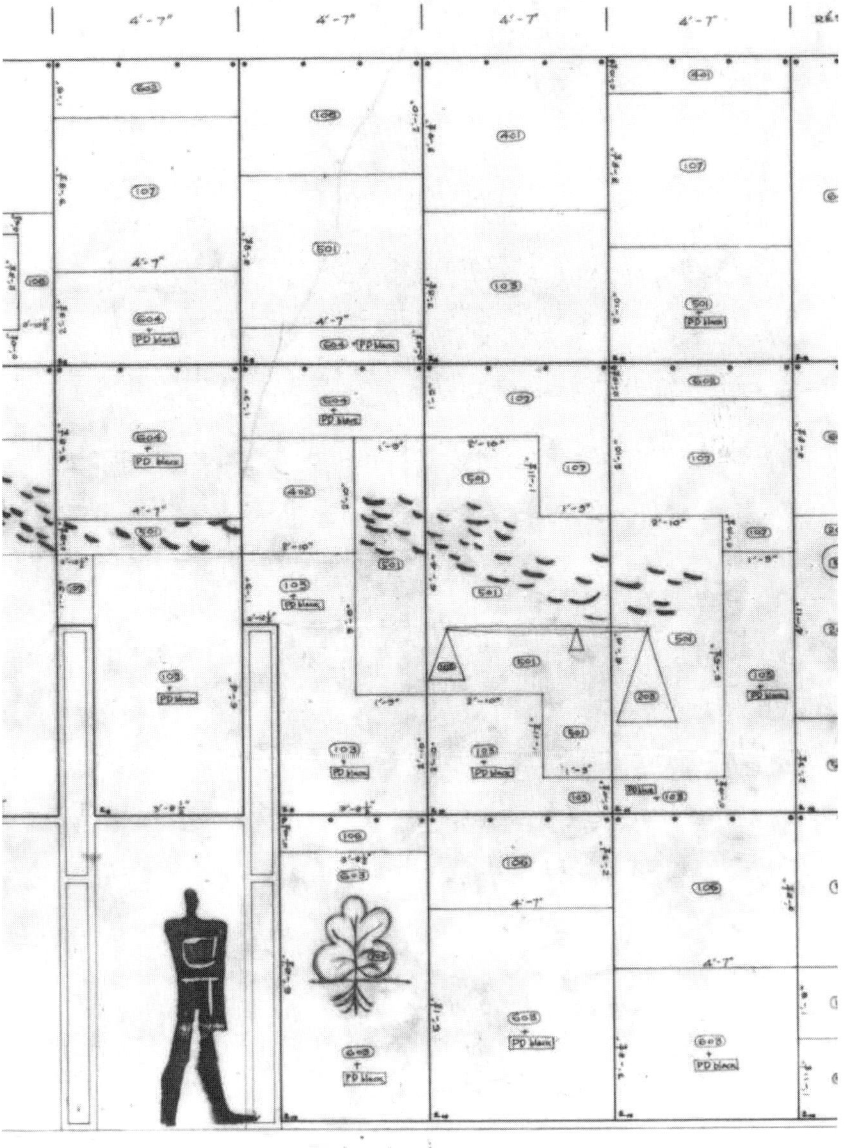


**Figure 8.5:** Le Corbusier, Palace of Justice, Chandigarh (1954), from *Le Modular II*, 1955. 2005 Artists Rights Society (ARS), New York/ADAGP, Paris/FLC.

 **Figure 8.6:** Le Corbusier, *The City of Tomorrow* (Detail) (Cambridge: MIT Press, 1971).

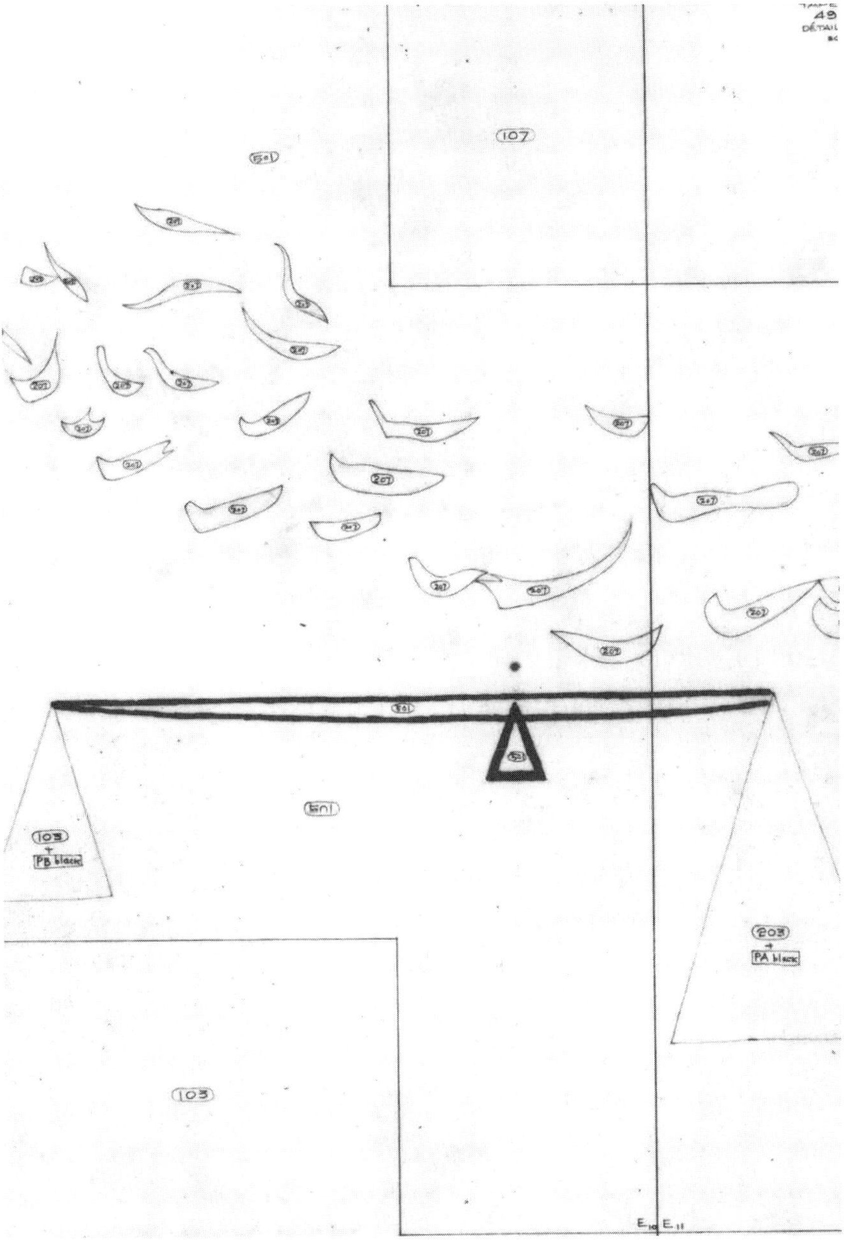


**Figure 8.7:** Le Corbusier, Palace of Justice, Chandigarh (1954), from *Le Modular II* (Detail), 1955. 2005 Artists Rights Society (ARS), New York/ADAGP, Paris/FLC.

(recovering Krauss), but the assembly of the whole, as mentioned above, requires an implied—even if notational—bodily movement through it. So, always, in architecture, a restless movement works its way in.

This system of presenting architecture as diagrammed movement held sway from the Renaissance to the late twentieth century and was based, in part, on projective drawing systems made possible by the discovery/invention of mathematical space and perspective that governed the drawing of plan, section, elevation and, later, photographic and filmic representations of architecture. However, and in spite of significant and astounding work on architectural representation, particularly in the late twentieth century before digital representation began to make the subject both more and less interesting, it still seems as if the problems presented to architecture by the Renaissance invention of perspective—in particular, problems of subjectivity and objectivity—have not yet been fully treated. Many of these discussions have been among the most significant in art and architectural history: discussions of the mobile eye/I as it scrutinizes and is, in turn, scrutinized by its surround; the peculiar ongoing persuasiveness and self-evidence of homogeneous space; the complexity of co-constructed meanings and hermeneutics; the adaptation of historical work to its own instability, and so forth. Some of what we have learned: to be an object, by definition, means to have extinguished the subjectivity that is a defining attribute of life. Nontheless, multiple conditions of objectivity continue to invoke and provoke the subjectivity implicit in the object's production, perception, usage, display. There is no pure object. But neither is there, as Derrida reminded us, pure subjectivity.[26] The object and its reception in the field of life, the eye and its grasp of the object, the "grey matter" that is the milieu of the eye,[27] the life and environment that are the milieux of the grey matter, are all in active negotiation.

In this context, part of what remains unsatisfactory for me is how we, as human beings, continue to enlarge on and embellish, architecturally, our own isolated humanity by means of the space-box and perspectival or wire-frame cage in a way that keeps the meaning of our occupation of that space, and the meaning of the milieux of that occupation, opaque and art historical in the worst sense. In other words, architecture, like the positivist science it is, still, after hundreds of years, almost devoid of specific comment on its relation to the life within it. "Sustainability"—recent theorizations of architecture as part of an ecosystem—falters around precisely this issue. For example, aren't the multiple forms of captivation in architecture—figurative (e.g. the logic of the plan) and literal (e.g. the dominance of certain scales)—related to the captivity, both figurative and literal, in which (other) animals live? The artist Francis Bacon observed that the cage binds the animal to its viewer and makes it possible to see the animal.[28] The cage doubles an animal's captivation. Architecture has taken care to bind us in multiple ways, using cages both literally and figuratively, to our own world-forming.[29] We see only the stars, as Norbert Wiener wrote in the 1950s, whose thermodynamics are like our own, although this statement now seems too modest an assertion for the cyberneticists, whose ambition was to control the neurology of the world, or, rather, to make of the world a neurology. Architecture, among other things, is the ubiquitous evidence of a unidirectional world-forming. In standing for world-forming, architecture also stands for Heidegger's "open" in human existence. We nod—all is as it should be. However, as I have been arguing, there is a catch. The human that architecture has housed (since the Renaissance, for my purposes here) is, for the most part, a human defined through architecture's various doctrines of humanism—not quite the modern human we conceive of ourselves as being and have been told we have become. For one thing, the ideal architectural occupant lacks, not in reality but in conception, the complex psychological dimensions of the modern human. Like the post-animal animal, this architectural human has been partitioned in order to be understood spatially; its living spaces are broken up, its mind separated from its body. Architecture itself must be both open and closed. It is a place, in other words, where humans live not just in the "open" but in a kind of "*disclosed* open captivation," or, in the terms of the twentieth century zoologist Jacob von Uexküll, architecture is a "world-environment" for a kind of being we thought we eradicated with the dawn of the age of reason, the human-animal, a hybrid, maybe even a monstrous being. An "animal that has learned to be bored," as Agamben puts it.

# 9: BIRDS (FROM BELOW)

There is a startling moment in Claude Lévi-Strauss' *Totemism* when he asks, echoing Radcliffe-Brown's quizzical remarks about the ubiquity of bird totems in certain cultures, "Why all these birds?"[1]

The moment arrives in Lévi-Strauss' narrative as a turning point, an exemplary instance of the famous *coup de grâce* of structuralist analysis, which cuts into a mass of data and quickly grasps a set of complex and incisive relations, in this case, the diverse data presented by the phenomenon of totemism.[2] It is not, as Lévi-Strauss argues, either the symbolic or real utility of the totemic animal that makes it attractive as a totem, but the system, the structure of similarities and differences between and among specific animals, that provides a homologous structure for the organization of human culture. Specific sets of attributes that differentiate and relate one species of bird to another result in totemic designations that are used to implant a "system of differences" into human society, which can also, therefore, be differentiated. The birds fly along a particular vector, a mental vector.

Although structuralism was, in every sense, related to cultural anthropology and linguistics—not specifically biology—

one of its main interests was to critique the classical philosophical opposition between nature and culture. To do this, culture had to be rewritten such that "random details of cultural practice . . . emerge as a set of ordered transformations, the logical restatements of a single, generating, pair of oppositions."[3] As Rosalind Krauss remarks on this practice:

> The semiotic square, or the structuralists' graph (the Klein Group), is a way of picturing the whole of a cultural universe in the grip of two opposing choices, two incompatible possibilities. Cultural production is the creation of an imaginative space in which those two things can be related. The conflict will not go away. But it will be, as it were, suspended. Worked and reworked in the space, for example, of myth. The imaginary resolution, as Lévi-Strauss projects it, of conflicts in the real is . . . the site of Jameson's Political Unconscious.[4]

Lévi-Strauss's category of totemism both rests upon and resists the Darwinian idea that species relate, although Darwin's work had no specific role to play in structural anthropology, which was primarily interested in symbolic associations. Birds and humans acquire a common ground through structural association, which is entirely human and intellectual. However, these structural associations, or almost any other relation between living beings theorized in the twentieth century, rest on Darwin's seminal theory that all species literally share a common ancestry with other species. Differences arise out of long periods of adaptation and relatively rare instances of mutation. Thus, birds and humans, while following radically different evolutionary paths, share, in a general sense, a sphere of evolutionary reference. Darwin's extremely odd inference of this common lineage—which precipitated numerous reactionary responses and for which there is meagre visible evidence in the fossil record—makes it possible for structuralism to operate quite freely in the world of the animal. It creates a biological, as well as semiotic, field of operation by which the animal is able to pass into the world of cultural production. This use of the word "biological," which lies uneasily next to the word "semiotics," as if playing a more primal or basic role than the semiotic, is not meant to uphold some essentialist nature/culture divide. It refers, instead, to a slightly broader field for the animal in "nature" than the word semiotic implies—a field that reaches into a deeper historical time and space frame than the cultural, although any idea of the biological as radically separate from the cultural is impossible. The biological, in this context, suggests the need for a kind of "double think" about the birds in question.

Differences relate, in structuralism, and organizational systems are exchanged between the animal and human world, but the exchange is weighted on the side of human culture, as it must always be, since, particularly after the eighteenth century, we are always operating from inside the human enclave. The return engagement, whereby animals would somehow import lessons from human cultures, is already rendered meaningless by the word "culture" itself. The question—it occurs only incidentally as an unnatural thought—of what the birds get out of a totemic system can only be answered tautologically. Perhaps their very survival depends on being marked or not marked as a totem, but the marking is inconsequential to their existence. Totemism, like speciation, is a naming system that tells us many things about culture but tells us almost nothing about the place, or beings, from which the opposing term "nature" emanates. Nature is, among other things, the obtuse, animal, side of the opposition. Its absorption into culture, in a post-animal world, is nearly complete, the opposition nearly ready for dissolution. As always, however, there is more to the story. We pretend to know that there are no species "in nature," but this formulation can't, ultimately, make much sense to us, since nature has opposed culture since antiquity and differences between animals (under different names at different times) have served culture since Aristotle. The connection of Darwin, who studied the operation of sameness/difference in nature, with Lévi-Strauss, who studied the operation of sameness/difference in culture, continues, in a different direction, the "problem of birds" that I began to outline at the beginning of this section. The problem of birds here is centerd on the problem of relation, association, and commerce across the nature/culture divide.

Part of the work of structuralism was to form semiotic relations in which terms can be compared along a linguistic axis. Thus, as already noted, an intellectual, rather than primarily visual or artistic, relation between human and animal is enabled by structuralist analysis. But there is a problem. The animal, in the post-animal age, apparently "cannot enter into relationships."[5] The nature from which the bird emanates—and, as a result, something about the bird itself—is a voided term/player in the nature/culture opposition that Lévi-Strauss seeks to "work and rework." It can't hold down its end of the bargain, and this turns out to be precisely Lévi-Strauss' point.

Lévi-Strauss' answer, or set of answers, to the question "Why all these birds?" starts with an amazing analysis of the relation of birds to human twins in the Nuer tribe. It is a long quote, but gives a succinct statement about how structuralism worked:

> In order to characterize twins, the Nuer employ expressions which at first sight seem contradictory. On the one hand, they say that twins are "one person" (*ran*); on the other, they state that twins are not "persons" (*ran*), but "birds" (*dit*) . . . As manifestations of spiritual power, twins are firstly "children of God" (*gat kwoth*), and since the sky is the divine abode they may also be called "persons of the above" (*ran nhial*). In this context they are opposed to ordinary humans, who are "persons of below" (*ran piny*). As birds are themselves "of the above," twins are assimilated to them. However, twins remain human beings: although they are "of the above," they are relatively "of [the] below." But the same distinction applies to birds,

> since certain species fly less high and less well than others: in their own sphere, consequently, while remaining generally "of the above," birds may also be divided according to above and below. We may thus understand why twins are called by the names of "terrestrial" birds: guinea fowl, francolin, etc.
>
> The relation thus postulated between twins and birds is explained neither by a principle of participation after the manner of Levy-Bruhl, nor by utilitarian considerations such as those adduced by Malinowski, nor by the intuition of perceptible resemblances proposed by Firth and by Fortes. What we are presented with is a series of logical connections united in mental relations. Twins "are birds," not because they are confused with them or because they look like them, but because twins, in relation to other men, are as "persons of the above" to "persons of below," and, in relation to birds, as "birds of below" are to "birds of the above." They thus occupy, as do birds, an intermediary position between the supreme spirit and human beings. . . .
>
> Although it is not explicitly set out by Evans-Pritchard, this reasoning leads him to an important conclusion. For this kind of inference is applicable not only to the particular relationships which the Nuer establish between twins and birds . . . but to every relationship postulated between human groups and animal species . . . this relation is metaphorical . . .
>
> An interpretation of the totemic relationship is here, then, not to be sought in the nature of the totem itself but in an association it brings to mind.[6]

What is particularly important for Lévi-Strauss about Evans-Pritchard's insight, which is under discussion in this part of *Totemism*, is that it understands the link between birds and humans to be primarily homological, resting entirely in the analogic and structural associations that totemism brings to mind. The natural characteristics of the bird serve the totemic designation but the bird itself—which lives on different terms than that of its characteristics—is merely the pretext for a cultural operation. Thus, the logic that binds together the operation of the human mind and objects in the world to which mental activity is applied (such as the "pairs of opposites" suggested by bird totems) is, as we have known for a long time, wholly a cultural logic. The irreconcilable oppositions of the structuralist graph, "suspended and reworked in myth" as Krauss wrote, can be suspended and made mythological precisely because of what I earlier called the "voided term" on one side of the opposition—the animal, the bird, nature. All the terms of the discussion that weight the opposition only, finally, weight it on one side, the side of culture. And that, in a sense, was the rich material that Lévi-Strauss' work offered to us: a meaningful, rather than bludgeoning, way of extending human social, political, and linguistic structures into the complicated and still largely unintelligible space of nature. It made it possible to go into nature and come out again relatively untouched, with structural system in hand, just as Lévi-Strauss himself could venture into the wilds of the Amazon jungle to grasp the culture of the Nambikwara tribes without foregoing the intellectual rigor of French philosophy or falling prey to the jungle itself. Occasionally there are stories of such anthropologists being killed by the tribes they are trying to study, or getting lost or attacked by wild animals. But little of what the actor Klaus Kinski referred to, in a vicious tone, as "the fucking jungle" in *Burden of Dreams*,[7] a film about the making of the film *Fitzcarraldo*, is ever evident in Lévi-Strauss' accounts. His are mid-twentieth century versions of scientific "eco-adventures" rather than the harrowing voyages into nature of earlier periods.

The problem with birds in this context is that they become, at the same moment, both fully available to and fully absent from the world of human production. We have no problem with their availability, the name of which is bird, but there is no name I can think of that describes their absence other than the inadequate ones already used—

a reserve, a wildness, an exclusion, some kind of continuing, complex, but small fluttering or nervousness in a dark unknown space.

I want to look more closely at the philosophical work of this (huge) opposition between nature/culture, although not with the hope of finding a way out of its dominance. The Cartesian struggle—Descartes' search for a syllogistic logic between nature and culture[8]—to interrogate the link between objects brought to mind and objects in the world is both upheld and undermined by structuralism, as is Kant's view that the operation of the mind itself plays a role in what is known of the world. On the one hand, objects of the world, both living and non-living, can be made specific in human cultural and intellectual systems because there is nothing outside this system. On the other hand, specific differences, between kinds of birds, for example, matter. The natural world is, thus, simultaneously a construct, a library, and an enigma, impossible to know in and for itself. Descartes and Kant would argue about where our knowledge of the world comes from, and what the status of that knowledge might be, but structuralism solved both problems—in a kind of virtuoso empiricism—by gathering its material from what appears to be a compliant and inventive nature, but situating its knowledge completely "in the intellect."

Lévi-Strauss' analysis of totemism, like Freud's analysis of hysteria, proved to be a radical proposal about both the mind and the world that had enormous consequences for the analysis of human culture during the structuralist period and after. Structuralist analysis also had its moment in architecture, although it ultimately faltered around the difficulty of isolating an architectural "sign" that was comparable to the linguistic sign. Was the architectural sign a unit or component or material part, such as a door or window, that materially makes up a building? Or was it a sign-system that one could read synchronically or diachronically and thus a form of hermeneutics? Architecture appeared to be a natural subject for something like structural analysis—largely because of the word "structure"—but it turned out to elude this form of philosophical and linguistic analysis. As is so often the case, architecture lumbered by most of the nuanced philosophical arguments of both structuralism and poststructuralism—asserting its materiality and scale as a form of rebuttal to arguments that asked, in effect, that it self-evaporate as a material object. I don't mean to say this fondly, as a way of excusing architecture from the discussion. There are both interesting and uninteresting reasons why this was the case—many of which come up in other parts of the discussion.

Much of the mode of argumentation used in structural anthropology, and later in poststructuralism, adopted the opposition as part of what is classically given to us when we embark on discussions of nature and culture.[9] The purpose of sustaining the opposition, while suspending and mythologizing it, was not to uphold classical modes of argumentation but the reverse, to subvert the essentialism implied by classical argumentation. Thus, in the clever parable cited by Leland de la Durantaye on the occasion of Jacques Derrida's death:

> [At a lecture given by Derrida] an audience member stood up and recounted the scene from *The Wizard of Oz* in which Dorothy and her friends finally meet the wizard, who is powerful and overwhelming until Toto pulls away the curtain to reveal a very small man. "Professor Derrida, are you like that?" the audience member asked. Derrida paused before replying, "You mean like the dog?"[10]

Derrida (as Toto) might "pull back the curtain" on the seemingly large presence of the Wizard of Oz to reveal the small person of the wizard of Oz in order to see aspects of the scene that the curtain is, literally, hiding. Both the large and the small wizards remain in the scene. But the pairs of opposites that appear in the phenomena of totemism—eagle-hawks to crows, twins to non-twinned children—and that seem to create a structural fit between human and animal culture use oppositional relations, according to Lévi-Strauss, as a "generative" force. Through oppositional relations, within and outside animal species, the relation between birds serves to smooth the operation of social relations between human beings. One way in which structural anthropology guarded itself against, and offered resistance to, the existentialism (1940s–1950s) that dominated the intellectual climate of France during the development of structural anthropology was to invest, in the animal world, a means by which the human world could regain the possibility of a generative, rather than negative, oppositionality that would then serve human social existence.[11] The animal world regains a certain stature through its analogic role as a parallel, almost symmetrical, world of animate beings by means of which humans—applying ritualistic, fetishistic, metaphoric, and symbolic forms of association—can solve specific problems, such how to get along in a group, how to resolve differences inside a particular cultural milieu, how to identify friends and enemies, how to avoid incest by establishing exo-gamous marriage rules, how to classify and correlate the natural world with human reason, perception, and so forth.

Lévi-Strauss writes further:

> Our question "Why all these birds?" is thus widened in its scope. . . . The comparative method consists precisely in integrating a particular phenomenon into a larger whole, which the progress of the comparison makes more and more general. In conclusion, we are confronted with the following problem: how may it be explained that social groups, or segments of society, should be distinguished from each other by the association of each with a particular natural species? . . . In other words, instead of asking "Why all these birds?" we can ask "Why particularly eagle-hawk and crow, and other pairs?" This step is decisive. It brings about a reintegration of content with form, and thus opens the way to a genuine structural analysis, equally far removed from formalism and from functionalism. . .

[I]f we examine some dozens of these tales [similar to eagle-hawk and crow] we find that they have a single theme. The resemblances and differences of animal species are translated into terms of friendship and conflict, solidarity and opposition. In other words the world of animal life is represented in terms of social relations similar to those of human society.[12]

And, concluding: ". . . Totemism is thus reduced to a particular fashion of formulating a general problem, vis, how to make opposition, instead of being an obstacle to integration, serve rather to produce it."[13]

Thus, animals used as totemic forces are, as Lévi-Strauss puts it, "not good to eat" but "good to think." Ultimately, animals serve the mental relations of humans, although it will be important to question the use of the word "good" in both eating and thinking the animal, a point to which I will return. Totemism is thus, not incidentally, a theory of human origin and identity: "It is because man originally felt himself identical to all those like him (among whom, as Rousseau explicitly said, we must include animals) that he came to acquire the capacity to distinguish *himself* as he distinguishes *them*, i.e. to use the diversity of species as conceptual support for social differentiation."[14]

The power of distinction—the ability to distinguish between self and other—belongs to both animals and humans, and must be one of the most fundamental expressions of aliveness. But the power to classify, to observe and invent a taxonomy of difference that is then named and numbered, is, as least as far as we know, chiefly a human attribute. Much of Lévi-Strauss' most important work constituted writings from field observations.[15] He mentions frequently in these observations how the science of classification—an attitude toward the world's diversity that results in hierarchical systems of relation—exists equally in both "civilized" cultures and "primitive" cultures. A scientific attitude toward the world, for Lévi-Strauss, is not a mark of civilization but a mark of human culture itself, because in order to have social culture, one must have systems of relations and ways of relating that control the multiple relations between what lies inside the human enclave and what lies outside. Culture is already a structuring force in a way that its putative opposite, the natural world, presumably is not. But the natural world, in a limited way, can be made to co-operate.

Structuralism organized, as Krauss remarks in the passage quoted earlier, "an imaginative space" for a certain mythical resolution of the opposition of nature/culture. In spite of the general failure, mentioned earlier, of the structuralist approach in architecture—particularly around the isolation of a sign system that would have opened it to semiotic analysis—architecture, like structuralism, clearly also organizes and structures imaginative spaces for mythically resolving conflicts between nature and culture. The transformation of raw materials into buildings, the concentration of energy fixed in built forms, and the transformation of animal life into architectural life all suggest a reconciliation and generative force toward the good, without any apparent reservation (without reserve). Of course, the word "mythical" is not irrelevant. Just as Lévi-Strauss' birds still stand in opposition to the use to which they are put, architectural space harbours forms of nature that cannot be fully assimilated: structures bend to pressures from site and climate, human needs take a nasty turn, materials express their instability, asymmetries apparently reconciled for the greater good reassert themselves and so forth. The bird somehow escapes the cage, not heroically or romantically, but through the slow inexorable openings in the opposition "nature/culture" itself.

It often seems, I am aware, that no sooner does a particular idea gain ground—such as a co-operation of ideas about nature and culture in anthropology, natural science, mathematics, architecture—than it is disrupted by some further remark such as this one: "The bird somehow escapes." It is as if one wants to have it all ways—

nature, yes, and culture, and nature/culture, capture and freedom, and so forth. This is true, in part, because nature and culture belong to us, our species, so we are free to roam in the domain of these terms. There is, however, still some content to this complaint. Among other things it is important to keep in mind, and make time for, an historical specificity that insists we look specifically at which cage, which animal, which escape (metaphoric or real?), under what circumstances, a specificity certainly not as well served in this book as it could be. The problem in this discussion—and the reason for disrupting attempts to settle the opposition between nature and culture by allowing the bird to escape—lies in the juxtaposition of two events, both paradoxically necessary to the existence of post-animal human and animal life (which professes to have successfully eliminated the autonomy of the animal, among other things), each inseparable from the other at what might be called the apotheosis of a post-animal age: First, Lévi-Strauss' bird, in its relation to other birds and for itself, is at our intellectual and material disposal, and second, Lévi-Strauss' bird doing something in the jungle apart from its work on our behalf. In the first, the bird is in the cage and the implications of that are immense for bird, humans, jungle and analytic method. In the second, the cage is irrelevant and the bird is essentially unknown in every respect, even in the respect by which the bird might be said to have regained some kind of autonomy. To stop this circulatory argument in one or the other of these places would be to divest the categories of human and animal of their formative complexity and to trivialize the pivotal operation of the nature/culture opposition. There will, no doubt, come a time when this opposition is rendered irrelevant. It seems premature to announce its death now.

Lévi-Strauss' discussions in *Totemism* add another piece to my earlier remarks on the transformation of the perspectival cage into the taxonomic cage. It is not incidental that architecture organized itself in the late eighteenth century as a natural science, with branches of development that signify organization, origins, and hierarchy.

The civic sphere evolves, after the Enlightenment, according to a far more specific architectural history, typological and material, rather than a quasi-naturalist history with human bodies landing and aggregating in space fortuitously, using uncoordinated technologies, drawing in animals as beast of burden or nourishment as needed. Post-animal life is animal life that no longer has its own field of expression, although still somehow existing "in the jungle," and human life that takes advantage of this fact. Animals and humans both reach, in the Enlightenment, a kind of structural gate through which most living beings eventually pass into structures. Post-animal life is mostly caged life—life inside fully realized structures—for both human and animal, and this is, almost, as fully true of wild animals as it is of literally caged animals. Post-animal life is also the swamping of the diverse field of life with the singularity of humanness: a calling out of human life. Caging implies not merely structure and enclosure but, in addition, powerful and productive cultural and political forces. The dwindling reserve of wildness—the nothingness we can't know signaled by the "bird in the jungle"[16]—remains poorly named and almost completely un-explicated, even, possibly, incapable of explication.

This structural gate or crossover of animal into human habitats is manifested in architecture, in a preliminary way, by what we now might call attenuation in built structures—the ability of structures to resist the import, if not the reality, of gravity. Although there are many developmental and historical scenarios for architecture from the eighteenth century forward, in almost all cases heavy anchoring technologies of antiquity are replaced gradually by lighter, more attenuated, structures. This implies, among other things, a distinct ecological shift. As Deleuze and Guattari noted in *Nomadology*, the mining and metallurgy that sustains this attenuation contributes to the disruption of the natural habitat of the animal. Foucault, writing of eighteenth century economies, suggests that, like developments in natural history that attempt to control the infinity of relations between things, the coinage of metals "makes those things that are brought into being by the hands of man correspond with the treasures buried in the earth since the creation of the world."[17]

The ability to frame larger spaces with lighter and stronger materials allows both a thinner barrier between the inside and outside of human structures—part of the opening to interior structures mentioned in earlier chapters—and the potential for housing a flood of movement and animate life, a kind of exodus from nature, that henceforth is invited in, and even trapped, by these structures. Nineteenth century natural history museums are literally built to exhibit a new captured animal population in the arrested forms of taxidermic specimens, fossilized bones, diverse cultural artifacts, dioramas. The human-animal is also included, although never as taxidermic specimens. Many of these museums still use the heavy stone building technologies of antiquity—in other words, they resist the attenuation that is technologically beginning to be available to architecture in the nineteenth century. They are also built in Neoclassical styles. These buildings still express the antique weight of the nature/culture opposition—the difficulty, for example, of bringing a hostile nature into a desirous culture—and continue to perform, in some way, as honorific and momumental structures that testify to the magnitude of this task. To put it another way, these museums feel the weight of the historically paradoxical need to contain a growing body of evidence for the complex existence of a nature, as it now must appear in culture. Thus, they are also the quintessential palaces of culture. The heaviness of these tasks fights with the lightness of modern materials for a long time. In Vienna the Natural History Museum and the Museum of Fine Arts, designed from 1872–91 by Gottfried Semper and Karl von Hasenauer, are mirror images that stand facing each other across a large open space. One building is for stuffed animals, the other for paintings, but they balance and support each other, through their architectures, across the divide. Both museums, as works of nineteenth century Neoclassical architecture, are indebted to the Renaissance, specifically, the Italian Renaissance, for the confidence with which they imitate classical structures. They have added, however, an expansive concept of interiority that belongs to the eighteenth century, and they take specific account of a modern constituency: a new public that makes of the Sunday museum/zoo visit a form of cultural solidarity. In addition, these buildings adhere to a *beaux arts* ideal in which highly ornamented buildings were constructed according to detailed mathematical drawings in which the interior of the wall, as well as the interior of the building, are rendered as equally available. There is no wild space in these buildings. Natural history museums take full account of the enormous expenditure of cultural energy on the collection of art, bizarre relics, bones and carcasses, artifacts from a century of visiting diverse cultures, digging around in the earth and foraging for specimens and concrete evidence to support abstract principles, such as the nature of biological time, in remote regions of the world.

A totemic animal is one that has already been vetted, so to speak—found, in its attributes or behavior, to be worthy of the comparative and metaphoric role it is meant to play in human culture. The animals in the natural history museums are, in this sense, totemic, although they also stand in some way for other animals that are not. Elected by humans as a substitute (a deputy, a bishop), the taxidermic specimen brings with it a continuing impropriety because it is absolutely and without any question from outside, from some other place. It maintains this externality as part of the active effect of its representation, and this externality keeps it from ever being at home. In some way the purpose of the animals in these museums—from what I recognize to be a problematic, even impossibly omnipotent, point of view—is to maintain an uneasy relation with home, to keep the line of reference to an original landscape, the infinite world of both perspective and of Enlightenment knowledge, open and active. This line of flight is always romantic, even in Deleuze, where it is a refusal of the striated architectures and the Oedipal containment of the classical building. And it is increasingly impossible.

But museum structures are the easy cases, because everything we need to know is, in some sense, on display. The harder cases are nineteenth and twentieth century commercial architectures, about which I speak only generally in a later chapter about Louis Sullivan's stock exchange building. And the hardest cases are domestic structures in which post-animal life dissimulates most convincingly as modern human life.

Lévi-Strauss remarks, in the opening section of *Totemism*:

> The first lesson of Freud's critique of Charcot's theory of hysteria lay in convincing us that there is no essential difference between states of mental health and mental illness; that the passage from one to the other involves at most a modification in certain general operations which everyone may see in himself; and that consequently the mental patient is our brother, since he is distinguished from us in nothing more than by an involution—minor in nature, contingent in form, arbitrary in definition, and temporary—of a historical development which is fundamentally that of every individual existence.[18]

Without reinstating the "reassurance" associated with regarding the mental patient as a "rare and singular species,"[19] states of mental illness offend against mental health by showing the fragility—and also falseness—of precise and stable states of being that we invoke constantly with words such as "I," "we," "here," "there." We are all part of the game—stable, unstable—but entire edifices, cities, political and social structures are built on the back of these words. The mere "involution" that throws these terms into jeopardy is, in fact, catastrophic to all human structures, however specious. The animal offends in the same way. The animal's "outsideness" is not some pure functioning of "otherness" that holds instructive lessons for ourselves, but a series of existential and ontological confusions that push life in one direction rather than another. There is no pure functioning of otherness; it is always only substantiated by its connection to *its* other, its "reflection back" of the self–other relation. As will become evident somewhat later in the discussion, animals are prohibited from this relationship. In architecture, Deleuze notwithstanding, the animal traditionally has been a metaphor for formal space, not for the human occupant. Alberti looked to the animal for its orderly and symmetrical arrangement of limbs, as well as its sensitivity to weather and site conditions. Unearthing the animal in the human occupant, or, rather, "extending" the animal from building to occupant, would be to risk breaking what has become a modern covenant between life and architectural form based on need, function, occupancy. It might also mean supplying speech to the speechless, mind to the mindless, content to the form. "Not our job," we, as architects, would say.

•

I have said most of this badly because, after all, what does it mean to say that we have reserved a niche—an architectural niche such as the natural history museum—for representing an imprecise and non-psychological living being that has been brought out of the wild? Totemic relations, according to Lévi-Strauss, have to do with the structure of the human brain itself:

> Associationism . . . was an original logic, a direct expression of the structure of the mind (and behind the mind, the brain), and not an inert product of the action of the environment on an amorphous consciousness . . . it is this logic of oppositions and correlations, exclusions and inclusions, compatibilities and incompatibilities, which explains the laws of association, not the reverse. [There is] . . . a homology of structure between human thought in action and the human object to which it is applied.[20]

As Giorgio Agamben, quoting Carl Schmitt, reminds us in the epigraph at the head of this section, all sovereign associations such as this between mind, structure, and object contain both incidental exclusions and profound and often unfathomable banishments.

The character of the relation between human thought and objects in the world (human or other), as well as human culture and its environment, an environment that includes other live beings, has occupied human thought since the dawn of the idea of culture, although structural anthropology redefined this relationship in quite specific ways. My question of "reserving a niche," however, has to do, specifically, with the history of architecture and architectural reasoning. One of the theoretical problems that fell out of structuralism and poststructuralism, and fell into architecture, was the critique of structure mentioned above: a critique, as we know, that had a unique set of reverberations for architecture, since architecture is, so to speak, nothing if not a discipline of structure. In anthropology the idea of structure, as Lévi-Strauss states above, belongs to the logic of the human brain as it forms associations that produce, in turn, human social and political structures, in some cases through totemic correlations. In architecture, I am suggesting a similar scenario. For some reason—we could call it loosely the structure of the body, mind, and brain themselves if we needed a seat of executive power—humans are magnetized by structure and form. Yet because architecture not only proposes to build structures in the world to house social structures (as well as being a social structure itself) but also claims for itself, at the moment it formally shapes itself, a particular kind of structural thinking that formalizes, summarizes, and postulates *exemplary* structures, it privileges or exaggerates structure in a way that ordinary social practices do not. Thus, if architecture can be said to "think" post-animal life, this thinking draws the animal into a human/object/world relation such as Lévi-Strauss elucidates, as well as into the problem of form, content and structure that comprises the architectural act. And because the animal is a living being and a formal physical entity, it provides a useful detour around the difficult problem of human occupation inside architecture, which is always the difficulty of form and movement plus psyche. Thus, the being for whom architecture builds its structures—the being architecture has in mind—is this being I have been calling the human-animal, which is the same name that Kojève gave to post-historical man,[21] although the resemblance is somewhat serendipitous. To summarize again, this human-animal is neither the human with animal drives of the nineteenth and twentieth centuries, nor the humanist human of the fifteenth or the eighteenth centuries, nor the modern human of the twentieth century. It is an architectural hybrid of some kind that intersects with large cultural formations and also with the weird specificities of biological life.

There are many problems with maintaining the theories of associationism I have been using to cross the gap between a work of architecture, human life and the realm of the animal. This is certainly a trope of some kind, although in the midst of crafting such a trope, paradoxically (and this is the balancing act of the argument), I must use, like Lévi-Strauss, literal aspects of the animal. The animal is a metaphor that one must, nevertheless, take literally in order to feel the full force of its meaning. A further problem is the common-sense arguments that would generally point to the complete implausibility of substituting any animal for any human in architectural space. "Where are the examples of this?" these arguments might ask. These problems are not trivial and yet they cannot, either, be directly addressed. What counts as evidence in this discussion is an enormous and interesting question, which I began to take up in an earlier chapter and continue to explore in subsequent chapters. The common-sense objections are true, as far as they go. But post-animal life is not part of the world of common sense; it exists in a precarious world in which common sense is generally a liability. Part of the force of the animal in this discussion is precisely its inability to fit the patterns of exemplary argumentation, historical or otherwise. This may sound like an avoidance tactic; it may even be an avoidance tactic. If the category of post-animal means anything, though, it means an interrogation of certain grounding ideas in architecture; a casting into another light of life, common sense, history, argumentation; and an inviting in of an enormous herd of complex and hybrid forms of life.

There have been many different theories throughout history of how humans come to represent themselves and others in their art and technologies, and, also, there are many theories of architectural meaning. To suggest the theme of post-animal life, at first, sheds light on only a small part of the very large and complex histories of architecture and the human being. It helps us, as I mentioned earlier, at first speculate on some curious phenomena: the almost complete absence of human figures in the representation of architectural work mentioned earlier, and, related to this, the simultaneous ridiculousness and pleasure of any resemblance between buildings and human or animal bodies. There is, as well, the difficulty of arguing architecture from the point of view of the psyche and the question of why such accounts routinely invoke accounts of spatial experience—narratives that are like dream narratives, revealing and distorted at the same time—as the primary way of marking the presence of aliveness.

# 10: SPACE:
## THE ANIMAL-FIELD



> Hence [there] is reason to admire at the wisdom of the Creator . . . in this wonderful contrivance of annually carrying off and burying the corruption and nauseousness of the air, of which flying insects are little collections . . . and especially the strange way of bringing this about in spiders, which are collections of these collections . . . flies being the poison of the air, and spiders are the poison of flies collected together.
>
> —Jonathan Edwards, *A Jonathan Edwards Reader.*

> If [post-historical] man becomes an animal again . . . it would have to be admitted . . . man would construct their edifices and works of art as birds build their nests and spiders spin their webs.
>
> —Alexandre Kojève in Giorgio Agamben, *The Open*

The mid-twentieth century, again, and a prequel to the question of asymmetry and a different theory of the divide.

Henri Lefebvre, Lévi-Strauss' contemporary, in his culminating work *The Production of Space*, builds the familiar China Wall between nature and culture:

> Nature . . . does not produce . . . nature does not labor . . . one of its defining characteristics [is] that it creates. What it creates, namely individual "beings," simply surges forth, simply appears. . . . Nature's space is not staged.[1]

In some way we recognize as true, nature and culture both share and compete for space, although only culture "stages" space, which frequently gives it the advantage. Sharing space means there exists, between the human world of labor and production and the "simply appearing" nature, an often fantastical but compelling potential for crossovers, associations, and contaminations. Nature and culture vie for the resources that space offers and suffer from its limitations. Roger Caillois' essay on mimicry articulates that one such limitation is the tendency of space to tempt the differences between things, to augur collapse. Gaston Bachelard, from a different position, attempts to capture everything in one mesh: "Objects of knowledge," he argued in the now canonical (in architecture) *Poetics of Space*, "are not intrinsically complex" but are "enmeshed in psychological complexes."[2] Bachelard's influence on architecture, particularly during the 1970s, was based on the perception, by architects, that phenomenology could finally deliver, to architecture, the means by which it could enact in space a complex human psyche. Consequently, architecture, for a time, hypothesized houses for the poet, towers for the mad, cities for the pursuit of the sublime. What was interesting about these projects, John Hejduk's in particular, was how they sought to establish a concordance between space and human consciousness, including the so-called "space of the unconscious,"[3] which architecture would be able to read and then enlarge upon. The architectural became a quasi-dream-like sequence of psychological thoughts that took the form, in Hejduk's case, of blunt civic injunctions and part-animal, part-human, forms—houses in the shape of animal bodies with human faces or conventional houses with no face but with high legs, ears or other protrusions. This architecture was episodic and used the tactics of its own figurality as a bid for psychological complexity. Using narrative techniques from linguistics, psychology, and cinema, it sought to write a spatial drama. The recounting of spatial experience by the architect on behalf of the occupant was particularly important in these architectures. Thus did the architect write the stage directions and script, and then build the theater in which the occupant enacted the play.

As a Marxist philosopher participating in the poststructural debates in France during the 1970s and 1980s, Lefebvre finds any idea of space "for itself" is problematic. Absolute space implies transcendental space, the absolute space of Descartes or Spinoza.[4] Lefebvre is interested in implanting specific bodies into space in a way that implies a reciprocity between, a co-production or counter-qualification of, spaces and bodies. Unlike the phenomenologists, he is not interested in accounts of psychological experience so much as concrete accounts of bodies themselves. In his view, the specificity that bodies carry with them clarifies, and makes less abstract, the concept of space. Animals, however, which he considers at some length, threaten to topple this plan. Animals, according to Lefebvre, do not labor and their specificity is, paradoxically, imprecise. Lefebvre gives the example of the spider:

> Marx wondered whether a spider might be said to *work*. . . . Is it aware in any sense of what it is doing? It produces, it secretes and it occupies a space which it engenders according to its own lights: the space of its web, of its stratagems, of its needs. Should we think of this space of the spider's as an abstract space occupied by such separate objects as its body, its secretory glands and legs, the things to which it attaches its web, the strands of silk making up that web, the flies that serve as its prey, and so on? No, for this would be to set the spider

> in the space of analytic intellection, the space of discourse . . . thus preparing the ground too inevitably for a rejoinder of the type: "Not at all! It is nature . . . which governs the spider's activity and which is responsible for . . . the spider's web with its amazing equilibrium, organization, and adaptability." Would it be true to say that the spider spins the web as an extension of its body? As far as it goes, yes. . . . As for the web's symmetrical and asymmetrical aspects and the spatial structures (anchorage points, networks, center/periphery) that it embodies, is the spider's knowledge . . . comparable to the human form of knowledge? Clearly not: the spider produces . . . but it does not "think.". . . [H]ere the production of space, beginning with the production of the body, extends to the productive secretion of a "residence" which also serves as a tool. . . . [The spider] is capable . . . of demarcating space and orienting itself on the basis of angles. . . . It is able to project beyond its own body those *dualities* which help constitute that body as they do the animal's relationship to itself. . . . We may say . . . that for any living body, just as for spiders, shellfish and so on, the most basic places and spatial indicators are first of all *qualified* by that body. . . . It seems that it is not so much *gestures* which do the qualifying as the body as a whole.[5]

The spider, without too much exaggeration, gets the better of Lefebvre in this passage. The multiplication of ontological inquiries into the spider's status as a living being is an indication of this. Lefebvre must first establish, for example, that the spider is not a "thing"—as if, in the twentieth century, there existed any persuasive philosophical way of putting into question a spider's aliveness. And then he must cope with the various problems of a non-thinking animal that still needs "something like thought" to do "something like work" and whose work is "admirable," the quotation marks thus suspending our admiration in the midst of it. Further, Lefebvre must establish that the spider has a sense of "right and left" and that it can develop "networks" and "relationships," and so forth. If the spider secretes a residence, as Lefebvre wants to argue, it seems to do so only to satisfy a general lack of co-operation of the animal in Lefebvre's bigger project, which is, as is well known, to form a "science of space."[6] In some respects the theoretical, philosophical and political problem of the spider is that it is all too much like human aliveness—it acts as if it were thinking, building, designing. Why not just say, as someone said to me in a conversation we were having about this material: "Of course the spider thinks, why wouldn't it?"[7] And then proceed to find out how it thinks, as we would proceed with any other thinking being.

Lefebvre becomes entangled in the venerable philosophical task—in which almost all become entangled in the end, the pleasure and company of spiders (E. B. White) notwithstanding—of trying to dissect the spider's specific cluster of energies and effects into parts that work with a theory of space and parts that don't work. This is, perhaps, more the task of discerning the meaning of spiders-in-the-house rather than of thinking spiders. Lefebvre's larger task is to account for—not simply describe but treat in a comprehensive analytic way—the "real spaces" of Greek and Renaissance cities. This kind of analysis, Lefebvre feels, has been muffled by the insistence in philosophy, especially poststructural philosophy, Foucault's work in particular, on the incessant analysis of discourse. His ambition is to unify theories of discourse (which he calls "modalities of genesis" of space) with the specific analyzes of "real" spaces: "to expose the actual production of space by bringing the various kinds of spaces [marketplace, room, public place] and the modalities of their genesis [discourse] together within a single theory."[8] For this task, the spider is uncooperative on all counts. Its secreted residence is temporary and filled with holes; the categories of public/private, domestic/urban, marketplace, room, public place, do not apply in any meaningful way; the web's modality of genesis requires massive ontological adjustments that, like the increasing contortionist quality of Ptolemy's calculations, suggest there is something fundamentally wrong with the original premise. As for the architectonics of the web itself, Lefebvre soon descends into unsupportable anthropomorphic projections, such as the notion that a spider's sense of orientation, of left and right, are evidence of a spatial consciousness not unlike human groups, while being unwilling or unable to say at any point that the spider is a web designer, without quotation marks.

One question—a recurring question for me—is why Lefebvre needs to bring the animal into his study of space at all. I asked the same question of Le Corbusier's use of the donkey, an animal that is trotted out at pivotal moments, particularly when Le Corbusier needs to establish the hman birthright to the right angle and straight line, in order to act as the all-too-familiar foil, the comical figure of crooked/dim thinking and irrational path-making. The answer to these questions/dilemmas seems now slightly expanded. Birds kept cropping up in the history of artistic and architectural representation, particularly with respect to the representation of movement. Spiders (and bees) keep cropping up in theorizations of architectural work, particularly with respect to questions of design, labor, and organization. Certainly, in all cases, these animals become important at the moment it becomes philosophically necessary to account for some kind of base, or core, meaning of a living body in space. It is important to note that neither birds nor spiders nor bees ever stand directly for the animal drives that we still associate, however loosely, with human sexual and instinctual life (in spite of the "birds and the bees"). Base life, in these cases, is not another word for base animal life inside humans. Such animal drives are, typically, represented as mammalian, not avian, arachnid, or insectoid. And although the donkey, a mammal, is not the usual choice for representing human sexual drives, its animality, in Le Corbusier, clearly threatens human rationality and, to use his word, "manliness."

Birds (continuing the theme of birds), such as those in Alfred Hitchcock's psychological thriller *The Birds*, or in Peter Greenaway's film *The Falls,* are less metaphors for repressed sexuality than sophisticated emblems of a broad human psychological complexity, parts of which have escaped the confinement of the head and taken the form of a bird(s). As Lévi-Strauss said of birds, a statement in which I think spiders should also be included, these animals serve the intellect. They are not bare bodies in space but bare "thoughts" in space. This distinction seems important to me in light of Lefebvre's argument, which takes so little account of salient differences in the way a donkey, versus a spider, might be said to produce space. Because animals, at least since the Enlightenment, have been radically generalized in philosophy and the multitude of other discourses in which they have made an appearance, we ultimately get very little service out of them in either metaphoric or non-metaphoric terms. The literal use of animals for farm work narrows, literally harnesses, the animal to a single line of thought, the furrow. The use of animals as meat, which attempts to use every single part of its body as a matter of economy, represents, nevertheless, a reduction of animal life to one idea, food. It is the same with zoos. The radical reductionism, through generalization, that we associate with animal usage of any kind, as well as our profound distrust of any discourse that might enter into the pleasure or company of spiders, keeps almost all thought about the minds and bodies of animals circumscribed by the pseudo-psychology of behavioral sociology or the wildly imagined but controlled realm of children's literature. It is interesting, though, particularly in philosophical discussions, that in spite of a meager and begrudging use of the specific complexities of individual animals, the philosophical tasks to which animals are put are enormous. They hold down, in a profound sense, an entire region of other life against which, and from within which, human life has found its way. So it could be said that animals don't just come to mind in some kind of crisis, such as Lefebvre's, where we need to account for the human microcosm in terms of the life macrocosm,[9] but they come to mind *always, continuously,* and in *all* aspects of human life and thought. Their roles and usage are dauntingly diverse, although rarely in the interest of maintaining a complex idea of the animal for itself. Animals, somehow and against all odds, are still complexly alive in their own skins, but the idea of animals is condensed and reduced whenever it appears in human thought.

We bring animals constantly to mind, in other words, in order to condense or sublimate them and, through this condensation we gain, presumably, various forms of self-definition. This is Derrida's primary critique of Heidegger's definition of animals as "poverty-in-the-world." "Yes, animal, what a word!" he exclaims. "[A]nimality in general" opposes human life in the specific. "Animal is a word that men have given themselves the right to give."[10] There are, in other words, vast and multiplicitous differences between a donkey and a spider.

Lefebvre is working somewhat later than the Hegelian theorists, such as Kojève, who, in the 1930s, explored the possibilities of "the death of Man," but the remnants of these debates are still at work in his thinking about animals. One of the most difficult questions in these post-historical discussions was whether once man has ceased to be historical and become completely biological he would become an animal again. The word "biological" refers to a range of freedoms and pleasures that, presumably, would be more fully available when history ends. Kojève ruminates, as I wrote in the introduction, that post-historical man, in becoming natural once again, would build like a spider or bee. After the end of history, "Man indeed is an animal, but a happy one, 'in *harmony* with Nature. . .' . . . he has plenty of . . . consolations: 'art, love, play, etc. etc.—in short, everything that makes man *happy*.'"[11] Post-historical human pursuits—which would lie outside of time, history, and action—would be mostly physical.[12] A purely biological human being, for Kojève, is, then, a human-animal that pursues animal pleasures and becomes natural again but is not possessed of any "animality—that is, of [any] purely unreflected-upon behavior." Post-historical human life no longer needs governance because it can live, in harmony with others, in a state of the "mutual recognition of free subjects."[13] I do not take up these discussions in any detail here, provocative as they are, but I want to note several things. First, as I briefly mentioned in the last chapter, the human-animal of these post-historical debates bears a superficial resemblance to the human-animal I am claiming for architecture. Both of these human-animals indulge in the possibility of animal existence with almost no animality left in it. Kojève's speculation, like Lefebvre's and, indeed, most philosophers in Western culture, maintains "nature" as a preserve that Man can retreat to in the event that all culture, i.e. history, comes to an end, but does not imagine that this nature is already full. The return to nature, in the post-historical movement, is a colonial return. The human-animal, during what I have been calling the era of post-animal life, is not a human that has returned to nature but a human that has evolved as a technological animal. There is no longer any meaningful animalness in this human-animal, but, like the post-animal animal, it is understood to be without an inner life. Also like the animal, the architectural human-animal is a subtractive being, one in whom something was once gained and then taken away. In Kojève, opposition remains in a post-historical world, as does self-consciousness, human wealth, and animal poverty.

It is also interesting that Lefebvre's difficulty in finding a way to speak of a spider's web-spinning is, in part, due to a kind of mimicry: a spider spins a web "almost like" humans build bridges; a spider's sense of orientation is "almost like" that of humans. This "almost like" is exactly the means by which architects have traditionally admired spiderwebs, beaver dams, and honeycombs and it, too, evokes a world of subtractive presences in which human work, minus humanness, which also means minus the concept of work, is done by spiders. The spider, in other words, has nothing to do with human work.

To pursue Lefebvre's discussion a little farther. The animal body, whether ox (the ox appears shortly) or spider, is crucial to the task of discrediting philosophies of absolute space, where the container (space) and the contained (bodies) do not "impinge on each other in any way:"[14] Lefebvre searches for a general theory by which bodies can be said to produce space, so that ideas of space can acquire both specificity and motivation, a reality in the midst of abstraction. "Can the body," he asks, "with its capacity for action, and its various energies, be said to create space?":

> [T]here is an immediate relationship between the body and its space, between the body's deployment in space and its occupation in space. Before *producing* effects in the material realm (tools and objects), before *producing itself* by drawing nourishment from that realm, and before *reproducing itself* by generating other bodies, each living body is space and has its space: it produces itself in space and it also produces that space. . . . [C]onversely, the laws of space, which is to say the laws of discrimination in space, also govern the living body and the deployment of its energies.[15]

In Lefebvre, the laws of space are both produced and verified by means of their reciprocal effects between bodies and space. The existence of symmetry in living bodies, for example—in a plane or around an axis, bilateral or dual, left and right, in reflection or rotation—is offered as proof of how laws of space produce bodies, and of how bodies are already in space. "[S]ymmetries are not properties external to bodies," he writes. Lefebvre cites studies by Hermann Weyl in which Weyl argues that "bodies . . . produce space and produce themselves, along with their motions, according to the laws of space . . . [T]his remains true . . . whether we are concerned with corpuscles or planets, crystals, electromagnetic fields, cell division, shells, or architectural forms."[16] "Here then we have a route from abstract to concrete," Lefebvre writes, and "this path leads also from mental to social."

It is clear that for such a theory of space to work—to get from the abstract to the concrete, mental to social—all living beings, as well as anything that exists as an object in the world must be included. And in order for such a theory of space to work as a refutation of the indifference of so-called absolute space, it is particularly necessary to show that space is counter-produced by a body (a spider body, for example) that exists *before* the production of material effects by means of tools and objects (such as in human culture), *before* the use of space as a place to live (as a habitat or milieu), *before* "reproducing itself." This body must be, essentially, a living being without hands (tools), psyche (intellect), eye (optics), reproductive organs, or mouth (speech). Agamben's blind tick, hanging from a branch, waiting for a warm-blooded animal to pass by, almost qualifies.[17] The spider almost qualifies, but only in a post-animal world, where one might agree to a partitioned animal that secretes or constructs a web, but where one is able to readily suppress other parts (eye, intellect, milieu, language, reproductive organs) as well as any idea of a whole animal in a whole environment, where the word "whole" is a pejorative term for separate, autonomous. As Stanley Cavall puts it, the "problem of the other is the problem of knowing the other."[18] To slightly expand my above statement, animals are beings that result from the subtraction of history and self-consciousness from humans, and they are also beings from whom things may continue to be readily subtracted.[19]

It is interesting, and confusing, that Lefebvre's evidence for a motivated relation between space and body—the existence of organic symmetries in crystals and living bodies due to spatial laws, for example—leads, with apparent seamlessness, into "architectural forms," to which "Weyl attributes great importance."[20] Architectural form is one of the concrete social realms that supposedly inhere in the abstract mental realm of space. And architectural forms, like organic bodies, follow the laws of geometric space. Here we meet again Galileo and Gould[21] in a different guise. Classical architectural symmetry has, on occasion, been used as evidence for the imperatives of spatial laws and proportioning systems, in spite of the fact that we know these surface symmetries cloak, in most cases, structural asymmetries. Architecture is a body that contains other bodies, usually human, but rather than the radical disconnect between container and contained that subsists between an organism and its milieu (which do not "speak to each other"), Lefebvre suggests an "immediacy," which he makes a symmetry, between contained and container—"bodies *are* space and *have* space." The requirement for a lawful spatial concordance between organism and milieu, connected with the "social realities" that Marxist theories of nature and production frequently mistook for a self-evident corroboration of mental constructs, implies that the concrete realm of architecture, itself subject to the laws of gravity, is further evidence of some essential symmetry between body and space.

But symmetry, in architecture, is ideological; it is not part of a biological or gravitational default setting.[22] And the idea of symmetry—even beyond the critique of classicism—requires the erasure of complex animal and human life. Architecture, precisely *because* of its connection to physical geometric laws—gravity, for example—is profoundly asymmetrical in its structure; its symmetries are, to reiterate, ideological propositions. And the spider and human, precisely *because* of mouth, psyche, hand, organs, eye, are profoundly asymmetrical. The presence of *two* hands, as Derrida noted, each of which moves differently, rather than "the hand" of Heidegger, is, paradoxically, the means by which bilateral symmetry in humans substantially changes its meaning.[23] Nor can architecture and the body, as I have been arguing, be made symmetrical to each other.

There are also other problems, in my view, with Lefebvre's theory. For one thing, the alternative to an immediacy between space and bodies is not necessarily abstract and absolute Cartesian space. Space can be, at the same time, contingent—formed at the moment of its use, territorialized, and then dissolved—homogeneous for all practical purposes and at a large scale, and yet discontinuous and heterogenous in its minute detailed operations. It can be subject to analytic deconstruction and synthetic construction. Maintaining an asymmetry between architecture and life is another way of saying that while space might be defined by the animate and inanimate bodies inside it, it is not possible to account for space in terms of those bodies, even if it is literally produced by those bodies. Space is, by definition, that which defines difference in bodies and objects and, by doing so, exceeds them. Space can envelop bodies and objects but in order to do so, it must also depart from them—unaffected, indifferent. This excess does not necessarily become a theology of excess. We have no clue at all to the spider's relation to space. It may be that Jacob von Uexküll, who was a biosemiotician as well as a zoologist, was right in arguing that spiders, as living beings, inhabit an environment-world that has nothing to do with any other living being or any other space-world. The spider and the bee offer us crude ways to form analogies about how labor and life conspire to "secrete" residences—the web, the beehive, architectural space—but the word "residency" may not describe, in any articulate way, where or how a spider lives. In this we might be said to be following the physicists, the string theorists, the "M" (membrane) theorists, the graviton theorists, the parallel universes theorists. In effect, I am only asking Lefebvre for a little more space to be placed around the spider, some continuing and unresolved perplexity, but not wonderment, about the meanings of its web as architectonic space or residence. Or perhaps I am asking for a lot more space.

In a later, even trickier passage, Lefebvre seems to situate the animal as an analogic medium. Still speaking of bodies in space, Lefebvre asks the question: "But what body, precisely, are we talking about?" To which he answers:

> Bodies resemble each other, but the differences between them are more striking than the similarities. What is there in common between the body of a peasant leading his working ox, shackled to the soil by his plow, and the body of a splendid knight on his charger or show horse? These two bodies are as different as those of the bullock and the entire horse in whose company

we find them! In either case, the animal intervenes as *medium* (means, instrument, intermediary) between man and space. The difference between the media implies an analogous difference between the two spaces in question. In short, a wheatfield is a world away from a battlefield.[24]

•

So we have come full circle, back to Lévi-Strauss' birds and laws of association between nature and culture. As Lévi-Strauss might say, human bodies are not independent of the company in which we find them, but this company is especially useful if it is animal, since the animal, after the eighteenth century, is understood chiefly in terms of differences (species difference) that can be used to analogize differences between human beings. The animal "intervenes as *medium*." Where do these animals come from? From what kind of place do they arrive in the human world? Horse and bull analogize the difference between knight and peasant and, in a somewhat companionable way, share the fields made by human differences. But this is not really a shared space; it is not on the same plane, nor does it have the same character for the animal and human. Lefebvre is interested in extending the power of analogy to the difference in the spaces occupied by these beings, wheatfield and battlefield. In this passage, the difference in human bodies is signified by the difference in each human body's penumbra of relations to labor, space, and other beings—i.e. animals, which are in Lefebvre's words, "a vulnerable flesh," "an accessible symmetry."[25] The animal thus stands as the instrument of mediation between two other differences, human and spatial. It would not make sense—although it would be an interesting exercise—to differentiate the animals in this passage not according to their genus and species, but according to the type of "labor to survive" unique to each of them. However, for Lefebvre and other scientists, survival does not count as labor; labor is part of the accumulation of excess energy that exceeds mere survival.[26] "To labor," in Marxist as well as Heidegger's theories, pointedly means to be human. It is odd—but, of course, the whole point—that the ox and the horse, two different species of animal with no genetic bond we know of, should be used as means for differentiating peasant from knight, who belong to the same species. It is as if we had repressed our own role in inventing taxonomic science in order to use that science henceforth as an apparently natural mechanism that would re-inscribe, over and over in every utterance, by means of animals, our differences from animals and from each other. And, indeed, something exactly like this was at work at the end of the eighteenth century—an enlightenment and a forgetting. But I want to say one more thing about this passage.

The laborer in the field keeps the company of animals that have been drafted into labor: animals who supplement the laborer's work and belong to a particular pre-industrial scene. Again, as in Lévi-Strauss' structural anthropology, the relation between ox and laborer in Lefebvre is not a relation between a laboring ox and a laborer, but between the ox that is not-a-horse and a laborer who is not-a-knight. The ox and horse, in Lefebvre's example, remain outside the wheatfield and the battlefield. Lefebvre's human and animal bodies seem to have reached a kind of pact; they agree, equally, to be understood as objects, material beings that are symmetrical, standing in fields at a particular point in place and time.[27] The human bodies, according to Lefebvre, qualify the spaces they stand in through their labor, farming in the wheatfield, conducting war in the battlefield. The ox, on the other hand, does not "farm," nor does the horse go to war. The ox pulls a wagon, the horse carries a rider; the spaces defined by their labor would not be fields but roads, paths, lines, and territorial space that might resemble a field, but has neither an agricultural nor a mathematical meaning of a field. Animals may be used as a medium of differentiation (indeed, anything whatsoever can be analogized), or as a kind of labor engine, or as a companion in space, but the specific space of their labor, the animal-field that exists alongside the wheatfield or battlefield, is radically incommensurable with the space of human. It is, for one thing, not a field but, instead, a space frequently formed by what one could call a running measure, a measure on the run, lines laid down at the moment of passage, lines of approach and of flight, with temporary moments of occupation that might change throughout different seasons. A hyena is different from a lion—one seemingly less settled than the other, one running in a pack, the other hunting in small groups—but it would not make sense to speak of either's habitat as a "field."

Symmetry, as a geometric ideal, emanated from antiquity and was reinforced in Renaissance humanist architectures and classification—a practice that differentiates and distributes beings through space in the eighteenth century. Classification, in particular, eventually organizes human beings in relation to space in such as way that animals, and the animal part of humanness, can be almost fully captured by the idea of space itself. I say "almost" because there is still, as I have been arguing above, a reserve. The animal's resistance to geometric ideals, its resistance to contributing the essential symmetry that Lefebvre claims for it to an agricultural field, for example, keeps the animal, in effect, always outside the philosophical category of space, always outside the field to which concepts of modern space aspire. Human beings inhabit these spaces without apparent reserve. Nothing about the wheatfield or battlefield, in principle, remains unknown to humans except the ox and the horse.

# 11: PRAYING MANTIS:
## TOTEM ANIMAL OF THE THIRTIES



The female praying mantis will choose to build her egg case, given the choice, on a smooth wire gauze or mesh with symmetrical openings rather than the rough asymmetrical surfaces she uses in nature. The beauty of the mesh—as Frank Gehry knows—is its simultaneous simplicity and complexity. For the praying mantis, the openness and regularity of the mesh would seem to mimic, but improve on, the irregularity of a natural surface. Some of this adaptation lies in the nature of the egg case itself—how it is attached to the mesh and the weird "life fluids" that make that egg-case. Henri Fabre, observing, writes:

> It is a marvel . . . whatever the support, the upper surface of the nest is systematically convex . . . lying along the axis of the nest and shaped like a date-stone is the cluster of eggs, grouped in layers. A protecting rind, a sort of solidified foam, surrounds this cluster, except at the top along the median line, where its frothy rind is replaced by thin plates set side by side. The free ends of these plates form the exit-zone outside [for the larvae to

> escape]; they are imbricated in two series of scales and leave a couple of outlets, narrow clefts, for each layer of eggs.[1]

The "solidified foam" or "frothy mass" consists mainly "of air imprisoned in little bubbles." This air is produced by the mantis whipping up, with movements of her abdomen, the sticky substance she secretes and into which she deposits her eggs at almost the same moment. This foam greatly increases the volume of the nest and provides insulating properties to protect the eggs during winter. In addition, what solidifies as a spongy covering for the eggs is also the matter that produces the harder, completely different, outer coating of the nest. ". . . [C]an it be," Fabre the experimenter asks, "that the Mantis really employs two different products? By no means. Anatomy, to begin with, assures us of the unity of the materials."[2] He continues:

> [W]hat a wonderful mechanism is this, which emits so methodically and swiftly the horny matrix of the central kernel, the protecting froth, the white foam of the median ribbon, the eggs and the fertilizing fluid and which at the same time is able to build overlapping plates, imbricated scales and alternating open fissures![3]

The mantis and the mantis' paradoxical motion ("chilling portrait of life's mechanical double"), "totem animal of the 30s,"[4] in its constructive ingenuity exceeds the wire mesh a thousandfold.[5] It *imbricates*, overlaps, structure on structure. In this, the mantis is simultaneously architect and inhabitant, able to literally "excrete a [complex] residence" for its offspring in (genetic) memory of its own place of birth. Fabre's description brings to mind Sanford Kwinter's observations on Sant'Elia's study sketches for Musei Civici in Como:

> [A]n architecture of conjunction, one that does not posit forms primordially, but rather stratifying systems whose expansivity

and acenteredness preclude classical individuated expression. Here the very notion of conjunction takes on its maximal significance: these are conjunctions not of buildings or isolated structures but of imbricating systems . . . at the molecular level of interpenetrating guided, rotating, or sliding masses. . . .[6]

Or, as Rosalind Krauss says of modernist painting logic, there is "[n]o figure, then, either; but a limit case of self-imbrication" in which vision becomes a form of cognition. The merest motion of the eye is simultaneously the formation of perception and space. Life motion, in these cases, animates/fabricates structures in a way that, subsequently, makes structure a perfect vessel for life processes, such as the protection and nourishment of the mantis larvae, the housing of a moving eye, the macrocosm of metropolitan life/urbanism of Como. And the mesh need not be steel or fabric. It could be synthetic, a polymer mesh like those used by the Tissue Culture and Art Project, which "grows" objects on these meshes, such as miniature "victimless" leather jackets and "disembodied cusine."[7]

To essentialize architecture in the classical sense, which a symmetrical wire mesh seems to sustain, meant, literally, to keep it from moving in any of these ways. Once the mantis stops moving and imparting movement—when the eggcase is frozen into its final form—life and architecture separate, once again, into their classical mode of animate versus inanimate. Architecture recovers what seems to be an unavoidable stasis, and the power of the oppositions inside/outside, alive/inert reassert themselves. The nest joins the mesh as a ground, the mantis and her offspring, the figures.

It is the simultaneously static and motion-filled quality of architecture that gives us what I am calling the "asymmetrical condition" between post-animal life and architecture. Were we to attempt to embrace an architectural type that imitated the mantis—such as digital architectures that overlap and blur wall and ground—and refused the tendency of architectural work toward stasis, this asymmetry

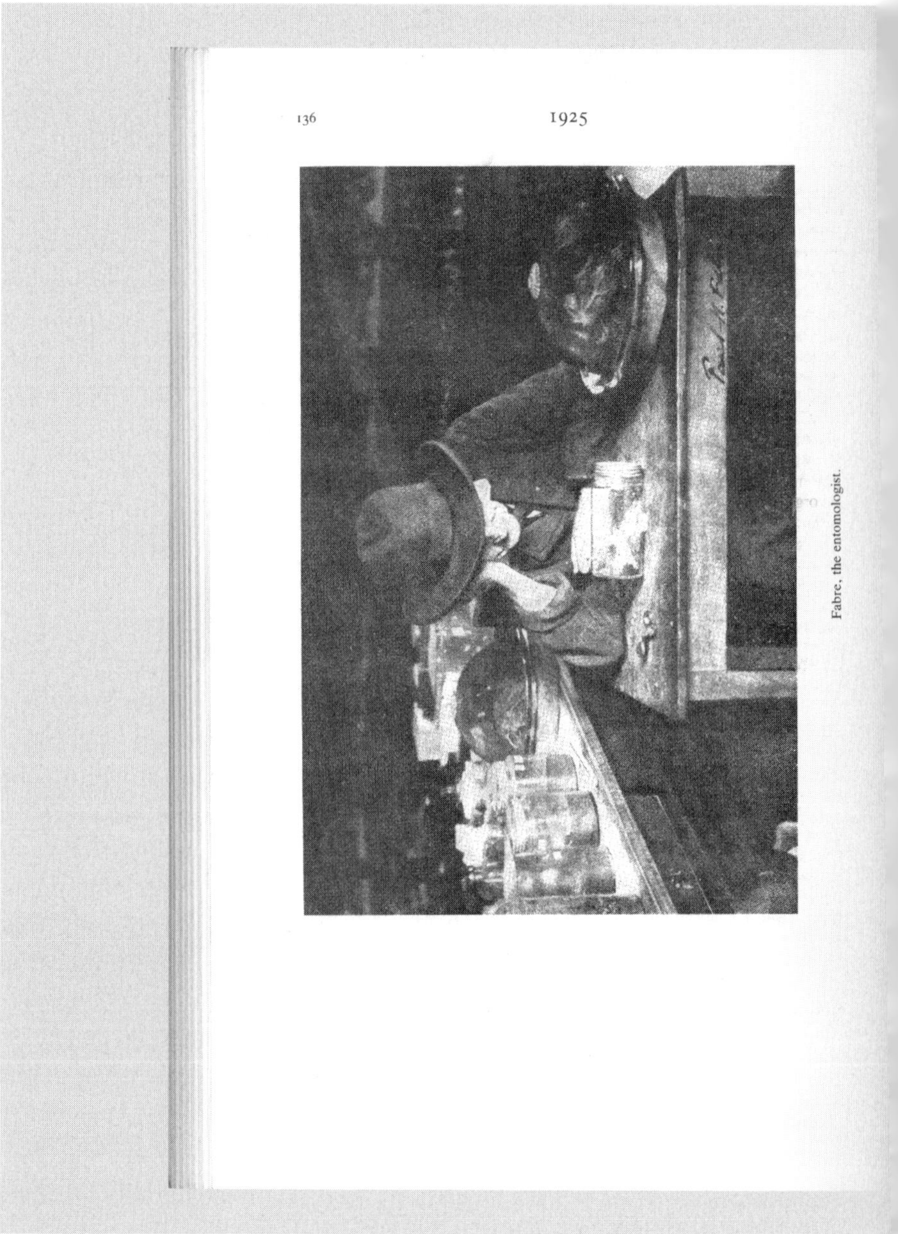




 **Figure 11.1:** Le Corbusier, *The Decorative Arts of Today* (Cambridge: MIT Press, 1987).

the agony of the previous age. We expended our manhood on seeing clearly, on grasping the meaning of what was coming, on spring-cleaning . . . and how! Around 1880 the factories were black with soot, the machines ugly and filthy, and they turned out cast-iron leaf-ornament and *papier-mâché* borders in profusion and almost for nothing. Industrialists with large whiskers extending railways everywhere were engaged in acts of mental cruelty, for everything had to be pushed aside: the peasants would fire on the trains as they advanced into the fields. The *Forge-master*, etc., Zola! etc. No art, oh no, not at all, not the least thought for that sort of thing. The poets were disgusted and indignant. Huysmans' *The Cathedral*. And also his *Against Nature*. The machine was hideous; the age is prostrate before it, the world was collapsing, etc. Protests. The past was regarded with longing.

The sweet voice of Ruskin – 'Look, here are the flowers, the insects, and the beasts of the Good Lord.' Soul of Giotto. Delight in primitives. *Pre-Raphaelitism*. Here in rational France the appeal to nature; analysis. The entomologist Fabre excited us.* We realised that natural phenomena have an organisation, and *we opened our eyes*. 1900. An outpouring. Truly, a fine moment!

Then Germany, working twenty-four hours a day, seized the moment. Her painters built houses – Darmstadt and after. But houses have no life without structure. All that great noise was for nothing. Nothing came out of it all. Still, it was a stimulus. The Munich people came to Paris in 1912. The Salon d'Automne. The *ensembliers*. 1914: the event that upset everything. Then it was just a question of bullets. In our minds also. Everything was said and done. The old world was shattered, trampled on, rejected, buried. Cubism, so profoundly serious in the hands of its authors, is evidence that everything was called into question. Around 1910 it already showed the pressures for revolt and the ascetic virility appropriate to conspirators bent on overturning the established order. This was achieved. While the affair took its course, technology could dare everything. The technology of building was purified. The framework became clearer.

A new conception has been born. Decoration is no longer possible. Our effusions, our vivid awareness of the beauties and power of nature have found their place within the framework of architecture.

Architecture is there, concerned with our home, our comfort, and our heart. Comfort and proportion. Reason and aesthetics. Machine and plastic form. Calm and beauty.

*Jean-Henri Fabre, who published his *Souvenirs entomologiques* in 1870–89, chiefly noted for his observations of social relationships among insects. J.I.D.

would not exist in the same way. The mantis produces, in her elaborate nest, other animals of her kind. She does not throw the nest open for random occupation. Her specific act of imbrication, in other words, is intended for a specific occupant, schooled in the specific nature of that space. Agamben mentions Uexküll's example of a bee whose abdomen has been cut away, that will continue eating honey even as the honey pours out of the opening in its body. The bee has been "taken by the food," Uexküll writes. The mantis and her offspring are, in some way, taken by the automatically processed structure of the nest. The relation between life and the space of the nest is thus not indifferent, in spite of the eventual presence of all the oppositions named above—static/dynamic, alive/dead. Animate architectures have been architectures that do not literally move but are produced by motion in much the same way that the mantis builds her egg case: as a series of both homogeneous and heterogenous surfaces and meshes that at one moment are wall, the next floor, the next ceiling, the next door and so forth. But animate architectures are also architecture; they aspire to a general condition of building just as human life aspires to a general condition of life. They have a kind of life in mind the human-animal I have been exploring—but they also have themselves in mind. Animate architectures also have, at least to date, a moment we find ourselves routinely cringing in anticipation of, the moment of "falling," and those are the very words, out of the computer with an enormous crash—falling away from generative motion and back into (this is why we cringe) the refused stasis and indifference of architectural work. "Imbrication" and the hardening of the dynamic into the static are present in both fluid and rigid versions of architectural production.

Among other things, I am suggesting that we re-admit a kind of stasis (not, however, in the form of ideological reduction) back into our contemporary digital practices, not in order to celebrate its certainties or exploit its promises, but in order to see *now*, *newly*, how movement and stasis negotiate their respective privileges. The point is perhaps simply academic. It is not reactionary, however. Into Deleuze's becoming, Stephen Wolfram's computational naturalism, and our ecstatic hopes for an escape from the classical, something like what Derrida would have called "turning the page on philosophy" has crept in—a repression of the form and structure within which we are theorizing the dismantling of form and structure. The mechanism by which that repressed structure comes back into play, I am proposing, is in a resurrection of the problem of "life" and architecture as a life-world. On the one hand, then, the asymmetry between life and architecture results from the virulence of philosophical and architectural essentialism (which has reappeared as a classical formalism in digital architectures) and, on the other hand, this asymmetry belongs to the anti-essentialist task of recasting the question of life away from its usual architectural terms, "program," "inhabitant," "occupant," and so forth, and into architectural form and form-making.

Architecture is technical—it seeks to obey laws of gravity, or whatever the laws of gravity have been called at any given point in history. Materiality has evolved a separate logic from life. And to pursue the logic of materiality (inanimate objects) it is necessary to generalize, in order to objectify, the logic of life (animate subjects). At the same time, life privileges itself and its own logic; life is pressured by its milieu, whether artificial or natural, whether internal or external, but its goal is to keep, to reiterate, the "first word." As Jacob wrote.

> Living beings are always imbued with magic to a certain extent. . . . They sum up all the forces of nature. In them, matter possesses miraculous properties: it is activated, influenced, transformed. With its train of images, metaphors and sympathies, the living occupies a privileged place in the world. From the outset it is placed above all other bodies. It is always given the highest rating. In comparison, inanimate objects lose their color and relief. The passage from objects to beings, from dust to thought, expresses a hierarchy of values as much as an increase in complexity.[8]

Questions of symmetry and asymmetry, particularly as they relate to movement and stasis, are philosophically venerable. The philosopher G. E. R. Lloyd argues that there were two types of logical argumentation in Greek thought down to Aristotle: first, philosophical argumentation by means of pairs of opposites: e.g. being/not being, one/many, like/unlike; and, second, argument by analogy, where something is likened or "assimilated to something else."[9] Lloyd is interested in looking at the history of logical techniques in philosophical arguments, but his book is unusual in its use of theoretical observations from twentieth century anthropologists, Claude Lévi-Strauss among them.

According to Lloyd, the relation of "pairs of opposites" that Lévi-Strauss notes in his treatment of birds in *Totemism*, which I discussed earlier, and which Lévi-Strauss attributes to an archaic, but not primitive, form of structural reasoning occurring in all cultures, is not unlike early forms of Greek thought. To briefly summarize where Lloyd comes into these anthropological debates: at various points in history, distinctions have been made between "logical" and "mystical" thought. The anthropologist Levy-Bruhl, in his work in 1910, hypothesized a "pre-logical" mentality in primitive cultures. This idea is discredited later by Durkheim and Lévi-Strauss, who argue that logical and mystical thought are ultimately indistinguishable from each other. One of Lloyd's questions is how to evaluate the various stages of Greek philosophy, from the pre-Socratics, who seemed to use a more "informal" logic, to Aristotle, who "is generally held to be the founder of formal logic."[10]

As Lloyd states in his introduction, Aristotle "put forward the first fairly complete theory of what may be called 'scientific method'. . . Pre-Socratic 'philosophers and the medical theories of the Hippocratic Corpus [also] attempt to elucidate a wide variety of natural phenomena."[11] His investigation seeks, in part, to discover what these pre-Aristotelian thinkers and practitioners "expected of an 'account' of a natural phenomenon" versus what we might call, in Aristotle, an early form of scientific reasoning.

Looking at various instances of Greek philosophy that support his hypothesis that "pairs of opposites" commonly occur in Greek thought, Lloyd turns to Plato's theory of Being. *Being*, in Plato, is, as is well known, opposed to *Becoming*. This particular example is interesting, and has been interesting since it was initially thought, because it defines, for human beings, an entire arena of existential inquiry. Here, Lloyd's examination of this canonical philosophical opposition, Being/Becoming, sheds some light on the role symmetry and asymmetry play in philosophical argumentation. And the example also explains more about what an opposition needs to do in order to work. "Being" in Plato means "divine and immortal and intelligible and uniform and indissoluble and ever constant and true to itself." "Becoming" means "human and mortal and manifold and not intelligible and dissoluble and never constant or true to itself." "Being" belongs to a different order of reality, mainly the divine, whereas "Becoming" belongs to everyday human realities. The incompatibility of the divine and human is rendered symmetrically: One is immortal/immovable, the other mortal/motion-filled; one is uniform, the other variable; one is intelligible, the other not intelligible. And it is also rendered asymmetrically: the divine is all powerful, the human subordinate; the immutable is truth, the mutable, less than truth. Oppositional relations depend on both symmetry and asymmetry. In order to render an opposition such as Being and Becoming, it is necessary to see a relation of equality between them. But in order to feel the weight of the opposition, this relation must be uneven, oscillatory. Birds, in Lévi-Strauss, are homologous to human life—sharing a structure of difference. Inside the homology, however, the the force of specific differences between human and bird drives the opposition.

In the case of biological life, the symmetrical/asymmetrical opposition is between the organism and its external milieu, which is also a relation between the organism and death. Part of the classical reason for the over-valuation of life, with respect to its milieu and death (an inanimate state portended by the world of objects), is due to the tautological fact that life is motion-filled. It is the presence of motion and mutability, the manifold vitality of life, that produces an excess of meaning on that side of the opposition. "Movement," as both a metaphysical category of being and as a description of information and feedback systems, has gradually overtaken, in contemporary genetics and computational sciences, the opposition between being and becoming. And with the dissolution, or gradual meaninglessness of this opposition, many other oppositions (subject/object, body/machine) have also begun to unravel. Even non-authentic motion, the synthetic motion of digital animation, for example, begins to make classical dialectical argumentation if not impossible, at least irrelevant.

The ascendancy of motion and movement in our thinking about architecture (and the world) is tricky. There have been, historically, multiple forms and definitions of movement and aliveness, some of which are meant literally and others metaphorically. At one moment, as we saw earlier, aliveness means adaptability and plasticity,[12] at another, life means resistance to death. Cuvier's definition of life included death.[13] Motion could refer to the relation of environmental forces (respiration, for example) between occupant (alive) and building (not alive); or the movement of the building itself, which, from the moment of its completion, as Aldo Rossi once characterized it, enters into a continuous trend toward disintegration and collapse; or the movement implied by representation, which necessitates a gap between orders of being and is a precondition for the existence of space itself; or the animation of space by means of physical forces such as gravity, electrical currents, connections to urban grids (sewers, gas lines, telephone systems), shear, wind loads, circulation; or the counterfeit movement produced by computers and film; or the movement of the culture, history and discourse within which buildings and architecture reside over time. At certain moments one or the other, or all, of these kinds of movement are referred to in architectural, technological, and philosophical histories.

The definition of movement specifically with respect to life, diverse as it is, is always classically framed and limited by its opposing term, death, which ends movement but does not end biological processes. The inertness of non-living objects, in which no "chemical activity" is exhibited, a totally unreactive state,[14] has been better understood in architecture, as Deleuze knew, through mechanics and the principle of inertia. "Inertia is inactivity and indifference," Canguilhem writes, "Life is the opposite of indifference to one's surroundings."[15] But inertia is also the tendency, in a resting body, to resist movement, or a tendency in a moving body to resist deviation—in general, a resistance to a change of state. Thus, it is a stillness or movement that is fabricated inside the potential for movement or stillness. Inertia acknowledges movement even as it resists it.[16] The arguments that link life with death or movement with stillness are reasoned in just this way, as arguments about potentials. The mechanical realm of architecture is endowed with these potentials, as is the material building itself.

Whereas movement is an indisputable sign of life, and life is indisputably multiple, regenerative, and hermeneutical, inertness is almost always either a rehearsal for death or death itself, an irreversible state, the endpoint of the arrow of biological time. The asymmetry between life and architecture results from an over-estimation of the value of life—which is the over-estimation of movement—inherent to the opposition life/death. "To live is to attach value to life's purposes and experiences. . . ."[17] The very "postulate that [human knowledge] exists—which is the first condition of its possibility—lies in the systematic negation, in any object to which it is applied, of the reality of the qualities which humans, knowing what life means to them, identify with life."[18]

In the postclassical age, an age "dominated by images and models of flux—not simple mutability but complex and usually in(de)terminable dynamics,"[19] classical philosophical oppositions have been opened in such a way that the terms life/death, motion/stillness still make sense but no longer describe opposing states of being. Motion and flux characterize death as well as life. We could say that, as a species, we are almost no longer under the control of classical oppositional structures, although this is, for the moment, too sensationalist a way of speaking to the entanglement of speech, culture, identity, history, and life itself. We are not yet the mantis-architect nor is it clear that we desire such a hybrid state.

# 12: MIMICRY

Birds are of the high ground and the sky. Mammals are, for the most part, of the middle ground and the animal-field. What more can we say about the low ground? What more can we say about the mantis, spider and other insects?

Uexküll founded the *Institut für Umweltforschung* at the University of Hamburg at the same time that quantum physics and avant-garde art were altering ideas and views of the world in the mid-twentieth century. Uexküll's investigations "express the unreserved abandonment of every anthropocentric perspective in the life sciences and the radical dehumanization of the image of nature." "[I]t should come as no surprise," Agamben wrote in *The Open*, a highly compact and thrilling account of Heidegger's long treatise on boredom (among other topics), that Uexküll's studies "strongly influenced both Heidegger, the philosopher of the twentieth century who more than any other strove to separate man from the living being, and Gilles Deleuze, who sought to think the animal in an absolutely non-anthropomorphic way. . . ."[1]

Rather than adhering to the hierarchies and classifications of classical natural history, Uexküll supposed "an infinite variety of perceptual worlds" linked together but unknown to each other. There is no single space, time, or world. The external place or habitat of each being, calculated from the outside by humans, is not the environment-world of the animal, only the environment-world of the human. Points of view—privileged in classical science and gathered around the idealized points of view from which sciences of objective measurement emanated—are plural in Uexküll's natural science, dependent on each animal's "receptor organs" and "marks." Agamben offers the spiderweb as an example:

> The spider knows nothing about the fly. . . . [A]nd yet it determines the length of the stitches in its web according to the dimensions of the fly's body, and it adjusts the resistance of the threads in exact proportion to the force of impact of the fly's body in flight. Further, the radial threads are more solid than the circular ones, because the circular threads—which, unlike the radial threads, are coated in a viscous liquid—must be elastic enough to imprison the fly and keep it from flying away. As for the radial threads, they are smooth and dry because the spider uses them as a shortcut from which to drop onto its prey and wind it finally in its invisible prison. Indeed, the most surprising fact is that the threads of the web are exactly proportioned to the visual capacity of the eye of the fly, who cannot see them and therefore flies toward death unawares. The two perceptual worlds of the fly and the spider are absolutely uncommunicating, and yet so perfectly in tune that we might say the original score [image, archetype] of the fly . . . acts on that of the spider in such a way that the web the spider weaves can be described as "fly-like."
>
> Though the spider can in no way see the *Umwelt* of the fly (Uexküll affirms . . . "no animal can enter into relation with an object as such," but only with its own carriers of significance [marks]), the web expresses the paradoxical coincidence of this reciprocal blindness.

The marks of the insect are like isolated gestures that reach out of one impenetrable world into another ("uncommunicating . . . yet so perfectly in tune") to acquire something and then are retracted. This is drastically opposed to Henri Lefebvre's human and animal whole-body-in-space analysis, nor does it share much with Lévi-Strauss' theories of association or the evolutionary developmental biological theories of the early twentieth century. It does share, however, something with Roger Caillois, who was working later in the twentieth century than Uexküll but earlier than Lefebvre or Lévi-Strauss. Caillois was also a member of the College of Sociology and a colleague of Georges Bataille and Michel Leires. His well-known essay about mimicry in insects, as instances of what he called "spatial temptation," argues that neither the independent body of the insect nor its gestures/marks prevents the mimetic insect from being drawn in, threatened, by the space it simultaneously forms and inhabits. In this, Caillois' theories might be seen as somewhere between Lefebvre's "unified" and Uexküll's "dis-unified" view of life. Caillois was neither an architect nor a zoologist. His interest in insects, particularly the phenomenon of mimicry,[3] reflect his interest in the human mind.

In his remarkable article on mimicry in nature, Caillois explores a condition called legendary psychasthenia, a pathological neurological condition in which a human subject is in a perturbed relation to space.[4] Legendary psychasthenia is a breakdown and decline in the relationship of the subject to the space he/she inhabits. It often manifests itself in clinical psychiatry as schizophrenia and in nature, Caillois argues, as the act of mimicry. The spatial aphasia of a schizophrenic person has to do with an inability to find a precise location in space because specific powers of differentiation, between figure-ground in particular, are missing. There are multiple spatial aphasias. Schizophrenia is among the most serious. Less serious conditions of optical aphasia and lack of visual depth perception, such as those recounted by Joanna Greenfield, the woman bitten by the hyena several chapters ago, make it hard to differentiate human faces from their backgrounds. Greenfield remarks

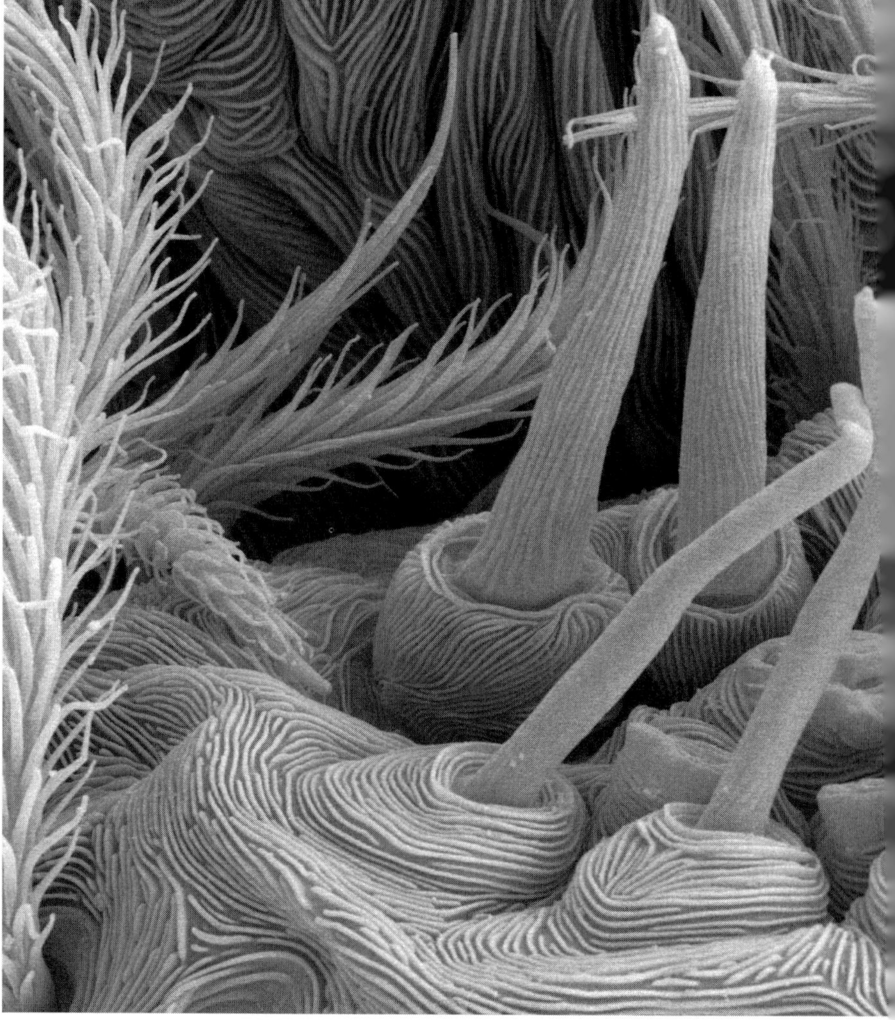





**Figure 12.1:** Spider Spinnerettes. Photograph by Diana Silva, courtesy of the Center for Biodiversity and Conservation, The American Museum of Natural History, New York.

on how it was difficult to identify who was speaking to her. She found refuge, in her own words, in the more recognizable formal morphology of animals—which, as it does not rely on the face as a guide, presents a less specific figure-ground identification than we usually associate with human perception.[5] In ways that we now increasingly understand in medical terms, the ability to see and live in the world is intimately related to the ability to differentiate form from background, figure from ground, pattern from body.

I will return to Caillois in a moment, but it is important to pause for a moment on this recurrent question of perception and identity. Kant was the first to articulate the fact that the world we go to, in order to learn things, is front-loaded with and constructed in advance, a priori, by our ideas about what knowledge is and what it might look like. This is a metaphysical predisposition, but it is also physical. We mostly only see, as I note in the introduction, the stars that have light moving toward us—those that have, as Norbert Wiener wrote in *Cybernetics*, a thermodynamics like our own. Contemporary astrophysics now has far more sophisticated theories about dark stars, for example, but there remain whole categories of bodies in the world that we, very likely, not only do not see but also don't want to see. Animals, in some sense, fall simultaneously into the category of objects we can and can't see because animals rarely look back at us in intelligible ways. And it is interesting, in certain theories of aphasia or identification pathologies, that living form does not primarily oppose inert form. Instead, living forms (animals) oppose forms with faces (humans). In contemporary animation technology it is still far easier to represent animals than humans for precisely this reason. Humanness—to identify and to be identified as human—is largely a function of the mobility of the human face, expressions of the eyes, mouth and so forth.

If Uexküll is even partially right, animals, even or especially our own animalness, are not directly available to our perception. Agamben's book opens with a fascinating description of the illuminations in a thirteenth century Hebrew Bible in which the survivors of the history of humanity, in its final hours, are represented by people with animal heads. "Why the animal heads?" Agamben asks. He provides, subsequently, a commentary not only on the possible "theriomorphous" character of "man." but also—in his perplexity (shared by other scholars) over the appearance of the animal at the end of man's history—on how we cannot see any animal directly, least of all the animal so notoriously lurking within us. Our possibly animal-shaped heads are perhaps the most emphatically invisible.[6]

Uexküll's theory of animal life also indicates that in addition to not seeing the eyes or faces of any other animal, we know nothing of any other environment-world. I have been arguing, in various ways, that architecture, which was the first art to make use of the mathematical construction of the human eye/space, in creating an environment-world for the human perceives/constructs that human as a body without a face—as a human that is "animal-headed," in other words. This body almost always has eyes, but they deliberately are not the eyes of an optical unconscious.

I encountered Caillois' essay on mimicry well after its appearance on the art theoretical scene, and, at the time, nothing about it seemed meaningful for architecture. The question for Caillois (and others) was: Why do some animals, insects especially, adopt protective coloring or protective morphologies? A common example is the butterfly with large eyes on its wings that makes it resemble, in a certain posture, a giant bird of prey. There have been a number of theories about this, not least of which is the idea that mimicry is a matter of self-defense. If the butterfly looks like a bird of prey it will frighten off its enemies. In fact, studies in the phenomena of mimicry seem to show that nobody is taken in by the dissimulating attempts of the mimic. As Caillois puts it, many remains of butterflies with large eyes on their wings are found in the stomachs of their predators. Beside being unsuccessful as self-defense, mimicry can make the insect vulnerable to all the perils that face the thing or being it is imitating. If you adopt the morphology of the twig, you're likely to get snipped off. As Rosalind Krauss writes,

"The animal's camouflage does not serve its life . . . because it occurs in the realm of vision, whereas animal hunting takes place in the medium of smell."[7] Mimicry is neither a particularly effective defense nor, for other reasons, does it allow the insect to be more aggressive. The question, then, for Caillois and others is: "Why mimicry?"

Caillois' discussion is interesting in general for its overturning of functionalist explanations—explanations to which the natural sciences, and architecture, have paid so much deference. But the point at which Caillois' article becomes riveting in architectural terms is when he begins to elaborate on the relation between mimicry and the crisis of space induced by it. Since mimicry is, through imaging, an act that toys with likeness and similarity between beings that are different, it pressures the space of differentiation that subsists between things. Space offers its temptations—to neutralize difference, to swallow up the living—to the mimetic insect edging toward its brink. The mimetic insect, in imitating all or part of another creature, affects to disregard the space between the two. Even if the insect is only pretending to be a bird of prey, there are real consequences. In the case of mimetic insects that convey only an image, not the morphology, of some other being, the whole animal—bones, skin, organs—is still poised behind the image, and lives or dies by the image. The loss of formal specificity and classifiable differences, by which we classically see, and place ourselves in, the world in the first place, is the triumph of space and the death of the living. As Caillois writes:

> From whatever side one approaches things, the ultimate problem turns out in the final analysis to be that of distinction, distinctions between the real and the imaginary, between waking and sleeping, between ignorance and knowledge. . . . Among distinctions, there is assuredly none more clear-cut than that between the organism and its surroundings; at least there is none in which the tangible experience of separation is more immediate.[8]

Or, in the same vein, Krauss' *figure-ground*: The "universe of visual perception, the one that is mapped by a distinction between figure and ground so basic that it is unimaginable, we could say, without the possibility of this distinction. . . . no figure-detached-from-ground, then no vision."[9]

Mimicry puts the distinction between subject and surroundings in danger, and endangers, therefore, the possibility of vision itself. But who is looking? The butterfly may count on distinguishing certain figures from certain grounds, but its eye, and the objects of its eye, are very different from the human eye.[10] The answer for Caillois would appear to be: *we* are looking. Mimicry is *our* game. The breakdown in the difference between space and the inhabiting subject, and between inside and outside, is, among other things, always an architectural crisis. In the face of the failure to "maintain the boundaries between inside and outside, between, that is, figure and ground" the body "collapses, deliquesces, doubles the space around it in order to be possessed by its own surrounds. It is this possession that produces a double that is . . . an effacement of the figure. Ground on ground."[11] The loss of the figure, which is also the loss of the potential for an "interiority" that informs the architectural whole, is a monstrous condition of space acting on its own behalf. The collapse of the body, ours and its, is an endgame.

Although Caillois gives no specific account of the theory of space he imagines, it is most certainly modern space, space with no ruptures or black holes in it through which an insect might escape were it to fall into the clear spatial interregnum that its mimetic posture bends toward. Modern spatial practices in architecture attempted to define objects in a clear, rationally understood milieu, but by doing so it also gave space a privileged status. Architectural practice—which partitions space so that people can live in it—is invested, at the same level and with a similar interest, although seemingly not with as intense a preoccupation as the organism, in maintaining differences in the face of undifferentiated space. Such an idea of abstract space, apart from its various manifestations, will prove, as always, problematic. The mimetic insect and the schizophrenic sit at the threshold of this dilemma: taunting the boundary condition of objects in space, visibly pressuring simultaneously substantial and airy boundaries. That this might be a moment of real danger for life, and for life's relation to its milieu, only makes sense if we can draw a more specific scene.

I once suggested—obliquely, because I was trying to find the right role for the animal in the world of architecture and was not willing to do what others have done, not willing to make the animal a fellow architect, admiring its built structures, nor to see the animal as part of a rich vocabulary of ornament that includes the vegetative—that architecture "animalizes" itself by maintaining a distinctness as object apart from the realm of the inhabiting subject. This is precisely like the distance and distinctness, but not autonomous separation, maintained by animals in the post-animal world. Alberti might have agreed with part of this formulation. This is the distinctness of a "living object," all of whose parts have been classified and named, but whose primary presence in the world is one of form. Architecture thus would act *as* animal in the sense that it makes culture and is made by culture in much the same way as the post-animal animal: by filling in the place of a speechless simplified other, almost without identifiable life attributes such as sex, gender, a face, just as, in our generalized perception, all animals in the contemporary world are without sex, gender, or face, meaning they remain un-constructed, un-revealed, in cultural terms. Of course, architecture is not alive and has no business in the world of a live formalism. We cannot, as yet, override distinctions between live form and inert form, except in fleeting and mostly irrelevant ways. Even if the coupling architecture/animal were meant as a metaphor by which we might understand something new about architecture, its absurdity prevails over its philosophical persuasiveness. The suggestion, at that time, was meant only to deal with one problem, one "surprise" already mentioned: the radical absence of the human form in architecture. The one form that architecture never assumes—except in perhaps one or two cases such as the Statue of Liberty or the Colossus of Rhodes, where architecture becomes confused with statuary—is the form of the human body. The strangeness of this fact is made only more strange by the existence of a classical tradition that takes the human body as a proportioning and scaling mechanism.

From Vitruvius on the relation between body and geometrical objects, ultimately, the inscription of the body in architectural space, has been dependent on an analogy where no analogy could seem to exist—an analogy between one thing that is in motion, psychological, dynamic and animate, and another thing that is inert, without mind, an object, inanimate. What architecture attempts to mimic are salient properties of the body—bones, skin, bilateral symmetry, the equipoise of the feet. "Mimics" in this case means the formation of an approach to, the formation of a desire. The desire for movement and wholeness compel architecture in the direction of body—a neoclassical dance enacted through the symbolic homage of the motif and the gesture. Yet the last thing architecture wants is a state of confusion between itself and the bodies that inhabit it. Confusion represents architectural failure, the failure of a claim to cosmological stature. Thus, the approach to the human body, whether inscribed geometrically as in Leonardo's man or Le Corbusier's modular, or literally, as in the caryatids (the special case), requires that the body become more biologically and psychologically simple, more animal-headed and formal, but less distinct than human beings.

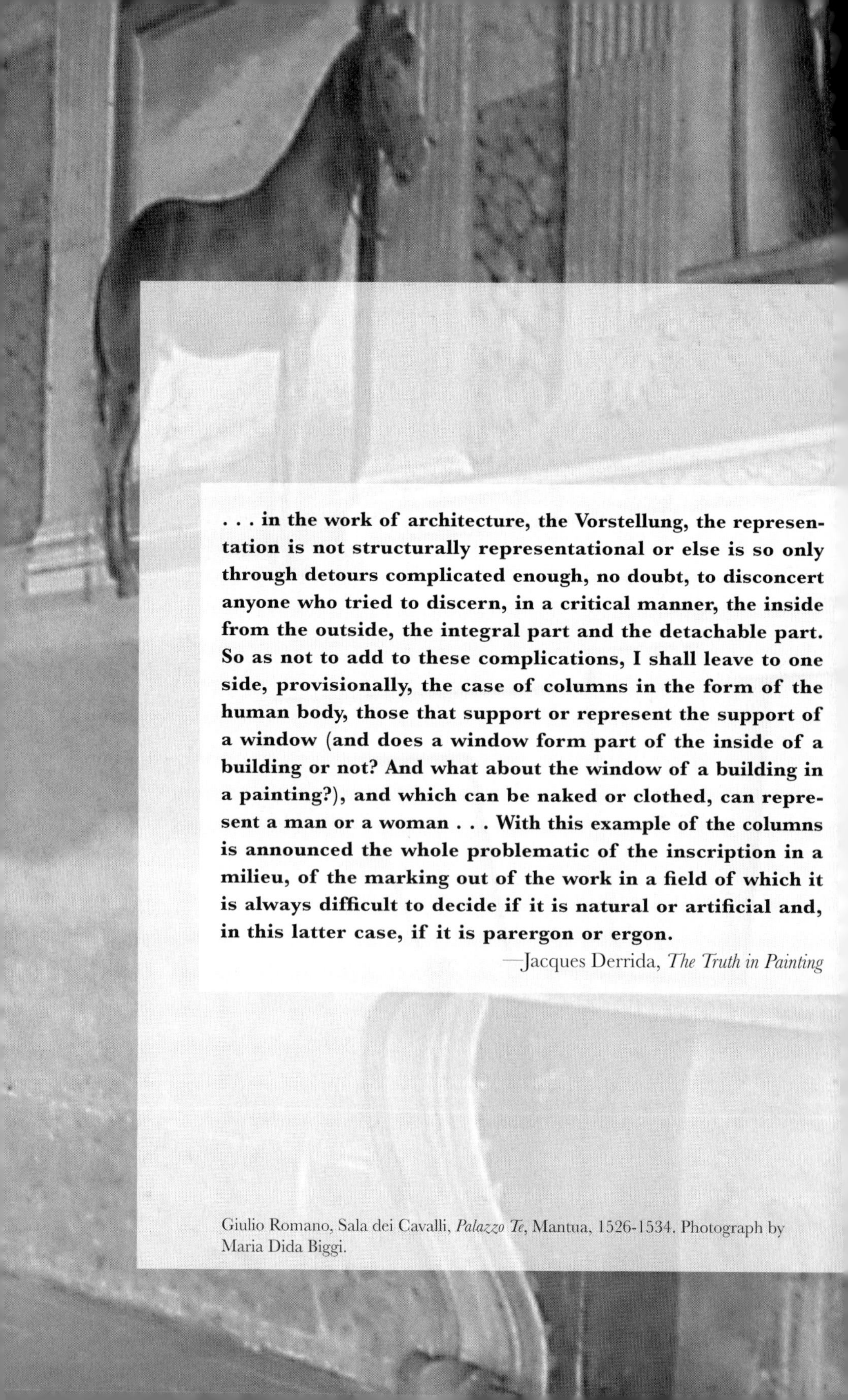

**. . . in the work of architecture, the Vorstellung, the representation is not structurally representational or else is so only through detours complicated enough, no doubt, to disconcert anyone who tried to discern, in a critical manner, the inside from the outside, the integral part and the detachable part. So as not to add to these complications, I shall leave to one side, provisionally, the case of columns in the form of the human body, those that support or represent the support of a window (and does a window form part of the inside of a building or not? And what about the window of a building in a painting?), and which can be naked or clothed, can represent a man or a woman . . . With this example of the columns is announced the whole problematic of the inscription in a milieu, of the marking out of the work in a field of which it is always difficult to decide if it is natural or artificial and, in this latter case, if it is parergon or ergon.**

—Jacques Derrida, *The Truth in Painting*

Giulio Romano, Sala dei Cavalli, *Palazzo Te*, Mantua, 1526-1534. Photograph by Maria Dida Biggi.

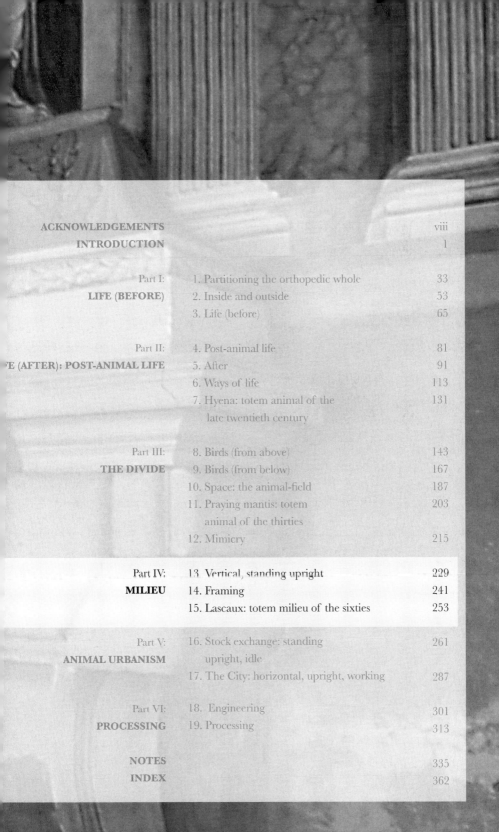

# 13: VERTICAL, STANDING UPRIGHT

"Milieu" has among its meanings the words "middle" and "mean." The middle of Leonardo's man, the (altered) navel, is the mean of the proportions taken from that figure that were sometimes used, with approximate results, to harmonize architecture with the human body. The animal is the mean between building and human, and/or the human is the mean between animal and building, and/or the building is the mean between human and animal. We could imagine all of these ratios in one form or another, and all of them contribute to the operation of the architectural "milieu."

Diderot's collection of words begins the nineteenth century, and the century ends with the "inventory of objects in the world," fantastic examples of which can be seen in the Paris museums discussed in the next chapter. The understanding of "living beings . . . through inanimate objects"—trying to fathom life by looking at the surface of things—begins to change in the late eighteenth century when, as Foucault remarks, the "character" of living beings is subordinated to function.[1] Fossilized bones are from the inside of the body but they are found outside the body, usually as fragments from a body that remains inarticulate. Even when evolutionary theory begins to concentrate on soft, rather than hard, structures, scientists continue to collect bones and hard artifacts for comparative purposes because, for a long time, there was no way of recovering or excavating the deeper internal structures that carry genetic information. It is only relatively recently that scientists have found ways to turn bones into gene pools.

The discovery of fossils but, more importantly, the new status of those fossils, had enormous implications for many of the disciplines that were formed in the late eighteenth and early nineteenth century. In the biological sciences, in philosophical circles, in literature, in civic and institutional life, and in the new human sciences of ethnology and anthropology, geological, human, and animal time is deepened. The "new human' literally emerges from the ground and descends from the air—from buried fossils and from Darwin's birds.

The French paleontologist Leroi-Gourhan's contribution to evolutionary literature, in the middle of the twentieth century, is connected to the two hundred year controversy surrounding that most crucial of bifurcations in the evolutionary tree—the bifurcation between ape and human.[2] The social and urban theories that resulted from Leroi-Gourhan's work in paleontology and anthropology, most of which are not read anymore, were influenced by work being done in the 1960s on metaphoric and morphological relationships between cellular biology and forms of human settlement. The idea of human settlement as a cellular structure—a unitized developmental organism—managed also to contain some of the lessons of social Darwinism that intellectual Marxists were interested in at the time.

Connected in an oblique way to theories of settlement were Leroi-Gourhan's main theoretical arguments about how humans evolved. These arguments are still influential in paleontology as well as in art history and histories of technology.[3] Most theories of evolution that predate the 1950s maintain that human beings were a slowly evolved form of monkey, arriving at various half-monkey and three-quarter monkey stages on the path toward humanness. Leroi-Gourhan theorized that the arrival of the human could only be an evolutionary leap—not a theological or idealized leap away from the primate so much as the arrival of a definitive "humanness" in the midst of primateness. Once the human appears, Leroi-Gourhan argues, its salient differences from the primate guarantee a different evolutionary path. The key difference, the crucial moment of departure from the primate, is the ability of humans to stand up, to maintain an erect posture.

All human fossils show erect posture—or, more accurately, humanness has been attached only to those fossils that show erect posture. The evolutionary significance of erect posture is that it frees the hand during locomotion and shortens the face. The frontality of the face shrinks its length and increases the acuity of the eyes over the sense of smell. These four things—the posture, the face, the eye, and the hand—create a cluster of effects that, according to Leroi-Gourhan, make up the distinctness of the species known as human. Further, he writes:

> [F]reedom of the hand almost necessarily implies a technical activity different from that of apes, and a hand that is free during locomotion, together with a short face and the absence of fangs, commands the use of artificial organs, that is, of implements. Erect posture, short face, free hand during locomotion, and possession of movable implements—those are truly the fundamental criteria of humanity. The list includes none of the characteristics peculiar to monkeys and makes the midway form of human . . . completely unthinkable. . . . Backbone, face, and hand . . . were indissolubly linked from the very beginning . . . as soon as erect posture was established there was no more monkey in humans and, consequently, no half-human.[4]

The leaving behind of the "monkey" is not a theological expurgation based on the problem of human lingering in the animal kingdom, which to the theological mind has always been a state of corruption and ethical threat. It is an evolutionary theory that contains a further theory about technology: that is, a theory about how human beings create a world simultaneously filled with themselves and their technologies and tools.

The moment of humanness that is marked by standing up is also, for Leroi-Gourhan, the beginning of a withdrawal of the biological human body from the process of evolution. In another words, no sooner does humanness assert itself than it begins to transfer its biological power to tools. In the case of *Homo sapiens*, the opportunism of an evolutionary being, which exploits its successes genetically, is externalized into the environment or milieu in which that being lives. This externalization is part of the extreme adaptability that accounted for the success of the human species, although the entanglement of genetic success with technological success is notoriously tricky. Speaking generally, human beings, more than apes, created mediating technologies between interior and exterior milieux—between body and habitat, body and landscape. And these mediations increased and eventually detoured around biological opportunities for adaptation. Thus, Leroi-Gourhan's very provocative theory of technology is that tools, and the constructions made possible by tools, are a series of extruded bio-anatomical and bio-neurological structures that eventually take over the evolutionary development of the human body. The increase of the human species—all evolution is based on reproductive advantage—was enhanced by the extension of the human body outside its own biological autonomy into inanimate objects that share, and sometimes take over, the evolutionary work. Technologies are always attached to living beings with reproductive potential, and as a direct result of this attachment, technologies evolve. But they evolve at a different rate (faster) and in a different way from their hosts.

Human beings have not stopped evolving as biological beings. However, to briefly cover the same ground again, Leroi-Gourhan proposes that a large portion of human evolutionary energy was redirected very early in human evolution into the evolution of tools, which are given incredible evolutionary impetus by the sudden re-posturing of the ape body into erectness, a re-posturing that frees the hand from its former locomotive functions, frees the face from the ground, and allows for the development of the brain. The modern human body, therefore, remains remarkably similar to the bodies of the first human beings; modern human tools, on the other hand, are radically different.

The end of this story is hard to predict. One scenario—Leroi-Gourhan's and others, including science-fiction writers—envisages that the body will continue to de-evolve as human tools continue to take over almost all aspects of human work, not just the work of the hand, but also of the brain. Tools still need, however, as the fantasy of the cyborg reminds us, human bodies and brains that pass along both genetic and cultural knowledge. Tools—if the computer, for example, can any longer be thought of as merely a tool—will also need to take over a certain responsibility for maintaining distinctions between, say, the realities and fantastical illusions that are characteristic of historical perceptions of the human body. It may do this, as well as other tasks it cannot easily do, by continuing to plug itself into living bodies, as Sanford Kwinter has theorized. The computer has long been advancing its own metaphysical and physical arguments by means of the interaction of software and hardware. The cyborg, a stopping point on the way to this transference of the body to the brain (and which combines software and hardware), will eventually give way to the fully wired offspring of brains that no longer need to be in that most ingenious and humble of containers, the human head, no longer need the generative contradictions between inside/outside that have attended the development of human beings since they first stood up. It will not be the robot, or robotic hybrid, that realizes this fully externalized state; it will be, as said earlier, the clone, who we will strive to make look just like us. An exaggerated future for the human in a late post-animal world would be the replacement of the slow editorial work of generational adaptation by the relatively fast editorial work of genetic engineering. Genetic engineering typically models life in the computer. This circularity, by which the inside and outside are no longer radically split and the tool makes us, rather than us making the tool, might well produce new possibilities for architecture; among other things, architecture may become the physical replacement for the obsolete head, that is, the reactive/interactive center of an externalized nervous system. Digital architectures are, in some sense, engaged in research and development for these new possibilities.

We are also only too familiar with the hyperbolic aspects of these claims, having experimented with them both before and after Leroi-Gourhan's paleontological version. Norbert Wiener, in *Cybernetics*, spoke in similar terms, as does *Wired* magazine today. From the standpoint of this discussion the question is not so much how wired our bodies will be in the future or how our architectures, for example, might accommodate this future. These questions about the future are exhilarating but, for me, still unanswerable in almost any terms other than the hyperbolic. Perhaps I am too mired in the philosophical problems and developmental questions that attend the scene of a vertical body, standing on the savannah, his/her eye oriented to the horizon line. Perhaps I am too captivated by the idea of a collaboration between the posture of the human body and the visual orientation of the human brain that produced both the human mind and the tool/machine, each of which still demands psychological and physical autonomy from each other, each of which demands its own space. Architecture seems to have been a crucial player in this process. It is not incidental that architecture has been built, at least since the Renaissance, according to the crosshairs of the vertical and the horizontal; that architecture has always embodied, in precise if somewhat regressive ways, technological culture; and that architecture has insisted on its likeness, simultaneously, to organic and inorganic life.

Following Leroi-Gourhan a little farther: the human body stands up, the hand is free, the brain expands, and the tool is formed. The developmental/evolutionary process that belonged previously to the biological body is subsequently given over to tools and technologies, "artificial organs" that extend and exteriorize the body in space. These tools are, in some sense, extruded from the musculature of the human body but are ultimately governed by the human mind, which acts, in a sense, as the recursive environmental niche into which the tool enters. The circularity of the process is not usually included in our thinking about tools. As tools take over evolutionary development from the body, the crude primal hammers and knives increase in sophistication and eventually both produce and themselves evolve into complex mechanisms that mediate between the hand that pushes a button, the machine that cuts the cloth and so forth. The brain, under this theory, is a beneficiary of developmental steps in locomotion and the technological effect of hands that have been liberated from the ground, not the other way around.[5]

Giancarlo Scoditti, who spent many years studying Oceanic cultures because he was interested in the relation of art and technology to culture,[6] has argued that both technology and art are so patently different from the body that it seems futile, and impossibly general, to link them together in some causal or instrumental way. And I think he is right to resist the deterministic, and somewhat one-way, aspects of Leroi-Gourhan's extrusion theory. Scoditti's "associationism" of the tool and the hand, not unlike Lévi-Strauss's associationism, is a theory of artistic representation and cultural mediation that evokes a more metaphoric relation between hand and tool, brain and external world. In any case, these are clearly circular economies and literal exchange systems. The production of technology depends on feedback, both technical and neural. I will return to this idea in later chapters, but I remain intrigued by the way Leroi-Gourhan brings the tool, hand, posture, face and theories of evolution into such an intimate, and such a literal, developmental relationship.

Instead of the body dropping out of the evolutionary picture, we could say that the body is everywhere extruded into a world that, for complex reasons, then produces a theory of radical separation between the body and the tool. The body, in other words, extrudes itself both materially and theoretically, as a site of difference from the material it produces. At the fantastical moment of evolution when the body extrudes its musculature, its nervous system, its psychological modes, its hard and soft systems into language, tools, technologies and material inventions, all aspects of the human world might be pronounced as simultaneously alive and dead. Ancient philosophical and psychological distinctions between inside and outside, tool and body, are reopened by this theory, and we reenter the Middle Ages, where the real potential for the monstrous comes back into play.[7] A theory of an intimate relationship between body and technology—even if discredited because it is, finally, too simple, just as extrusion is a time-honored but weirdly false and simplistic move in architecture—moves the relationship between architecture, human and animal into more hazardous and provocative territory. The metaphoric status of this relationship coexists with a more-than-metaphoric connection. That is, we cannot entirely erase the gap between the animate and the inanimate, but this gap is no longer as empty as we imagined it to be.

Leroi-Gourhan details, in subsequent sections of *Gesture and Speech*, the moment-by-moment development of the human species, showing how locomotion, mobility, the freedom of the hand, erect posture and a larger brain had a massive effect on the positioning of the human species in the evolutionary chain. The human being developed as a "general" being, rather than a specific one. As most paleontologists would agree, the general and broad adaptability of the human species is the reason it has, so far, succeeded so brilliantly. The interesting final discussion of Leroi-Gourhan's theory of technology, as mentioned at the beginning of this chapter, is the production of the city. He envisions the city not as some inevitable outcome of social or collective human development, but instead, as evidence of the continuity between human posture and human production.[8]

There are other questions. In the history of philosophy, it has been an ongoing project to explain the connection between mind and body because the mind is an idea that, at least in the West, has completely swamped and upstaged the idea of the body from the time for the Socratic dialogs onward.[9] And the mind's will-to-power necessarily places itself, its own image, above that of the body. The existential pressure we feel in architecture around the replacement of the hand drawing by the computer—as if the computer had nothing to do with the hand—is an ancient anxiety associated with this will-to-power of the mind. Before the computer, this anxiety expressed itself around issues of language, among others. The body/brain distinction, which is not quite that of the body/mind, does not go away, even as the brain and body extend themselves into the world. As Leroi-Gourhan puts it, the "relationship between brain and body is one between the contained and the container. Every imaginable evolutionary interaction may occur between them, but contained and container cannot, by their very nature, be identified with each other."[10]

When Lévi-Strauss remarks, in *Tristes Tropiques*, on the fact that "architecture" seems to arrive in cultural history at the same time as the idea of "empire," he is referring, in part, to what he perceives as the irreducibly empirical nature of architecture, a nature that impels it toward the outside, toward the external material domain, where it finds its resting place and makes its argument. The political definition of empire—an anthropological and ethnographic term for a coalescence of forces, an efflorescence of culture that results in specific hierarchies—has more than an etymological relation to the word "empiricism." Empires are created through a massive infusion of political and hegemonic force into the material world. Architecture routinely is used as one of the symbolic markers of this empirical dominance, since it can concentrate material wealth, natural energy, and political process into one act, one site. It also uses itself this way. In contemporary architectural culture, there are still vestiges of the division between "making" and "thinking," "practice" and "theory," as if these things had to be kept far away from each other in order to prevent very specific contaminations. But these things cannot be held apart anywhere in human life, and they cannot be held apart in architecture especially, a quintessential symbolic-empirical practice.

Yet again I am not saying it quite precisely enough. The evidentiary, empirical aspect of architecture allows it to shift its loyalties from one place to another; it is the model for and about reality, but it also differentiates itself from mere building by claiming a symbolic dimension. Symbols "both express the world's climate and shape it."[11]

In evolutionary theory, there are, of course, competing theories, some of which follow the hand, others that follow the brain. Leroi-

Gourhan follows the hand and the posture. Because of this, I think his theory is architecturally seductive; it seems to touch two of the most important spheres of influence in architecture, the tool-mind and the postural event which is the building. The development of the brain, as mentioned above, follows rather than leads the hand and the posture.[12] And, as is already clear, I am interested in the upright posture of the human as a parallel development to the "uprightness" of buildings, in which one can see not only the structural or morphological analogy but also architectural associations with civic appropriateness and human propriety. Against this uprightness, though, the question of horizontality poses itself.

The history of trabeated structures—the arrangement of post and beam into the various architectural orders—is a structural and technological history, but it is also the morphological history of the animal, which evolves by means of "quadrupedal locomotion . . . pillars carrying the body high above the ground."[13] This (mammalian) development and the evolutionary path it set forth was not the path taken by the anthropoid apes. So some part of architecture sustains an animal relation to the ground. Animal horizontality, which erect posture overcomes, is atavistic, a buried skeletal idea that, in fact, allows architecture its appearance of uprightness. Uprightness is the central attitude of architecture. However, the problem of keeping a building vertical is solved through bracing. Buildings do not stand upright through balance, an equipoise that the human body acquires by using the bone and muscle structure of the spine, although there are always fascinating moments of almost human-like balance in any building's structural solution. The relation between the vertical and the horizontal in architecture plays to the forces of gravity, but then so does the human and animal body. The animal, like the building, experiences a more stable relation to gravity by being on all fours, "the body riding high above the legs." It uses this stability to develop other characteristics—balance, speed, flexibility, stamina. In architecture, this animal stability attempts to root itself in one place, which causes it to move against itself. As Rosalind Krauss writes of moments of failure in human uprightness: "the architecture of the human will be transformed in moments of greatest pain or greatest pleasure . . . which [will assume] the animal "geometry," fallen into the horizontal . . . to attain the formal coherence of the animal's structure is nonetheless to descend into a condition of *informe*. For it is to blur the distinctions between human and animal.[14]

•

The change in representation[15] that I discussed in the beginning chapters of this book began at the end of the eighteenth century with the formation of disciplines—"positivities," Foucault called them—which had a cluster of effects, one of which was to break the parallelism between names and nature. Architecture, in some sense, uses this break as a way of organizing itself as a life environment, a milieu, that subsequently houses a living being whose own being has, more or less, just been born, but is immediately put to work. This moment, as is evident, is theoretically dense. Not only is a newly definite human being living in a newly definite milieu, but being and milieu are linked analytically (both are produced by the same epistemic shift), mimetically (both exercise sovereignty over exterior and interior, skin/surface/room/organ/air), organically (both need the structure of the other to survive), and metaphorically (organic metaphors are linked with technological and urban concepts—brain, cell, skin). As I also suggested earlier, however, architecture—in spite of being newly organized during the late eighteenth century in light of natural history, and, in the nineteenth century, struggling toward an aesthetic of lightness profoundly and paradoxically influenced by capital, production, and labor—is already on this path when human life begins, very late, its own self-definition. This is a biological being, *Homo sapiens*, but also the idealized humanist human for whom architecture, newly inscribed inside the new natural histories and the civic, secularized, domain, begins to design increasingly autonomous and public structures. The newer man is a being who looks at nature from ever deeper inside the enclosures of culture. The milieu is only waiting, in some sense, to become the mean, to be included, as a kind of fulcrum, in the life picture. Like a biological milieu, architecture pursues its own developmental path as a physical and technical practice during the centuries preceding the eighteenth century. And in the nineteenth century, it gathers knowledge about its physical and economic properties alongside the discoveries of the physical and political sciences. Unlike the biological milieu, however, architecture registers, more intricately and with greater consequences, not only the history of physical time, as well as biological time, the time of the life inside it.

The Renaissance, Enlightenment, and nineteenth century, are, along with the classical age, probably the most scrutinized periods in architectural history. These four periods, in different ways, increase and make more complex the distance of everything human from everything not-human. The nineteenth century "radicalization of the dividing-line between organic and inorganic" follows, as discussed earlier, from the analysis of the invisible, rather than visible, organic structures of life. The more the organic is differentiated from the inorganic, on the basis of structure, the more the human is differentiated from plants and animals. Making the internal structure visible, at this stage, leads to different conclusions than it will later, when the internal anatomical and organ structure becomes a molecular structure, at which point human and animal begin to reunite. "Seeing," in biological terms, goes through its well-known transformations from the eighteenth century to the late twentieth century: seeing surface identities and differences (classification and taxonomy), seeing beneath the surface (comparative anatomy and analysis of organic structure) and seeing inside the organic structure (molecular biology, embryology and genetics). The third kind of seeing breaks definitely with the first two in that it is fully instrumentalized and mediated by technology. By the early twentieth century the naturalist is increasingly not the one who tells us about nature. But we still need the naturalist, and the paleontologist, as well as the evolutionary biologist, to describe the surfaces and morphologies of the world as we see and manipulate them from our upright, two-handed, poised, moving, frontal, intensified optical point of view.

## 14: FRAMING

Giulio Romano's spectacular horses, barely able to be inscribed, in fact, ultimately not inscribed at all between the classical columns of a Renaissance palazzo, nevertheless are at home there, perhaps because the architecture and horses are (merely) a painted scene.[1] Romano is one of the most perplexing of the mannerist architects and master painters. The painting is clearly, on the one hand, a Renaissance diorama, and, just as clearly, inseparable from the architecture of the Palace of Te in Mantua. The horses have been disciplined by the columns, but the columns are given scale and a hyper-attenuation by the bulk and density of the horses. Each touches upon, but does not exhaust, the other. Vicki Hearne might say that each side reaches its moment of artistry not as a painting, but as a column and a living being. The fact that the horse is a military horse, schooled in dressage and somehow particularly available to this architectural scene by means of this training, would not change Hearne's view. The horse trained for war or pleasure cannot, in her view, be trained against its will, nor can it be trained to mimic the reason or lack of reason of war itself—anger, politics, greed, vengeance, mayhem. It is again, in this context, trained to some standard of art that Hearne would maintain is within the horse's repertoire of possible ways of being.[2] Romano's horses bring to a point some of the issues of the *Vorstellung*, the issues of taxidermy, mimicry, and the caryatids, columns in "the form of the human body."

It is commonly said of Leonardo's man that he is a figure of ideal proportions—a human form that aspires to the ideality of geometry. Taxidermic specimens, as Donna Haraway articulated fifteen years ago, aspire to a similar ideality that depends on the absence of viscera, which is, of course, the absence of life. As Haraway discussed, in the dioramas of the nineteenth and twentieth century museums, animal life is portrayed in idealized family tableaux that correspond with nineteenth century experiments with human eugenics.[3] Taxidermy is slowly dying out as we become habituated to image-based animals, although hunters still process the trophy heads of their game and an entire domestic taxidermy industry still flourishes in America. Typically, taxidermy retains the skin of the animal, but replaces perishable parts—eyes, soft tissue and bones—with various plastics, resins, or metal. Taxidermy, ironically, is an art that evolved during a period when the nineteenth century sciences of the internal structure, paleontology and comparative anatomy, were in their ascendancy. I say "ironically," because the one point of taxidermy is to present the animal as a calm surface, unmotivated and unstimulated by internal life. Because it would be impossible to reconstruct such an animal accurately without an understanding of its internal structure, the missing inside of the animal is dissimulated by its exterior, which is the true virtuosity of the art.

The benign naturalistic settings of the diorama in which taxidermic animals are placed—glass-enclosed "living rooms"—are typically *trompe l'oeil* reproductions of the animal's habitats. The always noticed, but repressed, caesura between scene and animal, scene and cage, is also an interesting instance of how the human eye assembles space by stitching together gaps and imperfections to create the illusion of a natural scene. It is the drama and beauty of the natural scene that one is after in natural history museums. Much is held in the taxidermic eye—the eye of the animal. The manufacture of these eyes depends on sophisticated techniques that almost always cast them in a state of peacefulness that would be induced by the occupation of a habitual and safe space. There is rarely any alarm or anxiety in the eyes of taxidermic animals; they are responding to nothing because they are, truthfully, entirely on ideological display in front of another eye, the human eye, that is deeply invested in—to use Haraway's words, "in communion with"—the animal as part of a completed scene.[4]

Taxidermy is not unlike legendary pychasthenia. It too tampers with the space between the animate and the inanimate and is a mimetic act that blends, in strange ways, nature and culture. Taxidermy is reserved for the re-staging of the animal body, never the human. It is sly in its politics, as Haraway's work enlightened us, but it is also safe.[5] It does not threaten what we see as the inviolate sanctity of the human body, nor does it offend what we expect, or desire, to see.

When I was first working on some of these issues a number of years ago, I happened to visit the Field Museum of Natural History in Chicago, financed by Marshall Field, the Chicago department store magnate. Like most natural history museums of the late nineteenth century, the Field Museum features extensive dioramas that are arranged according to the geographical origin of the animals—North America, Asia, Africa, etc. The uncanny quality of the stuffed animals in their meticulously crafted spaces, looking straight out of the dioramic cage with their glass eyes, to me has always seemed to offer a moment of intensive commentary on space and life. During this visit, something even stranger was happening. In the spirit of the new mood of animal conservation of the early 1990s, museums of natural history in the United States began to imitate zoos by building three-dimensional, rather than painted, habitats for animals that attempted to more closely resemble the animal's real habitat. This was a reversal. Formerly, zoos had copied natural history museums;

 **Figure 14.1:** Giulio Romano, Sala dei Cavalli, *Palazzo Te*, Mantua, 1526-1534. Photograph by Maria Dida Biggi.

cages of live animals were frequently painted with the same scenes used in museums. Now, however, the problem for museums became how to take the stuffed animal out of its former cage, the diorama, and put it in open, un-caged, space. The resulting "nature walks" in these museums attempted to enlarge the field of the animal, in the interest of education. The chance for conservation or salvation of the animal, which these settings argued for, was, of course, already long gone, the taxidermic specimen already long dead. Thus, part of the educational lesson of the exhibit seemed to be that conservation as an idea was unaffected by the morbidity of the animals in question, that three-dimensional—structural and sculptural—imitations of nature could redeem some of the false consciousness that surrounded the fake habitats of the dioramas. However, any attempt to critique this scene for its "lessons" is thrown into oscillatory confusion. At one moment we walk through the museum, appreciating, in a classical way, its architectural gestures, peering, in darkened rooms, into cages out of which elk, bison, chipmunks, lions, weasels, bears, birds, snakes and gorilla stare. At another, we walk though a jungle of fake trees behind which are hidden the same stuffed animals and for whom the museum architecture itself has become the vitrine.

Steve Baker, in *The Postmodern Animal*, argues that the zoo cage belongs equally to the evolution of technologies of capture and containment and to the evolution of representation.[6] Certainly, painted perspectives, classification, taxonomy, and the taxidermic arts cohere in multiple ways in both the zoo and the museum. With twentieth century innovations in representing natural settings, we begin to see a break in the concept of the cage, a thinning. Zoos began to use very thin wire in order to melt the cage into the scenery; older Victorian cages are now understood to be symbols of brutality and abuse, as if the idea of "degrees of freedom" made sense. Still, increasingly, the cage seems all-too-real. Virtual caging, which is the introduction of the image and image technologies into the museum, newly captures the animal in such a way as to finally, completely, obliterate the need for the animal itself, either philosophically or in actuality. The image carries forward, in a new way, the seduction and virulence of curiosity—watching the animal in the wild, the animal wearing an electronic collar or a camera mounted on its head, the animal planet that the cage promised but could deliver only in a crude manner. Yet, as Mark Collins, a student in one of my seminars, astutely pointed out, digital representation in museums has not entirely done away with the taxidermic animal or the diorama.[7] They linger, even in contemporary museums that have redesigned many of their exhibits into very sophisticated digital displays. His observations as to why this is the case are not unlike Haraway's. Taxidermy, Collins argued, continues to provide ways for humans to assuage large-scale civic guilt for the murder of animals. In this, it is like George Hersey's classical architectures, in which the animal is sacrificed and then restored through a surrogate structure. I discuss this process in greater detail in a later chapter on the stock exchange.

Taxidermy, as one possible existential condition of the animal, suggests, in ways I have been exploring, that the animal is not one body among many from the point of view of architecture. The animal in the post-animal age represents a special sphere of animation that contributes its vitality to architecture in limited ways—a being with a formal body, devoid of interiority, nameless, genderless, passive, without psychological import. These are not the "full" terms of the human, which is an informal body with an interior, identity, gender, and psyche. It is this animal, as I have been repeatedly indicating, that describes the architectural occupant far more accurately than this human.

To a certain degree, all objects refuse the human body in the same way that architecture refuses it. The human is the "user" of objects which means that objects are assumed to pre-exist their use and to be autonomous. More than any other object, architecture also acts as a frame as, to use Derrida's word, a *parergon*, a "surrounding work," to the human body. And, to recover Hannah Arendt's word for the more general surrounding structure within which we live, architecture is also a "preserve"—a surrounding work that is designed as a particular kind of geographical or ecological perimeter and field. Were architecture to look like what it framed and preserved it would risk an isomorphic confusion similar to the one Roger Caillois describes between the mimetic insect and space. In such a crisis of identity, we might collapse into our interior structures, losing our functional illusion of orthopedic wholeness, or dissolve into our outside structures, losing our envelope of space, our shelter.

The caryatids, or any other instance of the human body literally figured in architectural structure, are worth looking at with respect to these issues, and I want to touch on these hyper-mimetic moments in architecture through a few of Derrida's remarks on the *parergon*. Derrida examines the painting frame, in *The Truth in Painting*, as something that stands around, *par*, in excess of, supplemental to, the *ergon*, the "work itself."[8] "The column in the shape of a human figure," and the accompanying problems of natural/artificial, inside/outside, framing and supplementing, that Derrida enumerates as the problem of any "inscription in a milieu" troubles the definition of architectural work. Are these columns ornamental (outside the work), or structural (inside the work), or decorative (inside the work), or symbolic (outside the work), or all these things? There is an historical tendency in architectural treatises and practices to avoid these kinds of questions in favor of simply asserting that architecture is an *ergon*, a central work. However, every time we walk into or out of a building questions of "inscription in a milieu" and the *parergon* are posed. To fend them off, one could say that architecture has found a "safer," less threatening way of engaging with the body that it surrounds as milieu, and by which certain distinctions between inside and outside, body and building, ornament and structure are maintained. This safer parergonality would consist of imagining that architecture contains a human-like figure with the interior attributes of the post-animal animal I mention above. Through this substitution—in which the human being becomes, also, a kind of parergon, with a central animal interior and a human-like epidermis or framing—the building is rendered safe and free from spatial temptations and unhealthy acts of mimicry.

The column in the shape of a human figure, which is often embedded in the classical wall as well as supporting the classical porch, thus presents a moment of crisis for architecture. It opens up a territory that architecture has rarely ventured into, the territory of direct structural reference to the human body, among other things. Although we have an historical understanding of the caryatids as sculptures of human prisoners that are incarcerated, by means of their symbolic posture, in the building, the directness of reference to a relation between building and human body—not coincidentally, a relation that refers to an enormous weight borne on the head, a Sisyphean labor of bearing the weight of stones for centuries—is rare and confusing. Is architecture primarily punitive in this way? Do these sculptures supplement the columnar structure of the building or do they refer to those other, live, human beings who walk casually among their columns or, perhaps, the slaves who built them?

There are several other museums that are interesting to look at in light of these issues, for example, the Museum of Arts and Culture *(Musée des Arts et Traditions populaires)* in Paris, one of whose curators was Claude Lévi-Strauss. This museum is about to succumb to the current French idea of museum craft, best demonstrated by the new Galerie d'Evolution in the Jardin des Plantes, which has the by now obligatory interactive information technology, freshened-up taxidermic animals set in life-like settings, glass cabinets with butterfly species pinned and backlit, a pretty good café, and so on. The more obvious antithesis to the Galerie d'Evolution is not the Museum of Arts and Culture but the old Paleontology Museum, also in the Jardin des Plantes. These rooms and herds of bones—the old archive of skeletons collected by Cuvier for comparative anatomy studies—have been given back their skins and a semblance of aliveness in the new museum. The Galerie d'Evolution seems to stage (indeed it is very stagy) a return to a nature in which the human ancestor has only minor representation, whereas

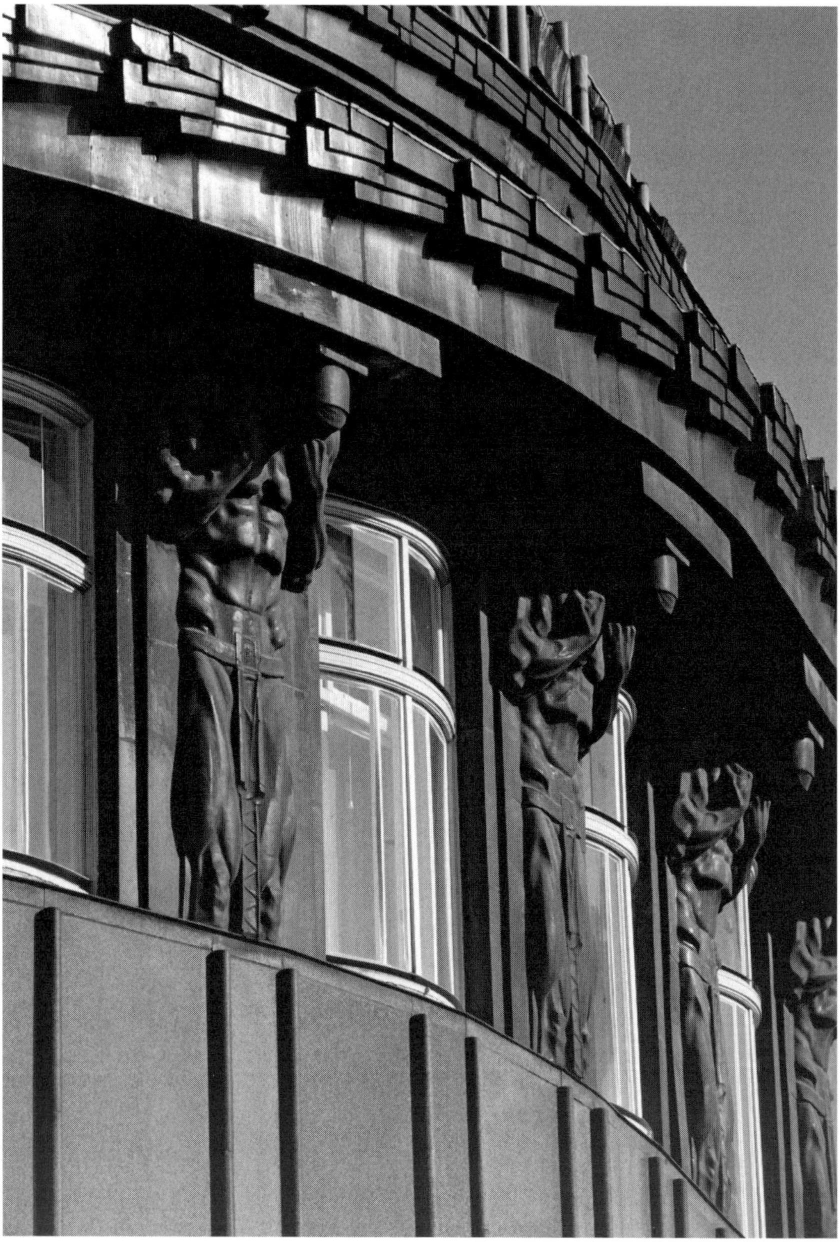





**Figure 14.2:** Jože Plečnik, *Zacherl House*, Vienna, 1904. Photograph copyright of Roberto Schezen/Esto. The telamon sculptures by Franz Metzner carry the beams of the building on their necks and heads.

the Paleontology Museum places the figure of the human, its skeleton, at the head of the pack, the triumphant leader of all life. Part of this reflects old and misguided theological ideas about a motivated evolution, but part also reflects how bones say one thing, human artifacts another, taxidermic specimens still another, and digital representations—moving images—yet another.

At a symposium in New York in 1998, sponsored by the Architectural League, entitled "The Architecture of Display" all these questions of display—which are always changing (slowly) in civic and cultural institutions such as museums—became synonomous, for me, with what I called "the problems of evidence." This is a longer discussion than I will present here,[9] and one that belongs as much to the history of criminology and law as to architecture, but the problem of evidence was well summarized for me in the natural history dioramas examined above that predated museums such as the Galerie d'Evolution and post-dated museums such as the Paleontology Museum. While the diorama-as-image of stuffed animals in a vitrine is picturesque, both naturalistic and calculated, the diorama-as-evidence is about a murder, that is, the murder of the animal for display purposes. Once we connect with this scene of evidence, a certain distance necessary to the spectacle collapses and a certain madness associated with the cultural display of stuffed animals becomes apparent.

The Museum of Arts and Culture, which also falls somewhere between the Paleontology Museum and the Galerie d'Evolution, offers us evidence of how humans are known not by their skin or body but by the evolution of their tools. In this museum, again in a darkened interior, French cultural history is recorded by means of the eerie display of tools and artifacts. These tools are not exhibited in a famikliar way, as a series of objects arranged on shelves; instead, they are suspended from ceilings and set on tables in spaces that seem cast in amber. There are no mannequins, no models or stand-ins for the human user; the plows, anvils, tables, forks and religious wands are often suspended from wires, precisely located with respect to the missing bodies that seem to have just left the scene. Part of the idea behind this staging was an attempt to exhibit the concept of utilitarian beauty: keeping the idea of labor, its history and economies, active in material objects while subjecting the objects themselves to the always desirous and dissipated attention of the museumgoer.[10] These dioramas of the interiors of French rural life during the nineteenth and early twentieth centuries—meaning both interiors of specific work spaces and the missing interior of working bodies—thus sustain themselves as a different kind of spectacle than the spectacles of the Galerie d'Evolution, which shows the new networked and informational skin of the animal, and the Paleontological Museum, which shows the residual evidence of former life, its inner structures. This museum, unlike the other two, brackets life in the midst of life's sublimation into objects. The central work, the live human, is absent—or perhaps has been displaced and condensed into the eye of the tourist pressed against the window of the glass display case. The various labors of the central work, however, are displayed as both a supplement to something missing and an end in itself, a technological object. In this, the Museum of Arts and Culture is not about the history of tools but about how our architectures frame hybridized occupants.

# 15: LASCAUX:
## TOTEM MILIEU OF THE SIXTIES

Lascaux is a Paleolithic museum of life and art.[1] The puzzling ubiquity of animals in human culture was Kenneth Clark's general justification for assembling a book about animals represented in art and sculpture. I say "puzzling" because the power of animals proper—and at certain points in human existence animals have been exceptionally powerful, both literally and symbolically—is matched by the human fascination with the representation of animals, such as we find in the murals in the caves of Lascaux and Chauvet, although this division between powerful animals and powerful representations rings immediately false. Representation—this is Baudrillard's point—proliferates in such a way as to erase, after a while, both the need for, and possibility of, the original animal and, after a little while longer, the need for, and possibility of, the original drawing of the animal. Representation turns the animal toward an economy of knowledge (enlightenment disciplines, industry, systems of production, data collection) that continues the fascination, but further reduces the animal as an animate force. Baudrillard used Lascaux, with its replicant tourist cave, as a salient example of these processes of "precession"—the simulacra that betters, in advance, the original. The most powerful animals in human culture, furthermore, usually have been the ones capable of being rendered as magical; capable, that is, of a hyberbolic form of symbolic representation. This magical symbolic power has sometimes been accorded to animals with actual muscular or venomous power, but just as often to animals with relatively little physical power: birds, for example.

From an architectural and artistic standpoint, Lascaux also is filled with originary promises. The portraits of bison, deer and rhinoceros are not merely images of prehistoric animals but ornamental adornments that follow the curvature of the rock upon which they are drawn, and, in so doing, draw out the "line" of the rock, separating it from the monolithic mass of the rock wall. They are structural, dimensional. The images use the surfaces of the cave's walls and roof as a way of reacquiring an anatomy—a bone and muscle structure—for the animal represented. Thus, a protrusion of the rock supplies the missing anatomy ("missing" because we are talking about a two-dimensional image, a drawing) of a rhinoceros' front quarters—a part of the animal body itself where a tremendous amount of muscle is concentrated. The reason for this is not clear. The animal is re-enlivened in the cave by being rebuilt as a three-dimensional image. Whether this belongs to a curatorial or some other impetus is the question that Lascaux poses. The idea of the cave itself, of course, both as an instance of natural shelter and also as a place for the enactment of art and beauty, belongs to architecture's most deeply held beliefs about its own origins and the origins of art and beauty.

This cave also presents questions of technology. The two worlds, the two arguments, exchanged back and forth inside Lascaux are the world of the hunter, who hunts by day and at night draws his/her prey by firelight as a record of the hunt, and the world of the artist, who hunts in order to survive such that he/she may paint as a record of his/her creative existence. The images themselves do not decide between their documentary or artistic status. These worlds are connected through the presence of both the technology of hunting wild animals with spears and knives and the technology of drawing on cave walls with charcoal. They are also connected through different processes of digesting the animal, literally and figuratively. Lascaux's walls were painted at a time when, as far as we know, humans understood representation not as a form of capturing and classifying, but as a form of spiritual homage. A continuity existed between the animal and cave dweller to which the acts of killing, eating and drawing contributed. In the case of Lascaux, it is likely that the animals are killed to be eaten, and are drawn or thought in relation to those acts. Drawing animals and killing animals have been related throughout human culture. Killing and art are routinely united not only in antiquity, through ritual, but also in modern history. This is why the hunt itself, particularly in ancient art, is often part of the tableau. At the same time, representation and the existential condition of the animal are not entangled as they become once animals are made to sit still and be named, which is the beginning of their general caged condition within, and existential extinction from, the human scene. The paintings in Lascaux are somewhat like taxidermic art; the animal is sculpted in three dimensions (using the rock as a form of "stuffing") and the reproduction necessitates the death of the animal.

That the animal is interested in its own survival is one of the premises of all contemporary theorizations of it. In *The Postmodern Animal*—a survey of different treatments of the animal in contemporary art[2]—the existential difficulty of the animal in art, in which killing and representation are intimately related, becomes the main focus. Audubon's elephant folio *Birds of America* cost forty thousand dollars when it first came out in 1840. He had meticulously drawn birds, hundreds of them, most of which he killed and "rearranged" into tableaux. The existential status of the animal—its survival, the conditions of its survival—becomes the primary question that dominates the many different postmodern artistic attitudes toward the animal: the understanding of the animal as radical other; animal as emblem of a natural nature;

environmental/ecological attitudes toward the animal; the animal as projection screen; the animal as embodiment of the body; the "animal-endorsing" and "animal-skeptical,"[3] and so forth. In postmodern art, the difficulty of maintaining a classical and authoritative relation to authorship, self-identity, humanness, animalness, and the difference between what is alive and what is dead makes the animal a particularly fraught, but strangely appropriate, subject and object of art. Even as the animal is cut up, stuffed, painted, alluded to, revered and vilified in contemporary art—often cited as a form of understanding—a preoccupation of this art is with maintaining a line of reference to the animal as a being whose existential status in the human world is threatened. In modernist art, the art of Henry Moore, for example, the problem of animal ongoingness was more casual.[4]

Aside from the question of absolute survival, one of the paradoxes, which is also a morass, is that the animal, even the most fugitive, is a being that can be made representationally and categorically precise in the contemporary world, but whose being, whose place in the post-animal world, is always imprecise. The extreme and luminous beauty of wild animals, such as lions, is a precise beauty with an opaque interior. To put it another way, the animal fills a particular existential niche that is somehow reserved for an imprecise live being with an precise form, impenetrable psyche, and no language; in Heidegger's terms, a place of no being at all. This "precise imprecision" of the animal accounts for both its ubiquity as representation in human culture, and its vulnerability and diverse amorphous effects.[5] In the same way, autistic, deaf, aphasic or otherwise physically or mentally handicapped people are also understood to be imprecise, as if they did not belong to the human race in a full way, even if the specific pathology is not in itself about locating identity, such as schizophrenia or autism might be.

**Chicago showed us the way . . .**

—J.M. Coetzee, *The Lives of Animals*

Rem Koolhaas, *Ville Nouvelle Melun-Sénart*, France, Competition, 1987. Courtesy of the Office of Metropolitan Architecture.

# 16: STOCK EXCHANGE:
## STANDING UPRIGHT, IDLE



> It is clear, in any case, that mathematical order imposed upon stone is really the culmination of the evolution of earthly forms, whose direction is indicated within the biological order by the passage from the simian to the human form, the latter already displaying all the elements of architecture. Man would seem to represent merely an intermediary stage within the morphological development between monkey and building.
>
> —Georges Bataille,
> *"Architecture," in Documents*

One room, the second-floor trading room, of Louis Sullivan's Stock Exchange Building (1863) in Chicago, has been preserved (1977) in the Chicago Art Institute for museum visitors to see and for the museum to use for banquets and fund-raising events.[1] Housing architecture, or parts of architecture, in a museum has always been odd. Short of leaving architectural fragments lying around where they fell—the scenic architectural ruin that becomes its own museum—architecture is typically brought into the museum in miniaturized, schematic, or cinematic form;

as a model, drawing, photograph, or film. On some occasions—the Stock Exchange trading room is one such occasion—architectural parts are brought into a museum context and completely reconstructed at the original scale. The Pergamon Museum in Berlin houses pilfered building fragments (gates, walls) from Babylon that seem almost plausible architecturally, perhaps because the museum building itself and the colossal fragments are in rooms whose scale is already so large that nothing but architectural remains can be imagined inside them. Even the reconstruction of Babylonian walls inside the Pergamon does not complete an architectural scene; the remains are still artifacts, pieces of a larger, missing, whole. The Pergamon houses trophy architectural fragments, some of which were collected during Heinrich Schliemann's colonialist adventures in Greece and the Middle East. Schliemann was an import-export merchant and amateur archaeologist who unearthed the ancient site of Troy. The Pergamon is not meant to be a naturalization of ancient architectures into another context: the Babylonian remains are not meant to be used or inhabited in any way. The Pergamon was part of the museum island in East Berlin—maintained but stranded from the Western idea of museum culture that lay on the other side of the Berlin wall. West Berlin itself was formerly an island of the West inside a country of the East. The eastern part of the city has been reunited with its Western half, as has the Pergamon. These types of irony are not unusual in either art or architectural museums.

The peculiar thing about Sullivan's trading room in the Art Institute of Chicago is that it is not a ruin, nor does it act as a building fragment, nor does it act as a fully scaled built artifact in a larger system of cultural classification. Its assimilation into the Art Institute is virtually complete and the building from which it came, the Stock Exchange Building, is only incidentally present in archival photographs and a few other (albeit large) fragments; for example, the former entrance arch to the Exchange is now a free-standing arch placed outside the back of the Art Institute.[2] The question therefore arises with respect to the restored trading room: What is it?

The history of stock exchanges, and stock exchange buildings, in America—particularly Chicago and New York—is, as might be expected, largely a history of how money and architecture collaborate to produce buildings, often highly ornamented, where cattle, sheep, pigs, chickens, corn, wheat, soybeans and countless other products of American agriculture and commerce are transmogrified into speculative capital that, in turn, fuels the building of public and private structures and infrastructures: office buildings, department stores, roads, schools, utility companies and so forth. The character of this exchange is both abstract and concrete,[3] and symbolic and material aspects of architecture are often uniquely engaged by these building commissions. Certainly, some of the usual questions—such as how to address questions of power and wealth architecturally—attend these projects. The Chicago Stock Exchange was built during the 1893 financial panic and was designed as a thirteen-floor office building with only one large room, the trading room, reserved for the Stock Exchange itself. The "Exchange was given a fifteen-year, rent-free lease" partly in exchange for the use of its name as the name of the building. Sullivan's extraordinary use of space and ornament in the design of the trading room—he saw ornament as integral to the architectural structure and form—figure somewhat more prominently in accounts of the building than theories of wealth and capital. The question of ornament will return, but I want to go back to Bataille's quote at the head of this chapter before proceeding.[4]

Georges Bataille's "theory of evolution," which extends the reach of Darwinian evolution into the mineral realm (stone), places architecture at the end of the typical monkey–human evolutionary development. The human already displays "all the elements of architecture." This ladder of development by which, as Denis Hollier observes in *Against Architecture*, humans are imprisoned in their own form (breaking with the monkey line) and then imprisoned in exterior forms (architecture) is a matter of social and political, but also architectural, interest to Bataille.[5] Hollier remarks on the evolution of the slaughterhouse, from a place where time and money are in a kind of equilibrium, to the art museum, where time

 **Figure 16.1:** *Members of the Chicago Stock Exchange in the Trading Room*, circa 1894. Courtesy of the Art Institute of Chicago.

**Figure 16.2:** Adler & Sullivan *Chicago Stock Exchange Trading Room.* Photograph by Richard Nickel, Courtesy of the Richard Nickel Committee, Chicago, Illinois.

and money are "wasted." This succession illustrates a single economic continuum in which Bataille's theory of *dépense*, translated usually as "loss" or "expenditure," plays a significant part. Hollier writes:

> The question thus is one of knowing whether a theory of *dépense* can work without the difference between high and low, between dirty [slaughterhouse] and clean [museum]; whether a theory of *dépense* is not, first of all, a theory of the difference between two expenditures, a proper clean one and an improper dirty one.[6]

The stock exchange, as a system of expenditure that brokers the dirty to make it clean and is tied to repositories of wealth and culture, might thus be placed somewhere between the slaughterhouse and the museum.

The slaughterhouse/museum system of spending and expending time and money—application and suspension of work, different attitudes toward offal/waste—is also a system that brings animals, humans, buildings, and the coalescence of buildings and infrastructures into cities, into entangled relations with each other. Animals are, in effect, spent in the slaughterhouse in order to fuel the economic and biological transfer of energy from animal to human. This could also be understood as a symbolic and conceptual transfer of natural energy from the rural sector to cultural energy that revitalizes the city on a rhythmic basis, a food chain transfer that returns vitality to the rural in the form of work and finished products. This is not, however, a perpetual motion machine. In capitalist terms, it is also an opportunity for speculation and an increase of wealth that tends to accrue to the city, returning, over time, less and less energy, and energy of a lower quality, to the country. The slaughterhouse building, like other industrial building types, is spatially adaptable to other purposes once the smells and residues of butchering have been erased. A slaughterhouse that becomes a park, as it famously did in the case of Bernard Tschumi's endlessly interesting Parc de la Villette in Paris, is still residually engaged with this energy transference, although now it is the romantic ideal of the open fields of the country—where the whole animal supposedly grazes in open pastures—that is recovered or revamped in the form of a park.

As Siegfried Giedion's chapter "Mechanization and Death: Meat" in *Mechanization Takes Command* articulates, the La Villette slaughterhouse, built over three years beginning in 1863, the same year as Sullivan's Stock Exchange Building, was the "first central slaughterhouse to cater to a population of millions."[7] Georges Eugène Haussmann's master plan for Paris included this central slaughterhouse, locating it on the outermost limit of Paris. Abattoirs—which process raw meat and byproducts and are sites of technological innovation and horror—are often unofficial indicators of city limits. La Villette, according to Giedion, became "*the* abbatoir, a prototype for the rest of the century."[8] The slaughterhouse was notable for the "care with which the individual animal was treated . . . each ox had a stall to itself . . . in which it was felled."[9] Giedion notes this survival of "handicraft" techniques in the killing of animals at La Villette, techniques later superseded by automation and mass slaughter, the first examples of which were the slaughterhouse assembly lines developed in Chicago between 1860 and 1885. "It may well be," he writes, "that this treatment in separate booths expresses the deeply rooted [largely European] experience that the beasts can be raised only at the cost of constant care and attention to the individual animal."[9] By contrast, the Great Plains of the Midwest seem to suggest to Giedion a different sort of animal-raising experience; an almost carefree maintenance of herds of cattle on open ranges. This, Giedion remarks, may account for the invention of the assembly line method of slaughtering in America. When La Villette was being built, Chicago was expanding and concentrating its cattle market. The Union Stock Yards, founded in 1864, had no stalls, and no plan per se, only open yards in which the cattle gathered and from which they were driven "directly up the open gangway into the top storey of the packing houses."[11] The slaughtering process started at the top of the buildings so that the weight of the dead animal could be used as a motive force in bringing a gradually partitioned carcass down through different levels of processing. The city of Chicago was felt at that time, again according to Giedion, to have "incalculable potentialities" and a "readiness for achievement unlimited in scope." "As soon as the industry began to process animals by the million," he writes, "the necessary instruments [raw material such as grain and cattle, mechanization of processing, transportation and storage facilities] lay at hand."[12] So, in spite of the economic instability within which Louis Sullivan was designing and building the Stock Exchange Building—ingeniously inserting a large void into the middle of a skyscraper for financial speculators who were responding simultaneously to the panic and the explosive economic potential residing in specific forms of matter and means—the idea of "stock" was rich with immediate and literal promise. The animal was still fully in the coin, so to speak.

The animal as stock, rather than symbol of bucolic ideal, was, in 1873 (and is still) transporte *en masse* to the periphery of the city and taken through a series of compressions that bring the animals into crowded pens, herds them into the killing factories, breaks them into digestible parts, and separates the parts into different strands of processing, packaging and shipping. The space of processing establishes a physical link between the slaughterhouse and the stock market because stock is, in cases where the commodities are actual animals, literally the animal as a whole body subjected to speculative bargaining that breaks it into digestible commodity parts, both literally and figuratively. In the same way, the stock market breaks corporations into parts (shares) in order to finance their growth through profitable exchanges. Stock, in an agricultural sense, means the animal is predestined to the market. Livestock, with the exception of horses, is already understood to be a form of animal life that is valued for its imminent death and transformation into parts ("meat on the hoof"). The stock market was thus, at a certain moment in the late twentieth century, particularly poised to ride the wave of processing technologies. Information, like the animal and the corporation, is broken into parts in order to be brokered in the marketplace of computational and non-computational work. It is not a coincidence that we speak of a computer "crashing" and of stock market "crashes." Both refer to a catastrophic loss of faith and capacity in the potential exchange of virtual and actual parts.

The marketplace is a space of accreted parts and its (always) urban and civic character consists in its myriad relations of part to whole. The space of the marketplace itself, such as the trading floor of the Stock Exchange and, in America in particular, the large animal yards where buying and selling takes place, are open, relatively undifferentiated spaces with multiple possibilities. Museums and malls are public spaces that maintain some aspects of this openness and continue to benefit, in some form, from the crude delivery of the animal to an abstract system and the recirculation of the abstracted animal in the form of speculative capital within the city, and from city to country. In America today visits to the museum commonly coincide with shopping trips where one might buy, for example, a stuffed animal for a child or have a hamburger for lunch. One peculiar twist is that animals, who are slaughtered as the dirty expenditure that fuels the clean culture of the museum, store and café, are quintessentially not the museum, not the store or café, not shopping or dining. The animal is the being that does not shop but underwrites, in part, the building of the place of its own brokering—the Stock Exchange—as well as shopping centers.

A Marxist account might theorize the breaking into parts (the death of the whole animal) primarily as an enchainment of the labor of the animal on behalf of capital, where the animal stands not primarily for itself but for a set of material potentials and processes such as those understood and exploited by the Midwestern capitalists of the nineteenth century.[13] The animal's life is understood as part of a system of production. As Henri Lefebvre writes, "What constitutes the forces of production, according to Marx and Engels? Nature, first of all, plays a part, then labor, hence the organization (or division) of labor, and hence also the instruments of labor, including technology and, ultimately, knowledge."[14] Insofar as architecture is built with the resources accumulated from these exchanges between life energy, work, wholes and divisions of whole, it becomes, as many have argued, part of the style of economic exchange that belongs to the power of the state—power that uses up resources and sends down its roots into the city in reductive ways. But insofar as there is something in this system that comes from outside (although, at first, it seems easily incorporated)—that is, the animal—architecture's affiliation with the official power of the state is less clear.

Lefebvre argues that "the properly historical period of the history of space corresponds to the accumulation of capital, beginning with its primitive stage and ending with the world market under the reign of abstraction."[15] Animals, as we saw in Lefebvre's account of the horse and the ox, are a "medium" between man and space.[16] To the extent that animals are part of man's world, they are said to work. To the extent that they are part of nature, they do not. To repeat Lefebvre's view of natural labor: "Nature does not labor . . . one of its defining characteristics is that it creates."[17] Georges Bataille, also a dialectical materialist, differentiates man from animals partly on the basis of work; animals do not work, whereas man does. These claims constitute a slippery slope, but their import is not ambiguous. The consciousness of work, not just its fact, is never attributed to animals because animals, in effect, have no independent consciousness. If animals work, they work at the behest of human consciousness. No other kind of work—such as animals' instinctual drive to provide for themselves—matters. The possibility that useful structures and spaces (the Stock Exchange, museum, slaughterhouse) are produced, at least partially, by segmenting a being from a place radically outside systems of labor, production and capital accumulation would be hard to entertain in a Marxist account. Nature is always already understood in productive terms in the industrial societies for which Marxism attempted to account. And yet the need for what are, in reality, extremely violent acts required to bring the animal into a productive relationship with human culture is evidence of some strain or tension in the delivery of the raw and natural beast to a system of production. How would a Marxist theory account for this particular violence? Is it the violence of war and economic accumulation? Deleuze and Guattari's violence of the hunted animal?[18] Or is it the quotidian violence of human life itself, which is biologically sustained by animal life? Lefebvre uses the category of "abstraction" to capture what initially appears to be, in his view, the most significant and errant category of historical and contemporary human life, "space."[19] The concept of Marxist abstraction, however, does not account fully for the field from which the animal arrives or the attendant problem of violence. For one thing, the animal remains outside any history of space because the history of space is tied, in Lefebvre, to capital accumulation (its "proper" historical beginning). Abstraction cannot completely absorb, for example, the question of wildness that remained an issue in animal slaughter long after the industrialists imagined themselves to have fully resolved the problem of animal usefulness—the belief in and formation of animal as stock.

The question of what kind of power and natural/cultural forces are, therefore, enacted in an architectural space such as the Stock Exchange Trading Room, continues to be difficult. Since I have posed the question of wildness, we might attempt to ask the question of power and force from the side of the animal, or, rather, the side of our viewpoint that might be uneasily (in all the ways we have already encountered) called the "animal side." Animals themselves, in the process of being herded toward their slaughter, have typically been thought to understand enough about their destiny to introduce fear and the consequences of fear into the equation. Many studies that take up this question are concerned with increasing productivity and the central question they ask is: "What is the cost of this fear?" Fear is, not surprisingly, expensive. Fear produces anxiety that results in weight loss and the pumping of adrenaline into the animal's muscles, which subsequently affects the taste and quality of the meat. But this is not the whole story of the animal's fear.

One of the most intriguing, and certainly quirkiest, studies on meatpacking plants and slaughtering systems, *Thinking in Pictures*, was written by Temple Grandin, an autistic woman who became an animal scientist and a specialist in designing animal-handling facilities.[20] Because

 **Figure 16.3:** Adler & Sullivan *Chicago Stock Exchange Trading Room.* Photograph by Richard Nickel, Courtesy of the Richard Nickel Committee, Chicago, Illinois.

of her own clinical terror of being touched by human beings, Grandin became interested in what comprises animal fear. She suggests that it is not a foreknowledge of death that produces anxiety in cattle, sheep or pigs being herded toward slaughter. Georges Bataille would agree with her, but his conclusions are different. In Grandin's view, it is, instead, small anomalies in the animals' surroundings—a chain hanging from a fence or a person standing near the chute in an unfamiliar way or a plastic soda bottle lying on the ground—that produce a sense of chaos and fear in the animal.[21]

In response to her own fears, Grandin designed what she called a "squeeze machine" in order to acclimate herself to a controlled touching. This machine is a place where Grandin goes when her hyperactive nervous system—"the nervous system," she writes, "that is common to autistic people"[22]—needs calming. She puts herself into a mechanism that applies particular kinds of pressure, a "language of pressure,"[23] to her body, and it is this tactile language that informs her designs of animal-handling plants. One of the significant, although relatively simple, innovations Grandin has introduced in her processing plant designs and veterinary apparatuses (she has designed many) has been to change straight chutes to curved chutes—to calm animals by allowing them to circle—and to adjust the width of a chute so that an animal is "held" rather than corralled. She also designed a linear automated belt system that carries the animal to its death more comfortably than typical assembly lines; the animal remains in physical contact with the animal on the belt in front of it throughout.[24] In the apparatuses Grandin has invented, in particular for kosher slaughter, she emphasizes that the animal be held comfortably and compassionately before the moment of slaughter. The animal should be, she remarks, "nursed" into its death.

The adjustments to these apparatuses seem minor to us from an architectural standpoint, and, further, Grandin's complicity with the slaughtering of animals seems to discredit her identification claims. The animal is, indeed, very minor in the contemporary world, but its import in this particular scene is profound. The consequences of ignoring the accumulation of small pressures on a herd of animals is to potentially induce, in time and space, the living chaos of a stampeding herd. Identity-related aphasias (of which autism is an extreme version) sometimes are thought to open a portal into animal consciousness. Part of this reflects the mistaken belief that aphasia is a return to a childhood that is an arrested, more primitive, stage of human development. Grandin's interest in animals is not primitivist in this sense. It is related, instead, to acute and highly developed observations about spatial sensibility. Grandin writes that she establishes a deep emotional connection with places she has designed and, whenever she returns to these places, she surveys the territory the "way a wary animal surveys new territory to make sure it has safe escape routes and passages, or crosses an open plain that may be full of predators."[25] Animals in small spaces, or on open plains, possess these survival strategies. When Grandin wants to evaluate an animal's "experience" she insists that she "really becomes the cow and not a person in cow costume."[26] She contends that there is still a large degree of wildness in domestic animals and it is this wildness that one must understand in order to "become the cow." Among other things, prey-species animals are acutely aware of their flight zone, the space that exists between them and any perceived threat or danger. Invasion of the flight zone can happen in innumerable small and large ways to which humans, a predator species, are usually oblivious. Only under rare circumstances, such as hunting animals for food, do modern humans need to become aware of the flight zone of their prey. Typically, humans view domestic and farm animals as no longer possessing any wildness, or at least not any wildness that matters. Domestication is, by definition, the removal of the problem of wildness and the insertion of the animal into a system of production, even if it is the leisure system of the domestic pet.

Aphasia, in both mild and severe forms, also dislocates normal identification pathways and intensifies attachment to a different set of meanings. It is often the case with autistic children, as Grandin comments, that visualization and drawing skills increase as verbal skills decrease. This is, perhaps, the usual neurological visual-for-verbal

verbal-for-visual economy but, in this case, the visualization of space comes to stand for the pointed absence of the "social." Grandin's architecture of the animal-handling plants is, at least in part, derived from a spatial consciousness that is "pre-social," outside the operation of collective labor and social production and, in some respects, outside the operations of history. The social is figured, particularly in Grandin's adolescent world, as a set of abstract symbols that stand in for, but are abstracted from, the animating force of the social. Later, as part of a related adaptation, Grandin remarks on how she was able to visualize the animal plants she was designing completely "in her head" before drawing them. She was also able to draw an almost perfect perspective of the building without ever having been trained in projective drawing.[27] As a child, Grandin employed visual symbols of doors and windows as ways of understanding the abstract give and take of human relationships,[28] because, as she says, she had no idea of what it meant to "socially interact" with people. She had no "social existence." She also used the physical doors in the buildings she lived and worked in to symbolize crucial obstacles that she wanted to overcome. Gradually, over time, Grandin was able to program herself by means of accumulated experience to less symbol-dependent thinking. She learned to generalize,[29] something that many autistic people never learn how to do. It was Grandin's ability to articulate these ideas "from the country of autism" that attracted Oliver Sacks, the ever-ready-to-hand neurologist, to her story. Autism is interesting to neurologists for the same reason all neurological pathologies are interesting to those who study the brain and mind—because it sheds light on normative neurological function. But Grandin is also an unusual case. She was able to "adapt to autism"[30] and use its particular gifts to become an animal scientist and an architect. Part of this adaptation consists of bringing a pre-social animal (and architectural) consciousness into a system of production, which is partly a matter of generalizing the relation between specific (spatial) symbols and general (social) requirements. "There is some evidence," Grandin writes, "that facial recognition involves different neural systems from those used for imagery of objects such as buildings."[31]

There is a particularly interesting passage in Grandin's book that returns us to the question of the animal, the city, the slaughterhouse, and architecture. In one instance, when Grandin is asked to design a more humane holding machine for animals who are, as mentioned above, undergoing kosher slaughter, she creates a squeeze machine of sorts that holds the animal tightly but comfortably and practices running the machine by visualizing the machine controls as extensions of her hands. Over time, the movement of the hydraulic levers that regulate the pressure on the animal come to feel like her own hands holding the animal:

> . . . the parts of the apparatus that held the animal felt as if they were a continuation of my own body. . . . If I just concentrated on holding the animal gently and keeping him calm, I was able to run the restraining chute very skillfully. . . . During this intense period of concentration I no longer heard noise from the plant machinery. I didn't feel the sweltering Alabama summer heat, and everything seemed quiet and serene. It was almost a religious experience. It was my job to hold the animal gently, and it was the rabbi's job to perform the final deed. I was able to look at each animal, to hold him gently and make him as comfortable as possible during the last moments of his life. I had participated in the ancient slaughter ritual the way it was supposed to be. A new door had been opened. It felt like walking on water.[32]

*I was able to look at each animal.*[33] The site of biological/symbolic exchange or transfer represented by the slaughterhouse represses the question of animal identity in order to disassemble the animal into autonomous parts, although, as mentioned previously, this repression came about gradually in the history of slaughterhouses. *Looking* at *each animal* is a way of reestablishing the animal's identity—and, in some ways, its history as a domestic animal, its European history—which Grandin then isolates and holds in place for a singular moment in the above (ecumenical) passage. The slaughterhouse sacrifices the animal to its larger collective destiny as both the symbolic and material underpinning of wealth, but Grandin, unlike the owners, workers and foreman in the slaughterhouse, the speculators in the Stock Exchange, and the museum and shopping center visitors, *attends* the sacrifice. This does not mean that her methods of slaughter or her slaughterhouse designs are admirable or even better than the usual designs. It simply means that she looks at the scene of slaughter from a different perspective than most people. She follows—although not explicitly—the words of Elizabeth Costello: "Kill the beast by all means . . . but make it a contest, a ritual . . . Look him in the eye before you kill him, and thank him for it afterwards."[34]

Bataille's theory of the sacred, and the role sacrifice plays in the sacred—already forecast here with Grandin's understanding of this moment before the animal's death as "almost religious"—will be crucial to any discussion of the slaughterhouse and stock exchange as an economic, architectural or urban site. But it is George Hersey's taxonomy of classical building parts as they relate to animal sacrifices in ancient culture that gives us one possible architectural "outcome" of the sacrificial scene.[35] Underlying Hersey's discussion is, largely, Homeric evidence that the murder of an animal in ancient cultures was as much a matter of spirit as a matter of meat. The murder of the animal weighed on civic consciousness in a more profound way than a primarily functionalist relation to the animal would produce. Sacrifice and sacrificial procedures were necessary, according to Hersey, René Girard[36] and others, to address the guilt and potential civic chaos associated with acts of violence. It is a further act of violence that attempts to undo the effects of an earlier act of violence. The animal victim, often acting as a surrogate for a human victim in such a way that its foregone wholeness would be symbolically recovered, thus restores a sense of collective well-being in the disrupted human society. On the sacrificial altar, the slaughtered animal is thus laid out in a rough realignment of its "natural" position, with the bones placed in a proper, although supine, position and the skin draped over the top. The further gesture of expatiation of all that is portended by the animal murder—the guilt, the expense, the loss—lies in the transformation of the animal body parts into the myriad named and assembled parts of classical architectural buildings. The classical column is thus, literally and figuratively, as Hersey shows, a reassembled body with a capital (head), center section (torso), and base (feet); the runnels by which blood flows off the altar are the column flutes; the various decorative motifs refer to the fetishes and food that were routinely placed next to the sacrificed body and so forth. The "lost meaning of classical architecture" that Hersey explores is, by means of these tropes, a series of references embedded within classical architecture to sacrificial practices that ritualistically restore a partitioned body to whole life—a theological meaning embedded in an eventually fully secularized use of classical motifs.[37] The animal victim, however, is restored not to its own animal life as a four-legged beast, but to "humanized" life: it stands upright and becomes symbolic, a "working part" of architecture, a column. Because the animal victim was often, as mentioned above, a surrogate for a human victim, its restoration to uprightness returns us to the original substitution of animal body for human, and endorses a further substitution of architectural body for human. However, in Hersey's account, the linguistic and formal references of the column pertain to the sacrificial scene itself and the animal victim. The "life" of architecture, if it makes sense to speak this way, is classically understood to be referring to human life. Hersey suggests a more hybridized biological provenance.

As I discussed in the chapter entitled "Vertical, standing upright," the paleontologist André Leroi-Gourhan argues that uprightness belongs, in an evolutionary context, to humans, not to animals. So we could perform a slight revision to this scene by proposing that the classical column is not only a redemptive trope for the murdered animal but also a trope for an animal that has undergone humanization—one that can now stand up comfortably, with complete equipoise, on its hind legs.

This is yet another instance of the human-animal hybrid in architecture. The transfer of tropes, from the substitution of animal for human, the murder of the animal on the ritualistic altar, and the restoration of both human and animal in the classical building, does not stop at the column but goes on circulating, as a monetary, biological and technological economy. I examined part of the character of this economy already with respect to Leroi-Gourhan's work, in which standing upright is connected with the evolution of technology. Louis Sullivan's restored Stock Exchange trading room, extracted from the masonry (mineral) Stock Exchange Building that used innovative building technologies,[38] now redecorated with floral motifs and supported in part by faux-marble-clad columns with no flutes but with gilt-plastered leafy capitals, is certainly part of this economy. But Bataille's theory of *dépense* is now indispensable to the picture.

Georges Bataille, along with Roger Caillois, Alexandre Kojève, Michel Leiris, and others, was also a member of the College of Sociology.[39] To briefly reiterate a history familiar to most, Denis Hollier, who edited a collection of writings by members of the College, remarks in his introduction on how this group was "founded"—if the brief, volatile, non-group character of this group can be dignified with this institutional sobriquet—to polemicize against the Surrealists, whose own movement was winding up as the College began.[40] The Surrealists, as Hollier remarks, began with political models of avant-gardism (the "Leninist groupuscle") and ended with the art market. When Stalinism corrupted the political model of the Surrealists, there was no fallback position except "work,"[41] and work, in this case, meant the production of art for mass consumption. Against this background of cynicism Bataille, Caillois, and other members of the College were interested in conceptualizing human settlements that could de-politicize collective experience by restoring the wholeness of human life. This meant, for them, bringing the sacred back into play—a utopian project, as Hollier indicates.[42] De-politicization was necessary in order to avoid the "aestheticization of the political that Benjamin has just identified with fascism."[43] Thus, the overarching mission of the College was "the formation of an 'order developing and holding sway throughout the entire earth . . . *whose mission was to bring forth, from the heart of the profane world, from the world of functional servility, the sacred world of the totality of being.*'"[44] Bataille's idea of an "order" is of a totality that "does not let itself be cut apart;" it is like life, "whatever resists partition."[45] Animals (and women), in this scheme, undo the whole. Yet the partitioning of life, specifically animal life, as my earlier discussion suggested, is an important part of how the modern city establishes the wholeness of its internal and external orders through the construction of infrastructure and buildings. The city's aspirations toward wholeness and totality are financed through processes that partition living beings both literally and figuratively. Like the transformation of the sacrificed animal into a column, animate beings—substituted, partitioned and sacrificed—create inanimate (mineral) wholes.

For Bataille, architecture's monumental history is the anti-exemplar, the negative example, of a practice that has habitually and historically alienated humans from themselves, an anti-architecture/ "against architecture" sensibility. The first form of architecture we encounter, in our humanity, is, according to Bataille, the prison—we are imprisoned in our own form. Architecture, as an official practice, subsequently enlarges upon this imprisonment. Hollier remarks on how Bataille's is an extroverted architecture, not the introverted architecture of control and surveillance of Foucault. In both cases, however, architecture belongs to the "Commodore,"[46] the power of the state.[47]

In the second and third volume of the *The Accursed Share*, Bataille proposes a theory of humanity that will reveal the "intimate truth" about human life: that the "world of eroticism and the world of thought are complementary to one another."[48] Eroticism is human sexuality as opposed to the sexuality of animals. Eroticism exceeds the animal, in both its subject matter and practice, by calling out the fact of sexuality itself and ascribing to it prohibitions and rituals. Hollier writes that Bataille's category of the erotic, which includes the scatological, in philosophical terms is that which one can "have no idea of." It is formless, the notorious *informe*, the stain, "ridiculous, worthless, trivial" (as Plato entertains it in *Parmenides*), "speechless" (Plato in *Philebus*), a "heterological operation," a theory of the need for loss (as in making "thought lose its head"), the "horror."[49] "We," Bataille writes, ". . . need a thinking that does not fall apart in the face of horror, a self-consciousness that does not steal away when it is time to explore possibility to the limit."[50] The horror contained in the erotic, the *informe*, is the everyday horror of contradictions that philosophy will not look at, or embrace, directly. It is the horror of the man who is able to play with his own child one day and massacre twenty men the next. The intimate secret of humanity is this aphilosophical partition: violent and destructive contradictions that characterize humanity's daily life. The slaughter of animals counts as part of this secret. Totality in thought would, according to Bataille, consist in bringing the secret life (the erotic, the violent) and enunciated life (rational thought) together. It would bring the abbatoirs into the cultural heart of the city.

Bataille's theory circles, as it must, around the problem of "nature." Nature is both the site of the beginning of alienation and, later, the site, now changed, that we return to in our desire and need for the sacred. We can never get back, of course, to an originary nature. For Bataille, the first moment of humanity is a negation of nature, which is the given. All that is present at the beginning of humankind—"differentiation from animals and from nature, labor and the awareness of death. . . . "[51]—is still present in human culture throughout its history.[52] As he continues:

> A profound difference results from the fact that the "nature" that is desired after being rejected is not desired in submission to the given, as it may have been in the first instance, in the *fleeting* movement of animal excitation; it is nature transfigured by the *curse*, to which the spirit then accedes only through a new movement of refusal, of insubordination, or revolt.[53]

The initial revolt and subsequent return are not stages but an "integral ensemble."[54] The sacred, then, is what is always forbidden.[55] For Bataille, the world of practice and things (made by humans) is evidence of the originary negation of nature that humanized humans, for example, the fact that humans have work, which animals do not.[56] But alongside this world of practice and things are also sacred practices and sacred things.[57]

> [The] sacred is, in some sense, the natural given. But it is an aspect of the natural given that reveals itself after the fact, in the world of practice—where it is denied—through effects that have escaped the negating action of work, or that actively destroy the coherence established in work . . . it is an aspect perceived by minds that the order of *things* has shaped to meet the exacting demands of this world's coherence: even a person who rejects all those demands is well aware of them; only animals are oblivious of them.[58]

"The paradox of my attitude," Batille writes at the beginning of *The Accursed Share*, "requires that I show the absurdity of a system in which each thing *serves*, in which nothing is *sovereign*."[59] Eroticism is a sovereign form that "*cannot serve any purpose*."

The degree to which the sacred revitalizes animal origins (nature, the given, periods somehow prior to work, technologies, practices) is both obvious and elusive. We already know this to be true in architecture from the presence of gargoyles on medieval churches, but it is equally true of contemporary buildings with no visible animal or nature motifs except public and private spaces that ritualize daily life into eating, sleeping, gathering. The animal typically appears in some form (the animal mask, for example) in ritualized "scenes of excess," as well as sacred events. In Bataille's terms, though, the animal's appearance is not primarily erotic. It appears, instead, as a symbol of the nature necessarily abandoned by the condition of being human. Gargoyles are thus symbols of a world left behind, excluded, by the practice of architecture as a human practice. They are positioned on the outside of the building, often cantilevered away from the building (to draw water, as well as evil, animate spirits, away from the building interior). While animality is often seen as part of the erotic, it is not, again, the exposure or exploitation of so-called animal drives that brings animal symbols into scenes of excess that strive to pass beyond, or below, ordinary or normative life. It is, instead, the understanding that the animal claims a scene, an "elsewhere," an excessive scene, that lies outside the (human) scene—a scene of the wild that belongs to all, even domestic, animal life. It has often been said that the animal is the radical "other." Yet wildness is that which lies outside even the ethical pairing of the self and other, or the human and not-human. It is, literally, that which undoes the pairing of oppositions themselves—oppositions that structurally maintain the human enclave, the coherence of the human world.

In an urban economy, the free whole animal that inhabits the wilderness, like the prostitute who pursues an independent, street economy, like art outside the museum, represents an aesthetic surplus that architecture, insofar as architecture is that which exceeds building, is also part of. Architecture lives in a captured state (it defines the conditions of capture, Bataille's prison), but also in a wild state. Its wildness lies in both its aesthetic dimension (the idleness of ornament) and in its underpinnings—its economic, symbolic, and literal *legs*. Architecture walks on (at least) four legs. But it also claims the upright, both morally and literally.

Hollier examines the relation of architecture to the "unthinking expenditure of *dépense*" in Bataille's discussion of the relation of the slaughterhouse to the museum that I drew on at the beginning of this chapter. As in Temple Grandin's connection between the slaughter of an animal and the nature of sacrifice, Bataille gives the slaughterhouse "a religious dimension."[60] This dimension, however, is the reverse of Grandin's. Whereas Grandin sees the slaughter of the animal as a nursing of it into its death, much as ancient sacrifices cradled the animal into death, Bataille marks the slaughterhouse as a place that has been "cursed and quarantined like a boat with cholera aboard. . . . The victims of this curse are neither the butchers nor the animals, but those fine folk who have reached the point of not being able to stand their own unseemliness." . . .[61] It is what Hollier calls the "religious repulsion" shown by the "fine folk" in the face of the killing of the animal; evidence of how humans refuse to address the "totality" of their lives. Temple Grandin's autism already places her in a quasi-sovereign position with respect to the utilitarianism of the slaughterhouse factory. She does not need to abandon "social seemliness" because the autism has abandoned it for her. As an autistic person, her social existence is precarious. She is immunized, in some sense, against the sacred horror of the murder of animals in the slaughterhouse not, to reiterate, because of a primitive identification with animals but because of the aphilosophical pathways of autistic reasoning. She can therefore reenter the slaughterhouse and practice a kind of theology there. At the same time, Grandin is an architect. She not only attends the event of slaughter but also designs as if, under certain circumstances, she were an animal. There are things, therefore, in the slaughterhouse system as it presents itself (before she redesigns it) that repulse her. Any form of abuse of the animal makes her physically ill. The hoisting of live animals up by their hind legs before their throats are cut is, to her, a profound and shocking form of cruelty and humiliation. Grandin is able, in other words, to discriminate between different kinds of acts that take place inside the slaughterhouse and to associate these acts with the spaces in which they are happening. She sees the connection between the animal and the architecture not as a behavioral relationship but as a structural relationship related to specific aspects of symbolic and functional life. Her aim is to bring the architecture to bear, like the squeeze machine, on the life processes happening within it. She does not flee to the museum,[62] but instead dissects and differentiates the dirty, which results in a third economy, neither clean nor dirty: the social and spatial affiliation of mechanization, humane slaughter, symbolic exchange, energy exchange, and spiritual life that acknowledges the animal and the architecture as having a common ancestry, neither exclusively animal nor human, neither exclusively productive nor functionalist. In various ways, she revises, or unearths, the meaning of "stock exchange."

Hollier is particularly interested, in his work on Bataille, in interregnums, days when work is forbidden. He is also interested in links between productive and non-productive aspects of life and architecture:

> The slaughterhouse and the museum (religion and art) . . . are two sorts of enclave within the economic continuum; the sacrificial nature of the first, and the fact that it is on Sunday that one visits museums, connect both to a sabbatical . . . rhythm, that is, how one spends time on the seventh day, when work is forbidden.[63]

So we might visit, on a Sunday, Louis Sullivan's Stock Exchange fragment inside the Art Institute of Chicago. It is no longer connected to the slaughterhouse, nor is it a museum—although it now coexists—comfortably with the museum. Slaughterhouses are now so remote an urban phenomenon (on the far far periphery of our consciousness) and the speculative processes of the stock Exchange so heavily mediated that the word "stock" no longer reminds us of animate life. The trading room is the unusual instance of a room that has become a true void. Following Hollier, we could say that it is an instance of the *informe*, because it has been radically excised from the forms that gave it meaning, that is, the Stock Exchange Building. If so, it would be an instance of the *architectural informe*, an oxymoron, whose simultaneous lack of formal definition (the stain and the animal) and reference to a formal site (the building and the human) produce an oscillation that is pointedly summarized by the decorative motifs restored in the room. This decorative extravagance—Sullivan's designs for the colorful, complex patterns stenciled on the walls and ceiling, ornately formed column capitals, faux marble cladding—plays, among other things, a sanitizing role that returns the unseemliness of killing animals in order to acquire great wealth to the opaque domain of a mediated and picturesque nature, which is symbolically vegetative, not animal. Ornament classically embellishes structure, surface, and form, but Sullivan's previously mentioned theory of ornament was that it should be integral to the structure. As he wrote famously in *Ornament and Structure*: "ornamental design will be more beautiful if it seems a part of the surface or substance that receives it than if it looks 'stuck on'. . . . And this, I take it, is the preparatory basis of what may be called an organic system of ornamention."[64] Then what happens when the "substance" or structure is missing? The room is now nested inside a concrete shell that attaches to the Art Institute; the room has lost its building, so to speak, and the ornament is no longer attached to the surfaces and structures that gave rise to it. The room has been excised and then redecorated with replicated ornamental surfaces attached to an (irrelevant) surrogate structure. Both form and ornament are now running wild: no work is underway; all has been rendered idle. The symbolic life of this (new) ornament has acquired the same pre-social, all-symbol status that Temple Grandin ascribed to her doors and thresholds before she learned to generalize. These symbols are meant to help us back to the socialization we associate with buildings, in this case Sullivan's building, but in order to make this return journey we would need to grant them, among other things, a social economy. In Bataille's terms, ornament is dead economically and, thus, sovereign. Sullivan's ornament thus represents here, at least in part, a vegetative victory over the mineral, the masonry structure of the original building. It does not, however, represent a victory over the animal. Just as grain/plants are intensified in value in the stock market by being fed to animals as feed, Sullivan's vegetative ornament in the trading room feeds on the structure of the museum itself, which is part of a large circulatory urban economy, much of which is underwritten by the animal. Standing upright, even if on the back of the museum itself, the trading room belongs to its human ancestry. Idle, it is animal. Yet another form of animal urbanism, the *informe,* and the erotic: the idle upright.

## 17: THE CITY:
### HORIZONTAL, UPRIGHT, WORKING



When I first saw the legendary red light district in Amsterdam I was particularly struck by the way in which this district seems to expand on the everyday urbanism of the city. The prostitutes, for example, display themselves in larger-scale, but similarly proportioned, windows typical of the Amsterdam house. The front window, facing onto the street, is an important feature in Dutch houses. Objects are frequently visible from the outside, arranged along the windowsill. Often, for privacy, the lower part of the window is opaque and, for transparency, the upper part clear.

The iridescent black light interiors of the red light district are like black boxes that display, like spectral signboards, women standing by the large windows in glowing white underwear. Inside, behind the women, are beds that also glow, with white striped bedspreads. There is an irrefutably domestic character to these shadow boxes, where the bedroom is the only visible, and only meaningful, space of the house. Crowds of men and women, some of whom are tourists, are pressed into the narrow streets. Much of the startling force of this scene lies in its entangled exhibition of work, sexuality, beauty and architectural/urban space. “Beauty” is set aside from “work” in

Bataille's articulation of the sovereignty of the erotic.[1] To the scene of beauty as an aesthetic category, Bataille adds the problematic of desire.

"Beauty," Bataille writes in *The Accursed Share*, "is indeed the sign of *sovereignty*"[2] because it represents a mastery over the servile state, a freedom from work, an idleness and indolence. The prostitute, in particular, excites desire and concentrates beauty, desire, and the absence of (legitimate) work into one, usually urban, place. She is therefore, for Bataille, a sovereign figure. The prostitute resides in a world apart from work, if not literally, since the prostitute is working and the work eventually roughens her, then figuratively in the image of idle beauty presented to the men in the street by the women loitering in the Amsterdam windows. "Work," Bataille remarks, "is never favorable to [female] beauty, the very meaning of which is to be free of oppressive constraints."[3] Idleness, however, is not only necessary to beauty, but it also anticipates the inertness and death that a lack of work portends in human beings, and this is why sexual desire is sometimes linked with death. "In fact," Bataille continues, "she [the prostitute] is not just eroticism but also *loss* having taken the form of an object. . . . The essence of loss is this intense consumption that exerts a dangerous fascination, that prefigures death and finally attracts more and more."[4]

The red light district is a scene in which loss and recovery are managed through the assembly and disassembly of parts: The woman is seen as loitering just behind the plate glass of the window, an idle object of desire; her sexually provocative parts are partially covered but the covering is made iridescent—it is called out; all the traditional parts of the house, with the exception of the bedroom, are hidden from view. Some of this "management"—a word that Mark Cousins made more interesting than its modern usage implies, where the bureaucratic is given sexual, reproductive content such that the manager is a kind of "breeder"[5]—is to be found in the architecture. Female beauty, in this scene, figuralizes the peculiar potentiality of desire, a state that is never fully present but laden with promise. It also allows desire to pass through it to the dark void beyond, a condition precisely figured by the sequence of window, woman, bedroom, and dark unrevealed, even sinister, interior, a perfect case of the "carnal perspective."[6]

We can slide, at this moment, in many directions, along the idea of beauty into general problems of beauty or, say, into the question of animal beauty, which, like the beauty of the prostitute, often resides in partitioning the animal into parts: the arched neck, the glossy coat, the fur pelt.[7] The problem of parts, in the stock market, in Renaissance architecture, or in the sovereignty of desire, brings with it both the promise of materiality and the suspension of the material in its contribution to a whole building, city, or body. For Bataille, as mentioned in the last chapter, women are the name of "whatever undoes the whole."[8] Women do not contribute to an urban whole. They have been traditionally sequestered away from the work of urbanism, protected and/or exploited in this isolation, as the case may be. Animals, on the other hand, contribute their parts to the making of various urban and architectural wholes, as we have already seen in the case of the classical column, or city marketplace, or stock market.[9] There are multiple and different conditions for all these players and for the urban condition itself. But the conception of the city—in which a "district" such as the red light district is uniquely marked as illicit and yet fully accessible—is a conception that, as we know very well, depends on some idea of a whole city, Amsterdam in this case, however publicity-driven or specious this idea of wholeness might be in reality.

In the Amsterdam scene, the idleness of the prostitutes produces a certain female beauty (with a strategic deployment of light as the cosmetic that hides the marks of work and daily life) necessary to their occupation that is protected and displayed by the window that separates them from their clientele. The window is complicitous with this display function, as it has always been, particularly in the city, but it is not of the same order. The window, in a sense, is at work. Certainly architecturally, the lightness and light provided by windows is a lightness and light won by meticulous management of weight and forces such that, at the moment of the window, the right amount of pressure from inside and outside the building is exerted, withheld, negotiated within the tolerances.[10] In other words, a building typically works such that parts of its façade remain open and transparent. Certain structural triumphs over force in architecture, which result in lightness, are part of what have traditionally constituted architecture's structural or anatomical beauty. At the same time, completed buildings are understood to be more or less at rest, idle, and this idleness, like Bataille's account of female beauty, results in a deep visual field of objectification that is also part of architectural beauty, the field of aesthetics. The tricky interior of buildings is, at first, hidden.

So the window and the room it displays, in Amsterdam, count on functioning at the level of architectural, animal and female beauty while simultaneously transacting a series of exchanges between the sexes, as well as exchanges between human and animal desire. For the moment, this animal desire can be understood, as it is commonly, as the implicit and explicit sexuality of the scene, and human desire as the implicit and explicit urban economy, an economy of representation—exchange of money, value, advertisement, sign systems, language. Bataille suggests that the prostitute performs a kind of distillation, through signs, of animal sexuality, by concentrating on herself all, and only, the signs of sexual desire.[11] In addition, the exchange of gifts—gifts of money, gifts of sex—between client and prostitute is not an orthodox urban economy based on use-value, but a "surplus" expenditure, an "excess."[12]

The degree to which the sacred revisits animal origins—something we already know to be true in architecture from the presence of gargoyles on medieval churches, but that is equally true of contemporary buildings with no gargoyles and instead public and private spaces that ritualize daily life—or draws the animal out again in humans is, again, an instance of excess and surplus expenditure. My earlier discussion of taxidermy gave, to the post-animal animal, several options, some gruesome: the option of living "freely" as a biological fantasy; the option of living in a captured state as a zoological fantasy (the *trompe l'oeil*); the option of serving as symbol and analogy; and the option of being dead but represented as though alive through taxidermy. In an urban economy, the free animal, like the prostitute, like art outside the museum, represents an aesthetic surplus that architecture, insofar as architecture is that which exceeds building, is also part of.

•

Like the red light district in Amsterdam, where the color red stands in some obvious way for flesh, illegality, and blood, traditional Apache initiation ceremonies, which are staged to celebrate the coming of age of young girls, use the explicit sign of blood to stand for the temporary interruption of normal civic life. The ceremony itself is bloodless. Its objective is to "transform the pubescent girl into the mythological figure 'Changing Woman' who gives the girl 'longevity and the physical capabilities of someone perpetually young.'"[13] The ceremony—which consists of feasts for the entire community paid for by the girl's relatives, and to which other tribal members are invited, as well as tourists—is played out between two different spaces, the large interior space of an open-weave tepee made of tree branches, where the girls dance, and the large exterior space of an arena, where the medicine men dance.[14] The precise relationship of the tepee to the other structures at the ceremonial site, such as juniper branch ramadas set up for the exchange of food and gifts, is important, as is the separation of space between girls and medicine men. The ceremony differs from tribe to tribe and over the years has changed in various ways. For three to four days, food is served to whomever comes and the girls, six or seven of them, dance day and night in the tepee. They are attended by aunts or sisters ("sponsors"). The dance itself is very constrained; a swift but smooth and continuous shuffle of both feet, held together, from side to side over a surface made of hardened buckskin—two or three shuffles to the left and then again to the right and back and so forth. In rhythmic accompaniment to this shuffle are the sound of many rows of swishing beads that are sewn on the white buckskin dresses and serapes that the girls wear. The scene inside the tepee can be viewed by people gathering outside and peering through the openings in the branch structure, but the scene is detached from the public sphere.[15] The girls dance in a concentrated way, with occasional short breaks, to the sound of drums and to the rhythmic music created by the beads and their feet on the buckskin.

Outside the tepee, in the adjacent arena, is a large bonfire around which older medicine men dance. They are dressed in tribal attire, hold long spears, and dance in a line, around and around the fire. Occasionally, they stop and file by the entrance to the tepee. The men also dance to the sound of a drum, and the dominant sense of their space is, as usual, public.

This scene—which is reproduced in almost every culture in the world, with different ritualistic settings—is the almost universal symbolic scene of initiation where the young girl, still attired in her virginal whiteness, is introduced into the world of adult sexuality by older, fatherly, men. All such scenes are accompanied, typically, by the play and passage between public and private space, domestic and civic life, interior quiet and exterior noise, surveillance, spectatorship, and voyeurism.

What interests me here is not the scene itself, although this is extremely beautiful and appealing, but, rather, what the scene excites in the spectators and the space of the spectators. The girls and men are enacting a ritual that has to do with specific prohibitions (blood, sex) and, as such, the ritual is sacred. It is a parallel world to the profane world that watches it. The profane world is not, however, in a state of industrious everyday life but, for the duration of the ceremony, has stopped its ordinary work in order to watch the sacred ritual, just as one stops work, as Hollier remarked, to go someplace on Sunday.[16] The sacred world has always been present in human life and it allows, as Georges Bataille in particular has suggested, a return to the prohibitions of nature without interrupting, except momentarily, the rhythm of everyday civic life. It is a return to what Bataille calls the "natural given," but not a full return. Because prohi-bitions usually refer to an aspect of animality—sexuality that is recognized but not permitted (the occasion for the scene, but prohibited in the scene)—this animality is ignited in the audience, where it can be acted out in various forms. The audience, which is comprised of tourists, residents, relatives of the girls and men, and visiting families, absorbs the meaning of the prohibition and enacts it in secular, but not normative or productive, space as a kind of civic orgy in which excess, bans, blood and sex all play a part. The spectators get drunk and there are occasionally violent encounters; tourists are banned from the all-night reveries; the bathrooms (the woman's bathroom in particular) are covered with blood that has been splashed on the floor and walls. The normative spaces of everyday life are brought into play and newly rendered as part of the ceremonial space, but with an additional capacity to be sullied and literalized as altars or sacrificial sites, much as the slaughterhouse becomes a sacrificial site in Temple Grandin's account. The sacred ceremony and its designated spaces simultaneously release and control this return to animality in the spectators, in the same way that churches have traditionally released and controlled spiritual life, and this animality, in turn, reconstructs the city temporarily as an animal domain. Protected from the various violent effects of such a release, the space of the tepee and the space of the arena are maintained as strict ceremonial areas in which the dances are carried out in the contrapuntal way already described. At the end of the three days, everyone goes home, puts on normal clothing again, keeps things clean, and carries on normal human life—upholding laws, acting as citizens.

•

Architecture, in the two scenes elaborated above, is alternately a public space, a sacred space, a domestic structure, and the technological and evolutionary evidence of the existence of a profane and sacred world in the human world. It is patently not nature. Instead, as Rem Koolhaas has been telling us, architecture is shopping. It supplies the literal evidence of the recoil of humans from the "natural given," which is not-shopping, the animal. It also, however, houses a controlled return to nature through the profane and the sacred, and provides not only the space but also the accoutrements for all the existential attitudes that range from the sovereign to the horrific and final event of death. In order to escape the paralyzing chill of death that happens inside its spaces, according to Bataille, architecture also strives to be identical with itself in time such that it can stand, as much as possible, outside time. It is a structure for a kind of animal that has undergone the up-righting of humanization, but it also exists in a post-natural condition, like all technologies. It is an active form of the *informe* (the idle upright), but its form displays itself most profoundly when it is released, in some sense, from its usefulness. When architecture is relatively idle in space—when it asserts itself as (only) an aesthetic performance, as in the Stock Exchange room, or when we observe the life within it more intently than we notice the structure itself, as in the Amsterdam scene or the civic arena of the Apache village—we can see that its form is post-animal, both human and animal at the same time. To be idle in time, even in the interest of endurance, is also a flirtation with death. There is no time without life.[17]

•

Very little has been said, apart from Bataille's version, about sacred practices and the role they might play in architecture. There is, of course, an enormous amount of literature on architecture and the sacred, in part because this relationship qualified all pre-modern, in my terms, pre-Renaissance, architecture. Post-animal life carries vestiges of the pre-modern sacred forward in peculiar ways, largely through different theories of symbolic work. Clifford Geertz, in *The Interpretation of Culture*, discusses the adjudication of human religious practices to the world in which humans must live, the "actual state of affairs" as he calls it. His view is not unlike Lévi-Strauss'—structuralist, anthropological, ethnographic. Religious practices, which are symbolic, belong to the brain, although they also involve the body; the world in which "humans must live" belongs to the body, although it also involves the brain. "Religious symbols," according to Geertz, "formulate a basic congruence between a particular style of life and a specific . . . metaphysics, and in so doing sustain each with the borrowed authority of the other." He continues: ". . . religion tunes human actions to an envisaged cosmic order and projects images of cosmic order onto the plane of human experience. . . ." Because human beings are genetically generalized to adapt to multiple worlds, the symbolic world performs the specifying, instruction-giving role that is necessary to specific survival. As Geertz says: "to build a dam a beaver needs only an appropriate site and the proper materials—his mode of procedure is shaped by his physiology. But man, whose genes are silent on the building trades, needs also a conception of what it is to build a dam, a conception he can get only from some symbolic source—a blueprint, a textbook, or a string of speech by someone who already knows how dams are built—or, of course, from manipulating graphic or linguistic elements in such a way as to attain for himself a conception of what dams are and how they are built.[18]

And Geertz summarizes this process: "The perception of the structural congruence between one set of processes, activities, relations, entities, and so on, and another set for which it acts as a program, so that the program can be taken as a representation, or conception, a symbol, of the programmed, is the essence of human thought."[19]

The world made symbolically—and there is almost no better example than architecture (the architect, *"whose genes are silent on the building trades"*)—is a world made according to how humans think and what humans need. Together these form a culture of humanness that needs both symbolism and an idea of a world, since symbolic processes stabilize the world and vice versa. It is the exercise of symbolic work in the face of material realities, and the search, in material realities, for symbolic expression that characterizes the multiple arenas of human endeavor, not least the field of inquiry that is architecture.

Some of what Geertz is saying about the relation between world and symbol can be seen in the functionalism of architectural modernism, although that particular formulation of the "intertransposability" between "models for [reality] and models of [reality]"[20] removed from the idea of need/function the complexity of desire. Insofar as the world is man's labor, this labor necessarily includes the labor of symbolic life, which, at certain moments, will make any notion of labor as a repository of a more real reality impossible to hold. The animal, which acts routinely as the symbol of genetic inevitability and limited adaptability, is also, paradoxically, understood to be free of the need for symbolic life. The animal has no apparent equivalent to human art, politics, culture or language. Attempts to discover these things in the animal world are always caught in the cone of symbolic projection. Thus, the animal stands outside the most fundamental enclave of human thought itself, which is symbolized perfectly by an upright posture that is an absolute break, in Leroi-Gourhan's terms, with the animal world. This uprightness, then, is not merely postural, but an exact moment of entry into symbolic life and an exact moment of departure from genetic specificity. That architecture—an extreme act of symbolic expression that is almost completely detached from genetic knowledge—calls attention to the upright posture and historically maintains a relationship between its own symbolic repertoire and nature suggests a profound anxiety about its drastic removal from the realm of any other natural than the human natural. This is also, paradoxically, an anxiety about how embroiled with, even isomorphic with, human thought architecture is. In the face of this anxiety, the animal in architecture acts as the speechless form that provides the salve of a more "true" nature. We see some aspect of this animal in characterizations of an architectural occupant as a being who lives inside buildings as if inside a kind of nature, with natural light and a warm habitat. The animal occupant in these cases attempts to ground architecture in ancient and instinctual forces—ultimately, genetic forces—rather than the relentlessly adjudicating, symbolic forces of human existence. Architecture's horizontality, trabeation, which is the posture of the animal (and the human at rest), thus both accommodates and wars with its verticality, the posture of the human who moves.

As mentioned earlier, animals in the post-animal world are, primarily, useful. And the use of the animal includes its possible symbolic and structural usages, as ornament, as otherness. "What marks us [humans] so severely," Bataille wrote, "is the *knowledge* of death, which animals fear but do not know."[21] The knowledge of death, in Bataille, operates in tandem with both the knowledge and abhorrence of sexuality that informs the practice of eroticism. The animal, according to Bataille, does not anticipate or wait for death. Death is the sole thing that makes life possible; it is thus sovereign over life. It also exceeds the idea of life; we cannot bear it, we try to forget about it. The perpetual explosion of life "is possible on one condition: that the spent organisms give way to new ones, which enter the dance with new forces."[22]

Both of the ceremonial scenes—Amsterdam and Apache—play out sacred and profane aspects of death, life, excess, sovereignty, eroticism. The animal, per se, is noticeable in these scenes only obliquely as, for example, in the buckskin dress, or the fur rug on the floor of the Amsterdam bedroom. The open-work tepee in which the girls dance and the houses in which the prostitutes wait border, in spite of the "working window," on being illicit architectures, architectures that are no longer doing their normal life-sustaining work. It is only in such non-working architecture that, in a sense, our own life and death comes to mind. We are literally exposed to ourselves, as living beings, in an unusual way. In such provisional architectures—the Stock Exchange room was another example, as would be the architectural ruin—we paradoxically find the question of human sovereignty posed and challenged, in these cases, by means of the conditions of idleness and uprightness (particularly the combination) and in terms of cost. This idea of human sovereignty is, to repeat myself again, not that of the various humanisms of the sixteenth or the eighteenth centuries. Those humanisms clearly resisted the animal. Renaissance humanism calculated the cost of human life and found it to be of immeasurable, but necessarily transcendental, worth, because of its divine content. Eighteenth century humanism calculated the cost of human life and found that its value could be increased, in a secular mode, by excising its animal aspects. In Bataille, life's worth is measured against the worth of life's cessation, i.e. death. Death is the "most luxurious form of life," he writes, ". . . We could really not imagine a more costly process. . . . Everything within us demands that death lay waste to us . . . life is the luxury of which death is the highest degree, that of all the luxuries of life, human life is the most extravagantly expensive."[23]

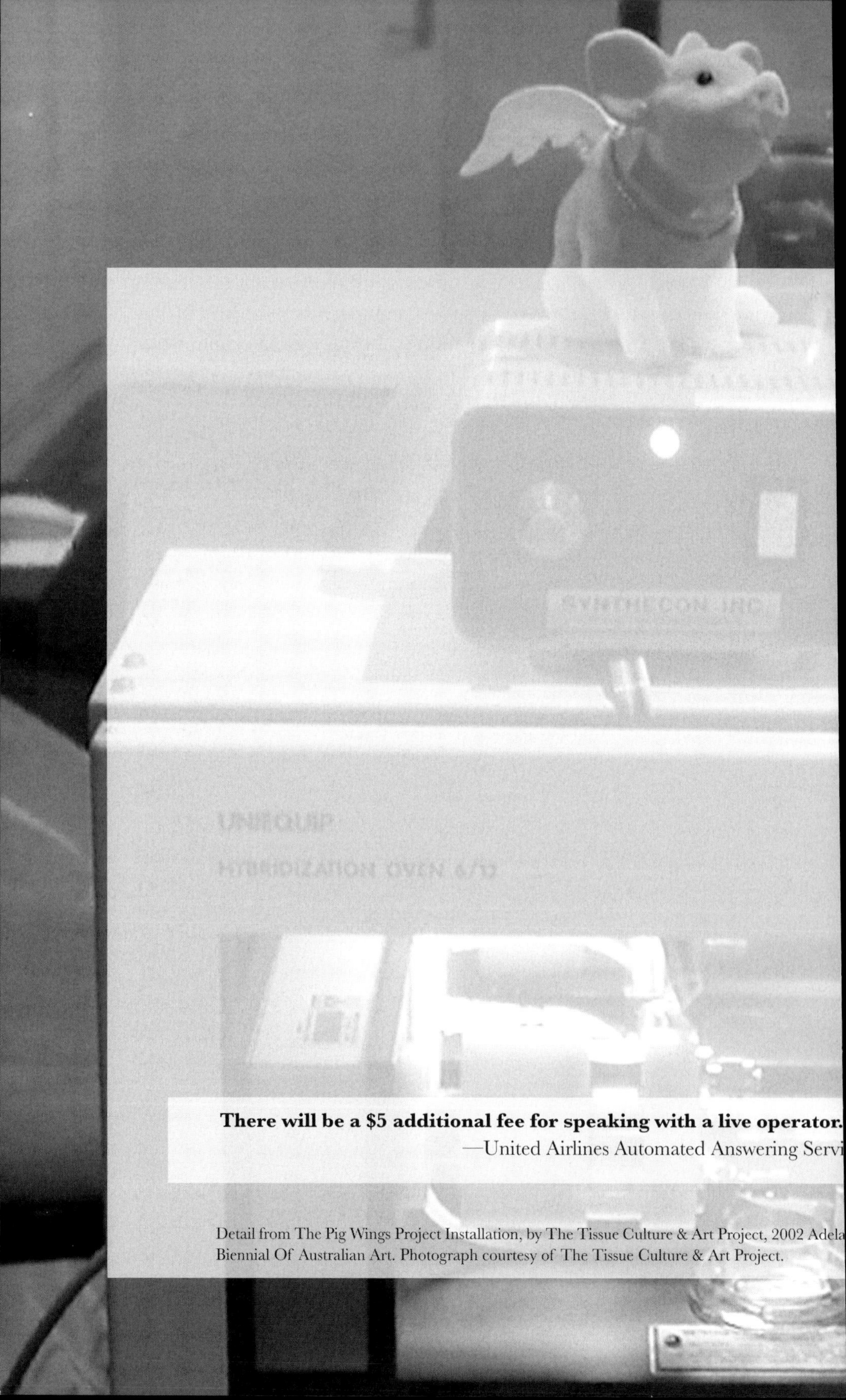

**There will be a $5 additional fee for speaking with a live operator.**

—United Airlines Automated Answering Servi

Detail from The Pig Wings Project Installation, by The Tissue Culture & Art Project, 2002 Adela Biennial Of Australian Art. Photograph courtesy of The Tissue Culture & Art Project.

# 18: ENGINEERING

The Tissue Culture and Art Project[1] (TC&A) has undertaken several tissue engineering projects, some speculative, that explore the "Art of the Semi-Living and Partial Life." One project is to grow wing-shaped objects out of pig-tissue (*Pig Wings Project*), another to sustain a partial body part, an ear, in a "technological environment" (*Extra Ear ¼ Scale Project*), a third, to grow frog meat (*Disembodied Cuisine*). These projects are not genetic engineering projects but they raise many interesting questions about how life and technology are seeking each other out after centuries of alienation. The Pig Wings Project was never about making the pig fly, yet from an architectural standpoint, and in light of remarks made earlier about the form and movement of birds, the import of attaching wings to a pig is always morphologically suggestive. If you attached a pair of wings to a pig, and you wanted the pig to fly (that is, you wanted the pig to live in a way that included flying), you would have the following problems: The wings might attach, but in order to fly the pig would have to be altered to fit the wings. The first alteration would require hardwiring moving wings into the pig's biochemistry. A pig is too heavy to fly. Its bones would have to be made hollow and its body mass leaner. You could attach a wing-engine to the pig, as if it were an airplane, but the interesting thing about the TC&A is that it is specifically testing certain ideological and technological limits and powers of living material, not mechanizing flesh. The pig, in effect, would have to become a bird. It might be a new bird species that resembled a pig although it would be more bird than pig because flight and all that it implies, or the presence of functional wings even if flight is impossible (as in the ostrich or penguin), has been a defining attribute of birds since at least the Renaissance, and surely before. A pig with wings that is not a bird is a fascinating "monster," a hybrid without transformative powers. And, clearly, it is transformative powers we are after.

Grafting a human ear to a mouse, which was done in the famous 1995 experiment by Dr. Charles Vacanti, poses similar problems. At first, the success of the graft seemed to promise an interesting future. But because the ear did not need to work, the mouse was burdened with a folly and the fate of the project was the fate of follies—fascinating for their visual provocation and experimental nerve, but a construction in which interesting surfaces become "mere surface" very quickly. The wings and pig, ear and mouse projects provoke, among other things, the idea that living tissue is species-specific. It may be possible, these experiments suggest, to return to certain forks in the road in order to remake the future of our own and other species, but the direction of this remaking, about which we hear daily, is quite tricky. There are, as the *TA&C* project elucidates in pointed ways, profound ethical issues in all such "life engineering" projects.[2] And, purely formally, you may not get the species, or hybrid (pig-bird), you planned on. It is additionally interesting that for many of these tasks computation has been an indispensable partner.

I want to look a little more closely at one of these digital biological projects, specifically the Human Genome Project. This project, in a shorter time than was expected, has successfully mapped approximately thirty million DNA units of the human nucleotide sequence in order, among other things, to better predict diseases, or proclivities toward diseases, that are genetically transmitted. This project continues a technical gambit that began with the invention of the microscope in the seventeenth century: determining how far biological instruments, technological and epistemological, can penetrate into the minutia of the body and, in a corollary but reverse fashion, into the diverse milieux of the world that the body inhabits.

The Human Genome Project is about engineering genetic material but it is also about finding, to use the prevailing metaphors, the construction mechanisms for the biological edifices called life. This project—made conceptually and practically possible by the computer—has more or less adopted the ideology of geneticists from an earlier part of the twentieth century that believed genetic action to be a front-loaded, "executive" system. The "gene" sends "instructions" to the secondary elements of the system, the cytoplasm and proteins, which in turn develop into the complex organism. Richard Lewontin has argued that the Human Genome Project will not solve what it thinks it will solve, because the complexity of life is not produced in this executive way. Instead, Lewontin and others claim, life is produced as a complex system of feedback loops between developing cells and proteins. Life that develops from a combined cellular and environmental milieu versus life that is driven by its DNA are two poles of an argument that has been under way, in some form, since the early part of the twentieth century. Several versions of this argument were transferred, in 1944, to another developing science, mainly cybernetics, which I discuss below in more detail. Cybernetics looked at models of biological intelligence in order to design, initially, war machines.

The genome project—which has been likened to the writing of a manual with instructions on building and running the human body—is a summary document of knowledge at a particular point in time, not unlike Diderot's encyclopedia. As such it is already an historical rather than a futuristic document, and a new, although encoded, register of how taxonomic and encyclopedic knowledge still serves as a paradigm for the assembly and distribution of knowledge. In some ways the genome "book" is like a pre-historic book in its compilation of an undifferentiated body of knowledge that can coalesce into almost any form. The human body, as we know, has always been inscribed in epistemological paradigms, and this is no less true of a body informed by a genetic model than of a body informed by linguistics, sociopolitics or medieval science. However, I think the two most staggering and impressive attributes of the genome project, for a lay person, lie, first, in the sheer number of "words," each of which represents a complex operation, that have been amassed in the genome document, and, second, the fact that it has been put on a public Website. This project has been, among other things, a twentieth century testing ground for the robustness of computer technology and a demonstration of how close we seem to be to fully computing our own genesis. However, the problems that Lewontin articulates with respect to this project—the problems of the "exemplary" potential of these gene sequences, which were taken not from a random sampling of population but from two Icelandic subjects,[3] its "readability," and its potential use and meaning—are immediately confronted by the casual Web user who visits the public Website on which the project has been published. It is, bluntly, incomprehensible as a life map not only because of the symbolic language in which it is written but also because it is only the beginning of another vast set of operations yet to be carried out.

In addition, there have been rapid cultural shifts toward new forms of empirical and evidentiary discourse, most of which are attempting to prove what empiricism has always attempted to prove, that life—that slippery and elusive thing—is hardwired. Life is concrete and life is real, and because of these things, it must also be predictable and subject to laws. This version of the concrete and real directs the internal milieu of biochemical processes outward toward external manifestations that correspond, in some sensible way, with orders emanating from a genetic command center. The human body, held tightly in that curious and highly detailed place between the internal and the external, is newly understood to be capable of an almost full externalization, an almost full exposure of its mysteries. The dream of the computer/genetic biology alliance is, in some sense, that internal life—the life that always confuses the question of the real—will finally yield to biochemical processes. New cures and the astonishingly seductive sovereignty of two terms, *computer* and *genetics*, are part of this evidentiary picture. The computer is a machine interested in the iterative production of evidence and the formation of signatures or patterns that can persuade us of specific orders and logics, and genetics is a field that is daily producing new evidence about biological life that will change the order and logic of life itself, biological and otherwise.

It is interesting, too, that the language of the Human Genome Project has been cast, for the most part, in what we would instantly recognize as architectural metaphors: structure, spatial relations, programming, building blocks, design and so forth. Architecture has, in turn, adopted the biological metaphors of variation, morphology, epigenetic surfaces, adaptation, evolution and development. In spite of these exchanges the Human Genome Project has no obvious relation to the daily practice of architecture, or, rather, in order for it to have serious consequences in architecture, we would have had to overcome innumerable obstacles. We would have to generally believe, as I have been arguing in this book, that theories of life and generation have architectural consequences because they affect both the idea and reality of human life as it is lived in the body and as it is lived inside enclosures. And we would also have to believe that an exchange, or an economy, of metaphors is consequential. This is an old discussion that belongs, in part, to the meticulous methods of inquiry of post-structural philosophy. One could, too quickly I know, summarize this discussion by saying that metaphors, like the language they belong to, are transitory, and therefore arbitrary, but also directed, and therefore not arbitrary, the notorious *arbitrary but fixed* condition of language that de Saussure articulated. It matters, in other words, that it is architectural metaphors that are used in biology, and biological metaphors that are used in cybernetics, because metaphors act, very precisely, as agents for the transfer of meaning, or, more strictly, as agents for the construction of meaning wherever it may occur. Postclassical theory, which brings theories of language and science together, has been very interested in these constructions of meaning, particularly as they apply to writings by geneticists.

Architectural metaphors have been used widely in many sciences because modern sciences, like architecture since the dawn of science, are always in need of a visible structure upon which to hang its theories. Architecture plays the same role for science that it has played for other disciplines: upholding, in its theory, history and practice, and in its claim to physical reality, crucial operational distinctions between the animate and the inanimate, interior and exterior, design and craft, theory and practice—distinctions between the concrete and the ideational itself. Architecture demonstrates, to itself and others, the proper in-the-world performance of these oppositions and distinctions.[4] The precise contribution architecture makes to this grounding of science and the specific reciprocities involved thrive in the midst of the metaphoric circulation I mentioned above.

The person who has given, I think, the most succinct and provocative history of the relation between the computer and biology is Evelyn Fox Keller in her book *Refiguring Life*.[5] One of several contemporary theoretical analyzes of the impact of the computer on biology, it answers the question, in part, why the computer has made many of its most significant advances, as a technology, through the biological sciences—medical science, embryology and genetics. It also argues that contemporary biological research and contemporary cyberscience have been uniquely formed by this biology/computer analogy. Other significant developments, such as the military applications that Manuel de Landa discusses in his book *War in the Age of Intelligent Machines*[6] and the role of telecommunications companies and the military in the economic and cultural advancement of the computer, are indebted in complex ways to the founding principles of cyberscience. These founding principles depend on both the differences and similarities between biological life and machine life and the idea of an informational system that acts as an "organic system."

Early in the twentieth century, as Keller recounts, with the re-discovery of Mendel's work in 1900, genetics was founded as a discipline that focused on the transmission of genetic information, ignoring, for the most part, the subsequent development of that information in the cytoplasm (the fertilized egg). Written into this history is, to some degree, a history of gender metaphors that emerge in Keller's account as an equation between "developmental milieu," i.e. the cytoplasm environment, growth of the embryo, and "transmission," i.e. genetic transfer of information. This has nothing to do with the sexual act of contribution by male and female to the fertilization of an egg, but the terms of debate are uncannily familiar and Keller is fully aware of the implications of this debate. Embryology continued to study embryonic growth and the overall development of the organism, but beginning with the re-definition of the term "heredity" to "refer exclusively to transmission," the two subjects of transmission and development became increasingly separate concerns. In part, Keller remarks, it was necessary for genetics to clarify its own investigative territory and establish itself as a separate discipline. At the same time, the concentration of genetics on the transmission of genetic information had its own compelling aesthetic: "geneticists . . . tended to assume that these hypothetical particles, the genes, must somehow lie at the root of development."[7] Or, as the geneticist R. S. Brink put it: "the Mendelian theory postulates discrete, self-perpetuating, stable bodies—the genes—resident in the chromosomes, as the hereditary materials. This means, of course, that the genes are the primary internal agents controlling development."[8] A large part of Keller's discussion concerns this assumption that the gene gives not only primary impetus to the subsequent development of life, but also *executive*, that is, the most important, impetus to the development of life, although at the time when genes and gene action were first discussed, nothing was understood about the gene itself or how it worked.

In the 1920s and 1930s genetic biologists began, by necessity, to speculate about embryonic development. Embryologists were concerned with how a germ cell develops into a multicellular organism: if the genetic content of all cells in an organism is the same, how is it possible to make sense of the emergence of the manifest differences among all the cells that make up a complex organism? To the embryologists it seemed self-evident that this problem of differentiation, so deeply at the heart of their own concerns, was simply incompatible with the notion that the gene was the exclusive locus of action.[9] Geneticists, in other words, could not account for why some cells of the embryo developed in one way, and some in another. There were various theories about development, one of which was the speculation that the gene, in its executive role, somehow delivered information about difference to the proteins, which in turn resulted in the complex differentiation found in higher organism. This speculative answer was confirmed and clarified with the discovery of DNA in 1953.

DNA is the means by which genetic information is transmitted. The discovery of DNA resulted in a re-formulation of the development equation that, nevertheless, kept the gene as an executive force: "DNA carries the 'genetical information' (or program), and genes 'produce their effects' by providing the 'instructions' for protein synthesis. DNA makes RNA, RNA makes proteins, and proteins make us."[10] More importantly, however, as Keller points out, Watson and Crick's research on DNA introduced the "information metaphor" to biological discourse. Information theory, fully under way in 1950 with Norbert Wiener's work on artificial intelligence and cybernetics in communication systems (*Cybernetics* was published by MIT Press in 1948), made the information metaphor available to Watson and Crick, but in different ways, genetic research had, in its earliest stages, suggested to theorists like Wiener that biological operations, and thus computational operations, had to be a front-loaded transmittal problem. As Wiener wrote:

the ideal computing machine must then have all its data inserted at the beginning, and must be as free as possible from human interference to the very end. This means that not only must the numerical data be inserted at the beginning, but also all the rules for combining them, in the form of instructions covering every situation which may arise in the course of the computation.[11] It is precisely this "front-loading" that Wolfram later attacks in his theory of simple random programming as the key to a level of complexity that resembles that of nature. The parallel one might also note here between "no human interference" and "no protein interference" are laden with the ever present ironies of this analogy. Wiener was interested in the function of the nervous system of animals and humans, the brain in particular, and he was interested in the feedback mechanisms of living bodies. The cybernetic idea of information, although dedicated to the ideas of storage and transmittal and therefore attractive to biologists, was nevertheless problematic. As Keller remarks:

> Because DNA seemed to function as a linear code, using this notion of information for genetics appeared to be a natural. Although geneticists recognized that the technical definition of *information* simply could not serve for biological information (because it would assign the same amount of information to the DNA of a functioning organism as to a mutant form, however disabling that mutation was). Thus the notion of genetical information . . . was not literal but metaphoric. But it was extremely powerful. Although it permitted no quantitative measure, it authorized the expectation . . . that biological information does not increase in the course of development: it is already fully contained in the genome. This move and, even more, the collapsing of *information* with *program* and *instruction* vastly fortified the concept of gene action . . . [genes] "are law-code and executive power—or, to use another simile, they are architect's plan and builder's craft—in one."[12]

The information theory/biology connection was not a perfect fit, as the above statement makes clear, but it was very fruitful for both sciences. Molecular biology, from the 1950s on, developed rapidly. If organic development is an "unfolding of preexisting instructions encoded in the nucleotide sequences of DNA . . . it makes perfect sense to set the identification of these sequences as the primary and, indeed, ultimate, goal of biology."[13]

However, at a certain moment, information theory and biology came to more serious impasses. Molecular biology tended toward reductionism, shaping developmental theory on the study of extremely simple organisms, such as the bacterium *E. coli*, in the belief that the action of the gene would express itself equally in the simplest life form as in the complex. The linear structure of causal influence, "from the central office of DNA to the outlying subsidiaries of the protein factory,"[14] used the cybernetic term "information," but the path of molecular biology was ideologically opposite to the path of information theory. Cybernetics was "using the organism to illustrate a new kind of machinery [artificial intelligence]," while molecular biology was "seeking to model the organism after the machines of yesteryear [linear, causal]."[15] In time, geneticists realized again that they would have to take on the old problem of embryology and development. As the geneticist Richard Lewontin put it:

> DNA is a dead molecule, among the most nonreactive, chemically inert molecules in the world . . . incapable of "making" anything else. . . . While it is often said that DNA produces proteins, in fact proteins (enzymes) produce DNA. The newly manufactured DNA is certainly a copy of the old . . . but we do not describe the Eastman Kodak factory as a place of self-reproduction [of photographs]. . . . We inherit not only genes made of DNA but an intricate structure of cellular machinery made up of proteins.[16]

Lewontin's observations were foreshadowed in the 1960s in work by a few developmental biologists who speculated on a more intricate series of exchanges between the biological concept of information and that of cybernetics, work that tried to import the more complex feedback models offered by cybernetics into the study of genetic development. Developmental biology (earlier known as embryology) re-imported, along with the idea of feedback, the terms expelled by molecular biology: old organist conceptions of purpose, organization, harmony, as well as other terms from physics and other branches of the physical sciences in order to acquire the concept "circular feedback" so inimical to the notion of executive gene action that molecular biology embraced.[17] Feedback was a fundamental part of information theory from its inception because it was one of the processes that would enable, at least theoretically, a machine to learn. Developmental biologists, as Lewontin later articulated, believed that it was the interaction of DNA with the cytoplasm that produced the complex development of the organism.[18] The attempt to directly model the computer, the computational machine, on life (the nervous system, the brain, logic, artificial intelligence) and to model life on the machine engages and troubles the relationship between the animate and the inanimate in a very different way from the philosophical conjecture that had been applied to this opposition throughout history.[19] Just as the ancient "invention" of the weapon structure man-horse-spear that Deleuze and Guattari discussed in *Nomadology* inaugurated a different theme of speed in culture—a theme elaborated on in subsequent periods until the body-propulsion-projectile equation is broken apart again by the industrial revolution—the conjunction of human-computer inaugurates a theme of correspondence, a continuum, between brain and world, most implications of which have yet to be realized. Such a continuum would, of necessity, revise almost every definition of human and animal that we are familiar with.

# 19: PROCESSING

> It is proposed that a machine be deemed intelligent, if it can act in such a manner that a human cannot distinguish the machine from another human merely by asking questions via a mechanical link.
>
> —Alan Turing, *Turing Test of Intelligence*



Norbert Wiener remarks in the preface to the second edition of *Cybernetics or Control and Communication in the Animal and the Machine*: "If a new scientific subject has real vitality, the center of interest in it must and should shift in the course of years."[1] Architecture, like many professions, is being computerized, and its interests are shifting. There are changes in the discourse, much of it neo-scientific, which has traditionally signified in architecture that we are in the spirit of things, in the spirit of our own time. It is no secret, or perhaps it's a disturbing secret, that our students, many of them, will become Web designers. A person trained in architecture, benefiting from five hundred years of the discipline's dedication to the visual, and now adept at computational logics, is perfectly trained for Web design.

How to characterize this shift in the terms of my discussion here? Certainly architecture has been caught, as always and, as always almost at the last minute, by events in the world—commercial, technological, ideological. But in the practice and discipline, architecture also continues significant internal debates. Commentary on computing in architecture continues its fascination with modernism, theories of signification, neo-scientific social theories, cinema, adding into the mix new theorizations of force, iterative processes, growth and form, sustainability questions, complexity and chaos theory, Darwin, genetics, robotics, biosemiotics, biocybernetics, dynamical systems theory, geodetics, d'Arcy Thompson, Gregory Bateson, Wolfram and many others. Some of the architectural theorists who were in on some of the seismic shifts in architectural thinking twenty years ago are now curators of that period. And some practitioners still have their teeth firmly clamped on the cord that snakes back to Deleuze and Guatteri. Practicing architects continue to be enmeshed in the problem of pointing the flexible and not-so-flexible mechanism of architecture toward the next thing, the next competition, the next commission, the next style and look. They have no choice but to do this. At the same time, it seems as if the practice of architecture is, as always, in danger of disappearing, so precarious is its hold on these events. It is also true, however, that these events are evidence of the way in which any practice and discipline works out the complex territory of its meaning at any point; the complex alliances and affiliations that are simultaneously associated with being in the world of architecture and being in the world.

There are still, however, serious differences in the positions one might hold at this moment in architecture. Architecture is political, or it is not. Architecture is media, or it is not. Architecture is a system of fluid dynamics, or it is not. Architecture is about form, or it is not. The formulation "architecture is . . ." is obsolete, or it is not. And so on.

Post-animal life in this account has been, among other things, a repository of a particular kind of post-Renaissance aliveness for humans and animals that, in architecture, becomes a hybridized, non-psychological form of concentrated energy (the "human-animal"). It is, as well, a symbol of slipped histories. Post-animal life is now also being virtualized in the digital world. This new incarnation for humans and animals is attuned to the re-mechanization of architecture by means of the computer, although, as I suggest earlier, the computer in architecture may also represent the beginning of a passage beyond post-animal life, which generally still privileges life and life-related processes. The transition of architecture from a twentieth century mechanistic practice to architecture as a twenty-first century digital practice, where technical aspects are tightly integrated with the process of design and both design and fabrication processes are in play from the outset, is a transition that may, finally and paradoxically, erase the self-privilege of the animate that produced the asymmetries I have been interested in exploring. This would not be because life disappears but because life becomes the model for everything. Interest in emergent systems of organization, for example, use scripting as a way of operating inside a live field of information. The classical oppositions between movement and stasis are an anathema to digital work and to the contemporary analysis of life itself. Yet nothing is farther from the truth. Contemporary computational architecture freely uses animation software to imitate the movement of living beings, but the production of those grotto-like interiors of digital buildings threaten to finalize Caillois' spatial closure on animate life. And, further, the all-surface character of these projects often expresses, yet again in history, a unified technical aim, not a complex skin with a complex interior. So the asymmetry between life and architecture still seems dominant; contemporary biological life, as it manifests itself in humans and animals, seems as self-privileging as ever, and architecture, in its technical and formal pursuits, more indifferent than ever.

Wiener predicted, fifty-five years ago, the life part of the processing machine/life equation would be too interesting to resist. Much labor is now expended, in architecture and elsewhere, on giving objects—artistic and otherwise—the status, nuances, viral infections and biological flexibility of live beings. The surprising conservatism that has come with this task—a conservatism that is built into computational processes and, one could say, into the maintenance of life itself—has, on occasion, returned a number of debates in architecture once again to questions of formalism. Part of this is due to the somewhat surprising desire of computational science to be of "use," surprising because the computer is, above all, a kind of toy that toys with what it would be like to be a limbless body—a head with a brain inside. As Turing said, the tasks to which the computer is put are tasks that do not require limbs, or, rather, require limbs at a distance in the form of our hands or robotic arms, not limbs, in either a Marxist or Renaissance sense, to do the work of the computer. The functionalist ethic that still seems present in computational work is also driven, in part, by old ideas about how machines should serve us. This ethic connects the computer to the world of material fabrication and production, where it serves, for the most part, what we still call capital, or, perhaps, late capital. The computer's use and politics is also still grounded in the conditions of its invention during the Second World War. It is, in many respects, still an instrument of the state; its informational networking potentials are still vastly easier to download than to upload. In addition, and as always, along with any connection with so-called reality and pragmatic concerns comes the desire to reproduce reality, not simply artistically, but now also genetically, since reality routinely fails the expectations of its admirers. It *asks* to be reproduced at every turn.

The history of these developments in architecture and other fields are hard to read carefully, because we are so close to them. On January 13, 2001, I read in *The New York Times* Science section—and this is how all such accounts begin—about the attempt of scientists to save an endangered species of ox from extinction by trying to reproduce it inside a cow, a biologically compatible species. A cow was successfully impregnated, and the baby gestated and born, but it died soon after. The scientists did not feel the death was due either to the genetic experiment or the cross-species incubation of the ox inside a cow. They reported the death simply as a "natural infant death."[2] All the ironies associated with the use of these words now, "natural infant birth," "natural infant death," were fully present at the scene of this birth, but it is these terms, as much as the ox and cow themselves, that are in the process of banishment. At what moment did the cow/ox become a natural infant? Was there any lingering sense of disjunction or *wrongness* about the cow/ox cross, like the wrongness that William Faulkner writes about when a boy falls in love with a cow (which is, admittedly, more drastic because it crosses the forbidden human/animal divide)? Also present at the scene of the birth was, perhaps, the image of a cheetah on the screen-saver of the laboratory technician's computer and, probably, leather shoes, leather purses, animal tokens attached to key chains, possibly even fur collars or hats, cups with images of dogs or bears on them, and so forth. Where we are now is, in part, a place where we are assimilating, banalizing, these life ironies, and this is simultaneously a revision of certain biological truths that, it so happens, have actually been true for only a few hundred years. The much promised erasure of irony—the tension between inner and outer meanings and one of the ways we have held oppositional structures in place while questioning their sacred status—carries with it the erasure of a certain kind of insight. It is nothing at all for us, we will find ourselves saying, to help cows give birth to oxen, oxen to eland, eland to kangaroo. We can now have the hybrid beings that were eradicated four hundred years ago through secularization, "accurate" representation, and theories of reproduction, in whatever form we wish, rather than these monsters having us. The re-branching of the evolutionary tree, which is based on finding common ground between formerly different species, is fully under way. Yet the transience of identities, across biological and species boundaries, across disciplinary boundaries, across ideas of sameness and difference, describes the course of biological and human history itself. And, further, irony gathers its force from language, which may or may not be fully subject to the events taking place in the visual field of the computer. We may be seeing, at this moment of transition, the internal operation of a very particular history that will close up again, like a fissure in the ice cap, once the assimilation of these relatively new scientific paradigms and theories of identity are complete. And it may not be as totalizing as the ubiquitous presence of the computer indicates.

The computer that has made many extraordinary investigations possible, in biology and architecture, is, in spite of its alliances, not primarily a piece of biological equipment. It is true that very early in the development of cybernetics, biological processes and metaphors became interesting because of the apparent similarities between neurological and computer operations. The visualization and virtualization of information that the computer also makes possible had some role to play in this attraction between the life sciences and cybernetics, but this visualization capacity has also extended the computer into almost every field of human knowledge. Many of the disciplines and practices that now are computerized had to invent a visual dimension for themselves to make full use of this visual capacity. The stock market was a good example. Hani Rashid's and Lise Anne Couture's virtual "kiosks" are information centers that simulate literal places in space; they take what was formerly electronic signboard information and give it a three-dimensional spatial reality. Desert Storm, for the United States and most of the world, was a war of the virtual; the instant visualization of remote places formerly understood through narratives. In addition to visualization, the computer is able to model complex systems of movement and animated sequences of action and behavior. Nothing could be more perfect for architecture—the animate technical, the technical organic, the technical visual, the visualized technical—except, of course, for the accompanying and annoying, even offensive to some, emergence of forms and interiors that float in apolitical, ahistorical space, that seem to have forgotten the old allegiances of architecture to limit, context, program, boundary and ground, and, of course, life. These floating forms are understood, by many, to be bastard or wayward forms, not quite worthy of the name of form since form has been in architecture, by definition, the fixing of process.

But the technology is still young, its future unclear. In work by the most interesting practitioners of this kind of architectural work, fascinating questions are being posed about architecture. One of the most interest-ing, if not *the* most interesting, is how computational work in architecture is directly engaged with "life problems"—not the classical life problems of how to build a pleasant shelter for a body, but the complex problem of how to understand the complexity of the world in which life lives and how to make or remake that world in light of this complexity. The early problem of "forces" that Greg Lynn, for example, used as a way to activate different generative systems in computational work—at the time, these were the somewhat large and undifferentiated forces of wind, traffic, sound—is now becoming far more differentiated and articulated. "Forces" are not reincarnations of Newtonian science, but evidence of a sudden new arena for intricate responses in architecture to everything around, in, and of it. The fact that Photoshop life figures continue to stand in for human or animal figures in most computational compositions means that the problems of sentient life forces and movement is still academic in these architectures. I think, though, that these Photoshop figures will eventually give way, as they already have in a number of projects, to something else—some kind of communicative force field that will have a human or animal surface in the architectural scheme but may become the fabled network by which architecture will break through many of its own limits. I think computational work will find its project, in other words, not in a re-hashed modernism or in some "unique form" production, but in life processes, in "sustainability"—not simply "green practices" but the deeper reaches of aliveness that are simultaneously biological, territorial, engaged in critiques of the various "fields" in which life exists, a play between constancy and motion, materiality and information and so forth.

Before that happens, the issues of form will, as usual, have to be settled. Along with the difficulty of form comes the difficulty of human life itself, which, like these new formless forms, is still historically illegitimate in the world of "proper" forms. Once again, post-animal life may solve, before its passage into something else, a certain dilemma for architecture. Life appears not as an ox born of a cow, nor as a monster—or, at least, its monstrosity is visible enough so that we can eliminate it—nor as the implied but faceless (the face turned away) human occupant of modernism, nor as the idealized human occupant of the nineteenth century, but as itself, humble and hollow, moving form alone, a translucent bubble of networked capacities and energies with motor skills and a path to follow.

Let me state more simply what I am thinking of in my title, "Processing." First, I am interested in the methodological question of what to do with computers in architecture. Second, I want to further explore the relationship, mentioned above, between cybernetics and biology, specifically, some of the ways these two fields have co-modelled each other over the last fifty years. Third, I think the computer hardware and software that we have been inheriting in architecture—from Hollywood, engineering, aerospace, SOM—is being structured, before we get it, around certain assumptions having to do with this cybernetic/biology alliance. There are a series of intricate, and old, questions associated with these things: how is architecture now connected with histories and theories of form?; what more can we say about changing definitions of "life" and the production of life in architectural space?[3]; what effect, one might ask, does understanding all these relationships between the organism and space have on architecture itself?; how might we build differently out of that knowledge? My too-abrupt answer here is that if these things and beings have nothing to do with each other, not merely in superficial ways but *really* nothing to do with each other, architecture would be out of business.

Many of the discussions documented in Wiener's still amazing and still politically disturbing book took place during the Macy seminars, which, as is well known, were funded by the Rockefeller Foundation. These seminars, about which much has been written, were exceptionally interesting. Convened by the federal government and attended by biologists, physicists, philosophers, anthropologists, geneticists, other scientists and students, the seminars were meant to explore the possibility of using computer science—at that time a very young science—for military purposes. The seminars also produced, or, rather, unearthed, a set of propositions about what kind of machine the computer was to aspire to be: primarily, a machine that could supplement, and perhaps even eventually fully imitate, human neurological function. Because of this early devotion to human neurological processes—to the human brain as a metaphor for the entire world—and because of biology's century-long interest in going into the details of the formation of life, cybernetics made many of its most substantive advances in the biological sciences. In the interest of getting as close as possible to "life" and all its processes, the computer's interest in its own future as a life-machine is inextricably tied to the future of generational processes in life. This is, by now, a circular and self-corroborating argument. The circularity is well known: The computer enables life to internally alter itself by means of genetic engineering made possible by vast computational data processing in exchange for the inclusion, in the definition of what it means to be human, of a genuine empirical and technological dimension, which, as we know, has been lurking in the definition of life even before mechanization and computation arrive as technological ideas.

If we believe Wiener's account, the Macy seminar participants were euphoric about the potential of "life-likeness" for the computer, and, in some respects, this potential has been fulfilled. But, as always, inside the process of attachment—machine to life, life to machine—old antinomies arise (atavistic, but no less powerful for their atavism) such that the computer perhaps found it a little more difficult, a little more laborious, to acquire forms of aliveness than it might have first imagined. On the other side, biology has found it to be a lot more difficult than was first imagined to figure out the mechanics of life. If the machine cannot become life, then perhaps life can become a machine. This idea was contained, also, in the original propositions of the cybernetic seminars. "The realization that Newtonian physics was not the proper frame for biology was perhaps the central point in the old controversy

**Figure 19.1:** Greg Lynn, *Ark of the World Museum and Visitor's Center*, Costa Rica, 2002. Photograph of model courtesy of Greg Lynn Form.

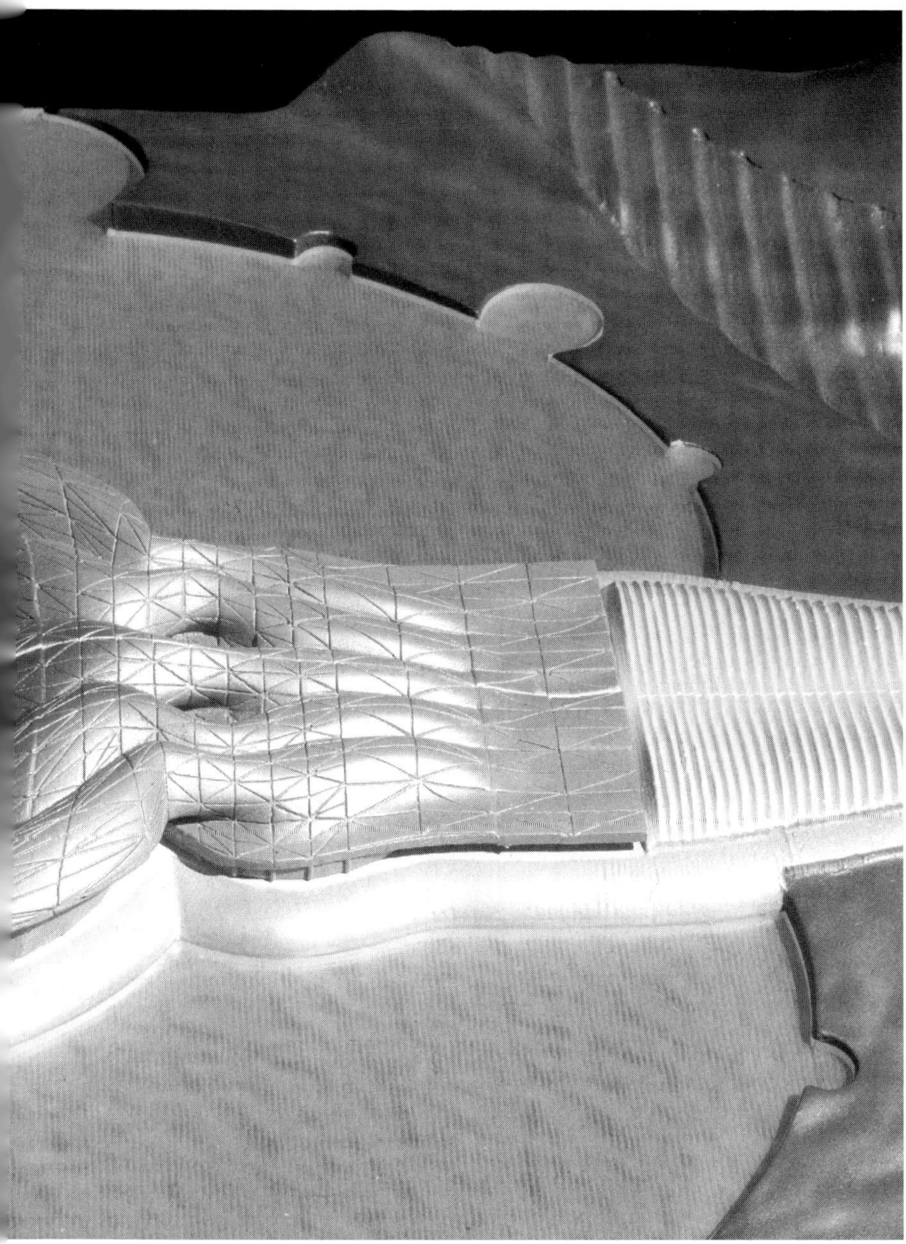

between vitalism and mechanism. In the end, as we have seen, the vitalist proved too much."[4] As Wiener writes: "At every stage of technique since Daedalus or Hero of Alexandria, the ability of the artificer to produce a working simulacrum of a living organism has always intrigued people."[5]

One of the central problematics of the cynbernetic life/machine equation was the problem of time—which, of course, engages the entire philosophical, mathematical, biological and metaphysical spectrum of existence. In architecture, the coupling of the two main contradictory conceptions of time—the reversible time of physics and the irreversible time of biology—makes up, in yet another way, the life/structure asymmetry. This coupling produces what one could call "architectural time:" the time in which a building endures or deteriorates, the time within which restoration and preservation is possible; the competition between materiality and abstract physical laws. Time's arrow, which in thermodynamics causes "populations of molecules to evolve . . . from order to disorder," in biology drives living beings "along a certain path by variation and selection" from which they cannot turn back.[6] All organized systems, whether living or not, increase in complexity over time and cannot reverse the sequence of their transformations. For Wiener, the problem of time was central to the potential of computational processes. In astronomy, he writes, "the music of the spheres is a palindrome, and the book of astronomy reads the same backward as forward." When this is formulated by Newton as "a formal set of postulates and a closed mechanics" the consequence was that ". . . the laws of mechanisms are unaltered by the transformations of the time variable. . . ."[7] On the other hand, writes Wiener, if we were to reverse a motion picture of the turbulence of clouds in a thunderhead, "it would look altogether wrong. We should see downdrafts where we expect updrafts, turbulence growing coarser in texture. . . ." The difference between astronomical and meteorological systems is the difference between a system with a relatively small number of almost rigid objects that interact in precise and predictable ways, such as the solar system under the influence of the laws of gravity, and a system with an enormous number of objects with complex interactions that cannot be predicted but can be statistically analyzed. Yet even in Newtonian systems, Wiener continues, "we are directed in time, and our relation to the future is different from our relation to the past. All our questions are conditioned by this asymmetry, and all our answers to these questions are equally conditioned by it."[8] One of the consequences of this directedness in time is (as already mentioned several times)that we can see only the stars that have the same past–future relation, the same thermodynamics, that we have.[9] "Within any world with which we can communicate," in other words, "the direction of time is uniform." In designing contemporary machines that, unlike the clock mechanisms of Descartes (which imagined animals to be forms of automata), are connected to external worlds and external bodies by means of energy and information flows, the question of time is also crucial. As Wiener writes:

> [R]elative input-output is a consecutive one in time and involves a definite past-future order. What is . . . not so clear is that the theory of the sensitive automata is a statistical one . . . it must give a satisfactory performance for a whole class of inputs. . . . Thus its theory belongs to the Gibbsian statistical mechanics rather than to the classical Newtonian mechanics. Thus the modern automaton exists in the same sort of Bergsonian time as the living organism. . . .Vitalism has won to the extent that even mechanisms correspond to the time-structure of vitalism, but . . . this victory is a complete defeat, for from every point of view which has the slightest relation to morality or religion, the new mechanics is fully as mechanistic as the old . . . the whole mechanist-vitalist controversy has been relegated to the limbo of badly posed questions.[10]

Of the biological sciences, as the previous chapter argued, it is genetics that has found the closest alliance with the computer. Genetic research could not have been fully conceived, in its current forms such as the Human Genome Project, without the computer. Almost all the priorities of computational development—repetition, additive processes, compiling, feedback—that characterize, in particular, visualization programs, as well as data programs, still belong to the idea that this machine can model itself after certain processes of the human brain such as learning and logic, as well as (although this is a secondary development) human and animal movement. It takes painstaking work, millions of dollars, millions of computational moments, and massive amounts of memory to "build" the animated animals of *Jurassic Park* or *Toy Story* or *A Bug's Life*—all of which, at the moment of their first presentation, were at the cutting edge of computational work in film.[11]

As a result, contemporary biological science and cyberscience have developed as intimately cross-referenced, although often conceptually opposed, systems. Architecture, in its dalliance with the computer, has run head-on into this cross-referenced system. The machine/body analogy that dawned in the nineteenth century as the possibility of a connection between the human body and brain and something outside the body, the force of electricity, for example—at the time, a monstrous connection—reaches a certain satiation with the biology/computer analogy. As Wiener says, the controversy surrounding the differences between machine and body has been, in some sense, tabled. Monstrosity, until the age of the machine, consisted of aberrant couplings and interchanges with animals or tetralogical beings from outside the human enclave. The gradual usurpation—or, if not exactly the usurpation, the co-occupation—by the machine of this category of monstrous otherness formerly occupied by some form of the animal is connected to the odd way in which the computer is being used to re-enliven old, especially mythological, animals that had begun to die in the imagination. It is important to note, however, that the relation of the body to the machine, like biology to the computer, is still an analogy, at most a homology, not (yet) the apparently desired collapse. The multi-faceted fantasy of intercourse between the animate and the inanimate is alive, but not fully consummated, by the match.

I have been arguing that in architecture, as in engineering and other building sciences, historical debates about building styles or, say, the political exigencies of practicing architecture have rarely directly engaged with contemporaneous debates about the definition of life or the definition of the machine. This is true partly because the architect began as a tradesman engaged in a manual practice, not as a scholar engaged in an intellectual discipline—the import of which is that metaphysical questions of life per se developed outside the practice. It is also true that the felt and literal distance between the body occupying a building and the building itself is very great. The question of the machine—from steam engines to computers—has been treated enthusiastically, for the most part, by modern architects, although largely for its potential application to technical tasks, such as those outlined in Giedion's *Mechanization Takes Command* or Le Corbusier's *Towards a New Architecture*.

In the same spirit, architectural practice, for the most part, has turned the computer into a dutiful office worker, a drafting machine. With the exception of a few practitioners who have been exploring generative computational principles—attempting to use animation and three-dimensional modeling programs in order to explore new territories of surface and force—most architectural offices have incorporated the computer as a means of efficiently producing building schedules, presentation and working drawings. Most are using AutoCad, the clumsy, linear, formally conventional computer software from Skidmore Owings and Merrill, a system that appears to accommodate both design and production, historically troubled areas of difference in architecture. Design, in architecture, which is simultaneously circumscribed by and antithetical to production and architecture, as a discipline and profession, has had to negotiate this delimitation continuously.

The computer would seem, in its idealist moments, to be the closest architecture has come, in both ancient and modern history, to importing, and depending on, a biological instrument, that is, an instrument that has aspirations toward biological movement and intelligence, whatever this might mean. None of the software or hardware we are currently using in architecture comes directly from the biological sciences per se, but the most provocative work being done in the profession is being done by practitioners who are fascinated by the potential for bringing life movements, motion capture, and vegetative and animal forms/energies into architectural forms.

Part of my overall discussion about how architecture has used the animal as a surrogate body—used it to get around the body/mind of the human being—is also at work in the architectural use of digital technology. If the computer is the new animal, organism, in contemporary culture—a new representation of the animate principle in culture—how does architecture's set of historical relations to animation, existential being and movement play themselves out in this new milieu? Or, if it is true, as Lacan says, that the locution "man has a body" is odd and archaic, how does this oddness and archaic condition manifest itself in architecture? These questions, the competition between the terms of the wet and the dry and the question of technological animation of the computer, are already at work in architecture in subtle and overt ways.

But compared to the success—perhaps success is the wrong word—compared to the ongoing and problematic interchange between the terms of biology and the terms of the computer, military and telecommunications systems seem bogged down in various kinds of hyperbole about computer potential, of which the suspension of extremely interesting moral and legal questions is only the most obvious evidence. Moral and legal questions about cloning are harder to suspend, which is why bioethics has developed concurrently with the Human Genome Project. Computer war—if I may speak in this disinterested (perhaps uniquely American) way about the archaic and deadly practice of war itself—is the same "war-at-a-distance" that guided missiles made possible long before GPS was employed during Desert Storm. Nothing has been substantially changed about the nature of war in spite of the large claims for what it means to be "tactically" capable of pinpoint attacks. The shape of the missile itself, an apparently "natural" by-product of efficiency functions, is very telling in this regard. As the history of technological development has instructed us, nothing is given in advance. I am not a military designer, but it may be that a drastically unlikely missile shape, say the shape of a hat or a bowl (emphatically not a projectile shape) is prohibited in missile design not because of aerodynamics but because of the importance of a certain aesthetic continuity between all projectiles (airplanes, missiles, cannons, guns), that is, an aesthetic class of projectiles. The production of this technology and its "look," however, is not a question I have time to take up here. In some respects, architecture shares with military science and telecommunications systems a certain detachment, a certain indifference toward the genuinely staggering questions raised by enlisting the computer in our everyday practices. It is, in fact, hard to see the reach of these questions in architecture unless one understands something about how the computer aspires to animate life. And, as I have been intimating, the history of this aspiration lies in parts of the history that biology and cybernetics share.

Several things need to be said before concluding: The first is that the Marxist-Hegelian proposition that "what the human mind discovers is . . . the record of its own operation"[12] and "man is his own labor" will be as true, in some respects, of biological and cybernetic science as it has been of earlier sciences, and that means we will be left with all the old problems of differentiation that currently populate our history as a species, as well as before our species had a history. Both cybernetics and genetics—and this is where architecture finds part of its own computational project at the moment—are interested in finding ways to dismantle the differences between man and machine that have been erected by linear and empiricist histories of technology. Human beings build computers out of the structure of logic, whatever it is, that is reserved for building persuasive machines that represent language, form and thought. We build the computer in our own internal image and attempt to give it desirable properties. Even the irrational things that were originally left out of the equation, such as laughter, white noise, irregular coastlines, are now being drawn into the equation. Finally, it is true that the computer is still a machine and probably destined to remain forever a machine. By this I mean that while it exteriorizes the brain and images it, plugging into our physical and mental labors, it remains an external, rather than an internal, milieu. Virtual reality and the various experiments for bringing this machine closer to our bodies by means of gloves, helmets and so on, as well as prosthetic medical devices, seem to be collapsing this distance. In fact, if a collapse were really to happen it would not be about donning a helmet or inserting a pacemaker, or any of the other possible forms of prosthetic attachment one might imagine, or even about taking over the visual field. It would be about abolishing the idea of the prosthetic and the representative itself, changing fundamentally the idea of the self in order for it to seamlessly include a mechanical dimension and changing the idea of the machine, the *word* "machine" itself, in order for it to seamlessly include an organic dimension. This discourse has been started and stopped along the way, but tenacious differences still keeps this discourse from being fully realized. One such difference is that if we close up the gaps—which are multiple—between machine and human, between architecture and animal, between animal and human, we will, in effect, have lost our lives. Perhaps new ones would arise, perhaps not. These (old) gaps damage the utopian promises of the genetic/cybernetic alliance that has also brought me to ask about life and architecture, but they also keep us going back and forth, back and forth, in an asymmetrical ping pong motion between the outside and the inside, the space and the body, the head and the brain, variability and constancy—between aliveness and that which is not alive. This is also why there is a constant and fundamental oscillation, in our lives and technologies, between the very smart and less-than-smart operations of our smartest ideas and machines.

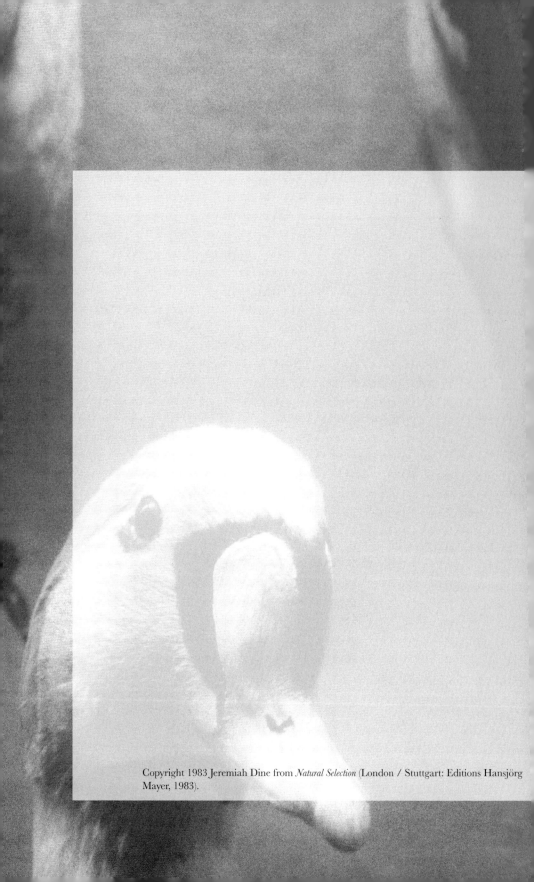

# NOTES

## INTRODUCTION

1. Erwin Schrödinger, *What is Life?* (Cambridge: Cambridge University Press, 1967), p. 3.
2. Ibid., pp. 4–5.
3. Ibid., p. 10. "All the physical and chemical organisms are of this statistical kind; any other kind of lawfulness and orderliness that one might think of is being perpetually disturbed and made inoperative by the unceasing heat motion of the atoms."
4. Ibid., op. cit., p. 20.
5. John R. Searle, *The New York Review of Books*, 2005, vol. LII, no.1, pp. 36–9. Mind is now defined in neurobiology as "consciousness."The "race to solve the problem of consciousness is now on," Searle writes. In his review of *The Quest for Consciousness* by Christof Koch, Vol. LII, No. 1, 13 January 2005, Searle summarizes current scientific objectives in the field as a quest to "find out how exactly the brain causes all of our conscious states and where and how exactly those states exist and function in the brain. . . . Part of the difficulty stems from the sheer technical problems of studying the system of a hundred billion or so neurons stuffed into the skull." And, further, "we have to get clear about what consciousness is."
6. Francois Jacob, *The Logic of Life* (New York: Random House, 1982).
7. Hannah Arendt, *The Human Condition* (Chicago, IL: The University of Chicago Press, 1958) p. xiv.
8. Rachel Whiteread, *Shedding Life* (Liverpool: Tate Gallery Publication, 1996).
9. Giorgio Agamben, *Homo Sacer: Sovereign Power and Bare Life*, trans. Daniel Heller-Roazen (Stanford, CA: Stanford University Press, 1998). Agamben is interested, as was Foucault, in the disciplining of the biological body in contemporary political life. Aristotle's distinction between *zoē* ("bare life") and *bios* ("public life") cannot be sustained, Agamben argues, in contemporary life.
10. Georges Canguilhem, *A Vital Rationalist*, ed. Francois Delaporte, trans. Arthur Goldhammer (New York: Zone Books., 1994).

11. Henri Lefebvre, *The Production of Space*, trans. Donald Nicholson-Smith (Oxford: Basil Blackwell Press, 1974), p. 362.
12. Barbara Herrenstein Smith and Arkady Plotnitsky, "Introduction: Networks and symmetries, decidable and undecidable," in *Mathematics, Science, and Postclassical Theory* (*The South Atlantic Quarterly*, Spring 1995, vol. 94, no.2).
13. Schrödinger, op. cit., p. 32.
14. Le Corbusier, *The City of Tomorrow*, trans. Frederick Etchells (Cambridge, MA: MIT Press, 1982).
15. Sanford Kwinter, *The Combustible Landscape*, Graduate Research Lecture Series, School of Architecture, Pratt Institute, 7 April 2005.
16. J. M. Coetzee, *The Lives of Animals* (Princeton:Princeton University Press, 1999). Elizabeth Costello is the mother of the main character in the book and is giving a series of lectures about animals. *The Lives of Animals* is a republished excerpt from Coetzee's book *Elizabeth Costello*.
17. Immanuel Kant, *The Critique of Pure Reason*, trans. Werner Pluhar (Indianapolis, IN: Hackett, 1987). As is well known, Kant argued that it is impossible to know anything "for itself" because the operation of the mind itself must be taken into account in this knowledge.
18. Charles Darwin, *The Origin of Species By Means of Natural Selection or The Preservation of Favored Races in the Struggle for Life*, ed. J. W. Burrow (London: Penguin Books, 1985), p. 120.
19. Allan Stoekl, "Round Dusk: Kojève at 'The End,'" in *Postmodern Culture*, 1944, vol. 5, no. 1. http://jefferson.village.virginia.edu/pmc/text-only/issue.994/stoekl.994. Page references are taken from the website reproduction of the paper.
20. Henry Miller, graduate architecture student at Pratt Institute, New York, made this insightful comment during my *Humanism Mechanism* seminar, Spring 2004.
21. Catherine Ingraham, *Architecture and the Burdens of Linearity* (New Haven: Yale University Press, 1998).
22. Cary Wolfe, ed., *Zoontologies: The Question of the Animal* (Minneapolis: University of Minnesota Press 2003), pp. 1–3.
23. Manfredo Tafuri, *Interpreting the Renaissance: Princes, Cities, Architects* (New Haven: Yale University Press, in press 2006).
24. Colin Rowe, *The Mathematics of the Ideal Villa and Other Essays* (Cambridge: MIT Press, 1982).
25. Anthony Vidler, *The Writing of the Walls* (New York, Princeton Architectural Press, 1987).
26. Siegfried Giedion, *Space, Time and Architecture* (Cambridge: Harvard University Press, 1977), p. xxxiv.
27. William MacDonald, architecture professor at Columbia University, New York, and Principal, Kolatan and MacDonald Studios, was the design critic teaching this studio.

## PART 1: LIFE (BEFORE)

### 1: Partitioning the orthopedic whole

1. Jacques Lacan, *Ecrits*, trans. Alan Sheridan (New York: W. W. Norton Books, 1977), p. 4. I refer only obliquely to Lacan's "orthopedic whole," although everything about the fantasy of the whole body within which we live is related to an "evolution" of fragmented parts into synthetic wholes. "The mirror stage is a drama whose internal thrust is precipitated from insufficiency to anticipation—and which manufactures for the subject, caught up in the lure of spatial identification, the succession of phantasies that extends from a fragmented body-image to a form of its totality that I shall call orthopedic—and lastly, to the

assumption of the armour of an alienating identity, which will mark with its rigid structure the subject's entire mental development. Thus, to break out of the circle of the *Innenwelt* into the *Umwelt* generates the inexhaustible quadrature of the ego's verifications."

2. Canguilhem, op. cit., p. 67.
3. Aristotle, *Parts of Animals, Movement of Animals, Progression of Animals*, trans. E. S. Forster (Cambridge: Harvard University Press, Loeb Classical Edition, 1993), pp. 53–73. As, for example, when Aristotle writes: "We must [also]decide whether we are to discuss the processes by which each animal comes to be formed . . . or rather the animal as it actually is. . . . I said earlier that we ought first to take the phenomena that are observed in each group, and then go on to state their causes. . . . the process is for the sake of the actual thing, the thing is not for the sake of the process . . . we need not concern ourselves with Soul in its entirety; because it is not Soul in its entirety that is an animal's 'nature,' but some part or parts of it."
4. Giorgio Agamben, *The Open: Man and Animal*, trans. Kevin Attell (Palo Alto: Stanford University Press, 2004), p. 13.
5. Peter Murray, *The Architecture of the Italian Renaissance*, (New York: Schocken Books, 1986), p. 51. The eclectic humanist spirit of the Renaissance architects was polemical. Alberti, for example, studied law and "wrote a Latin comedy which for a short time passed as genuinely antique." Humanism argued, in opposition to what Jacob Burckhardt called "the development of a genuinely politically independent and modern Florence," for a deep devotion to classical principles and learning. The Renaissance, and the humanists it cultivated, was thus a strange mix of adventurous classicism and conservative political principles. "Humanism"—a view of life that carries with it specific practices—begins as a kind of dedicated nostalgia for classical universality.
6. Rudolf Wittkower, *Architectural Principles in the Age of Humanism* (New York: Norton, 1971), p. 29.
7. Ibid., p. 67.
8. Canguilhem, op. cit., p. 74. In Aristotle's *De anima*, Aristotle "first proposed the traditional distinction between the vegetative or nutritive soul, the faculty of growth and reproduction, the animal or sensitive soul, the faculty to feel, desire and move; and the reasonable or thinking soul, the faculty of humanity. . . . [F]or the Greeks, *psyche* meant cool breath."
9. Wittkower, op. cit., p. 108. "It is probably right to say that rarely did Palladio or any other Renaissance architect use irrational proportions in practice. . . . We must repeat that Palladio's conception of architecture . . . is based on commensurability of ratios. This creed he expressed in these words: '. . . in all fabrics it is requisite that their parts should correspond together, and have such proportions, that there may be none whereby the whole cannot be measured, and likewise all other parts.'"
10. Ibid., p. 101.
11. *The College of Sociology, 1937–1939*, ed. Denis Hollier, trans. Betsy Wings (Minneapolis: University of Minnesota Press, 1988), p. xvii.
12. Franco Borsi, *Bernini*, trans. Robert Erich Wolf (New York:Rizzoli International Publications, 1984), p. 21.
13. Ibid., pp. 108, 147, 161.
14. See www.forbes.com/global/2001/0219/061.html. This is a report on a material that Nexia Biotechnologies is working on. It is an attempt to synthesize spider silk, specifically that of the Orb Weaver, a "palm-size spider that spins the world's toughest natural material," into a woven cable which can be used in lightweight "ballistic vests, medical sutures and

artificial ligaments." The Orb Weaver gene is injected into female goats whose "mammary glands are able to produce the complex proteins that make up spider silk." The proteins are filtered and made into a fine white powder that is then spun into extremely strong thread.

15. Manfredo Tafuri, "A search for paradigms: project, truth, artifice," *Assemblage*, 2002, 28, p. 48.
16. Greg Lynn, Graduate Research Lecture Series, School of Architecture, Pratt Institute, Spring 2004.
17. G. Deleuze and F. Guattari, *Nomadology: The War Machine* (New York: Semiotext(e), 1986), p. 98. The idea of an "asymmetrical condition" does not oppose Deleuze and Guattari's theories of a continuum between the animate and inanimate. Instead, it attempts to name some of the oppositional forces still presiding inside that continuum, which periodically break it apart.
18. Jacob, *Logic of Life*, pp. 6–9.
19. Wittkower, op. cit., p. 98.
20. Canguilhem, op. cit., p. 246. He is speaking of Auguste Comte's remarks about human life.
21. Ibid., p. 246.
22. Wittkower, op. cit., p. 117. Architecture's relation to universal mathematical principles, Renaissance science, elevated it from a manual to a liberal art. "This transformation was the great achievement of fifteenth century artists." Manfredo Tafuri suggests that Wittkower's "hypotheses require some correction. First, the 'architectural principles' of the age of humanism were not innovative: in fact they seem to indicate a theoretical regression." Tafuri, op. cit., p. 60.
23. Tafuri, op. cit., pp. 28, 50.
24. Ibid., p. 50.
25. Ibid., p. 51.
26. Ibid., p. 65.
27. Mark Rakatansky, in conversation, May 2004.
28. Tafuri, op. cit., p. 53. This rested on a fuller idea of secularity and individual judgment versus universal judgment.
29. Ibid., p. 54.
30. Tafuri, op. cit., p. 57. "Pursuing distinct paths, Leo Spitzer and Henri de Lubac, have demonstrated this, the first in a magisterial study of the concept of the *Stimmung*, the second in a study of Pico that recounts the history of 'man the microcosm.'" As Tafuri continues, "Adam's name—whose four letters in Greek seem to designate the four cardinal points of the compass—constitutes a 'miniature world' identified as the human instrument with a thousand voices that, according to Clement of Alexandria, plays in harmony with God's voice."
31. Ibid., p. 58.
32. Ibid., p. 59.

## 2: Inside and outside

1. Borsi, op. cit., pp. 40–42; Wittkower, op. cit., pp. 99–100.
2. Ibid., p. 44.
3. Ibid., p. 60.
4. Barbara Maria Stafford, *Body Criticism: Imagining the Unseen in Enlightenment Art and Medicine* (Cambridge: MIT Press, 1997), pp. 29–31.
5. Borsi, op. cit., p. 41.

6. Vidler, op. cit., pp. 160–1. Decoration, "attributes," in Quatramere de Quincy's words, "constituted the language of architecture" in the eighteenth century. Decoration is allegory. "By means of allegory, the art of architecture is made historian and narrator."
7. Wolfgang Lotz, "The Rendering of the Interior in Architectural Drawings of the Renaissance," *Studies in Italian Renaissance Architecture* (Cambridge: MIT Press, 1981), pp. 1-65.
8. Ibid., pp. 9–10. "It is significant . . . that for the most part Leonardo's studies . . . are limited to ground plans and exteriors drawn in perspective. Interiors are rarely shown." Leonardo had little interest, Lotz remarks, in "illustrating the space-limited function of the wall. No matter how strongly the exterior view stresses the three-dimensional physical appearance of the building, the old concept of an interior as a skeleton whose members signify the divisions of the walls in between apparently persists unchanged."
9. Wittkower, op. cit., p. 99.
10. Ibid., p. 99.
11. François Jacob, *The Possible and the Actual* (Seattle: University of Washington Press, 1982), p. 27.
12. Aristotle, *op. cit.*, p. 5.
13. Jacob, *The Possible and the Actual*, p. 29.
14. Foucault, *The Order of Things* (New York: Random House, 1970), p. 229.
15. Lotz, op. cit., p. 43. Filarete's drawing of The House of Virtues, Florence, was, according to Lotz, the first "interior perspective."
16. Agamben, *Homo Sacer*, p. 4.
17. Agamben, *The Open*, p. 75.

## 3: Life (before)

1. Jacob, *Logic of Life*, p. 20.
2. Ibid., pp. 21–2.
3. Ibid., p. 22
4. Ibid., p. 22.
5. Ibid., p. 27. Also see Foucault, op. cit., p. 23. "Man . . . transmits resemblances back into the world from which he receives them. He is the great fulcrum of proportions—the center upon which relations are concentrated and from which they are once again reflected."
6. www.tca.uwa.edu.au, The Tissue Culture and Art Project is a non-profit "tissue engineering" laboratory that explores contemporary biotechnological techniques in terms of the "art project." Current projects include the *Extra Ear – ¼ scale*, *Semi-Living Food: "Disembodied Cuisine*,*" The Pig Wings Project*, and *Victimless Leathe—a Prototype of Stitch-less Jacket grown in a Technoscientific "Body*.*"* The projects are all provocative and meant to challenge contemporary meanings of "life" as well as human life practices, such as wearing clothes, eating meat, and cloning animals.
7. Jacob, op. cit., pp. 27-28
8. Ibid., pp. 23–6.
9. Foucault, op. cit., p. 125.
10. Jacob, op. cit., pp. 28–9.
11. Canguilhem, op. cit., p. 128. "One might say that long ago Aristotle believed in a pathological mechanics since he admitted two kinds of movements: natural movements through which a body regains its proper place where it thrives at rest, as a stone goes down to the ground, and fire, up to the sky;—and violent movements by which a body is pushed from its

proper place, as when a stone is thrown in the air. It can be said that with Galileo and Descartes, progress in knowledge of the physical world consisted in considering all movements as natural, that is, as conforming to the laws of nature, and likewise progress in biological knowledge consisted in unifying the laws of natural life and pathological life."

12. Jacob, op. cit., p. 40.
13. Stephen Jay Gould, *Ever Since Darwin: Reflections in Natural History* (New York: American Museum of Natural History, 1977), p. 171.
14. Ibid., p. 175.
15. Jacob, op. cit., p. 34. This footnote refers to this quotation and the one following, which is Jacob quoting Borelli's *De Motu Animalium*, CCIV, Rome, 1685, p. 243.
16. The sky is still a largely unclaimed territory for the human race and yet it is included, in all the grasping terms that characterize space as the "next frontier" in nineteenth and twentieth century, particularly American, ideas of manifest destiny. The bird's flight is still used as an aesthetic and technical resource for these "space missions."
17. Baker, op. cit., p. 33.
18. Canguilhem, op. cit., p. 245.
19. Ibid., p. 68.
20. Ibid., p. 69.
21. Ibid., p. 68. The italics are the author's.
22. Ibid., p. 69.
23. "Ecology"—a later refinement of environment as an interactive milieu—is not named until the early twentieth century, when Ernst Haeckel, a German physician, biologist, and philosopher who advanced numerous (ultimately false) theories about evolutionary theory, coined the word.
24. Canguilhem, op. cit., p. 241.
25. Ibid., p. 242.
26. Ibid., p. 245.
27. Jacob, op. cit., p. 33. "The distinction generally made between animal, vegetable and mineral was used chiefly to establish the main categories of bodies in the world. That classification could just as well have been founded on the degree of organization of bodies, their faculty of moving or their powers of reason, as Charles Bonnet did." "Organization," Jacob remarks, "still represented only the complexity of visible structure."
28. Foucault, op. cit., p. xxiii.
29. Ibid., p. xxii.
30. Ibid., p. xxiii. Refers to this quote and the one following in the text.
31. Ibid., p. xxiii. Geoffrey Scott, author of the influential (in its time), but now largely dismissed, *Architecture in the Age of Humanism*, was infuriated by what he called the "biological fallacy" in architectural history, which, he claimed, insisted on "sequence" as a guiding organizational principle. But Scott also, in spite of arguing for the "precession" of time—looking not at the evolution of events in time, but at a "devolution" from, say, Bernini to Bramante to Brunelleschi—was neither willing nor able to dispense with either continuous history or an ennobled idea of humanness; in his case, humanism means a sentient human that fabricates architecture in its own image.
32. Ibid., p. 128.
33. Ibid., pp. 129–30.
34. Ibid., pp. 217–21.

## PART II: POST-ANIMAL LIFE

### 4: Post-animal life

1. K. Michael Hays, *Modernism and the Posthumanist Subject: The Architecture of Hannes Meyer and Ludwig Hilberseimer* (Cambridge: MIT Press, 1992), p. 273. Post-humanism means, among other things, the "dispersal of the subject."
2. Agamben, *The Open*, see editor's remarks on book cover.
3. Lotz, op. cit., p. 13.
4. Beatriz Colomina, *Privacy and Publicity: Modern Architecture as Mass Media* (Cambridge: MIT Press, 1994).

### 5: After

1. Martin Jay, *Downcast Eyes: The Denigration of Vision in Twentieth-century French Thought* (Berkeley University of California Press, 1993), p. 412.
2. Jay, op. cit., pp. 386, 411. Jay discusses "the panoptic reversal of enlightenment values."
3. Foucault, op. cit., pp. xx–ii.
4. Barbara Maria Stafford, op. cit., p, 1. For Stafford, the primary probative instrument of the eighteenth century is "metaphor."
5. Jacob, op. cit., p. 74.
6. Ibid., p. 74.
7. Ibid., p. 74.
8. See Vidler, op. cit., pp. 125–6. "[T]he problem of reconciling an external, context-related story of art objects [textual evidence] to an internal, formal, and aesthetic treatment" was a central methodological issue for art history. ". . . [textual evidence] proposed a normative, systematic arrangement, parallel to that of the natural and physical sciences; the other subordinated considerations of [aesthetic] judgment to those of relative significance and social change."
9. Denis Cosgrove, "Ptolemy and Vitruvius: Spatial representation in the sixteenth century texts and commentaries," in *Architecture and the Sciences, Exchanging Metaphors*, eds. Antoine Picon and Alessandra Ponte (New York: Princeton Architectural Press, 2003), p. 31. Cosgrove writes: ". . . by the 1540s the volume of descriptive cosmography resulting from geographical discovery was clearly outstripping the mathematical side and seriously undermining the authority of Ptolemy's original geography."
10. See Vidler, op. cit., p. 54. Diderot, in particular, was important in giving evidentiary, rather than hypothetical, knowledge (such as classification based on empirical observation) epistemo-logical force. His Encyclopedia entries expressed strong theoretical positions on a multiplicity of matters.
11. Martin Bressani, "Violett-Le-Duc's Optic," in *Architecture and the Sciences*, eds. Ponte and Picon, (New York: Princeton Architectural Press, 2003) pp. 119–39. Bressani's fascinating essay is on the influence of anatomy on Violett-le-Duc's dissections of Gothic cathedrals.
12. Jacob, op. cit., p. 114. With Bichat's account of anatomy as that which connects "simple tissues" with the formation of organs, "a new level of organization emerged," Jacob writes, "intermediate between the organ and the molecule. The tissue represented the ultimate point of anatomical analysis."
13. Ibid., p. 76. Buffon explains that ". . . animals and plants that can multiply and reproduce themselves in all their parts are organized bodies composed of other similar organic bodies."

According to Jacob: "The reduction of organisms to a collection of units was . . . derived directly from the corpuscular theory of matter, and in a sense completed that theory."

14. Geoffrey Scott, *The Architecture of Humanism: A Study in the History of Taste* (New York: Norton and Company, 1999), pp. 127–40. As mentioned earlier, Scott calls this the "biological fallacy." He believed it was a mistake for architecture to imitate the natural sciences because architecture is a "value-laden practice" depending on "taste" and artistic individuality.
15. Jacob, *The Possible and the Actual*, p. 32.
16. Christine Boyer, *Cybercities* (New York: Princeton Architectural Press, 1996), p. 93. Boyer refers to Barbara Stafford's remarks on Piranesi's use of anatomical techniques to "flay" architecture and the city.
17. Spiro Kostof, *A History of Architecture: Settings and Rituals* (New York: Oxford University Press, 1995), pp. 554–5.
18. Stafford, op. cit., p. 58.
19. Kostof , op. cit., p. 562.
20. Vidler, op. cit., p. 133.
21. Stafford, op. cit., p. 59.
22. Luigi Ficacci, *Piranesi: The Complete Etchings* (Cologne: Taschen, 2000), p. 47.
23. Ibid., p. 47.
24. Cf. Diane Kelder, *Canaletto/Piranesi: Views, Real and Invented*, a catalog by Kelder who was the curator for an exhibition of etchings at the art gallery of the graduate center, the City University of New York, 20 September–16 November 2002.
25. Philippe Duboy, *Lequeu: An Architectural Enigma* (Cambridge: MIT Press, 1987), p. 21.
26. Vidler, op. cit., p. 43.
27. Jay, op. cit., p. 386.
28. Vidler, op. cit., p. 36–47.
28. Kostof, op. cit., p.547.
29. André Leroi-Gourhan, *Gesture and Speech*, trans. Anna Bostock Berger (Cambridge: MIT Press, 1993), p. 7.
30. Ibid., p. 7.
31. Vidler, op. cit., p. 127.
32. Ibid., p. 127. "History was the realm of the philologist, antiquarian, and collector."
33. Leroi-Gourhan, op. cit., p. 7.
34. Vidler, op. cit., p. 12.
35. Ibid., p. 12. "The careful collations of ancient and modern examples of primitive life . . . had the effect, important for the history and theory of architecture, of establishing a belief in the intimate, if not instrumental, relationship between social customs and the forms of dwelling, between religious rituals and the iconography of monuments."
36. Ibid., p. 12–21. The word "principled" recurs everywhere in Vidler's discussion, but particularly with respect to the example of Robinson Crusoe as the exemplary eighteenth century settler, "a paradigm of economic man [as Marx noted], mercantile and colonialist." Vidler comments that "Crusoe, as Rousseau understood, was in no way a 'natural man'. . . . Defoe's materialist account of architectural origins [in Robinson Crusoe] . . . was both progressive and principled, embodying the simple and fundamental precepts of all good building, joined inextricably to economic and social development."
37. Canguilhem, op. cit., p. 70.
38. Schrödinger, op. cit., p. 21.

39. Evelyn Fox Keller, *Refiguring Life: Metaphors of Twentieth-Century Biology* (New York: The Columbia University Press, 1995), pp. 67–8. The word "device" used in this paragraph is Fox Keller's word for the "marvelous faculty of a living organism" to stay alive.
40. Vidler, op. cit., pp. 147–51. "[Type] derived from a more or less logical combination of the idea of origins . . . epitomized in the primitive hut as a paradigm of structure, and the notion of charactacteristic form [from] the classical tradition and newly adopted in the terminology of the natural sciences. In the early 1780s, this combination was expressed by the word 'type,' a term whose peculiar etymology and history of use lent itself especially well to to an idea that was vague and precise at the same time: vague in its general reference to a world of ideal forms and metaphysical beauties, precise in its application to the expressive qualities of different building types."
41. Ibid., p. 155.
42. Ibid., pp. 166–7. "In order to disentangle the true principles, to demonstrate them incontestably, one should make them stand out by bringing together all the monuments that deserve to be known; these monuments should be placed in a simple and clear order that makes their comparison easy, indicates their origin, their genre, their perfection, and their decadence."
43. Ibid., pp. 7–8.
44. Jacob, *Logic of Life*, pp. 173–7. All quotes in the following section are taken from these pages.
45. Ibid., p. 174. "The new attitude found expression in the appearance of statistical mechanics . . . Even though Darwin did not use statistical analysis, he had a statistical conception of populations. First, because variations only express the fluctuations of distributions inherent in every system; secondly, because selection acts only by slowly altering population equilibrium throughout the random interaction of organisms and their environment."
46. Ibid., pp. 175–7.
47. Vidler, op. cit., p. 9.
48. Ibid., pp. 13–15. Georges Canguilhem writes that health becomes synonymous with life in the nineteenth century. See Canguilhem, *A Vital Rationalist*, pp. 67–8.
49. Ibid., p. 15.
50. In part, the aesthetic theory of the monstrous and the grotesque. There is an excellent discussion of the Baroque in Anthony Vidler's *Warped Space* (Cambridge: MIT Press, 2000).
51. Jacob, op. cit., p. 163. "Geographical inquiry reached the same conclusions as investigation of 'paleontological archives:' in the course of time, a small number of similar organisms produces a large number of different descendants."
52. Ibid., pp. 163–5. Jacob quoting Darwin.
53. Ibid., p. 165.
54. Ibid., pp. 166–7.

## 6: Ways of life

1. William Shakespeare, "King Lear," in *William Shakespeare: The Complete Works*, ed. Alfred Harbage (New York: Viking Press, 1979), pp. 1065–106.
2. Canguilhem, op. cit., pp. 70–1.
3. Ibid., p. 85. "The organism is a society of cells or elementary organisms, at once autonomous and subordinate. The specialization of the components is a function of the complexity of the whole. The effect of this coordinated specialization is the creation, at the level of the elements, of a liquid interstitial milieu that Bernard dubbed the 'internal environment,' which is the sum of the physical and chemical conditions of all cellular life . . .

[homeostasis] provides regulated organisms with an assurance of relative independence. Bernard was fond of using the term 'elasticity' to convey his idea of organic life."

4. Rowe, op. cit., p. 2.
5. Ibid., p. 3.
6. Canguilhem, op. cit., p. 72.
7. Ibid., p. 72.
8. Rowe, op. cit., pp. 13–14. "Le Corbusier has an equal reverence for mathematics and would appear also, sometimes, to be tinged with a comparable historicism. For his plans he seems to find at least one source in those ideas of *convenance* and *commodité* displayed in the ingenious planning of the Rococo hotel. . ." Rowe continues, ". . . symbolically . . . Palladio's and Le Corbusier's buildings are in different worlds. Palladio sought complete clarity of plan and the most lucid organization of conventional elements based on symmetry as the most memorable form of order. . . . In his own mind, his work was essentially that of adaptation, the adaptation of the ancient house; and, at the back of his mind were always the great halls of the Imperial thermae and such buildings as Hadrian's villa at Tivoli. . . . Indeed, Rome for him was still supremely alive."
9. Krauss, *The Optical Unconscious* (Cambridge: MIT Press, 1993), p. 190.
10. Wittkower, op. cit., pp. 90–1.
11. Agamben, *Homo Sacer.*, p. 3.
12. Ibid., p. 4.
13. Ibid., p. 8.
14. Ibid., p. 8.
15. Krauss, op. cit., p. 186. "'Value,' Barthes writes, 'regulates all discourse.' He is speaking of the system by which culture generates meaning not by naming things, but by opposing two values within a structure."
16. Roger Caillois, "Mimicry and legendary psychasthenia," trans. John Shepley. *October*, Winter 1984, no. 31, pp. 17–32.
17. Krauss, op. cit., p. 186. As Krauss remarks about Le Corbusier, a Crusoe figure with the ambitions of Lear, "he undertook to reinvent [nature] as a rhythmic network of interlacing shapes. . . . The task was to speak the language of ornament. . . . The ornamental unit would be a microcosm in which 'everything' in the whole would be expressed. The triangle would be so charged that it would at one and same time invoke the tree, the cone, the clouds, the solar rays, and the very dynamic of growth."
18. Martin Jay, *The Dialectical Imagination: A History of The Frankfurt School and the Institute of Social Research, 1923–1950* (Berkeley: University of California Press, 1973), pp. 232–4.
19. Canguilhem, op. cit., p. 16.
20. See Jay, *Downcast Eyes*, op. cit., p. 83-86.

## 7: Hyena: Totem animal of the late twentieth century

1. *The New Yorker*, 11 November 1996.
2. Jacques Derrida, "L'animal que donc je suis," in *L'animal autobiographique* (Paris: Galilee, 1999). ". . . that which distinguishes in the last instance [the beast] from man, is being naked without the knowledge." As Derrida remarks, "*Nus sans le savoir*" is, in effect, not to be naked at all.
3. *The New Yorker*, op. cit., p. 76.
4. Ibid., p. 75.

5. Baker, op. cit., p. 143. In Francis Bacon's work, about which Deleuze wrote the book *Francis Bacon: Logique de la sensation* (1981), there are approximately twelve paintings where the animal is presented unambiguously. In these paintings, the "animal holds-to-form; the human does not."
6. Wolfe op. cit., p. 3. Stanley Cavall calls our view on animals part of "our skeptical terror about the independent existence of other minds."
7. Harriet Ritvo, *The Animal Estate* (Cambridge: Harvard University Press,1987), pp. 1–2. Animals had been fully relieved, by the nineteenth century, of the diverse moral accountability that had been attached to them earlier. "By the nineteenth century British authorities had stopped sentencing animals to suffer and die for their crimes . . . As animals were released from the burden of guilt for witchcraft, homicide . . . and other crimes, a sense of . . . power that had been implicit in the ability to intentionally transgress was also withdrawn . . . Nineteenth century English law viewed animals simply as the property of human owners, only trivially different from less mobile goods. It followed that they were no longer held morally accountable for their actions."
8. Joan Copjec, "Evil in the time of the finite world," introduction to *Radical Evil*, ed. Joan Copjec, *S* series (London and New York: Verso 1996), pp. vi–xxviii.
9. Wolfe, op. cit., p. 7. "Eating reveals our allegiances."
10. The cage "idea" is, as has been initially laid out, an optical, historical and legal idea. The cage is connected with the establishment of a "middle distance" by means of the mathematical calculations of perspective—perhaps one could call it the pursuit of an ideal balance between the view from inside the picture frame and the horizon line.
11. Ritvo, op. cit., pp. 2–5. This modern human is also the human who, through the eighteenth century acquisition of knowledge about "nature," is held newly accountable for the violent actions of animals: ". . . people who encountered or owned them [animals] were responsible for assessing the danger they might pose to person or property. . . . Thus, a plaintiff who attempted to recover damages after a nursing cat bit first her dog and then her hand was told that she should have been aware 'that cats rearing kittens are inclined to be savage and in a vicious state. . . .'" The "natural history" required in order to understand the idea of "savage nature" is acquired during the prior century (Rousseau). Animal behavior becomes, as cited in the earlier passage from Ritvo, the responsibility of humans to understand and account for. At the same time, the sentimental attachment of Victorians to animals, which replaced some of the earlier fear of nature, resulted in the increasing displacement of human characteristics onto the animal: " . . . when nineteenth-century dog breeders commented, as they did at great length, on the difficulty of persuading a prized bitch to mate with the male they had selected and only that male, their remarks were loaded with assumptions about the sexual proclivities of human females. By implication they linked a problem of management in the kennel to one of management in the home." Ritvo continues, "The discourse of popular zoology [in the nineteenth century] . . . presented a moral hierarchy in the animal kingdom based on the hierarchy of orders in human society."
12. Ibid., pp. 3–4.
13. Baker, op. cit., p. 34. Although this is changing. Animal "culture" is increasingly of interest to biologists.
14. Gilles Deleuze and Félix Guattari, *A Thousand Plateaus*, trans. Brian Massumi (Minneapolis: University of Minnesota Press, 1987), p. 242.

15. Becoming-animal, in Deleuze and Guattari, is to leave subject/object, representation, "animal drives," and identity-related existence. But it is not to become like Elizabeth Costello, Coetzee's "lecturer" in *The Lives of Animals*, who comments on how all animals in captivity are thinking about how to get home. She means home in the same sense the Oedipal human means home, that is, the place you imagine yourself as coming from, the place of your species origin.
16. Agamben, *The Open*, p. 64. Heidegger's description of the experience of "profound boredom" is worth repeating: "We are sitting, for example, at the tasteless station of some lonely minor railroad. It is four hours until the next train arrives. The district is unattractive. We do have a book in our rucksack, though—shall we read? No. Or think through a problem, some question? We are unable to. We read the timetables or study the table giving the various distances from this station to other places we are not otherwise acquainted with at all. We look at the clock—only a quarter of an hour has gone by. Then we go out onto the main road. We walk up and down, just to have something to do. But it is no use. Then we count the trees along the main road, look at our watch again—exactly five minutes since we last looked at it. Fed up with walking back and forth, we sit down on a stone, draw all kinds of figures in the sand, and in doing so catch ourselves looking at our watch yet again —half an hour—and so on." The absence of the "tasteful" or engaging architecture contributes to the occasion of profound boredom but, of course, boredom can happen anywhere. It signals detachment from the world of things that remain as they were, but now a matter of profound indifference. This is the "being-left-empty," Agamben writes, that makes room for our discovery of our own captivation. We are the animal that has "learned to be bored."

## PART III: THE DIVIDE

### 8: Birds (from above)

1. Kenneth Clark, *Animals and Men: Their relationship as reflected in Western art from prehistory to the present day* (New York: William Morrow and Company, Inc., 1977), p. 26.
2. Ibid., p. 108. Clark also writes: "[Birds] had an inexhaustible fascination for the medieval mind and eye. . . . [They] abound in the margins of fourteenth century MSS., the most beautiful being in the Sherborne Missal; and among the source-books which were circulated to the various scriptoria were drawings of the various birds and beasts that might be thought appropriate to the margin of a book, or on a piece of *opus Anglicanum* embroidery. . . . They were probably not done from life, but were derived from life drawings done with great accuracy and power of observation." And later in the same book, under the heading "Animals Observed:" "The way back to Nature was only fully opened by the Italian Renaissance, when the physical work became an object of passionate study for its own sake."
3. Ibid., p. 26.
4. Many medieval artists worked from models of life rather than life itself. In reproducing these models, the problem of flight, of *flightiness* in an artistic object, would have already been resolved.
5. The three most pertinent discussions on perspective are Erwin Panofsky, *Perspective as Symbolic Form*, trans. Christopher S. Wood, (New York: Zone Books, 1991); Hubert Damisch, *The Origin of Perspective,* trans. John Goodman (Cambridge: MIT Press, 1994); and Robin Evans, *The Projective Cast* (Cambridge: MIT Press, 1995). All these studies speak to the larger field of meaning embraced by perspective, not simply the mathematical construction.
6. Rosalind Krauss, *op. cit.*, p. 213. Krauss goes on to say: "If, in the art historian's perspective

diagrams, the eye is always pictured open and fixated, staring into the pyramid's tunnel, that's because it is an eye that sees with such dazzling quickness that it has no need to blink. It sees in a twinkling, before the blink. And this twinkling, this infinite brevity or immediacy of the gaze, is the analog to the picture's own condition in the all-at-once, for painting's ontological truth as pure simultaneity."
7. Ibid., p.12.
8. Clark op. cit., p. 28. "How did he ever persuade a hare to sit still long enough for him to record all that detail?," Clark asks, speaking of Albrecht Dürer.
9. Krauss, op. cit., p. 12. Krauss continues: "The whole of the external world. That, I can imagine the social historians saying, is a bit of an exaggeration. It's sea and sky, or dunes, sea, and sky, that have been segmented off from the rest of the world, from everything political, or economic, or historic, and themselves made into an abstraction of that world. . . . And they would be right, of course. The sea and sky are a way of packaging 'the world' as a totalized image, as a picture of completeness, as a field constituted by the logic of its own frame. But its frame is a frame of exclusions and its field is the world of ideological construction."
10. Damisch, op. cit., pp. 89–90. Damisch quotes Antonio di Tuccio Manetti, *The Life of Brunelleschi*, trans. Catherine Enggass (College Park: Pennsylvania State University Press, 1970) pp. 42–4: "And insofar as he had to show the sky, that is, where the painted walls stamped themselves against the air, he used silver burnished in such a way that natural air and sky were reflected in it, and even clouds that one saw pass by in this silver pushed by the wind, when it was blowing." The sky in the drawing mirrors the actual sky. Also see Hubert Damisch, *A Theory of Cloud: Toward a History of Painting* (Cultural Memory in the Present), trans. Janet Lloyd (Palo Alto: Stanford University Press, 2002) and, by the same author, *Skyline: The Narcissistic City* (Palo Alto: Stanford University Press, 2001).
11. Krauss, op. cit., p. 12.
12. Jacob, op. cit., p. 39. "Animism" was a classical idea by which all things in the world were animated. This is different from eighteenth century "vitalism," which referred only to living beings.
13. Diane Wells (illustrator Lauren Jarrett) *100 Birds and How They Got Their Names* (Chapel Hill: Algonquin Books, 2001).
14. Siegfried Giedion, *Mechanization Takes Command* (New York: The Norton Library, 1969), p. 17. Giedion writes about Bishop Nicolas Oresme (*c.*1350) who was "the first to recognize that movement can be represented only by movement, the changing only by the changing." This is achieved by "repeatedly representing the same subject at various times," p. 16.
15. Benjamin Aranda, "Hunger, fear; devotion and other rules for assembling a flock," in *Log 3*, Fall 2004, pp. 9–18. The Brooklyn Pigeon Project is an experiment in "developing a satellite that records the city as seen by a flock of birds."
16. Wolfgang Lotz, *Studies in Italian Renaissance Architecture* (Cambridge: MIT Press, 1981), p. 9. "The earliest systematically constructed examples. . . of [a] *bird's-eye view*, are found in the oeuvre of Leonardo da Vinci, who began as a painter and who was largely responsible for developing the basic forms of plane and perspective architectural drawings. . . . Interiors are rarely shown, and only appear relatively late in his drawings. A typical example, from the *Codex Atlanticus* dated around 1490, shows separate views of the exterior and interior of a centralized building."
17. Craig Reynolds, *Boids: Background and Update*, www.red3d.com/cwr/index.html. Reynolds

is interested in "computer modeling of life-like complex [human and animal] behavior."

18. Walter Benjamin, "The work of art in the age of mechanical reproduction," in *Illuminations*, ed. Hannah Arendt, trans. Harry Zohn (New York: Schocken Books, 1969), pp. 225–9. Portraiture is an interesting case. "It is no accident," Walter Benjamin writes, "that the portrait was the focal point of early photography. The cult of remembrance of loved ones, absent or dead, offers a last refuge for the cult value of the picture. For the last time the aura emanates from the early photographs in the fleeting expression of a human face." But gradually, as the exhibition value of photography gains ground, and film becomes the art form of the twentieth century, "man has to operate with a whole living person, yet foregoing its aura."
19. Panofsky, op. cit., p. 63.
20. Steve Bah and Ornament in the Frankfurt Project: An Interview,' in *Assemblage* 1998, vol. 5, pp. 51–7.
21. Steve Baker, The Postmodern Animal (London: Reaktion Books Ltd., 2000), pp. 11–12.
22. Arendt, Human Condition, p. 173.
23. See Mark Wigley's very astute discussion of ornament and structure, "The Displacement of Structure and Ornament in the Frankfurt Project: An Interview," in *Assemblage* 5 (1988), pp. 51–7.
23. Krauss, op. cit., p. 7.
24. Mark Linder discussed the question of the literal in a public lecture "Literal 1967: How *Art Forum* Stole Architecture," presented at Pratt Institute, Brooklyn, New York, 31 January 2002. See Linder's forthcoming book on the same subject, *Nothing Less than Literal: Architecture after Minimalism* (Cambridge: MIT Press, 2005). Linder discusses how architecture "invaded" minimalist art in the 1960s by looking at different artists such as Robert Smithson and examines the debates surrounding the relation of architecture to art.
25. This movement is somewhat like that created by early optical instruments such as the zoo-trope, in which the progression of openings and closings counterfeits the intervals between different positions of a bird's wings as it flies and thus is able to counterfeit the movement of flight. See images of the zootrope from *La Nature* (1888) in Krauss, op. cit., pp. 206–10.
26. Jacques Derrida, "Structure, Sign and Play," in *The Structuralist Controversy*, ed. Richard Macksey (Baltimore: Johns Hopkins University Press, 1969), 20. "Now I don't know what perception is and I don't believe anything like perception exists."
27. Krauss, op. cit., p. 213. Krauss elaborates: "If the Renaissance had diagrammed the punctuality of [the infinite vanishing point], it was modernism that insisted on it, underscored it, made the issue of this indivisible instant of seeing serve as a fundamental principle in the doctrine of its aesthetic truth." The counter-argument, the "antivision" argument, pits the "grey matter" (Duchamp) against the "retinal" (Greenberg).
28. Baker, op. cit., pp. 29–32.
29. Giorgio Agamben, *The Open*, p. 71. Quoting Heidegger, Agamben writes: "'The stone is wordless. Plant and animal likewise have no world; but they belong to the veiled throng of an environment in which they hang suspended. The peasant woman, on the other hand, has a world because she dwells in the open of beings.'"

## 9: Birds (from below)

1. Claude Levi- Strauss, *Totemism*, trans. Rodney Needham (Boston: Beacon Press, 1963), p. 85.
2. Ibid., p. 1. "Totemism is like hysteria, in that once we are persuaded to doubt that it is possible arbitrarily to isolate certain phenomena and to group them together as diagnostic signs of an illness, or of an objective institution, the symptoms themselves vanish or

appear refractory to any unifying interpretation . . . [T]he comparison . . . suggests a relation of another order between scientific theories and culture, one in which the mind of the scholar himself plays as large a part as the minds of the people studied; it is as though he were seeking, consciously or unconsciously, and under the guise of scientific objectivity, to make the latter—whether mental patients or so-called 'primitives'—more different than they really are."

3. Krauss, op. cit., p. 14.
4. Ibid., p. 21.
5. Agamben, op. cit., p. 54.
6. Lévi-Strauss, op. cit., pp. 79–82. Quoted from Evans-Pritchard's *Nuer Religion*, (Oxford: Oxford University Press, 1956).
7. *Burden of Dreams*, 1982 film on German film-maker Werner Herzog's film *Fitzcarraldo*; directed and produced by Les Blank.
8. Rene Descartes, *The Philosophical Writings Of Descartes*, trans. John Cottingham, Robert Stoothoff, Dugald Murdoch (Cambridge:Cambridge University Press, 1985) p. 81. From Descartes' "The World or Treatise on Light:" ". . . there may be a difference between the sensation we have of light . . . and what it is in the objects that produces this sensation within us . . . For although everyone is commonly convinced that the ideas we have in our mind are wholly similar to the objects from which they proceed, nevertheless I cannot see any reasons which assures us that this is so."
9. See G.E. Lloyd's *Polarity and Analogy* (Cambridge and Indianapolis: Hackett Publishing Company, 1966).
10. Leland de la Durantaye, *Village Voice*, November 2004, no.16.
11. In *The Savage Mind*, Lévi-Strauss's theory of history and social change opposed Sartre's philosophy of human freedom (Chicago: The University of Chicago Press, 1966).
12. See Radcliffe-Brown, "The comparative method in social anthropology," *Journal of the Royal Anthropology Institute*, 1951, vol. 81, pp. 15–22, quoted in Lévi-Strauss, *Totemism*, p. 85. All Radcliffe-Brown quotes are from this volume unless otherwise indicated. Also see Lévi-Strauss, *Totemism*, pp. 87–8: Quoting Radcliffe-Brown ". . . the division eagle-hawk/crow among the Darling River tribes, with which we began, is seen at the end of the analysis to be no more than 'one particular example of a widespread type of the application of certain structural principle,' a principle consisting of the union of opposites."
13. Ibid., p. 89.
14. Ibid., p. 101.
15. See Claude Lévi-Strauss, *Tristes tropiques* (New York: Atheneum, 1972). This text is Lévi-Strauss'anthropological study of "primitive societies in Brazil."
16. See Wallace Stevens' poems, "Thirteen Ways of Looking at a Black Bird," and "The Snowman," for more on the "nothing that is not there and the nothing that is."
17. Foucault, op. cit., p. 173. Foucault writes: " . . . profound knowledge of the order of the world must lead to the secret of metals and the possession of wealth."
18. Lévi-Strauss, *Totemism*, pp. 1–3. Totemism is a "projection outside our own universe, as though by a kind of exorcism, of mental attitudes incompatible with the exigency of a discontinuity between man and nature which Christian thought has held to be essential."
19. Ibid., p. 2.
20. Ibid. p. 90-91

21. Thanks to Anthony Vidler for historically situating Kojève's remarks for me. In conversation, January 2004.

## 10: Space: Animal-field

1. Lefebvre, op. cit., p. 70.
2. Canguilhem, op. cit., p. 72.
3. Lacan, *op. cit.*, 5. "[T]he formation of the I is symbolized in dreams by a fortress, or a stadium—its inner arean and enclosure, surrounded by marshes and rubbish-tips, dividing into two opposed fields of contest where the subject flounders in quest of the lofty, remote inner castle whose form. . . symbolizes the id in a quite startling way."
4. Lefebvre, op. cit., p. 169. Leibniz calls space "indiscernable," neither "nothing" nor "something." It is necessary, according to Lefebvre's interpretation of Leibniz, for "space to be occupied." What then occupies space?, he asks. "A body . . . a specific body." So space is "absolutely relative"—both abstract and concrete.
5. Lefebvre, op. cit., pp. 173–5.
6. Ibid., p. 7.
7. Conversation with Mac Wellman, Obie-award winning playwright, MacDowell Colony, Spring 2004.
8. Lefebvre, op. cit., p. 16.
9. Agamben, op. cit., p. 3. ". . . the 'shadowy' kinship between animal macrocosm and human microcosm."
10. Wolfe, op. cit., pp. 19–20. Heidegger's sentence "Apes, for example, have organs that can grasp, but they have no hand" is answered by Derrida in the following manner: "The hand of the man, of man as such . . . Heidegger does not only think of the hand as a very singular thing that would rightfully belong only to man, he [Heidegger] always thinks the hand in the singular, as if man did not have two hands but, this monster, one single hand." The ethical and identity questions that the animal is currently posing to philosophy will, no doubt, fade over time because philosophy depends on discussion and from the animal side there is no discussion. It can play the silent philosophical partner—as it must since it is not simply a subject of inquiry, but a living subject as well—for only a short time before, in a sense, the argument will be, once again, settled in the direction of those who are talking.
11. Stoekl, op. cit., p. 6.
12. Ibid., p. 6.
13. Ibid., p. 6.
14. Lefebvre, op. cit., p. 170.
15. Ibid., pp. 170–1.
16. Ibid., pp. 170–1.
17. Agamben, op. cit., pp. 45–7.
18. Wolfe, op. cit., p. 3.
19. Ibid., p. 23.
20. Lefebvre, op. cit., p. 171. "It would not be a matter," Derrida writes in his essay "The Animal that Therefore I am" (Wolfe, op. cit., p. 126), "of 'giving speech back' to animals but perhaps of acceding to a thinking . . . that thinks the absence of the name . . . as something other than privation."
21. Stephen Jay Gould, *Ever Since Darwin* (New York: Norton, 1977), pp. 171–8. Gould linked

the modern geometry of space to the size and shape of animals as evidence of a "lawfulness" in the basic "design" of organisms. "We are prisoners of the perceptions of our size," Gould writes. Like Weyl, he includes architectural forms. Medieval churches were built in "an enormous range of sizes before the invention of steel girders, internal lighting, and air conditioning permitted modern architects to challenge the laws of size." "Like tapeworms," Gould writes, these churches lack internal systems and must "alter their shape to produce more external surface as they are made larger."

22. Greg Lynn made the point a number of years ago that symmetry is not a default setting for organic development. Symmetry, in organisms, requires "additional information." Symmetry is not "natural."
23. Wolfe, op. cit., p. 22.
24. Lefebvre, op. cit., p. 194. Thanks to Michael Hays for alerting me, a number of years ago, to this passage.
25. Ibid., p. 174.
26. Ibid., p. 177.
27. Lefebvre, op. cit., p. 175.

## 11: Asymmetry: Praying mantis, totem animal of the thirties

1. J. Henri Fabre, *The Insect World of J. Henri Fabre*, trans. Alexander Teixeira de Mattos (Boston: Beacon Press, 1991), p.158.
2. Ibid., p. 160.
3. Ibid., p. 161.
4. Krauss, op. cit., p. 171.
5. Ibid., p. 171. Even when it is decapitated the mantis can "play dead." "I am expressing. . .'" Caillois says, "what language can scarcely picture, or reason assimilate, namely, that dead, the mantis can simulate death."
6. Sanford Kwinter, *Architectures of Time: Toward a Theory of the Event in Modernist Culture* (Cambridge: MIT Press, 2002), p. 82.
7. Tissue Culture and Art Project website, www.tca.uwa.edu.au.
8. Jacob, *The Logic of Life*, pp. 36–7.
9. See G. E. Lloyd's *Polarity and Analogy* (Cambridge, and Indianapolis: Hackett Publishing Company, 1966), pp. 6–10.
10. Ibid., p. 6. "In particular, the evidence for ancient Greek thought in the period down to Aristotle provides us with a unique opportunity to consider how far the invention or discovery of formal logic merely rendered explicit certain rules of argument which were implicitly observed by earlier writers, or to what extent the analysis of various modes of argument involved the modification or correction of earlier assumptions."
11. Ibid., pp. 2–3.
12. Canguilhem, op. cit., p. 17.
13. Ibid., pp. 74–5.
14. *The American Heritage Dictionary, Second College Edition* (Boston, MA: Houghton Mifflin Co., Boston, 1985), p. 658.
15. Canguilhem, op. cit., pp. 72–3.
16. Ibid., pp. 73–4. "It may be paradoxical to attempt to explain a power such as life in terms of concepts and laws based on the negation of that power . . . ."
17. Ibid., p. 74.

18. Ibid., p. 72.
19. Herrenstein Smith, op. cit., p. 379.

## 12: Mimicry

1. Agamben, *The Open*, pp. 39–40.
2. Ibid., pp. 41–2.
3. Mimicry, Homi Bahba remarks, is a common form of representational adaptation of a colonized population to its colonizers. It is a form of political camouflage.
4. Caillois, Mimicry and legendary psychasthenia, *October* 31, Winter 1984, p. 28.
5. Krauss, op. cit., p. 19 and on the Klein Group graph, p. 19.
6. Agamben, op. cit., p. 3.
7. Krauss, op. cit., p. 155.
8. Caillois, op. cit., p. 18.
9. Krauss, op. cit., p. 13.
10. Butterfly eyes are large spherical structures composed of thousands of sensors. "Collectively, they are directed in every direction . . . butterflies are able to see in virtually every direction simultaneously." But they cannot focus their vision and therefore see only a blur. From the website http://www.centralamerica.com/cr/butterfly/
11. Krauss, op. cit., p. 155.

# PART IV: MILIEU

## 13: Vertical, standing upright

1. Foucault, op. cit., p. 218.
2. Leroi-Gourhan, *Gesture and Speech*, trans. Anna Bostock Berger, (Cambridge: MIT Press, 1993).
3. A large portion of Leroi-Gourhan's work was translated into English and re-published in the 1990s by October Books.
4. Leroi-Gourhan, op. cit., p. 19.
5. The controversy among anthropologists is whether it was the erect posture or the brain that developed first. The question would be "why stand up?" unless the brain were already in a different developmental mode.
6. Giancarlo Scoditti, "The man remembers," in *The New Yorker,* 15 February 1999, 50–1.
7. The monstrous is back in play in a way that we recognize instantly in genetic experiments, and less instantly in children's movies about dinosaurs that have an entirely new cinematic life, or in the material sciences where apparently inert materials are biologically alive and apparently live materials are biologically dead.
8. This evolution by means of the exteriorization of the body into tools, according to Leroi-Gourhan, which started at the moment human beings stood upright, reaches a point where the brain itself begins to exteriorize itself into automatic processing machines. However, before this the hand already has turned over its evolutionary development to the tools, which continue to evolve, from the hammer, the knife (taking over from the teeth), and the loom, to the weaving machine (Jacquard loom), and the computer.
9. See Pauline Sargent's study of relation between brain, mind and image. Pauline Sargent, *Imaging the Brain, Picturing the Mind: Visual Representation in the Practice of Science*, Doctoral Dissertation, University of Minnesota, August 1997, UMI Dissertation Abstracts

Database, Michigan.

10. Leroi-Gourhan, op. cit., p. 59. This neo-Platonic formulation is contested at various points in the history of philosophy. Descartes, for example, regards the container's existence to be proved by the ability of the contained to announce the existential alliance between the two; the *cogito* is a proposition about how mind is proof of the body.
11. Geertz, *The Interpretation of Cultures* (New York: Basic Books, Inc., 1973), p. 95.
12. Leroi Gourhan, op. cit., p. 37. Bataille privileges the mouth, because it acts as a switching station between brain and the hand. Out of the mouth comes speech, which comes from the brain, and into the mouth goes the food gathered by the hand. At the site of the mouth the various competitions between mind and body are staged.
13. Leroi-Gourhan, op. cit., p. 47. Also see pp. 26–7. "The design whereby the entire organism is placed behind the aperture for ingesting food . . . is the normal design of animal bodies. . . . Mobility implies that for purposes of nourishment the organs that ensure orientation, adjustment of position, and the coordination of the organs of food capture with those of food preparation [arms] must also be situated in front of the body. From the first acquisition of mobility to the present time, the general structure of the animal . . . has not changed."
14. Krauss, op. cit., pp. 156–7.
15. Foucault, op. cit., pp. 229–30. "The parallelism between classification [delimitation] and nomenclature [denomination] is . . . dissolved. . . . Names and genera, designation and classification, language and nature, cease to be automatically interlocked. The order of words and the order of beings no longer intersect except along an artificially defined line . . . [T]hings . . . take place in another place than that of words."

## 14: Framing

1. *Giulio Romano—Architect, Exhibition Catalog*, eds. Christoph Frommel and Richard Schofield (Cambridge: Cambridge University Press, 1998).
2. Vicki Hearne, *Adam's Task: Calling Animals by Name* (London: William Heinemann Ltd., 1987), p. 150, 160. "When I say artistry," Hearne writes, "I mean that the movements of a developed horse, the figures and leaps, mean something, and an artistic horse is one who is capable of wanting to mean the movements and the jump perfectly. . . . The jump, like the complicated movements of dressage, is an imitation of nature, especially of various movements that horses perform for the sake of sexual display or . . . [for example] a stallion's claiming of a herd or a mare's claiming of a foal."
3. Donna Haraway, *Primate Visions* (New York and London:Routledge, 1989), p. 31-32, 38. "Taxidermy," Haraway writes, "was made into the servant of the 'real.'" Haraway talks about Carl Akeley, who founded the art of taxidermy in 1880 by stuffing P. T. Barnum's elephant, Jumbo, and who went on to create magnificent scenes of animal life in natural history museums. As Haraway says, "the end of his [Akeley's] task came in the 1920's, with his exquisite mounting of the Giant of Karisimbi, the lone silverback male gorilla that dominates the diorama depicting the site of Akeley's own grave in the Mountainous rain forest of the Congo, today's Zaire. So it could inhabit Akeley's monument to the purity of nature, this gorilla was killed in 1921. . . . From the dead body of the primate, Akeley crafted something finer than the living organism; he achieved its true end, a new genesis. Decadence—the threat of the city, civilization, machine—was stayed in the politics of eugenics and the art

of taxidermy."

4. Ibid., pp. 29, 54.
5. Gunther von Hagens, *Bodyworlds* exhibition, Mannheim, Germany, 1997. The artist exhibited flayed human bodies preserved through "plastination" (a process he invented) in various postures of everyday life—sports, chess playing, walking. Like Vesalius and Cowper, the double exposure of the inside tissue and organs and the outside expressiveness of the bodies is uncanny. The exhibition caused immense controversy.
6. Baker, op. cit., pp. 129–30. "Cagedness is a condition of art, an expression of art's entanglement with desire." Baker is speaking of Deleuze and Guattari's writing on Franz Kafka. "It is the matter of an intensive and inventive looking," Baker continues, "a rigourousness of investigation, which has to be coldly unapologetic in its attitude to the looked-at thing, the caged thing." Francis Bacon thought the cage was a "means of focusing in, concentrating the image down: 'Just to see it better.'"
7. Thanks to Mark Collins for his research on modern taxidermic practices, including specific information about the fabrication of the animal body. Columbia University, School of Architecture seminar, Fall 2004.
8. Derrida, *The Truth in Painting*, pp. 59–60. ". . . not every milieu, even if it is contiguous with the work, constitutes a parergon. The natural site chosen for the erection of a temple is . . . not a parergon. Nor is an artificial site: neither the crossroads, nor the church, nor the museum. . . . But the garment or the colulmn is. . . . What constitutes them as parerga is not simply their exteriority as surplus, it is the internal structural link which rivets them to the lack in the interior of the ergon. And this lack would be constitutive of the very unity of the ergon. Without this lack, the ergon would have no need of a parergon."
9. Catherine Ingraham, "Architecture and evidence," in *Drifting: Architecture and Migrancy*, ed. Stephen Cairns (London: Routledge, 2004), pp. 61–81.
10. Thanks to Alessandra Ponte for first alerting me to this fascinating museum. It is in a modernist structure designed by Jean Debuisson. The question of utilitarian beauty returns, in a later chapter, around Georges Bataille's remarks about female beauty and its relation to animal beauty. Also see, with respect to the problem of evidence, Michel de Certeau, *The Practice of Everyday Life*, trans. Steven Rendall, (Berkeley: University of California Press, 1984), p. xi. De Certeau goes into the "obscure background of social activity" in order to bring to the foreground, more explicitly, the meaning of "everyday practices."

## 15: Lascaux: totem milieu of the sixties

1. Krauss, op. cit., p. 168. "If art began in the caves, its starting point was not the space of architecture, with light differentiating vertical pillar from horizontal slab, but that of the labyrinth, with no light, no differentiations, no up, no down."
2. Baker, op. cit., p. 12.
3. Ibid., p. 9.
4. Ibid., pp. 22–4.
5. Lévi-Strauss, *Totemism*, pp. 3–13. The whole first section this book speaks to the question of "imprecision." Like Freud's hysteria, the effects of totemism are too general and diverse. The animal is always present, but nothing else is always present: totemism is fetishism plus exogamy and matrilineal descent; totemism is the association of animal species and a human clan. Lévi-Strauss formulates the question eventually as the problem of under-

standing the "logical power of systems of denotation that are borrowed from the realm of nature" (p. 14). The imprecision of the animal also puts it at risk because it cannot, for example, be legally or even philosophically protected.

## PART V: ANIMAL URBANISM

### 16: Stock Exchange: standing upright, idle

1. The Chicago architect John Vincy coordinated and designed the meticulous reconstruction of this room, as well as its removal from the Stock Exchange building and insertion into the Art Institute. See John Vinci, *The Art Institute of Chicago: The Stock Exchange Trading Room* (Chicago, IL: Art Institute of Chicago, 1977).
2. Vinci, op. cit., p. 10. "The Art Institute of Chicago . . . decided that, in place of miscellaneous fragments, it would be more rewarding to request the ornament from the Trading Room[;] the City of Chicago generously offered the museum the Stock Exchange entrance archway. It has been reassembled at Monroe Street and Columbus Drive, adjacent to the new wing."
3. Stock exchanges necessarily spawn additional layers of speculative possibility. The futures market and The Board Options Exchange in Chicago (designed by Helmut Jahn) does not even deal with hard goods. Instead, they trade on the infinite realm of speculation itself; the number of pork bellies that may sell next year, or the multitude of possible options to buy and sell goods and services. In these markets, the hard goods are, ideally, always in motion from one broker to the next. The grains market and the futures markets use, for example, six month to one year weather predictions to speculate not only on the sale of grain but also the use of this grain as feed for animals and, thus, on the sale of animals. Animal parts are not, of course, brought onto the trading floor and, for example, in the New York Stock Exchange, it is stocks in agribusiness companies, rather than specific animals, that are brokered.
4. Epigraph is from Georges Bataille, "Architecture," in *Documents*, trans. Dominic Faccini, 25, *October* 60, (spring 1992), p. 25.
5. Hollier, op. cit., p. xii.
6. Ibid., p. xiv.
7. Siegfreid Giedion, *Mechanization Takes Command* (New York: W.W. Norton and Company, 1969), p. 209.
8. Ibid., p. 210.
9. Ibid., p. 211.
10. Ibid., p. 211.
11. Ibid., p. 212.
12. Ibid., p. 219. Also see J. M. Coetzee, *The Lives of Animals*, op. cit., p.53. Elizabeth Costello's full remark is: "Chicago showed us the way; it was from the Chicago stockyards that the Nazis learned how to process bodies."
13. In *Architecture and Utopia*, Manfredo Tafuri speaks of the enduring contradiction between mobile values and stable forces that shape the city. See Tafuri, *Architecture and Utopia*, trans. Barbara Luigia La Penta (Cambridge, MA: MIT Press, 1987). The problem here is the nesting of the mobile (the animal) in the stable (the building).
14. Henri Lefebvre, op. cit., p. 69.
15. Ibid., pp. 128–9.
16. Ibid., p. 194.

17. Ibid., p. 70.
18. Gilles Deleuze and Felix Guattari, *A Thousand Plateaus*, p. 249.
19. Lefebvre, op. cit., p. 129.
20. See, in particular, "A cow's eye view: Connecting with animals," in Temple Grandin's *Thinking in Pictures* (New York: Vintage Books, Random House, Inc., 1996), pp. 142–56. Grandin mentions a number of studies on "animal fear" in her book, and has, herself, written extensively about livestock handling and transport. She writes that she is asked all the time if animals know they are going to be die. This is now part of an enduring mythology in which animals are both a source of anxiety and an ideal victim.
21. Ibid., p. 142.
22. Ibid., pp. 85–6.
23. Ibid., p. 63.
24. Ibid., p. 151.
25. Ibid., p. 93.
26. Ibid., p. 143.
27. Ibid., p. 74.
28. Ibid., pp. 34, 36, 95.
29. Ibid., p. 38.
30. Ibid., pp. 35–6. "Being autistic" she remarks, is like being "trapped between two panes of glass."
31. Ibid., p. 74.
32. Ibid., pp. 41–2.
33. In looking at each animal, Grandin, like Derrida when he looks at his cat, asks the question, in the midst of the sacrifice, of the animal's powers of "calculability."
34. Coetzee, op. cit., p. 52.
35. George Hersey, *The Lost Meaning of Classical Architecture* (Cambridge, MA: MIT Press, 1988). Also see my discussion of Hersey in Ingraham, *Burdens*, pp. 14–16.
36. René Girard, *Violence and the Sacred*, trans. Patrick Gregory (Baltimore, MD: Johns Hopkins University Press, 1972).
37. Hersey, op. cit., pp. 2–45.
38. Vinci, op. cit., p. 27. "A striking feature of the room was the contrast between the symmetry of the coffered ceiling and the asymmetry of the interior elevations . . . the development of the structural daring required to achieve such a space within a skyscraper can be traced to two earlier Adler and Sullivan projects; the Auditorium Building (1886–90) and the Schiller (later Garrick Theater) Building (1891–92), p. 27."
39. The *College of Sociology, 1937–1939*, ed. Dennis Hollier, trans. Betsy Wing (Minneapolis, MN: University of Minnesota Press), viii–xxix. The *College*, Hollier writes, was part of the "emergence of French existentialism in 1938, commencing with . . . the *Études kierkegaardiennes* in which Jean Wahl developed the negative form of cogito that Kierkegaard called the paradox: Since thinking existence is experience of incompatibility between thought and existence, how is it possible to think or measure the incommensurable? Man is a philosopher more because he exists that because he thinks" (p. ix).
40. Ibid., pp. vii–xxix.
41. Ibid., p. ix.
42. Ibid., p. x.
43. Ibid., pp. ix–x.
44. Ibid., p. 385. Italics Hollier's own. As Hollier remarks in a footnote, "Sade, Lautreamont, Hegel, Baudelaire, Rimbaud, Nietzsche were the names of some of these existences

that Bataille considered to be 'existences authentic in themselves to the extent that they all converged toward the formation of that order.' This order was, incidentally, to be based specifically on the unification of men, who then might confront women from a position of 'virile totality.'"

45. Ibid., p. xvii.
46. Hollier, op. cit., p. x.
47. However, as I have been arguing, the "orders" that attend the history of architecture and urbanism, classical, modern, are orders that have specific relationships not, initially, to the monumental or aspirations toward wholeness, but to the partitioning of life, a broken order.
48. Georges Bataille, *The Accursed Share*, vols 1 and 2, trans. Robert Hurley (New York: Urzone Books, 1991), p. 23.
49. Hollier, op. cit., pp. 98–107. This is also the "horror" uttered by Kurtz in the jungle at the end of Conrad's *Heart of Darkness*.
50. Bataille, op. cit., p. 14.
51. Ibid., p. 76.
52. Ibid., pp. 77–8. Bataille writes: ". . . the horror of nature, which was the first movement of the process, was ambiguous, and it anticipated a nearly simultaneous return movement. [A]s soon as nature, which a spirit of revolt had rejected as the given, ceased to appear as such, the very spirit that had rejected it no longer considered it as the given . . . it then regarded nature's antithesis, prohibition, as the given—that prohibition to which at first it submitted, as a way of denying its subordination to nature," p. 77.
53. Ibid., p. 78.
54. Ibid., p. 94. Bataille further writes that the "unity in the violent agitation of prohibition and transgression will be evident: it is the unity of the sacred world, contrasting with the calm regularity of the profane world."
55. Ibid., p. 214.
56. Ibid., p. 28.
57. Ibid., p. 212.
58. Ibid., pp. 215–6.
59. Ibid., p. 16.
60. Hollier, op. cit., p. xii.
61. Ibid., p. xiii.
62. Hollier, op. cit., p. xiv. For Bataille, the museum opposes the slaughterhouse. Those who are repulsed by the slaughterhouse seek the beauty of the museum. "Slaughterhouses," Hollier writes, "along with museums, make up a system in which the ambivalence defining the sacred nucleus is at work: the slaughterhouses are the negative pole, the generator of repulsion, the centrifuge (they are placed farther and farther away from the center of the city). Museums, the pole of attraction, are centripetal. But within the heart of one the other is hidden. At the heart of beauty lies a murder, a sacrifice, a killing . . . The main thing about this system . . . is not, however, the conjunction of these two poles but the space between them. One does not exist without the other, but it does not exist with the other either. . . ."
63. Ibid., p. xiv.
64. Vinci, op. cit., p. 35.

## 17: The City: horizontal, upright, working

1. Krauss, op. cit., p. 113. The displacement [of beauty] "from the empirical realm to the wholly subjective one [in Kant] preserved, in the act of judgment, a universal categorical dimension. . . . Their [i.e. aesthetic judgments] very logic is that they are communicable, sharable, a function of what could only be called the 'universal voice.'"
2. Georges Bataille, *The Accursed Share*, trans. Robert Hurley, (New York: Zone Books, 1991) p. 146.
3. Ibid., p. 145.
4. Ibid., pp. 141–2.
5. Mark Cousins, in conversation, Architectural Association 2004.
6. See Krauss' discussion of Duchamp, particularly "*Etant Donnés*," in *The Optical Unconscious* and the use of classical perspective ending (the vanishing point and viewpoint of the seeing eye co-identified) in the dark interior of the woman herself—the "carnal" perspectives, pp. 111–12).
7. Bataille, op. cit., p. 145. Animal beauty can be the beauty of the bird, which, like Bataille's fantastical female beauty, appears to move without restraint in a sovereign space, or it can be the beauty of the work horse or oxen, "their beauty is bound up inescapably with the idea of a movement of energy triumphing over the hardest physical tasks." Animal beauty, in the post-animal world, is the linking of a certain idea of freedom (not absolute freedom) and a certain idea of constraint (not always noble).
8. Hollier, op. cit., p. xv.
9. Women, in relation to men, have traditionally been given a subordinate status that is frequently married to the idea that women are biologically inferior to men, i.e. they are closer to the animal. But animals, particularly in relation to traditionally male collective groups such as the army, are often given elevated status.
10. Beatriz Colomina, *Privacy and Publicity* (Cambridge, MA: MIT Press, 1994), Colomina, in a discussion of Le Corbusier's use of the window, argues for the powers of the moving eye ("media") in the construction and geometry of the modernist architectural scene.
11. Bataille, op. cit., p. 140.
12. Ibid., p. 142.
13. Keith H. Basso, *The Cibecque Apache*, University of Arizona (New York: Holt, Rinehart and Winston, 1970), pp. 64–5.
14. For several full accounts of this ceremony, which is routinely cited as a highly significant Apache ceremony in general (for the entire tribe, not just the girl in question), see Basso op. cit., pp. 53–72 (cited above), and Morris E. Opler's *Apache Odyssey, A Journey Between Two Worlds*, (New York: Holt, Rinehart and Winston, 1969), pp. 98–101.
15. Krauss, op. cit., p. 119. "The visuality Duchamp proposes, he says, is carnal, not conceptual. It views the body as a psychophysiological system." "The optic chiasma that Duchamp suggests . . . is unthinkable apart from a vision that is carnal through and through" (p.114).
16. Hollier, op. cit., p. xiv.
17. Agamben, *The Open*, p. 47. "He [Uxeküll] then drew the sole conclusion that without a living subject, time cannot exist." Also see Foucault, op. cit., p. 226. Time is connected to organic labor. The concept of "labor" brings to the study of economy "the interior time of an organic structure which grows in accordance with its own necessity and develops in accordance with autochthonous laws—the time of capital and production."
18. Geertz, op. cit., p. 90. Includes quote in the preceding paragraph.

19. Ibid., pp. 93–4.
20. Ibid., p. 94.
21. Bataille, op. cit., p. 82.
22. Ibid., p. 85.
23. Ibid., pp. 84–6.

## PART VI: PROCESSING

### 18: Engineering

1. See Tissue Culture and Art Project website (http://www.tca.uwa.edu.au). Andrew Colopy, a graduate student in a Columbia seminar I taught in Spring 2004, first introduced me to this website. Thanks to all the students from that seminar for their inventive research and thoughtful contributions to these questions. Also see Oron Catts and Ionat Zurr, *The Art of the Semi-Living and Partial Life: Extra Ear—¼ Scale*, p.1. They write: "The work of The Tissue Culture & Art Project (TC&A) is the first attempt to explore the prospect of combining the techno-scientific knowledge of tissue culture and related technologies with an artistic practice."
2. Catts, op. cit., p. 3. "The Tissue Culture & Art Project have made three major decisions in regard to its work; the first was not to kill animals or inflict suffering in order to obtain the cells and tissues, the second was not to directly refer to the human body or its parts, and the third was to always construct a fully functioning tissue culture laboratory when we present our semi-living creations."
3. Iceland, because of its lack of pollution, is presumed to be a more pure environment from which to take a tissue sample for genetic mapping. But, as always, how are we to understand this idea of "purity" in light of the nefarious roles such ideas of purity have played in human culture?
4. Architecture that overtly or tacitly uses biology or bio-technical metaphors—such as Greg Lynn and Reiser + Umemoto's competition projects for the Cardiff Bay Opera House Competition—has done so in order to arrive at new forms and geometries. That is, they are still architecturally proper in some sense in spite of their dramatic inventiveness.
5. Evelyn Fox Keller, *Refiguring Life* (New York: Columbia University Press, 1995).
6. Manuel de Landa, *War in the Age of Intelligent Machines* (Cambridge: MIT Press, Zone Books, 1991).
7. Ibid., pp. 5–7.
8. Ibid., p. 7.
9. Ibid., p. 13.
10. Ibid., p. 18.
11. Weiner, *Cybernetics*, p. 139.
12. Fox Keller, op. cit., p. 9. The last sentence is a quote from Erwin Schrödinger.
13. Ibid., p. 21.
14. Ibid., pp. 24, 92-93.
15. Ibid., p. 21
16. Richard Lewontin quoted in Keller, op. cit., p. 23.
17. Keller, op. cit., pp. 89, 93, 103.
18. Ibid., p. 99.
19. Ibid., p. 108.

## 19: Processing

1. Weiner, op. cit., p. vii. The epigraph by Alan Turing is the well-known "Turing Test of Intelligence," of which there are different versions. This version is taken from www.abelard.org/turpap.htm#learning-machine.
2. *The New York Times*, 13 January 2001. "Scientists attempt to save an endangered species of ox from extinction by trying to reproduce it inside a cow . . . ."
3. Speaking loosely, architecture is still well within the Newtonian universe of the direct, and reversible, action of forces on bodies, and also still within the aesthetic implied by the industrial revolution at the turn of the century that architectural modernism attempted to actualize.
4. Weiner, op. cit., p. 38.
5. Ibid., pp. 39–40.
6. Jacob, op. cit., p. 176.
7. Weiner, op. cit., p. 32.
8. Ibid., p. 33.
9. Ibid., p. 34. "Our observation of the stars are through the agency of light, of rays or particles emerging from the observed object and perceived by us. We can perceive incoming light, but can not perceive outgoing light. . . . In the perception of incoming light we end up with the eye or a photographic plate. We condition these for the reception of images by putting them in a state of insulation for some time past. . . . This being the case, we can see those stars whose evolution is in the reverse direction, they will attract radiation from the whole heavens. . . . Thus the part of the universe which we see must have its past-future relations, as far as the emission of radiation is concerned, concordant with our own. The very fact that we see a star means that its thermodynamics is like our own."
10. Ibid., pp. 43–4.
11. The animation in *A Bug's Life* simulated the movement of the body, not the movement of the brain or genetic forces that drive the body. Motion capture, such as that used in *Polar Express*, 2004, seems to be attempting to model the interior motivation of human life—expressed, for example, through the eyes—by attaching sensors to an actor's body and then fabricating the animated body as a mirroring of actual movement. The inside, in other words, is being sought, once again, from the outside.
12. G. W. F. Hegel, *The Phenomenology of the Mind*, trans. J. B. Bataille, (New York:Harper and Row, Publishers, 1967), p. xxiii.

# INDEX

## S



## T